The County Books Series

GENERAL EDITOR: BRIAN VESEY-FITZGERALD

KU-520-132

YORKSHIRE
NORTH RIDING

THE COUNTY BOOKS SERIES

A series comprising 57 volumes. It covers every county in England and there will be five books on Scotland, two on Ireland, two on the Hebrides, and one each on Orkney, Shetland, Wales, the Isle of Man and the Channel Islands

THE FOLLOWING THIRTY-FIVE VOLUMES
HAVE NOW BEEN PUBLISHED

PLEASE WRITE TO THE PUBLISHERS
FOR FULL DESCRIPTIVE PROSPECTUS

YORKSHIRE
NORTH RIDING

by

OSWALD HARLAND

Illustrated and with a Map

London
ROBERT HALE LIMITED
18 Bedford Square W.C.1

PRINTED IN GREAT BRITAIN
BY WESTERN PRINTING SERVICES, LTD., BRISTOL

CONTENTS

CHAPTER I

THE SOUTH-EASTERN CORNER
AND SCARBOROUGH

THERE are children of all ages for whom maps possess an
irresistible attraction, and you would think, perhaps, that
such children become great travellers, intrepid explorers,
Marco Polos to a man. It does not follow. Map-worshippers
are often introspective fellows whose journeyings take them
only through lands of the imagination. The Himalayas and
the Kuen Lung, the Tian Shan and the Mountains of the
Moon, tower together into the skies above a single planetary
landscape where the pampas and the llanos, the deserts and
the dark rain forests sweep into a blue distance in which the
peaks of the Andes may be superimposed upon the Urals and
the Caucasus. Why should such children ever step across
their own doorsills? Yet it may come to them in the way of
war, business or pleasure to watch new constellations rise in
the night sky and to see the domes and minarets of eastern
cities, the skyscrapers of the west. And what then? I can only
tell you what my experience has been. First, dreams grow
dim and the landscapes of imagination blur and vanish. Then,
too, it becomes impossible to hold steady in the mind's eye the
lately seen realities. Lastly, the landscapes of one's own particular patch of country grow clearer and dearer to one's
sophisticated and rather tired eyes. Although in my time I
have travelled somewhat, I have few strong memories of the
foreign places I have known, but, on the other hand, many
vivid impressions of my own district.

That district is the North Riding of Yorkshire.

It does not matter that my home lies within the boundaries
of the West Riding, near the summit of the sharp rise out of
Wetherby on the turnpike road to Harrogate. The front
windows, facing south and a little west, overlook the reaches
of the Wharfe from Collingham Bridge. There is a view, but
not a view to remember. At the back of the house, where the

B   I

windows face north and by east, the country slides down into the vast saucer-shaped depression (or so it seems from my windows) of the Plain of York, and I look across that plain to the ridge of Black Hambledon, Whitestonecliff, and the White Horse of Kilburn. Hidden in the trough of green lie the towns and villages of the Vale of Mowbray. Invisible on the heights stand the little hamlets of Scawton, Old Byland, and Cold Kirby. Beyond these, deep in the north-eastern dales, lie Helmsley, Kirbymoorside, Gilling, Hovingham, Pickering, and Old Malton, and, miles away beyond them, Whitby, Staithes, Runswick, Bay Town, Scarborough, and the wrinkled plain of the North Sea.

Through this land, straight as the Romans made their roads, runs the great highway A1, the Great North Road, across the border of the West Riding into the North, unrolling massively towards Catterick and Scotch Corner. In that direction, pushing westward into the folds of the Pennines, lie Teesdale, Swaledale, and Wensleydale, famous in the memory of those who love beauty in landscape and splendour in antiquity.

Here I have it all before me. I take the bones of the country and without reference to the map I clothe them with the comely flesh of the land. The details are there, definite and precise, of moor, headland, valley and mountain, river and plain and sea. And yet they change, they change from season to season and from year to year. I take, for instance, a familiar path along the cliffs north of Scarborough, and I find I have to revise my memory-image of it because since last I passed that way there have been subtle changes in contour and colouring and the ecological build of the scene. No topographical survey of the North Riding can ever be absolutely and accurately up to date. I try to annotate my landscapes with a fresh mind and a recent eye. The ink of the annotations is, in places, hardly dry. And within the capabilities of my mind I try to be accurate. Still, I know, some reader, following in my tracks, will come to some commanding point overlooking a view, and, setting his finger on what I have written, will say, "But it is not like this at all : it is not like this at all."

People will tell you that they can cover a country by motor-car. Stevenson wrote that landscapes may profitably be studied from the windows of a railway-carriage. Young people with bare legs, corduroy shorts and black alpaca jackets ride the roads on bicycles and claim to know every dip and rise, every pothole and newly tarred surface, from Greta Bridge to the crossings of the Swale and from Keld to Scarborough. I have found only one profitable mode of journeying through the country : I have gone on foot. In a car I am rather on the country than in it. Rubber tyres insulate not only my body but also my mind, which is not absorbent and retentive enough to take in and register all the impressions that crowd upon the eyes. The sense of smell is also in suspension, the hearing is muffled, and I lose all the tactile sensations that are so necessary to me. The smell of meadowsweet and heather and pigsties is overwhelmed by the smell of car-travel, and the grip of the hands on the wheel is no substitute for the roughness of rock under my hands. My first foot-journey in the North Riding was made at the age of seven when on a fine Sunday morning I ran away from home. My last, I hope, has not yet been undertaken.

In the North Riding dialect there is a verb *to allack*, which means *to proceed energetically on foot from place to place without set or serious purpose.* I think I may claim to have *allacked* all over the North Riding of Yorkshire, and if you were to follow the line of my journeyings you would see it like the track-chart of a four-masted barque during a spell of gales and wild weather. Following it on foot, you would find yourself in difficult places, walking on mountain-tops and open moors with dead darkness around you, or the uncanny livingness of moving mist. You would wade up to the knees in peaty water, up to the thighs in soaked ling, and up to the neck in bracken. You would fight your way up crags and struggle down steep-sided gills choked with rocks and rotten timber. You would proceed across country without landmarks, and often you would be very lost.

A great acreage of the North Riding is not tamed country, and to know its wildness you yourself have to be a rather wild person—wild enough and tough enough to match and master this wild, tough country. You ought, too, to know the sort of people that have made the Riding what it is to-day. The gentleman in the parlour, you remember, if he had to have company, preferred that of a Quaker or a man from the West Riding of Yorkshire; I would have a North Riding man who was either a Quaker or a heathen. His dialect is purer and his outlook not so twisted. He lives closer to the earth than his West Riding brother.

I try now to estimate what qualities of mind a man should have if he is to describe the Riding as it is to-day. I have already suggested that he should have a physical roughness and toughness. Now I am going to assert that his mind also should be tough of fibre yet not lacking in sensitiveness. He ought to have a working knowledge of many sciences, arts, and crafts; he should be swift with the literary allusion, a free talker, an antiquarian, an agriculturist; he should wield a lively pen and have some small gift of prophecy so that he may describe the land not only as it is but also as it is likely to become. William Shakespeare himself would fall short of the ideal, but I shall not spend time in apologies, lamentations and denials. I purpose now to begin upon the work which is also my pleasure. The map, if you please!

The map measures six feet one way and over seven feet the other, and includes the whole county. It is in three strips which fit together without overlap, and to examine it properly I have to spread it out on the floor and lie on it. "To the Nobility, Gentry, and Clergy, of Yorkshire, this Map of the County, constructed from a survey commenced in the year 1817, and corrected in the years 1827 and 1828, is respectfully dedicated by the Proprietors. London, published by Henry Teesdale and Co. and C. Stocking, Paternoster Row. April 21, 1828. J. Bingley sc., Sidney St., Islington."

It sounds well. It is meritable. It is dignified, and even noble. The wapentakes are shown in colour—West Gilling, Hang West, Allertonshire, Birdforth, Gilling East, Hallikeld, Langbarugh, Rydale, Bulmer, Part of the Bishoprick of Durham, Pickering Lythe, and Whitby Strand. The North Sea is the German Ocean, and, incidental to the map, there is a large engraving of "York Cathedral viewed from the North-West" which shows no steps at the west door and only a low-roofed cottage in the background. In the foreground a mason busies himself with mallet and chisel.

Out of date? Precisely so, but why complain? Observe that

no railways existed, and that alum-workers were busy at Kettleness, Sandsend, and the Peak. Watermills and windmills were worthy the marking. There were lead-mines on the fells north of Wensleydale. The ironstone of Rosedale was not opened out. Middlesbrough was the tiniest of hamlets. Between Gillamoor and Ingleby Greenhow there were coal-workings. At Thornton Dale there was a paper-mill, and there was a tanyard. Times change. Saxton's map of Yorkshire, dating 1577, shows the Riding as largely forest and wilderness. Times change, and the face of the land puts on different expressions. The North Riding of yesterday is not the North Riding of to-day, and to-morrow, if certain people have their scientific way, it will be alarmingly different again. Though nobody can replace alluvium by granite or limestone by syenite, atomic fission may rearticulate the bones of the country, and a thousand years hence the skylines of the Riding may be strangely contorted, with new hills and dales and levelled areas. How they will be peopled is another matter.

Impatient with maps and fireside talk, I want now to take to the road. Before I do so, however, I ought first to tell the reader that I have a habit of unrolling the one-inch survey map and clipping out the section I want to cover. I will not be cluttered up with a big map, nor will I fight to control the thing in a high wind and a slant rain.

The first portion I cut out covers the country and the coastline south of Scarborough. I begin, that is, upon the south-eastern corner of the Riding.

Years ago I used to make my way along the sands from Scarborough without having to slop and splash round the wall-foot of the South Bay bathing-pool. There was then no bathing-pool. If to-day were a winter's day I should certainly scramble over a set or two of iron railings to avoid the sea-weeds and tide-pools below the wall, but in high summer I make no trouble of the slime and sea-water lying an inch deep on the foundation course of the wall. I climb a flight of broken steps to the sea-wall girdle of Holbeck Gardens and follow the weathered asphalt as far as it will take me. Then I go down to the sands and the rocks again.

It is all much as it was forty years ago. The Children's

Corner, famous in photographs, is still less crowded than Sandside. The children play sedately, though there are fewer nannies. Rock-pools are still most carefully explored and sand-castles are still built with an eye to barbican, curtain-wall and moat. Yet there are changes. To-day there is no Punch and Judy, and, looking back towards the town, the Sitwells would miss Will Catlin's pierrots on the sands by the Spa wall, and the rival show of Tom Carrick; but still they would hear, drifting downwind, the intermittent noises—music at a distance becomes a series of noises—from the Spa orchestra, and they would be completely gratified by the nineteenth-century smoothness of the sands and the timeless sparkle of the sunlight on the sea—a sparkle that would bring George Crabbe to mind and lead Osbert to happy quotation. They would miss brown lugsails on the bay, the donkeys and the ice-cream stalls, but, perhaps, would remember how B. C. Hucks, pioneer of flying, landed his primitive plane upon the beach two hundred yards from this spot. A memorable day.

I make rather heavy going through dry, dark-brown patches of sand under the cliff, and there comes into my mind the picture of a small boy making the discovery, which had, of course, been made before, that the stuff contained a high percentage of magnetic hæmatite—and of the same small boy tapping the rocks for fossils, and wondering how much the carnelians of Carnelian Bay, round the next point, would fetch at Hatton Garden. Sidling round rock-pools without thinking to poke a disturbing finger into the rose-red sea-anemones or lift up brilliant stones for the grey-green dog-crabs under them, I make towards White Nab and the bay of worthless jewels. Out amongst the bigger, deeper pools—I still think of them as lagoons—a single blue-guernseyed fisherman looks for bait. He is the survivor, the last of the dozen or more thigh-booted veterans I used to see there, yet still as then there stands by him, inevitable as fate, a middle-aged man in flannels and blazer, holding the old man in talk about fishing and the sea.

At the southern end of Carnelian Bay the rough sand falls more steeply towards the sea, and there I find fifty little girls in the water. An energetic woman in tweeds stands upon a rock and has her charges bathing by numbers. Twenty elderly women sit upon the dry sand and talk in the sun. There is no occupation more satisfying and more natural. The one man amongst them looks sad and abstracted. He does not or dares not speak at all.

I am not such a fool now as to work through the chaos of sea-worn boulders at the foot of Osgodby Nab. As a lad I should have kept to the foreshore and raced the tide round the point, but as a man of middle age I mount up and over the *nek* of stout, stiff, red boulder clay remembering how once I went up the cliff at a more precipitous spot and found myself on a razor-edge with a hundred-foot drop below me. I halt to make a small experiment. Does boulder clay, under the friction of the sole of a shoe, still take on a strange, steel-blue patina?

It does, and I make a safe and leisurely descent into Cayton Bay.

There was once a time, and I remember it, when a bathing-suit at Cayton Bay was a despised superfluity. Now I could not go into the water without harrowing the morals of many people. Once Cayton Bay was a summer solitude; now it is a resort. I make it my business merely to stroll along the stretched bow of sand with my eyes open and my attention casually fixed. All the while I have been conscious of a presence walking with me, and now in Cayton Bay it takes shape and reality as a bright-haired youngster—myself when young. He prods me, asking, "Do you remember?"

"Do you remember," he demands, "pitching camp on the flat area of turf to the south of the wood there, and going down to the tide-edge at sunrise, when only the prints of the gulls' feet marked the smooth sand? Do you remember tearing dead wood out of the sea-fretted and wind-tormented trees for firewood, and walking along to the spring for fresh water? Do you remember, and do you remember?"

On Sunday afternoons the brawny young men of the Scarborough Amateur Rowing Club used to bring their boats into Cayton Bay, and the Scarborough girls walked along the cliff-top from Holbeck Gardens and came down the woods to the beach. There was bathing, and there were ball games. Fires of driftwood were lighted, and there were picnic teas, and there was more bathing, until the sun went down over

7

Gristhorpe and the cool twilight came. Then the men of the Amateur Rowing Club pushed out their skiffs, climbed aboard and set off for home; the girls collected their gear and went up the woods, laughing and chattering, and the beach was left to the silent gulls and to the campers in their solitary tent just south of the neglected woods.

The iron laws of the Victorian Sunday were then at last being broken. The young men undressed on the beach, the girls behind little promontories of boulder clay. It was all very decorous, very innocent, and very long ago.

Now let me silence the insistent youngster who walks with me, and let me use my mature eyes. The bungalow at the seaward fringe of the wood, once so comely with tiled roof and white paint, looks derelict to-day, and there are two over-prominent notices displayed by its side. "N.A.L.G.O. Persons damaging this piece of property will be prosecuted." "Private Property. Trespassers will be prosecuted."

Associations and trade unions always remind me that force, fear and insecurity still rule the economic world, but I do not see that they should rule here in Cayton Bay. I am hardly inclined to praise an association which to fulfil its benevolent aims fences off a portion of Britain's foreshore, builds ugly huts upon it and threatens trespassers with prosecution. Once upon a time a man could walk from Filey Road down through the woods to the beach here, and there was no fence to stop him and nobody to prosecute him. But now, for him, there is no road through the woods.

This summer afternoon there are three hundred and six people in Cayton Bay and a dozen dogs. The people and the dogs are of all sorts and conditions. They are bathing, paddling, sun-bathing, playing ball, rushing about or resting. There is an almost total absence of books and newspapers.

I sit upon the steep slope of sun-warmed stones by the waterworks and, my hands clasped round my knees, watch the scene. It has a curious illusory quality. I am not sure that it is solidly three-dimensional or has any duration in the sort of time with which I am familiar. A very hairy fellow comes up out of the sea—a Mediterranean type, I say to myself, it is more hairy than the northern type—and dries and dresses himself ten yards away to my left. Two girls pass by, looking speculatively across the sands towards the sea. And, shortly, I climb the road past the waterworks and make for the farming country behind the façade of cliff. Four young men hurtle past me, going down to the sea. They talk loudly, but I cannot understand the town jargon of the West Riding, and the substance of their conversational bellowing escapes me. I go up-country with a desolation of caravans on my left, and, in front of me, the high road to Filey. I turn towards Filey.

The newly painted metal mile-marks tell me I am still in the North Riding. I pose myself the question, "Shall I go on until I stand with one foot in the East Riding, the other in the North?" Rejecting the affirmative answer, and indeed any answer at all, I turn off the main road into the village of Gristhorpe. In the carr to my right men are cutting corn. Girls and women are stooking with quick skill. Where the land sweeps up in a convex bulge towards the edge of the cliffs, most of the corn is still uncut, but in the first stackyard I come to men are piking sheaves.

In the North Riding a stackyard is a staggarth, rectangular stacks are stacks, but circular ones are pikes. Whether you are building a pike or a stack you pike your sheaves from the wagon to the men disposing them in place. Finished with piking, you go to work with loose straw, hairy band and stackprods, and you thatch your pike or stack. In the North Riding you use no staddle-stones.

Gristhorpe village was by-passed before by-passes had a name. Hence there is still a thatched dovecot in the place, and the cottages are much as they were a century ago. Many of their outward walls have developed perilous bulges, and the local mason has given them a hideous facing of concrete. The cottages are whitewashed and resemble rather East Riding than North Riding buildings.

The footpath through the village runs above the level of the road, and behind the houses there is a tangled, nettle-grown path so swampy as to suggest that the water-table is not far below the surface. From this path I cross a couple of old pastures that might be more fertile if ploughed up and resown, and a few minutes' walking brings me into Lebberston, a tidier village than Gristhorpe and more modernized.

Here I meet a rheumy old man hobbling across the road, and we stand on the crown of the empty road and talk.

"Yonder," I say, "is Lebberston Hall?"

The building is late Victorian or early Edwardian, with nothing remarkable about it but its size, ugliness, and fresh white paint. Someone is mowing the lawn in front of the house and I hear children shouting.

"Ay," says the old man, "yon's Lebberston Hall."

"And who lives there now?"

"Why, I can't tell you that : some folks that moved in last Wednesday week. Strangers."

"People don't usually want big houses these days. Where do these strangers come from?"

"From away," says the old man.

His answer is perfectly intelligible. Either you belong to a place, or you come from away.

"It's going to be what I believe they call a guest-house," the old man adds. He shakes his head doubtfully, disapproving of this modernism but helpless to resist it. I ask him to tell me where lies the boundary between the two Ridings, and we turn to look over the flat carrs towards the bare escarpment of the wolds. Shakily he indicates a belt of woodland, a planting, perhaps a mile to the south. The boundary runs eastward through this wood.

"And beyond that there's Muston," he says, as though Muston were Baghdad or the rose-red city of Asandivat.

Muston is in the East Riding and on foreign soil. I move on from Lebberston to Cayton, thinking first of Wordsworth's leech-gatherer with whom my old man has dignity in common, and of the high cliffs of Yons Nab and of white water breaking over Calf Allen Rocks on the southern fringe of Cayton Bay. In Cayton I find old men sitting in the sun opposite a pebble-dashed cottage called "Ye Olde Cayton Cottage, 1677." I help the village joiner's lad to fix the churchyard gate, newly mended, on its hinges, or, as they say hereabouts, on its crooks. The lad is a silent soul, and I stroll into the church.

"Twelfth-century—in places," I say to myself. There is no mistaking twelfth-century work once you are familiar with it. Intuitive knowledge succeeds upon scholarly investigation in such matters. I note an ancient font upon a new base. Above the door into the tower I find a wooden tablet, and, painted upon it, "These made by me Thomas Shaw: and Ralf Spenclay church wardens, this year of our Lord 1678." I fail to find out what "these" are. The south door by which I leave is twelfth-century, the tower is fifteenth-century, and the joiner's lad has gone.

From Cayton church the road swings coastwards to Osgodby and Osgodby Hall. It climbs, I slacken pace and work out the reason why Muston, Lebberston, and Cayton should have Saxon or Anglian names and why Osgodby should be Danish in origin.

"The low land down there," I say to myself, "at the time of the Danish Conquest was marshy and undrained, mostly swamp and reeds, the abode of web-feet. The Danes left it to the Angles because it wasn't worth occupying, and they put their own settlement in a strategic position on the high ground close to the sea, with the land falling away to the south." I am moderately well satisfied with this theory, and push on with the sun beating upon my back. Once there was a Hospital of St Leonard at Osgodby, but all that remains is a trifle of medieval walling and a gateway with a pointed arch in the outbuildings of Osgodby Hall Farm. I see it as I turn a corner, but it is not remarkable enough to attract the shy antiquarian that dwells in me, and I do not investigate more closely. I am more interested in an aspect of modernity upon the road itself—half a dozen scouts and their scout-master making slow progress towards Filey Road. Three of the scouts are flinging handfuls of road-grit at one another; the others whistle as they go for want of thought. They have no eye at all for medievalism, and no more has their scout-master.

The upper end of Osgodby Lane has been clutched by the builder and contractor. There is a group of red-brick and tile dwelling-houses. I learn nothing about the sanitation of these houses, but it is probably better than that of "Ye Olde Cayton Cottage, 1677," and no doubt the water-supply is first-rate, for the pumping-station is less than half a mile down the road. This Osgodby settlement has metalled, tar-sprayed roads. The roads at Gristhorpe, Lebberston, and Cayton look as though they rightly ought to be of limestone roughly rolled and heavily cambered, dusty in summer, muddy in winter, with wide pools of creamy water at intervals. But they too have had the tar-sprayer over them. Civilization has touched these villages with its massive little finger, and presently, no doubt, its whole heavy hand will come down upon them. I trust that the old men in the sun will duly rejoice.

Wheatcroft, on Filey Road, is now no more than a ribbon-developed suburb of Scarborough, and there is nothing more to be said of it. I walk at a huge pace into Scarborough.

Here, then, is the extreme south-easterly landscape of the North Riding: the rocky foreshore, with the boulder clay covering the lower limestone stratification, and Yons Nab, brant as a house-end, to the south; the wrinkled and pale patterned plain of the sea; inland, the convex rise of the land up to the scalloped edge of the cliffs, with crops growing almost to the verge. Farther inland, west of Filey Road, the land, sparsely wooded because trees hate to have their roots in water, yet heavy with crops, sinks in a slightly concave trough towards Seamer Carrs. Bluish-green along the southern rim of the landscape stands the marching line of the chalk wolds. A stiff soil, I should say, that tests the sinews of a man's back, but fertile when knowledgeably treated. Like the extreme north-west of the Riding, it is an outlier. It seems rightly to belong to the East Riding; I can sense the East Riding at every step I take through it. But, should They ever propose to transfer the area from North Riding to East, the indigenes would swell with wrath and swear that Seamer Carrs make a satisfactory boundary. Muston, they would point out, is inhabited by foreigners.

I find a note on boulder clay, of which there are massive deposits in the North Riding. Its presence has everything to do with the Ice Age. "It forms a great mass of glacial deposits," say Kendall and Wroot. "Boulder clay is a material unique in its kind in Britain. The most striking characteristic of boulder clay is that it presents a mixture of materials without order or arrangement. Its matrix is a clay composed of materials of the most exquisite fineness of grain, and in this are included sand particles, grit and stones through every gradation of size from minute pebbles to great blocks many tons in weight. There are embedded also masses of chalk, and of the older clays—Oxford and Kimeridge and Lias—and, in some regions, huge 'rafts' of chalk, slabs and sheets hundreds of yards in length and thousands of tons in weight."

It is, no doubt, interesting stuff. Varying in colour from brown to purple through intermediate shades of red, when thoroughly wet it is as slippery as soap; when dry, it resembles a rubbery sort of brick. Great cracks open up in it, rain-water and snow fill the cracks, frost and thaw break the bonds of the clay, and great masses of the viscous stuff slide down the hills and the cliffs into the valleys and the sea. Lumps of it, rounded and smoothed by the washing of the tides, are rolled about the beaches, incorporating sand and pebbles until they form a terrible and intractable conglomerate. The stuff used to present a problem to coastal engineers and to people who built houses near the sea. It is still apt to mock the farmer and the gardener. Quite useless until copiously limed or marled, it devours humus almost as fast as humus is put into it. Even grass does not naturally flourish upon the raw stuff, and it poses pretty questions to those who would drain the slopes and flats upon which it squats. If the agriculturist has learned to handle it, he cannot be said to love it. To the geologist alone is it precious. By sorting out the various kinds of stones embedded in it and tracing them to their sources, he is able to plot the intricate movements of the ice-sheets and glaciers during the remote Ice Age. Even to-day he is still concerned with the stuff, for he has not yet solved all the problems it presents. He finds black flints and pink flints, for example, and is baffled to know where they come from. Boulders of Shap granite, with deep glacial scratches upon their smoothed and flattened surfaces, are fairly common. I have found them myself, and there is one handsome specimen at the railway station of Seamer Junction. It came out of the old quarry which is now the cattle market, close by the railway track, in the middle of the nineteenth century.

Covering the carrs there is a black alluvium, light and sandy but extremely fertile when well treated. Below the alluvium lies a stiff blue clay, and there is much loose stone in the soil. I remember digging down to the clay and, in process, removing the stones. An old labourer watched me for some time. Then said he, "I've known folk 'at went to the trouble of digging out stones in this land and when they'd got 'em out they had to put 'em back again." He didn't explain why the stones had to go back and I didn't ask. I put the stones back and dug out no more of them. That old man had wisdom and I knew it. It was, after all, a matter of drainage.

This south-eastern corner, between Scarborough and Filey, is showing signs of development, but the signs are not yet extensive. The whole area is dominated by the radar masts on Seamer Moor. There is a good deal of intensive market-gardening, some of it tidy, some untidy. The population shows a blending of the stagnant agricultural strain with blessed but bungaloid retirement.

Those who visit the Yorkshire coast for their holiday by the sea may be divided into two categories : those who go to Scarborough and those who do not. The people who do not say that Scarborough is too hilly. "Everywhere you turn," they declare, "there's a hill, and a steep hill at that." If, however, these same people go to Runswick, Staithes, Saltburn, or Whitby, they seem not to notice the hills. Perhaps they even expect hills, welcome hills, rejoice in hills. Usually they go to Filey "because Filey is so nice for the children."

Scarborough is built upon a thick deposit of boulder clay which rolls and dips and stands up in hills because the Scandinavian ice-sheet impinged upon these cliffs and piled up its morainic debris upon a foundation of Jurassic limestone. This moraine blocked the gap between Oliver's Mount, Stony Haggs, and Seamer Moor, meeting there the ice that came crawling eastward from the inland moors. Deepdale, a little south of Scarborough, was an overflow channel where a grinding tongue of ice rasped its way through the limestone. When the ice finally melted, the Vale of Pickering became a lake dammed by a terminal moraine at its eastern end, and the Old English name of Seamer (Sea-mere) witnesses to the existence of a lake spreading its waters over the carrs, a wide, shallow expanse of flood-water left behind when the Vale of Pickering had become waterlogged marshland.

Scarborough should be proud of its hills. They give employment to the eyes, afford panoramic surveys of the sea, prepare the feet for the beaches, for the bold promontory of the Castle Hill, for the levels of the Foreshore Road, the Marine Drive, the Royal Albert Drive, the sweep of the two bays. To look down upon the Museum, the Valley Gardens, the Spa and the sea is as enjoyable as to look up Long Greece Street, Dog-and-Duck Steps, and Church Stairs Street, and to stand by the railings of the Esplanade on a summer night and look across towards the floodlit castle, the curved chains of light along the foreshore and the diffused glow over the town is, I am sure, one of life's major pleasures. Lights, plain or coloured, have become a chief instrument of publicity, as whisky-blenders, cinema proprietors and the town councils of Blackpool, Torquay and Scarborough are well aware.

Those who visit Scarborough cannot but be reminded that this town has a history. They probably know that Earl Tostig and Harold Hardraada fired the houses in 1066, and that William, Earl of Albemarle, built the castle. They connect Oliver's Mount with Oliver Cromwell though the connection has no basis in fact, and may have heard that Paul Jones fought an action off the town. What they do not commonly realize is that Scarborough has a fierce, vivid, contemporary life. "In winter," they say, "the place is dead," and they take to themselves the credit for its liveliness in summer. They are wrong. I do not know a town, unless it be some of the provincial towns of France—Bordeaux, for instance, or Marseilles—where the yarn of life is spun with such fury, where the issues of local politics are fought with such fierceness, where history, tradition, contemporary problems, and future programmes are so blended in a single concentration of spirit. Elsewhere the streams of thought are muddy and stagnant. Here they roar along the years like mountain torrents, and everyone knows who has had the controlling of them, everyone knows the great names.

And great names they really are. Scarborough has always had the habit of producing great men who, instead of entering the arena of national life, have given their energy and genius to the town. I could name you a hundred such from William

15

Smith, father of English geology, to Sir Meredith Whittaker and his brother Sir Thomas. It may be the stimulating quality of the northern air, the proximity of the sea, the shut-away situation of the town, the backing of the moorland country, the mixture of bloods and breeds in the population, an inherited boldness and originality of outlook—the reasons are complex and hard to establish or assess. There is a fierce turbulence of spirit in the youth of the town, moreover. Very early in their lives, the young men, and now also the young women, learn to consider their prospects, and their usual reaction is this : if they stay in Scarborough, they are cramped between the sea and the land, there is no outlet for their restlessness, no opportunity for their talents to develop. They cannot, like the young folk of Leeds and Manchester, play for safety, and they show themselves eager for adventure.

Perhaps I ought to prove what I have written above, and I will do so by setting down what I know of those who attended the Municipal School, now the Boys' High School, between 1906 and 1914. To mention names is to make distinctions, but the facts are accurate. Here is one man who holds a high position in the diplomatic service; another who was an important government official in Malaya; a third became manager of an emerald mine in Brazil and taught the inhabitants of the Matto Grosso to play hockey; a fourth became a wealthy timber merchant in Ontario; a fifth went into gold-mining in Johannesburg; several hold posts in British universities; many went to sea, and one was a professor of genetics in South America. The girls, even in those days, were almost as energetic. One went to South Africa, many to Canada. Some hold university posts in this country, and at least two went to South America.

I cannot estimate with certainty what part was played in all this by the headmaster of the Municipal School during those years, but the majority of those who came under the influence of A. S. Tetley will agree that he too was a great man. He was one of the William Smith sort, not born in the town but finding his genius when he settled there. Tetley was not a great scholar nor even a great teacher, but, as one of his old pupils said to me the other day, "There was something about him. Character? Yes, I suppose so, but Arnold of

16

Rugby had him beaten there. Organizing genius? Nothing like the genius of Sanderson of Oundle. Enthusiasm? Enthusiasm by itself is not enough. No, I know what he had. It was vision. There was a Wellsian breadth and sweep of imaginative vision in the man. He was a great character."

And there were others. Albert Strange, for instance, yachtsman and artist; Elihu Richard Cross, who was more than merely an amiable noise on the board of directors of the old *Nation*; Dr Rooke the antiquarian, who lived in a crazy battlemented house, authentically sham-Gothic, overlooking the Valley; Sir George Sitwell, to whom should be given something of the credit for the achievements of his children; "Advertiser" Smith, thwarted genius and stormy petrel of local politics and history; Tudor James, who claimed royal descent and held the mayor and corporation at bay for years on end; Will Catlin of Catlin's Pierrots; Fred Clark the ornithologist; David Bevan the natural historian; and Meredith Whittaker, newspaper owner and local statesman, whose pen was charged with vitriol and whose speeches had a Ciceronian tang. All these men were alive and active between 1906 and 1914. Something of the secret of their originality lies, perhaps, in their not having been put through the modern educational process. They all exemplified the Herbert Spencerian drive towards individuation.

Some men are great only while they live. Dead, their memories fade rapidly and their achievements are forgotten. Others, while alive, are minor figures who, having died, step into the foreground and develop greatness. Such a man was Harry W. Smith, borough engineer and surveyor of Scarborough, and no account of the town to-day would be valuable unless it took into account the work and achievements of Harry W. Smith.

Smith's father was, I believe, a landscape gardener, and Harry W. Smith came to Scarborough from Bournemouth. When last I was in Scarborough, I walked into the Borough Engineer's office and talked with two of the town-planning officials trained by Smith. It took them two hours to sing the epic of their master.

"According to the lawn-tennis correspondent of the *Daily Mail*," I said, "the tennis courts in Filey Road are the first in

Hackness: the Anglian Cross

the country apart from Wimbledon. Who was responsible for their design and execution?"

"Harry W. Smith," said Poole.

"And the Italian Gardens?" I asked.

"Harry W. Smith," said Milward.

"Peasholm Glen, which I remember as Wilson's Wood?"

"Harry W. Smith."

"Peasholm Lake and Peasholm Gardens?"

"Harry W. Smith."

"Alexandra Gardens, Northstead Manor Gardens, and the Open-air Theatre?"

"Harry W. Smith."

Obviously Smith was something more than the Capability Brown of Scarborough. He had an eye, that man! He had vision in two senses of the word, for he knew not only what to put his hands on, but also what to leave alone. There were places in his vision for art and artifice on the one hand, for natural, untouched wildness on the other. Whenever Smith used art, he improved. "He was a master of contour, skylines, and vegetation. He knew, moreover, when to be original and when to follow acknowledged genius," Poole told me. "The Italian Gardens, for instance, are modelled upon the Italian Gardens in the Spa grounds. They are frankly imitative."

"And who," I asked, "designed the Italian Gardens in the Spa grounds?"

"Sir Joseph Paxton."

"Paxton of the Crystal Palace? Paxton of the Great Exhibition?"

Poole nodded.

"And," added Milward, "Paxton of the original Spa buildings."

Genius at work. It was good to fix, also, the continuity of tradition from Paxton to Smith, from Smith to his capable successors.

"But," Poole went on, "don't go away supposing that Harry Smith was the only man who had a hand in the modelling of Scarborough. You've possibly heard of Sir Edwin Cooper, of Hall, Cooper and Davis?"

I nodded.

"Sir Edwin Cooper," Poole continued, "was an old Central

18

School boy. He designed the Municipal School when school architecture had no more status than Cinderella with her sisters."

"That," I said, "is good hearing. Anything else?"

"He designed the outdoor orchestral building on the Spa," said Milward quickly.

We went into a divagation upon the Spa's music and the influence of Alexander Cohen and Alick Maclean. Out of it emerged the information that a prominent British conductor, deservedly popular, had once been a boy clerk in Harry Smith's office.

"Talent," remarked Milward, "of an unexpected kind in an unexpected place."

At this point I brought out my bogy.

"What," said I suddenly, "about boulder clay?"

They laughed.

"Some years ago it gave us trouble, but——"

"Trouble!" I said. "The footpath and half the carriage-way of Queen's Parade were slipping. I remember huge fissures—you couldn't call them cracks—in the road, and asphalt ten feet below road-level. Trouble? I expected the boarding-houses on the landward side of Queen's Parade to subside and topple every time I walked that way."

"True, but——"

"And you called in professorial advice."

"We did."

"And you shifted Flagstaff Hill."

"Correct. Then we did a certain amount of remodelling, you remember. Seriously, though, once boulder clay is contained by a wall, it gives little bother."

My bogy, after all, was no more frightening than the turnip-lanterns we used to make forty years ago.

Turnip-lanterns? I was the only member of my family possessing patience enough to carve out turnip-lanterns for Hallowe'en. Raking in the dust of oblivion, I find that the inspiration came to me from a five-by-four picture in the *Boy's Own Paper* of a wretched traveller fleeing from a sheeted ghost like that which, in the Elizabethan theatre, cried miserably like an oyster-wench, "Hamlet, revenge!" And, under the picture, four lines of verse :

19

Like one that on a lonesome road
Doth walk in fear and dread
Because he knows a frightful fiend
Doth close behind him tread.

Thus was the Road to Xanadu opened to me by a turnip-lantern ghost carved out of a big swede in a ramshackle harness-room, smelling of mice, meal and leather, ten miles east of Scarborough.

I make no apology for this divagation. On the contrary I insist that there shall be more and better ghosts before we reach the closing stages of our journey together. Meantime I return you to the Borough Engineer's office.

"Scarborough to-day," I remarked, "is subtly different from Victorian and Edwardian Scarborough. I note changes."

"German bombs and land-mines are partly responsible," Poole told me, "but between the two wars we ourselves were not idle. We didn't interfere with the quayside and the fishing-village, but set to work on the indeterminate area, the no-man's land, between the fishing village and the new town, where the streets were sinking into slumdom if they hadn't already arrived there."

"Cross Street!" I said. "Dumple Street!"

"Precisely! And we made one or two interesting discoveries. While we were working down Cross Street we uncovered the lower courses of the old town wall, ten to twelve feet thick. We have the photographs somewhere, I believe."

He raised an eyebrow. Milward caught the query and produced the photographs. We looked at them together.

"And what happened to the uncovered wall?" I asked.

"We wanted to keep it as an exhibition-piece but unfortunately it had to go underground again : keeping it would have meant too much replanning. A pity!"

Poole ruminated over the photographs.

"That's me—just there!" he said.

"Then," said Milward, "there was that business at Friarage School."

"Go on!" I said.

"Friarage School was built on soft ground—a peaty deposit where there had once been a pond, most probably the fish-stew of one or other of the medieval religious houses in that area. If you visit the school you'll find that the ground floor now shows a subsidence of between four and six inches. That, however, is not the point. In this peaty area there must have been either a medieval cobbler's shop or else a dump for old footgear, because out of the peat we dug a whole lot of ancient sandals, splendidly preserved by the peat they'd been buried in, and a pair of huge boots with leather buttons, together with a scattering of smashed pots—products of the local Falsgrave pottery. The stuff, I believe, is on show at the Free Library."

The final sentence came out casually, and I understood why. A discovery once made, the fate of the trophies matters little to the discoverers. Do antiquarians haunt museums to gloat over their prizes? I doubt it much.

Town-planning demands special qualities in the men who give their lives to it. Particularly in a place like Scarborough it needs creative imagination—not the creative imagination that sees infinity in a grain of sand and eternity in an hour—*un coup de tonnerre sous un ciel de plombe*—but the con-structive-creative imagination that can remould what is into what may be, that can transform a Wilson's Wood into a Peasholm Glen, for example. This sort of imagination craves leisurely thought. It cannot be hurried. It has to be based, too, upon copious and accurate knowledge of things as they are and a shrewd estimate of the future. The town-planners of Scarborough are not, moreover, men to beat the bones of the buried. They have a right respect for antiquity.

"We proceed upon the assumption that the resident population figure will remain fairly steady at 37,000," they said. "In 1801 the population was 6,409; in 1851, 12,158; in 1818, 26,238. By 1891 Scarborough and Falsgrave had amalgamated and their total population was 33,776. In 1945 the resident population was 35,800. So far as these things can be foreseen," Poole went on, "Scarborough is unlikely to grow much bigger. I think and I hope it has reach optimum size and is not eager to digest the surrounding villages. Our plans for the town——"

21

"My apologies!" I said. "I think I ought to look at the town as it is now. Then I'll come back to hear about your plans for the future."

"And then we'll try to show Scarborough as it will be. Meanwhile keep an eye upon the sky-lines," Milward advised.

As I walked down the steps of the Town Hall into St Nicholas Street I thought about horizons. Wherever the earth cuts the sky the silhouette has value. West Riding windows, for instance, look across valleys filled with industrial gloom towards groupings of mill chimneys against a concave sheeting of greenish sky. Those distant chimneys develop a vivid pictorial symbolism. Sunset floods the valley of the Aire and throws into sombre relief the workshops and warehouses of the river-front, and they are lovely. Plumes of engine-smoke, trees, ships' cordage, a broken wall, colliery workings, a mountainside and a sequence of pylons, all may develop pictorial magnificence in silhouette. Something, but not everything, depends upon the kind and quality of the lighting. Here at Scarborough, summer or winter solstice, the light has a peculiar clarity and there is a plenitude of horizons. The long sea-line is never more lovely than when a full moon rises over it, with bars of white light across the water, and, in summer, the counter-blaze of Spa lighting diffused across the tide-rippled sand. Look southward after sunset at the dark finger of land thrusting into the sea-haze and ending at the flashing light of Flamborough. Consider the Castle Hill in noonday sunshine, or floodlit, or faintly visible through an October sea-roke. The sky-line of the South Cliff has the beauty of the sequence of horizons along Lake Como, but without their ramshackle romanticism and southern garishness. As you walk slowly along Quay Street amongst the old houses, the curved roofs and ridge-tiles lean against the sky with exactly the right irregularities. Looking inland, you suddenly catch sight of the high horizon of the race-course, with Baron Albert's Tower squatting upon the straight line of the headland and reminding you of the last line of "Childe Roland." And, of course, there is Oliver's Mount with its conspicuous obelisk. When the town's war memorial was first set up I suspected the good taste of those who selected the site. Now it has grown familiar, I praise their judgment. So much for sky-lines. Now for another matter, the matter of history.

Whenever the past gets in the way of the present, the past is sure to suffer. I used to consider this a matter for regret, but within the last ten years I have developed a changed attitude. I recollect talking to Albert Strange on this subject, reminding him of Steeth Bolt and the old tarred sail-lofts that occupied the frontage close to the south entrance to the Marine Drive. He tugged at his trim white beard and looked at me with an amused expression in his clear blue eyes.

"You're thinking of the pictures and not of the rats and mice," he said. "The sail-lofts were incredibly verminous, they were tumbling to ground-level and their day had gone. Picturesque they may have been, but they were cluttering up the quayside and the time had come to get rid of them."

He was right. The past has to give way to the needs of the present. How long ago nobody can precisely say, the flat acreage of the Castle Yard was inhabited—one might almost say infested—by prehistoric pit-villagers, who dug holes in the ground and lived in them. What they lived upon, I don't know. Then came the Brigantian Celts to dispossess them, and the site of the pit-village was abandoned. The Romans in the days of Theodosius erected a hundred-foot tower, a beacon and signal-station, on the headland. The Anglian pirates destroyed it. Their christianized descendants put up a little chapel there, not only to worship in but also to be landmark and beacon for coastal traffic and homing ships. Skarthi built his Viking village in the shelter of the headland. In 1066 the village was burned. Then followed the Norman harrying of the north, and Domesday Book makes no mention of Scarborough. In the twelfth century the chapel on the Roman site was rebuilt to form part of the story of the great castle put up by William le Gros, serving as the garrison chapel. Outside the castle walls arose the Church of St Mary to minister to the spiritual needs of the haven folk. Two or three Cistercian monks dwelt there, and a vicar of Scarborough. The fishing village became a walled town, and the friars arrived, Franciscans and Dominicans, to build their friarages within the shelter of the walls.

The pit-village was lost, the chapel on the headland was

lost, the Roman signal-station went below ground, Skarthi's Viking village was utterly destroyed, and the Church of St Mary preserved little indeed of its original structure. The shell of the castle, but only the shell, remained. The friarages vanished and the town wall disappeared. Man the destroyer was followed by Nature; she laid a healing hand upon the scars that man had inflicted, slowly the level of the soil was raised by earthworms and decayed vegetation, couch-grass invaded the hummocked sites, young trees rooted in the crumbling lime between the tumbled stones, and then, finally, man once more cleared and levelled the ground for new and necessary building operations.

In Scarborough antiquity is overlaid by modernity because within the walls of the old town there was little room for expansion. As the old became antiquated it had to be pulled down to make room for the new, yet the past is almost everywhere still alive, the present, the immediate past, and the remote centuries blending together into a composite in which old Long Room Street and modern St Nicholas Street, old Tanner's Row and modern St Thomas Street, become one, Theakston's Library and the modern Free Library amalgamate, and the modern high schools are identified with the old school known simply as Back o' Danyell's. The present, it appears, is also history.

The middle-class residential districts and the boarding-house quarters have, I find, changed little during the last half-century. Many big houses on the South Cliff have been turned into flats, new private hotels have sprung up to overlook Peasholm Gap, the Burniston Road area has been developed and the down-street population has been moved into North-stead. There has been building activity along Scalby Mills Road and elsewhere on the fringes of the town. But the lines of this development, which is neither change nor progress, were fixed long ago by the belief that the prosperity of the town lies in development as a holiday resort for middle-class families, tennis and bowls players, swimming and sun-bathing and dancing devotees, concert-goers and fun-fair haunters. These lines of development have meant decline in another direction. Not so many years ago, Scandinavian barques and barquentines brought cargoes of timber into the harbour.

Two general freighters, the *Buccaneer* and the *General Havelock*, called regularly to discharge and take on passengers and cargo. There were many privately owned yawls and cutters. During the herring harvest both harbours were crammed with trawlers and drifters from almost every fishing-port along the coasts of Britain. Scots lasses gutted the fish with incredible dexterity along the quayside, or walked about with clicking needles. Heavy carts laden with dripping barrels of salt fish climbed the cobbled street from the harbour-side. The departure of the herring fleet on the flood tide made many a picture for the artist and much money for the picture-postcard photographer. Those times have gone, the curve of decline has grown steeper and swifter, and to-day the harbour-side is little more than a survival upon which the fun-fair has already begun to encroach.

I had almost written "a picturesque survival." But the harbour-side is not so picturesque, either. Nobody has worried consistently enough about this part of the town. Nobody has cared enough. When I walked along the irregular frontage and looked up at the work of the Philistines sprawled over an eighteenth-century dwelling-house, or stopped to try to picture the grouping, gabling and pitching of the tiled roofs, I presented an unfamiliar sight—that of a man actually troubling his mind with something not worth patching and mending. When I went behind the frontage and walked along the old streets, intruded into courts and alleys, invaded derelict houses and peered through smashed windows, tested door-snecks and looked for eighteenth-century ironwork on broken shutters, I went alone. Nobody in the whole town was on a similar quest, nobody worried, nobody cared. Many of the houses were mere rubbish. They had once been clean and cared for; they were used as dumps for old fishing-gear; they had once housed thrifty and industrious people. Here the blistered paintwork on a warehouse door told me that a barker of sails had once plied his trade within; there the paint had gone altogether in a splintering of rotten wood. It was rather pitiful, the whole business, but I do not easily give way to this sentimental kind of pity. If the old has to fall into ruin by a process of natural decay, the shedding of tears is vain, and *alas!* has gone out of fashion. Still, if the old houses are to tumble down I do not see why the old ice-factory should be allowed to remain. It is a vile building and has long ceased to justify its existence.

When I got back to my lodgings I asked for a town directory and looked for the names of the seafaring families which for generations lived in the older part of the town. My suspicions were confirmed. The Owstons, Cammishes, Sheaders, and Capplemans had dwindled in numbers. Two wars no doubt partly share the responsibility, but the decay of the port and haven must take the rest of it. Very dimly I remember when fishermen walked about this part of the town in high-heeled boots, sealskin caps, and blue reefer jackets with sealskin collars, when they were a large, sober, religious community, when the bigger houses in Princess Street, Longwestgate, and Merchants' Row were furnished with shining mahogany and gleaming brass. Mahogany doors with brass handles.

In 1938 Professor Adshead and the Borough Engineer went through this area with inquiring eyes and speculative minds, making notes on what could be preserved and what should be preserved, on pulling down, renovation, repair, removal of unsightly advertisements, cleaning up and opening out. Their house-to-house findings were published in their report and ought to be diligently studied, but even when their recommendations are carried out in full and to the letter this ancient fishing village can now never be much more than a moribund museum-piece. Friars' Entry has now become Friars' Way, and I think I do not like the change of name. Auborough Street, though mostly Victorian, is worth preserving. Cook's Row is derelict. Many of the wrecked houses have old oak door-lintels. There are eighteenth-century wrought-iron knockers to some of the doors, but they would disintegrate if an attempt were made to detach them. Spreight Lane Steps is well kept. There is a good little house at the corner of Longwestgate and Church Stairs Street. It has a sensible steeply pitched tile roof, a staircase inside the wall, and a good high fireplace with a paltry Victorian kitchen-range in it. In Church Stairs Street there are signs of old stone stairways outside the houses. Part of the old town wall runs through the basement of Nesfield's old house at the head of Auborough Street.

In Paradise the Graham Sea Training School was the former residence of the Tindalls, who were builders of deep-sea brigs and barques at Scarborough from the late seventeenth century until 1863. There was a Tindall fleet, but ships were also built for other owners at Scarborough, Whitby, Filey, and Bridlington. The Tindalls built *Free Briton, Europe, Fortitude, Alfred the Great, Centurion, Knapton, Diligence Packet, Good Intent, Endeavour, Meanwell, Providence and Hannah, Sarah Margaret, Rose in June, Happy Meeting, Good Samaritan.* If Homer could catalogue ships, so could the Tindalls. When iron ships began to leave the northern yards the Scarborough shipbuilding industry died and the Tindalls left the house in Paradise with its country Adam dining-room and inlaid mahogany cornices, its acre of garden and its air of dignified importance. The garden is now waste land, the rooms are occupied by desks and blackboards. On the staircase walls is an interesting collection of old local prints, but about the house lurks only the faintest echo of its past, and the dimmest feeling of protest is awakened by the chalked diagrams on the blackboards and the dingy, rather battered desks.

The Ministry of Works and Buildings has taken over Scarborough Castle, and when I paid my visit to the ruin two or three masons were at work upon the keep. That morning, I remember, there were only three visitors—an oldish man, a Canadian soldier, and a schoolboy. Of these, the Canadian alone showed interest in the castle. He had that nostalgia for the past which is born of the loss of spiritual equilibrium and orientation. The schoolboy felt nothing of that sort. What he wanted to know was : how deep was the well in the ballium (he didn't call it the ballium) and was there water at the bottom? The oldish man blinked in the sunshine. His mind was "drowned in the golden deluge of the morn." He did not speak, his eyes were dull, he had no living curiosity. The schoolboy and I dropped pebbles down the well, counted and calculated, and determined the depth. And there was water at the bottom.

Twenty yards north-east of the keep, a man was on his

way to the brick-built cottage in the castle yard for a mug of tea, and though he wore no leathern apron and carried no rule he was certainly a joiner. Moreover there was something vaguely familiar in his build and walk. I contrived to meet him face to face and knew him at once.

"You're Payne!" I said. "You're Nancy's brother : I remember you."

"Ay," he said, "and I know you, too."

For a while we talked family history. Nancy was married, one of his brothers was deputy harbour-master, the other had been in China so long that he had to think in Chinese before talking in English. Then he opened his mind to me about the castle.

"I've known the old place," he said, "since I could toddle. I know every stone in it and every episode in its history. I don't mind saying I love it better than any place on earth, and it vexes me beyond everything when sightseers are sluggish and incurious or silly and ignorant. Truly," he said, "I'd like nothing so much as to be made warden of Scarborough Castle."

"And you would live," I told him, "in a state of perpetual vexation."

I suppose the truth is that only a few antiquarians and students of medieval architecture devote their days and nights to relics of bygone centuries. I am no Jonathan Oldbuck—I rather wish I were—but if the proper study of mankind is man then these relics form no mean part of it, since there is a great deal more of the past than there is of the present. That is half the reason why ancient things have a hold on me; the other half is that I share the Canadian's lack of right orientation.

I shall say little of the castle. It is there, and it is worth a visit. Its stone came largely from Hayburn Wyke, its timber —when there was timber there—from Raincliff Woods. Cromwell's men blasted out one wall of the massive keep. There was a barbican, a drawbridge, a barracks for redcoats, and a little sweetshop here. The ditch—the Castle Dykes— never contained water.

Across the headland towards the open water stands the solid wooden structure built to overlook F. G. Simpson's excavations of the Iron Age settlement, the Roman signal-station, and the medieval Chapel of Our Lady, all on the one site. I mounted to the platform, grasped the polished rail and looked down upon a tenth-rate desolation of Balclutha. The area was overgrown with white grass, mat grass, couch grass and monstrous docks. Of the neat lines revealed by F. G. Simpson's careful digging there was hardly a trace. The years of war had been years of neglect. Here was nothing of the majesty of ruin, nothing of its pathos. Here I felt anything but nostalgic. Vexed in spirit, I thought that the site should have been cared for even during the toughest war in history.

Now, at this halfway station between the two great bays, I interpolate a note or two of general nature. The first concerns the visitor more than the resident. August Bank Holiday, 1945, was a very wet day. It began with cold wind and heavy rain, the sea lay under a thick blanket, the Castle Hill was invisible and the town was vague and indeterminate in every line. When during the afternoon the range of visibility increased a little, the sea looked as it looks on a wild October day—old, white-haired and white-bearded, grey-faced and wrinkled. It was very fine. I, however, had business in hand. I made it my affair to find out what the holiday crowds were doing, and I started in Peasholm Glen. The shelters and the seats and the paths were deserted. At the yachting-pool there was a single schoolboy pushing his craft across the grey water. The bathing-pool at Peasholm Gap was a solitude. There was no line-up for the miniature railway, none for the booking-office of the Open-air Theatre, none for ice-cream on the foreshore by the wrecked Corner Café. The beach was tide-washed and smooth. The Royal Albert Drive carried no traffic. In the draughty shelters a few silent folk stared at the sea, or read newspapers, or knitted with blue fingers. On the Marine Drive a group of people gathered at the spot where incoming waves would fling spray over them. The Castle Holmes were totally abandoned to the wet. Along the South Foreshore Road the crowd began, but it was nowhere a dense crowd. I saw people carrying suitcases. Nobody cared for the sea or the sands. The amusement parks were shut. People wandered about. They had no aim, no goal, yet they seemed not indignant, not unhappy. The long shelter at the foot of St Nicholas Gardens was occupied by people sitting. They were merely sitting. It was not yet time for the cafés to open.

I thought, "I will visit the Museum." The Museum was locked up. The reading-room and the Public Library were closed not only for the day but for the whole week. An excellent library, a model library! A pity, I said to myself, it should ever be closed for stocktaking. The shops were shut, but the town streets were crowded with all sorts and conditions of people. They were wandering about because there was nothing to do and nowhere to go. At the bus-station there were no queues. Nobody felt like going to Whitby, Filey, or Bridlington. At the railway station folk were arriving in large numbers, many without raincoats and still more without umbrellas. They had come for the sunshine, and there was no sunshine.

I record my observations without acrimony and without comment, and there ends my first note. My second deals with the Scarborough Sunday.

The weather forecast spoke of a cold front advancing from the north-east, but the morning was fine though cool. Peasholm Glen carried crowds making for the sea. Nobody stopped to examine the name-plates of the rock-roses, veronicas, Japanese birches, gentians, and willows with which Harry W. Smith had beautified a steep-sided wilderness of gaunt trees once inhabited by owls and vagabond cats, but doubtless the general impression was one of peace and beauty that could not but furnish some contrast with Sunday morning in Market Street, Huddersfield, or Briggate, Leeds. The Peasholm yachting-pool was busy with children, and parents were thick on the seats. The bathing-pool was crowded. Over a hundred people were in the water. The beach bungalows were all occupied, the sands were crowded with sunbathers brown, lobster-red and pallid. The ice-cream queue was thirty yards long. There were not enough deck-chairs, and people were sitting on the edge of the promenade, on the cliffs, and on the sands. Nobody was reading. One fat man lay fast asleep in a deck-chair, his sun-glasses and eyelids shutting out the sea and the sky, his mouth a perfect O. A ventriloquist entertained a group of children. Two ex-service men stood by the hydrocephalous elephant they had created on the sand, but seemed uninterested in their own masterpiece. Many people used the promenade merely as a promenade, but not, as in Edwardian years, to pass comment upon fashions and frights. Has the fashion-parade utterly perished here? The miniature locomotive, trailing its miniature carriages, puffed along gallantly with its load of passengers. It whistled triumphantly and blew out imposing jets of steam. The little monstrosity surely knew itself to be—as it is—a marvellous attraction. "Worth its weight in gold!" Sam Poole told me. "And it weighs a lot!"

My third note concerns the Museum. When at last I found it open it had no curator and no regular attendants. All were in the services. The official in charge was from the Free Library and knew nothing of the place. He wished he did, but he didn't. Starting from zero, he would take half a hundred years to learn the Museum thoroughly. It needs cleaning up. For a museum the shape of the place is monstrous, and the exhibits look as if they had been shot into the place with little care, no thought, and no science. There is only the raw material of museum-stuff here. The large collection of prints and sketches of Scarborough and the surrounding villages ought to be housed in a single well-lighted room; I found them in chaos. The thirteenth-century door-hinges of Ebberston Church were ranged on the wall along with primitive rat-traps. Old iron. Below them was the carved oak counter of the *E.T.D.* of Nantes, driven ashore by a gale in 1872. I could not make out whether the whole *E.T.D.* had come ashore or only the counter of the *E.T.D.* Marine monstrosities mingled with Zulu war-shields and Polynesian skirts. The town ducking-stool was in the same enclosure as an iron bicycle leaning against a box mangle, and to the left of the ducking-stool stood a penny-farthing bicycle sold by Swift of Scarborough. The town crier's bell hung amongst rusty handcuffs, police batons, clay pipes, and an old-style sewing-machine. Flints and bronze implements showed more logic in their arrangement, and less humour. The fossil-room was a wilderness of ammonites. An inadequate attempt had been made to annotate a dinosaur's footprints, but the plaster cast of a plesiosaurus (or was it a pterodactyl?) failed to indicate whether it was authentic or a reconstruction. Rows of bones from Kirkdale Cave bore no notes as to what bones they were, how they were discovered, by whom they were collected, or why they were important.

The Museum was full of bewildered people. Outside, it was raining steadily.

Scarborough—a fourth note made from this vantage-point on the Castle Hill—shows three economic segregations : first, the South Cliff, a comfortable middle-class unit; secondly, the bulk of the town, a trading and artisan unit; thirdly, the port and haven. Each area merges into its neighbours not only as an economic unit but also as a linguistic unit, though the haven alone clings to the old dialectal forms, chief of which is the use of an unblurred initial *d* for *th* in words like *those, this, these, the* and *there*. This peculiarity of the coastal fringe, persisting also in the Shetlands, emphasizes the voluntary segregation of the fishers from the trading and farming communities. The fisherman turns his back upon the land. A sturdy build, yellow hair, and blue eyes are his Mendelian dominants; the swarthy skin, dark hair, and clumsy frame you meet occasionally result from a nineteenth-century admixture of southern and western blood that took place when trawlers ousted cobles and when the Silver Pit became a lucrative fishing-ground.

From the parapet of the castle wall I stare with some perplexity across the South Bay towards the Spa. Its grounds, terrace, and concert-hall used to be the social centre of the town; there was an atmosphere of rather stately luxury here, an air of moneyed culture. There was a brilliance, a spaciousness, a grace. The finger of change has touched the life of the Spa. As of old, the waters remain a very minor attraction, the orchestra is smaller than it used to be, the fortnightly firework display has localized itself at Peasholm, the crowd seems neither so smart nor so lively. Indeed I thought it grim. Perhaps I saw it on a bad night in a poor season, before Scarborough showed clear signs of recovery from the stress of war, but perhaps my observations also reflected the large-scale shift of wealth, the tremendous shift of values, that have taken place in the whole country during the war years. Hence

32

my perplexity, hence the rather puzzled frown with which I contemplated the distant, old-fashioned Spa buildings. That the Spa has at last begun to outlive its glory I doubt, but if I could by a single wish bring back an August night in the 1900's, with warships swinging their searchlights in the bay, the full moon rising over the sea, the Spa lights blazing, and the colour and the laughter and the leisure, I would wish with all my heart.

Turning from the South Bay to the North, I rest my forearms on the stone parapet. The Castle Holmes lie below me. They belong to the Ministry of Works, which has not yet seen how the slipping of the boulder clay has wrecked the footpaths and the steps by which one climbs to the *col* between the two bays. The stonework of the Albert Drive has suffered from storms and mines, and needs repair.

One of my confirmed negative habits is an avoidance of pleasure-piers. I have never been able to sympathize with the type of mind that plans their erection or with the unnatural urge that leads people to tread their planking. There was formerly a straddle-legged, steel-strutted, gawky pleasure-pier in the North Bay, and whenever I passed it I wished the sea would overwhelm it. By the autumn of 1902 it had become the nightly rendezvous of grey-faced, mufflered sea-anglers. In the winter of that year my wish was fulfilled, not exactly before my very eyes because the night was one of the blackest I have ever known. But, young as I was, I was there. That was what mattered. I was cold, drenched and dazed by the storm, but I was there and I knew what was happening.

The darkness was an opaque immensity without a glimmer in the sky or on the land. The lamplight usually visible at Scalby Mills was drowned in storm, and the length of the promenade was so overwhelmed in spray and scud that no gas-lamp could have survived. The wind burst the glass and dowsed the lights. But wide luminous sheets of foam made it possible to see what was happening within a range of vision limited to ten or a dozen yards. There was no distinguishing between rain, wave, spray, and wind. A heavy and steady pressure of air came in from the north-east. There were no gusts, no lulls. The gale was all of a piece. The waters were

D 33

piled, pressed, hammered and hurled against the defences of the land. Tubular iron railings were wrenched out of their sockets, tossed into the air, twisted and flung across the road by the last lick of a wave. Below the yelling of the gale a dull and immense roaring was audible, a monstrous procession of waves broke with vast explosions of sound against the sea-wall, and parabolic sheets of water rushed a hundred feet into the sky and vanished in the darkness. Then came a succession of vague crashings and grindings in the outer chaos, a wild hullabaloo of rendings, groanings, splinterings of wood and iron, and presently the first bits of the pier were tossed out of the sea. All night the storm tugged and tore at the carcass, and when at last the dawn broke with the gale still raging we saw a battered island of pier out to sea, windowless, splintered, completely gutted, and still subject to terrific rushes of foaming water. I was very excited and very gratified. At the same time I was a little afraid. I had witnessed the elements at play, and, myself considerably battered, had learned something of their strength. Not many hours went by before Harry Wanless came down to sketch the scene. His work shows the tide receding, the sky clearing a little, a few sightseers huddled below the empty windows of the landward wreckage, a sagging upright or two, three crazy girders and much half-submerged ruin out beyond the broken railings.

The owners of the wreck had, I believe, a notion to recondition the gutted island on its shaky legs, but their project was properly discouraged.

Before going down to the North Bay beach I walked along to the parish church, stopping on my way to look at the Hinderwell Memorial. I have owned my copy of Hinderwell for over thirty years : "*The History and Antiquities of Scarborough*, by Thomas Hinderwell, Esq.,, third edition, revised, with a brief memoir of the Author. Scarborough, printed and published by M. Bye; published also in London by Messrs. Whittaker and Co., and may be had of the booksellers of York, Hull, Malton, Whitby, Bridlington, etc., 1837." The volume, with its portrait of Hinderwell looking rather like the young Wordsworth and its fine steel engraving of the arms and seal of the borough, belonged when it was new to William Edward Woodall of Woodall's Bank (formerly at the corner of St Nicholas Street), of Manor Road and of the French Riviera, and is dedicated to Sir J. V. B. Johnstone, Bart., M.P. for the County of York, by his obedient servant, B. Evans.

We have lost the knack of composing a title-page and of writing the curiously stilted prose of former times. "To exhibit a topographic and economic view of Scarborough, and to rescue from obscurity the remains of information relative to its antiquities" has a starched-collar dignity impossible to our less formal age.

B. Evans of the third edition, dating his work from Hinderwell Place, July 1832, considerably enlarged Hinderwell's work, and in his thorough revision acknowledged the help received from Francis Palgrave, F.R.A.S.S., and from Dr Travis and Dr Murray. Mr Bean helped with the natural history. Of Thomas Hinderwell, Evans tells us that "his course was mild, uniform and settled." He was the son of Thomas and Rebekah Hinderwell, born at Scarborough on 17 November 1744, the eldest son of a family of four. Educated at Scarborough and at the grammar school at Coxwold, where the Rev. R. Midgley was "an able divine and an excellent classic," Thomas went to sea. In 1773 we find him master of a transport at St Petersburg; in 1775 he retired from the sea in easy and comfortable circumstances, in 1778 became a member of Scarborough Corporation and in 1781 a magistrate. He was president of the Amicable Society, of the Humane Society; he was a friend of William Wilberforce, and interested himself in the lifeboat. His *History of Scarborough*, not originally intended for publication but merely the amusement of leisure hours, was first published in one quarto volume in 1798, and the second edition, enlarged and improved, appeared in 1811. The first edition was inscribed "To the magistrates of the borough of Scarborough, the burgesses and the inhabitants at large," the second "To W. Wilberforce, esq., M.P. for the County of York."

"The author," we are told, "stands upon a pedestal which many will envy; he is adorned with a garland which will bloom with perpetual verdure, and Scarborough in her history will hand down to succeeding generations the name of Hinderwell as her first and greatest benefactor."

One Michael Kennedy, Esq., of whom I know nothing, burst into a series of dreadful couplets in a monody on the death of Thomas Hinderwell, Esq., of Scarborough :

> Ye who would sorrow o'er departed worth—
> Ye who would mourn when genius flits from earth—
> Ye who would sigh to bid the good, farewell—
> Crowd round the hallow'd tomb of Hinderwell.

Hinderwell's studied style is dull and prolix. His lists of monuments, priests, magistrates, and burgesses are not accurate enough to be of much value, and I weary of "this noble castle whose venerable walls defend the summit of a lofty precipice." All the same, I do not much admire Arthur Rowntree's *History of Scarborough*, 1931. It is planned too much like the *Cambridge Modern History* to suit my taste. The matter is good but the arrangement lacks discretion.

I come to the conclusion that local history is as hard to write, and as unsatisfactory when completed, as the British National Anthem in cuneiform, and I make my way to the parish church, with whose history Hamilton Thompson has dealt once and for all in Rowntree's *History*. Let me say that I admire more the graveyard than the church. This does not mean that I do not admire the church. It has a wonderful situation, it is solid and dignified, it has atmosphere, it is the right size, it has many claims to merit. But give me a graveyard overlooking the sea, with worn tombstones at all angles to the horizon, wind-combed tussocks of grass, and little evidence of regimentation of the dead. Ann Brontë was buried in this churchyard.

I wish the parish church were more like a ship, but as it is it is very well. The first record of its existence is dated the 11th of December 1189, when Richard the First granted the church in free alms to the Cistercians, which meant that from that date there existed in Scarborough a little group of Cistercian monks, a cell of the mother-abbey at Cîteaux. In addition there was a vicar. The Cistercians seem to have spent their time in the usual medieval occupations : praying, collecting revenue, and quarrelling with their neighbours. At the Reformation the chantry-priests went out of business, and during the eighteenth century so many parishioners wanted private pews that the interior became cluttered up with staircases, galleries, and oak partitions. Sir Gilbert Scott overhauled and renovated the building in modern times. In brief, the parish church has had its moments, but I doubt if its history is sufficiently chequered to interest anyone save the ecclesiastical historian.

The North Bay has never achieved the popularity of the South Bay. There is still a bleakness, bareness, austerity here, an exposure to the north-east wind, a total lack of natural shelter; and yet on a fine day in summer the foreshore car-park is crowded and there is a great deal of holiday activity.

At last I found my survey, though haphazard, fairly complete, and I went back to Poole and Milward in the Borough Engineer's Office.

"Well?" they asked.

"I've looked at Scarborough," I said. "What are you going to do about it?"

"Housing first," they replied.

In an auctioneer's office in the town I had been talking to a builder and contractor who at the moment was neither building nor contracting but who, describing himself as a vampire, was buying and selling bricks and mortar as fast as they came into the market. He had views on housing.

"There's a lack of vision," he insisted, "in the schemes of the Corporation. There's timid counsel, there's timid planning. The schemes are makeshift and there's a tendency to build piecemeal, a few houses here and a few there. I myself think," he went on, "that the town should think in millions of pounds, not in thousands. The job of reconstruction is urgent and essential, and I'm sure that ultimately the expenditure would show a profit."

In the Borough Engineer's Office I did not voice this criticism. It was not my concern, but a matter for council-chamber and town meeting.

"Housing," said Poole and Milward, "takes chief priority. Nothing will be done to improve the town as a holiday resort until the shortage of houses has been remedied."

"And then?"

"A crowded programme. New approach-roads to the town

and the provision of suitable sites for holiday-camps," said Poole.

"The rebuilding of the façade of the Foreshore Road between Bland's Cliff and Eastborough," said Milward.

"A replanned Corner Café at Peasholm Gap."

"The widening of the road there."

"A car-park, gardens, and an ice-rink where the Aquarium is."

"A new Olympia."

"Central area improvements."

"A country club and sports centre."

"A big bus station on Sandside."

"A huge amusement park at Scalby Mills."

I held up my hand in the manner of a traffic policeman.

"Slowly, slowly!" I pleaded. "Let me ask a question or two."

They permitted me to put my queries.

"You will preserve vistas and viewpoints?"

"Yes."

"Raincliff Woods and Throxenby Mere?"

"We shall leave them alone."

"The foreshore north and south of the town?"

"We shall make and keep it fully accessible everywhere. As farms along the coast come upon the market, we shall buy them."

"Allotment gardens?"

"We shall try to co-operate with the allotment-holders to make their gardens more sightly."

"Flowering trees along the highways?"

"Certainly. Not forest trees."

"The race-course?"

"The big wireless station has pretty well destroyed the natural beauty there. We can't do much about the race-course."

Milward fetched me a copy of *Scarborough, a survey of its existing conditions and some proposals for its future development, by Professor S. D. Adshead, Emeritus Professor of Town Planning, London University, and H. V. Overfield, Borough and Water Engineer to the Scarborough Corporation, 1938.*

38

"It's all here," he said. "Read this, and you'll know."

"I may borrow it?"

"You may have it."

Tucking the handsome volume under my arm, I left the office with two more calls to make. The first took me to the Shuttleworth Garden opposite the Clock Tower at Holbeck. I look upon that rose-and-rock garden as the most restful garden in the town. It is sunny and secluded. There I am reminded of the Chinese sundial inscription : *Enjoy yourself while you can; it may be later than you think.*

The second call took me to the cliff-tops south of Holbeck Gardens. I wanted to know if blue butterflies—the large and small varieties—were still to be found there. I found them both and was satisfied.

CHAPTER II

THE COUNTRYSIDE ROUND
SCARBOROUGH, WITH PART OF
THE COAST

IN 1829 John Cole of Cole's Library in Newborough, Scarborough, published *Historical Sketches of Scalby, Burniston and Cloughton, with descriptive notices of Hayburn Wyke and Staintondale, in the County of York*. I confess to a regard for John Cole, who seems to have been as mad as Dick's hatband and as thrang as Thrap's wife, and an excellent specimen of the topographical writers of the early nineteenth century. He was stimulated to write his remarkable little production of ninety-one pages by the discovery of what he calls a "Brigantian village" near Cloughton. "This," he says, "in a great measure incited me to become the Annalist of the contiguous and connecting parishes." Forthwith he explains Scalby as "the home of the scald or poet," and determines the existence of the poet by the beauty of the village, which is "seated in a vale, surrounded by majestic hills, in the wapentake of Pickering Lythe, in the North Riding of the County of York. In the landscape here presented, the eye of taste is fully satisfied. The hills of Hackness, especially one tabular projection, and the range of Raincliff, from the boundaries of the horizon on the right hand and on the left, these noble eminences and slopes of every size and form, are clothed with woods, in growth and quantity most picturesque, and disposed with the best effect on the very points where we should most desire them."

He stalks his Brigantian village with the cunning of a domestic cat creeping along a hedgerow, introducing first a digression upon church-going at Scalby, where "the excellent prayers of our church are offered by Mr. Thurlow in a meek tone of supplication which hardly gives promise of that compass of voice which is afterwards displayed in the sermon, when its deep intonations are brought forth with much

40

energy." Next follow two stories of the plague. "The introduction of that Plague which broke out in England in 1625 is
attributed to a seafaring man just returned from the East
Indies; whose wife being landed at Cloughton appeared on
the following Sunday in the church of Scalby, habited in black
silk. Whether the contagion was conveyed in this dress, then
put on for the purpose of attending divine worship, or the
disease, from which she had apparently recovered, yet lurked
in her frame, cannot be positively ascertained, but certain it
is that it quickly spread its baneful effects around, as many of
the congregation were suddenly infected, became sick, and
fell in their pews, which caused the officiating clergyman to
desist from preaching, and put into practice his labour of
love. The pestilential contagion was soon disseminated over
this and the neighbouring villages, and but few escaped its
ravages : the family of a medical man then resident at Scalby,
it is reported, preserved themselves, through the blessing of
Providence, from its sickening consequence by eating, every
morning, fasting, rue and figs."

"It is curious to observe," he goes on, "that a lady of
Scalby, who was, at this calamitous period, near the time of
her accouchement, and fearing she should take the disorder,
caused a cow-house, situated in a pasture near the village, to
be fitted up as the chamber of her delivery, and on the
emergency of the moment it was hung round with the
undressed, but no less serviceable, skins of sheep; and in this
humble abode she was, through the care of Providence,
sheltered from the effects of the Plague, and recovered her
wonted health. In the course of a fortnight, however, that
great natural calamity had reached Scarborough and was then
raging to so great a degree that carts were sent round, as in
London, with the cry 'Bring out your dead!' and on this
occasion the Corporation of Scarborough built a Pest-house,
in a retired place in the Holmes, for the reception of such of
the inhabitants as were infected. It is stated that the tanning
and tallow-chandlery businesses warded off its pestiferous
blasts, as persons engaged in those trades at Scarborough
escaped the contagion."

The topographer elbows the chronicler out of the way in
order to describe Scalby Mills, "romantically situated in a

delightful recess on the North-shore of Scarborough, about the distance of one mile and a half from the Castle, the ride conducting to which may be pleasantly taken along the sands. A branch of the river Derwent, which passes through Ayton, Hackness and Scalby, rolls with pleasing murmurs near the building, proving ornamental as well as useful. It is enclosed with hills of verdure, and of varied form; an elevated point of rock near the shore gives an effective finish to the scene. In the garden of this retreat appear several neat edifices, erected for the purpose of displaying the tea-equipage during the summer months, round which grow pendent laburnums and honeysuckles, this spot being much frequented in the Scarborough season by parties formed for the purpose of taking tea amid the charms of rural scenery. From the seats here a most delightful scene presents itself of the majestic ruins of Scarborough Castle, with the great expanse of ocean."

Then he looks the other way. "A road opposite Newby, to the south, leads to Raincliff, in every respect the most extensive wood in the neighbourhood of Scarborough. Through it, in the warmer seasons of the year, may be taken one of the most delightful rides that this country affords. The wood is entered by a gate on the right hand of the lane, which may be followed along the bottom of the hill, and will conduct strangers either to Hackness by way of Everley, or through the Forge-valley to Ayton, and thus returning to Scarborough by the York road. The variety of ground passed through in making this agreeable tour is abundant in diversified sylvan scenery. The succession of very dissimilar, but well contrasted scenes, almost every one beautiful in its kind, may, combining the effect of the whole, scarcely be rivalled within so small a compass. The river Derwent overhung with branching shrubs, and spiry alders, sweeps its winding course, rippling along at the foot of lofty eminences, thickly planted with trees. This river afterwards spreads a broader stream, meandering through more open ground, toward the picturesque village of Ayton, adorned by a handsome modern bridge, near to which are the remains of an ancient mansion, all so happily situated as if designed in succession to surprise and gratify the eye of the visitant."

Nature, aided perhaps a little by John Cole, sets out her

charms to provoke gasps of delight from stovepipe-hatted gentlemen and flounced, furbelowed, sprigged-muslined, and parasoled ladies.

Cole approaches his Brigantian village by way of Ringing Keld, "where, it is said, a Bell was rung on the hill above the spring, after sunset, to guide benighted travellers, who happened to be crossing the moors, to the public roads and places of safety." Bell-hill in Staintondale, he thinks, "retains that appellation from a similar custom having been practised at that place." He notes the celebrated quarry of freestone at Cloughton, whence Scarborough Castle is said to have been built; the petrifying spring at Cloughton Wyke, and another three hundred yards north near the defile called Salt-pan, on the estate of John Woodall. Coal has sometimes been wrought at Cloughton Wyke.

At last he reaches his destination, the Brigantian village. "The area upon which it formerly existed is called by the country people Hulleys or Hall-leys because, presumably, an old hall formerly stood there. The remains of the town are not spread over the whole of this surface; but they occupy several acres, and consist of squares, oblong-squares and semi-circles, of various dimensions; the foundations of which are of stone, some very large, and all apparently unhewn. Those divisions that have escaped the plough exhibit all that fertility and freshness of vegetation which is generally observed within the walls of ancient camps and settlements."

The investigator noted shallow pits, a surrounding rampart of stone, and a covered way, a fosse-road, running north to the moors. He also notes that the tumuli, "those interesting memorials of antiquity," have been carted away to mend a paltry parish road. In this district, they "are generally of a very singular construction; large blocks of stone, piled close to each other, composing the outer edge or boundary; in the centre of this circle the ashes or body appears to have been deposited, and cairns of various dimensions have been raised by heaping on stones of all sizes. No earth has been used, as far as I have observed, in those tumuli near Hulleys."

One tumulus, east of the ruins, had a diameter of about seventy feet, with unbaked fragments of pottery scattered over the interior, "but none were preserved."

The trackway crosses Ringing Keld, goes boldly up the hillside and continues in a straight course to three larger tumuli on the verge of Harwood Dale, and near a place called Gowland. North-west of Hulleys, a mile and a half away, to the left of the high road, is a vast assemblage of stones apparently without order or design. Contiguous are many tumuli, nearly surrounding "a remarkable and beautiful little relic," a stone circle of upright stones, of about thirty feet diameter; most of them in their original position, the highest of which is now nearly four feet above the surface. "And in the middle of the circle, the altar-stones are still clearly visible." Not far west from this spot is one of those singular clusters of pits called Dry-heads. Dry-heads, which is as much as to say, Druids !

Finally, "to the north and north-west of Hulleys, the scenery possesses all that wild and romantic character so peculiar to the Yorkshire moors; frowning, as it were, in wrath at their own desolation and dreariness, and deserted by the human race. Not so once : cast your eyes around, and everywhere you behold mysterious relics like the ruins of a former world, of a people long since mingled with the dust."

Not even in the age of nuclear energy can we afford to patronize writers like John Cole, for what we have gained in knowledge we may have lost in enthusiasm. I myself, sitting in the sunshine at the edge of Throxenby Mere, below Raincliff, am reminded that Scarborough has had the habit of producing amateurs of the vasculum and the geological hammer, sturdy and shrewd field naturalists in knickerbockers and norfolk jackets whose findings and recordings have not always remained in the faded brown ink of the proceedings of their society.

Throxenby Mere is almost overgrown with pondweed, flags, sedges, and rushes. The morning is very quiet. I watch dabchicks in the few open patches of water. They come down to the surface with their bodies at a steep angle, legs thrust straight down, necks stretched out and upward. They are unafraid. Swallows dip the surface of the water, and presently the dabchicks move off quietly into the reeds. Butterflies— meadow browns—settle on the hawkweed and ragwort by the side of the mere. The reflections of the trees in the water seem more real than the trees themselves, possessing a greater depth of colour; but perhaps this is an illusion created by silence and solitude. I think of Havelock Ellis's comment that we need solitude in order to find our fellows, and, as though in response to the thought, up ride two cyclists, their bicycles laden with camping-gear. Where can they find a site? I suggest the wilderness of caravans at Cayton Bay but they shake their heads. They have been there, and the place is choked with campers. I advise them to try Everley, Suffield, or Hilla Green, but express no confidence that they will find what they seek. These two are the first human beings I have seen since quitting Scarborough. So magnetic is the attraction of people for people! And yet, in the fourteenth century, the North Riding was densely populated by hermits!

From Throxenby Mere, instead of taking the narrow flagged packhorse trail usually and falsely called the Roman Road, or the steep path up to the race-course, I choose the Forge Valley road past the farm called Dogbark. The road is shaded by young broad-leaf trees, and there is little traffic; a cyclist or two, a farmer's car, but no walkers. There are no old trees in Raincliff, no giant oaks or beeches. At least since the twelfth century the wood has been a source of timber-supply, and during the 1914–18 war it was stripped of saleable stuff. A hundred years ago Dr Travis found wild daffodil in Raincliff, but there have been none in my time and primroses are fewer than they used to be. Except for children at Easter-time nobody walks in Raincliff for the fun of the thing, and the rides through the wood are choked with lop and top, overgrown with the lyre-stems of bramble and slippery with sodden clay. If I follow Cole's eye as he looks along the river-gorge I should now turn left, but, perhaps wilfully, I take the road to Everley and Hackness, with woodland clothing the slopes and the Derwent sliding through rich ings to my left. There is more corn than in former days. In the heat of the day everything is very still. By the little watercourse that gurgles through a culvert I stop again deliberately to listen. The grasshoppers are quiet; I hear only the noise of running water, the clink of a bucket in a garden by the side of the road, the call of a yellow-hammer and the bell-call of a great tit.

45

At Mowthorp I find a postal van standing on the bridge over the cut which carries flood-water from the Derwent to the sea at Scalby Mills. There is no flood-water now, in high summer. Twenty or thirty yards up the broad, shallow stream the postman is bending low over the water, very intent upon something. I wait for him.

"I've often a few minutes to spare at this point on my round," he tells me, "and I'm interested in aquatic plants. It's a good place for them, is this! I've just been watching young chub up there—a little school of 'em! You going that way?"

"Yes."

"You'll find musk in flower about three hundred yards up."

"Scented?"

"No."

Grinning, he climbs into his van. I bid him good day and take the high path along the sea-cut. Presently I sight the yellow flowers of the musk growing in the stream along with clumps of forget-me-not and a three-foot water-plant with rose-campion flowers and a look of mallow about it. I should be able to give the thing its name, but have to shake my head over it.

Here a horse stands aside to let me pass. Where the sea-cut leaves the Derwent stands a sturdy bridge of timber, and the river widens out into a broad, shallow pool. Though there is cool shadow under the bridge the cattle prefer the sun. They stand in the shallows stamping and splashing and swishing their tails, in two groups, the reds in one group, the brindles in the other. I stand and stare. Is this a breed or a colour segregation, or mere chance? In the empty landscape I listen to the humming of flies and the crackling of dry whin-pods, then I go on to Wrench Green, a tiny cluster of cottages built in the middle of the eighteenth century—such cottages as Marshall describes in his *Rural Economy of Yorkshire* when brick and tile were replacing mud and thatch. One of these cottages has an outside staircase of stone leading up to a chamber over a small wagon-shed. A baby is squalling up there; that's how I know the chamber is a living-room.

I look for horse-shoes nailed above the lintels of barns to

keep the luck in, but at Wrench Green they nail them to the walls at random. Crossing a pasture, I come into Hackness and find the sort of excitement I like begin to flood into my rather sluggish mind. Hackness is a very ancient village. It had a monastic establishment, a cell of Whitby Abbey, in the days of St Hilda, who turned all the snakes of the vicinity into headless fossilized ammonites. The church tower is almost massive enough for a castle keep, and the story of the church is recorded upon the north wall. Within the church I find a motoring family, man and wife and two daughters, examining the memorials of the Johnstone family of Hackness Hall. It was Sir Richard van den Bempdé Johnstone, Bart., who built the road from Hackness to Scalby about 1809 at a cost of £600, a good, cheap, and useful work. I also am impressed by the marmoreal calm of the Johnstone tablets and by the twelfth-century austerity of the church, but my attention is all for the Anglian Cross. It is in three fragments, and on all four sides there are Latin inscriptions, worn, weathered, and indeed lamentably indecipherable to all but skilled antiquarians. Obviously some mason, amateur or other, has been freshening up the name of Ædilburga.

I sit down in the now empty church, a few bubbles break the calm surface of my mind, they are followed by others, and soon I am thinking faster and harder than, on a day like this, is good for me.

"This cross," I begin, "is of the local stone, the Kelloways Rock which, soft when first cut, hardens on exposure to the air. It is heavily weathered, it has been subjected to summer heat and winter cold for many centuries, and because it bears inscriptions on all four sides it stood at a crossroads not far away from Hackness."

I fold my hands on my stomach and approve my theory.

"Now," say I, "where was the crossroads?"

Without consulting the map, I blot out the main road from Whitby to Scarborough because in St Hilda's time it did not exist, and similarly I expunge the road from Hackness to Scalby. Next, I consider the situation of the monastic community at Whitby. Occasion would sometimes demand that monks should leave the abbey on the headland and journey to York. How would they reach York?

I work out a monks' road from Whitby to the ford at
Langdale End and from there to Hackness. The next hospitium would be the nuns' priory at Wykeham and thence the
monks could make a short day's journey to Yedingham
Priory, from which they could reach the main road to York.
Now west of Hackness the land rises in a steep upward swing
to the southward-shelving summit of Hutton Bushel Moor,
and the headland overlooking Lower Troutsdale is called
Mount Misery.

My mind gives a wild leap in the dark.

"Mount Misery," I say, "is Mount Miserere, and that is
where this Anglian Cross originally stood."

Leaving the church I am too stirred in spirit to call at
Hackness Mill, and I hurry into Lower Troutsdale. The
woods are dark with the darkness of green foliage in high
summer, and with fresh vision I contemplate the dull, smoky
green of a planting of conifers growing low down the slope.
The sky-line of the headland is bare, sharp-edged, a long,
level line against the cloudless blue. At Hilla Green I quit the
metalled road and presently confront a wilderness of bracken
dense as a tropical forest, tough as new manila rope, and
taller than I am. The gradient is one in two. Brought to a
standstill I slant away to the right and plunge into a narrow
grain full of seeping water and tangled thorn, fight my way
up it, slant to the left, quit the area of bracken for an easier
patch of grass and ling, and presently top the summit of
Mount Misery.

Mount Misery is a mere 650 feet above datum-line; it
seems more like six thousand. The brick bridge over Troutsdale Beck is straight out of Lilliput, the Sugarloaf at Langdale End is a tiny nipple on the swelling breast of the moor,
the ford across the infant Derwent is exactly where I thought
it would be, and the band of pilgrim monks ought to be visible
as greyish beads on a twenty-mile string laid over the moor
from the blue north. The terrific sweep of country, however,
is empty, and on the crest of Mount Misery I am as solitary
as though I were the only man alive. This is a typical North
Riding landscape, and nobody in either paint or print has ever
given these North Riding landscapes their due.

What a man sees from the top of a hill he commands and

comprehends. His mind follows his eye. He dominates, he rules as absolute monarch, he is master of the scene and nobody can dispute his authority. But this is also true even if the country below him is tamed and populated; he may develop this state of mind at the top of Cleeve Hill or on the spurs of the Malverns or at the summit of Ingleborough. From such vantage-points, however, he commands only the coeval; what lies below him is his contemporary. Here at the edge of the headland of Hutton Bushel Moor, the crest of Mount Misery, there is a difference. What lies below is timeless. In the farther landscape there are no roads and no railways, there is neither farm nor steading, no smoke rises and there is no history. The solitary observer breaks through the limits of time. Moreover, the horizons are so indefinite that he feels on the verge of breaking the rims of space, and his domination of the landscape takes on the qualities of a vision. The observer becomes the seer.

Such visions lead to no outburst of magnificent prose or poetry. Wordsworth, looking westward at sunset from the scar of Black Hambledon, produced only a second-rate sonnet, and where he failed who shall succeed? The drifting lights and blurrings of shadow, the burning purples and fiery greens, the translucent blues and greys, are stuff neither for pen nor for palette. They are music, and whoever has broken the shackles of time and space knows that the sort of music I mean has the frightening, lifting effect of vision. If an impressionist painter, after mastering the solid light-patterns of Provence, had thought to paint the north beyond Normandy, this silent shifting of light and colour would have challenged his genius and laid his skill open to question. The masters of Renaissance Italy would have found subtler material than the ready-made stuff of the wind-grieved Apennine. John Constable would have flung down his pencils in despair, and though Richard Wilson could have caught the right timeless quality of the scene his canvases would have a false flatness which is not a quality of northern landscape. Truly the artist does well if he leaves the immensities of the North Riding moors alone.

In contemplation I have been forgetting why I climbed the steep pitch of the headland. Now turning my back upon the

Whitby Abbey

north and ranging through the self-sown birch and thorn of the plateau, I find the Great Moor Road, a broad green track running from this summit southward to the Vale of Pickering. It is old, yet still in use by foresters and, two miles to the south, by farmers. And here is a crossroads less than a hundred yards from the brow. The westerly track, curving along the fringe of Troutsdale, seems to make either for Cockmoor Hall or Annie Jane's, a mile south of Cockmoor Hall. The easterly track slips between young conifers down to Wrench Green, and at the crossroads lies a vacant plat of turf with a silver birch half-dragged from its roothold, leaving a pit with sides of peat and clayey subsoil. Ancient sites sink below ground-level in the course of centuries. I fear that the foundations of the Anglian Cross, if here, lie too deeply buried for scrabbling fingers to lay bare, and only a prairie-buster could clear the ground. My fingers are soon discouraged, I climb out between the tough roots, and follow the muddy track down to Wrench Green.

Again at Hackness I go into the church to study the cross, and a straight-backed, square-shouldered, bony old giant villager, following me, stands in the doorway half in light and half in shadow, watching me without moving and without saying a word. When I look at him he looks at me, and that, for a while, is all. Finally I leave the cross and speak to him.

"The cross," I say, "used to stand out of doors."

"Ay, it did. I was one of those that fetched it into the church and set it up where it is now."

"Where did it originally stand, then?"

"That I don't know. I can't say where it came from."

"Mount Misery?"

"Mebbe. There's nobody in the village can tell you."

"Mount Misery," I say, "is Mount Miserere, and I think your cross used to stand there."

"A sort of praying-cross?"

"Ay."

"Mebbe so," the giant says. Then, casually, he adds, "Mount Misery used to be called Mount Pleasant, y'know."

"Well," I say, "does that destroy my theory?"

He looks at me with a strange, doubtful eye, but does not

answer. Instead, he gives me a brief good day and goes about his affairs, leaving me with the shattered fragments of a fine, too-plausible conjecture. Yet, before I shut the churchyard gate behind me, I re-form my theory : Mount Miserere became Mount Misery; in the eighteenth century Mount Pleasant; in the last years of the nineteenth century Mount Misery once more. Mount Pleasant is decidedly eighteenth-century. It has the requisite picturesque false-seeming, and my theory may still be as valid as the holy Anglians whose names are faintly decipherable upon the Hackness Cross.

The road from Hackness to Scalby skirts the ornamental lake where swans are mirrored in the unruffled water, and past the old water-road into Whisperdales. In its layout Hackness Park is eighteenth-century. Red squirrels maintain themselves throughout its woodlands in spite of axe and saw. Hackness Hall is handsome neo-Renaissance, and looks shut up. The best view of the place is not from the road but from the hill above Wrench Green. Nobody comes to the park gate, which nowadays stands permanently open, and the climbing road brings me to Suffield, not quite moorland, not quite tamed, the land still in the intake stage of development, and to the top of Hay Brow, steep descent to the green coastal belt which, with a sharp turn to the left at the bottom, brings the traveller into Scalby. Should he turn to the right and follow the farm road, he finds himself at Scalby Nabs, which the family of Cross has farmed since the days, they say, of the Armada.

Seventy years ago, for a wager, a man rode down Hay Brown on a bicycle with an open umbrella in his left hand. At the bottom only the umbrella saved him from a broken neck.

I turn along the seaward-facing ridge of Silpho Moor. In peace-time summers charabancs brought people here to look at the view from the top of Reasty Hill, picnic on the moor and leave litter. Now I walk the empty road between the woods, go down the hill into Cumboots and make for Burniston. I want to talk to the blacksmith.

Mr Chew has worked Burniston forge for thirty-three years and was at Cayton for thirty years before that. He is a busy man, mending farm implements old and modern. "I've more shoeing of horses than I can cope with," he tells me, but this is only part of his job. He is a master of wrought-iron work, and only last week he had sent a set of hand-forged chandeliers to Wiltshire. The forge is electrically operated. The blacksmith is also the timber merchant. He grows his own timber and builds farm wagons and carts, being joiner, wheelwright, and smith combined. Blacksmith and forge together have made a Royal Academy picture.

At Cloughton Old Mill the original mill-race supplied electricity for the house, but the dynamo got out of repair and the mill-house is now lit from the mains. The mill is a coal store, but the half-breast mill-wheel is still in good shape. In the grounds is a swimming-pool, and the door leading to it carries a large number of horseshoes probably though not certainly made by the Burniston smith. Cloughton Hall has an ancient dovecot. Blown down in a gale long since, it has since been rebuilt, stands about eighteen feet high and is all stone save for a skep-shaped wooden top, a hole about nine feet up with a little shelf in front of it, and a wooden door at the bottom with a remarkably ancient lintel. This dovecot has historical interest. It is a relic, an Ancient Monument.

Cloughton has a ghost story, though the inhabitants of the village probably know nothing of it. The tale was told to me by an old woman named Susan Taylor. She was ugly with the ugliness that comes of a lifetime of drudgery, and had, in addition, a terrible cast of the left eye. She died about thirteen years ago in the Poor Law Institution at Scarborough. This was her story.

The wise woman of Cloughton never did anyone any harm; she never witched cattle or young married women or bairns, but when she was dying the doctor asked her if she would like the parson to call. She said no, she'd done without the parson for sixty years and she didn't want him across her doorsill.

"But you ought to have him," said the doctor. "You see——"

"Ay," answered old Meg, "I knaw weel enough I'm dying, but I tell you this, young man, that if you send the parson here I'll haunt ye in the likeness of an auld white hare."

The doctor laughed, and the parson called to see old Meg, who had not a word to say to him. She died, and there was a vast to-do as to whether she should or should not be buried in consecrated ground. The parson settled the matter. Whether she liked it or not, she had had spiritual consolation before she died, and Meg was buried in the churchyard. This was in summer. Now

> It fell about the Martinmas
> When nights are lang and mirk

that doctor and parson were called out together at midnight to the death-bed of a farmer living between Cloughton and Staintondale. Having watched the farmer die peacefully, they set off for home. They came to a stretch of road with high hedges and a steep cam-side, and at that point a great white hare louped across the road in front of the gig. The horse shied, swerved into the cam-side, the gig was overset, the doctor was killed instantly and the parson was never the same man afterwards. Old Meg had known how to bide her time. All through the rest of that winter people kept watch for the white hare but nobody set eyes upon it. Meg's spirit was at rest and has not walked again. The guests at Cober Hill may sleep in peace; it is not likely to trouble them.

Hulleys is a blunt-nosed, southward-facing plateau north of Cloughton village between the main road to Whitby and the minor road to Staintondale. It is certainly a prehistoric site, as John Cole said it was. The features upon which he reported are still there, and since there is nothing so satisfactory as getting into touch with the man on the spot, I ask Mr M. H. Dennisoun of Hulleys to put his knowledge at my disposal. Here it is: "Between a point south of the Hulleys and the woodmen's cottages on the Whitby Road there are definite traces of a prehistoric trackway. At the southern tip of the Hulleys there is an old square citadel with the remains of stone circles, these most likely being the remains of pit dwellings. Remnants of pit dwellings are also to be found in the valley north and south of the stone circle. In all probability this stone circle was a communal workshop, there being a trace of a square hearth the stones of which show signs of burning, and one stone of having been used as an anvil. The stone circle on the west side of the Whitby Road is still in good preservation. The raised way which runs from the Hulleys to the stone circle on the moor is still to be seen, especially where it crosses the sunken foss-way in the woods north-west of Hulleys farmhouse. The large stones shown on Knox's map at the north end of the Hulleys are still to be seen forming the base of one of the field walls. In 1938 numerous flint flakes were found in the various fields."

I approach Hulleys to make acquaintance with a mystery. The mystery is the existence of a stone circle at the very bottom of a steep-sided valley, the western edge of the snub-nosed plateau. Mr Dennisoun tells me, "Yes, the circle's there, but you'll not find it. There's too much growth down there."

"I'll try," I answer.

He gives me directions to find the exact place. "And," says he, "look out for snakes."

"Snakes?"

The last snake I saw was a whipsnake, a most poisonous reptile, and the one before that was a rather small adder in Dalby Warren. I pretend a scorn of snakes. Even a hint of disbelief creeps into my voice.

"I've warned you," says Mr Dennisoun.

I plod across ploughed land and skirt a ripening wheat-field until I come to a little wall fenced in by posts and wire. Over the wall is the valley I'm looking for, and it is deep in bracken, bramble, and sapling. Somewhere in the midst of all this growth is the mysterious stone circle.

Then I see the adder. He is a big adder, lying on the sun-warmed scree of stones on the other side of the low wall. I look at him. He looks at me. Then, without a sound and without haste, he slips into the scree and disappears. In a pair of thin flannel trousers and walking-shoes I am not dressed to cope with big adders whose tempers may not be very placid, and, looking down the scree and considering that where there is one adder there are likely to be dozens of adders, I reach the conclusion that amongst all the rampant growth in the hollow the stone circle will certainly elude my notice. The mystery remains a mystery, and I catch the Scarborough bus from the top end of Cloughton village.

Not that I have finished with the immediate locality, for though I have done with the red-brick villa and bungalow sub-urban areas of Scalby and Newby, I have yet a few notes to make. Near Suffield, for instance, is Northfield, and this would prove that the three-field strip system of the Middle Ages, which may still be studied at Laxton in Nottingham-shire, extended also to this area despite vast acreage of wood and waste. Moreover, when a Member of Parliament nowa-days wishes to retire from the political arena, he may apply for the stewardship of the Manor of Northstead, and North-stead lies between Burniston and Scarborough. Further, whatever you may think of the Scarborough Museum, you cannot deny that the freestone of which it is built is a very good building-stone. So too is the stone of Christchurch in Vernon Place, and that of the Philosophical Hall in Leeds. They are all from the quarry of Kelloways Rock at Hackness, and Hackness Hall is built of the same stuff. Cloughton quarries also furnish first-rate stone.

Extending now the range of my survey, I come into as close contact as I am ever likely to get with the vast-bodied, little-brained reptiles of the Jurassic Age. North of Scar-borough the coast was once a famous collecting-ground for the fossil fragments of these brutes; later it was discovered that what they had in number they lacked in variety and the fossil-hunters went elsewhere for specimens. In 1907 the footprints of a dinosaur were found by Harold Brodrick at Saltwick; in 1914 Arnold Wallis found more in the Upper Estuarine beds not far north of Scarborough. From Burnis-ton a by-road leads directly towards Long Nab, and from it a cart-track strikes south-east towards Crook Ness. Here a dinosaur coming to drink at the stream which ran this way hopped or waddled across a bed of soft clay, the sun baked the clay, flood-water of the stream washed sand into the foot-prints, time changed the sand into sandstone, disposed of the clay and left a positive cast of the feet of the three-toed reptile. The Scarborough field naturalists transferred the cast to their museum, and this transference, quite irrationally, gives me a vague feeling of dissatisfaction.

North of Cloughton lies Staintondale. I shall not sound a fanfare of silver trumpets for Staintondale, though it is a pleasant, unspoiled village. It straggles. It has a rural forge and the Shepherd's Arms, it is easily reached from Scar-borough by road or rail, it was once a manor of the Knights

Templars, it has the Staintondale pack, and it is an excellent
jumping-off place for an excursion into the wilderness. There
are many journeys in the North Riding which must be made
on foot, and this is one of them. The land is not merely wild,
it is Beowulfian. The railway station may be my point of
departure, but I do not take the train to any place. I cross the
line and plod over the fields towards the coastal rim, walking
up the convex curve of the land with my face to the north-
east wind. Almost without warning I come to the edge of the
world. I pause on the verge of Beast Cliff, and before and
below me lies the sea of that melancholy Old English poem
The Seafarer. At the moment, curtains of rain slant over the
grey waters.

A word about Beast Cliff. The name on the maps is Blea
Wyke, called Blewick or Bluewick, with the stress on the first
syllable, and *blea* is the Old Norse *blaa*, meaning *blue* or
azure, *dark* or *leaden-hued*. Ancient peoples were often
dubious about colours; they had no cultivated colour-sense.
Wyke is Old Norse *hvik*, a *creek*, a *bay*, a *haven*, and the
vikings or hvikings were the men of the creeks or havens. But
Beast Cliff? Cattle cannot be driven or coaxed down the steep
descent to the dark undercliff, but they may be lowered on a
wire rope to spend the summer months down there, and I
myself when young have on occasion descended the five
hundred feet of cliff by that same wire rope. Beast Cliff is not
so high as Boulby Cliff farther north, yet high enough to
dizzy the brain.

I turn northward along a narrow, overgrown cliff-top path.
For a hundred yards or so the going is easy, and then the
maquis closes in—bracken, bramble, hazel, mountain ash—
and I have a struggle to get through. Unexpectedly the track
begins to slant down the cliff, a steep, slippery, zigzag descent.
I move slowly and cautiously; haste would merely land me in
trouble. Fifteen minutes of this brings me to a rugged level,
not down to the sea-line but to the undercliff, and a wild,
strange place it is. Modern geologists ascribe it to a huge
subsidence of the cliff, but one old field naturalist I know,
brought up on Phillips's survey of the Yorkshire coast, still
maintains that this undercliff is the ancient sea-beach now
raised some twenty feet above the present shore. There is a

relic of that same old beach at Saltburn. I must, I suppose, accept the word of the geologists, yet I am reluctant to do so on two grounds : first, a raised sea-beach appeals to me; secondly, the vegetation down here is totally different from that on the height above me. There are botanical rarities here which will delight the ecologists when they come to make a detailed survey.

The undercliff of Blewyke is a little world of ling, boulder, bracken, bilberry, blaeberry, and a particularly succulent grass. At the foot of the huge cliff there is a narrow pool of black, stagnant water; a dying tree leans low across it, and there is a moorhen's nest. Under my weight the tree sags and sways, and I return to firm land to rake round for some sort of support. A twelve-foot stake will serve, and with it I go back along the sagging trunk. Arrived at a point of precarious balance, I thrust my pole lightly into the shallow pool. It sinks down, and down, and down. I push the whole twelve feet into the mud. It sinks, and I am ready to depart, backing slowly to firm ground and praising the caution that had saved me from stepping or falling off the trunk into the three inches of dark water and heaven knows how many feet of saturated mud. Beowulfian? Ay!

I may descend to sea-level here, but not by way of that mud-pool. I cross the undercliff, scrambling through the tough ling and round the big boulders, and find the place where a rope, not very trustworthy, is knotted to an iron crowbar. I slip down the rope to the wet rocks. Here is solitude. At full tide the rocks are submerged, but at low tide on a summer's day they are dry and warm.

The journey round Blewyke at sea-level is a vast labour even if it may be safely accomplished. The fossiliferous strata will tempt the geologist, though I trust not to an un-timely drowning. I scramble up the cliff and walk northward through the wilderness with hanging wood and crag to my left. The track by which I came down to the undercliff is lost in the *maquis*, and as I move steadily through the brush and boulder, looking, no doubt, like a not very intelligent ant, the hanging wood gives place to crumbling crag and rock. I reach a broken wooden fence, and plain in view are the high cliffs of the Peak, with the steep, zigzag path and steps mounting to the summit. Down below, the cliff first slants, then drops, to the sea. Above water-level stands a flat platform of rock, a rendezvous of sea-anglers, and beyond it the deep blue, almost a Mediterranean blue, of navigable water. Navigable, I mean, for submarines. There is a legend which insists that German submarine officers used, in the 1914–18 war, to land on the flat rock-level down there to stretch their cramped legs. I will not vouch for its truth.

Over the wooden fence lies a steep slope of loose shaly stuff, and the slope ends abruptly in a sheer drop. Across this slope lies my way, and there are no footprints, there is no path. All I need, however, is a cool head and a little judgment, and for once I have both. The slope is crossed and I toil slowly up the path to the Peak. Doing so, I suddenly recollect old Susan Taylor's story of the Staintondale poltergeist. When Susan was sixteen years old she was servant lass along with another wench of about the same age at a Staintondale farm. Unfortunately I can give no details of the farm, for Susan's geography, like her theology, was excessively nebulous. The two lasses slept in one of the attics, and at dead of night were often wakened by violent demonstrations on the ground floor. Then one lass would say to the other, "Harkstha! T'awd devil's at it ageean!" They were not so much alarmed as amused until one night Susan's fellow-servant crept downstairs for a drink of water and met the poltergeist at the foot of the stairs. It must, I imagine, have come straight out of one of M. R. James's ghost-stories, for with her shrieks the girl woke the household, the shrieks passed into low moanings of "that awful, awful creature! ..." and then the moanings passed first into a state of insensibility and then into brain-fever.

From Staintondale a by-road reaches the main Whitby Road a little south-east of the Falcon Inn, and not far north of the Falcon a sunken track leads southward over the moor to Keasbeck and Harwood Dale. Here an expanse of rich yellow sandstone on each side of the track contrasts so brilliantly with the purple ling that local artists are inclined to halloo with joy.

"It's easy," said one of them, "though not so easy as it looks. The lines of the picture, of course, are there already.

The artist can't improve upon them as Turner improved upon the lines of the Castle Hill at Scarborough. Here Nature gives him two or three birch-trees, an outcrop of rock, cushions of heather and bilberry, a few tussocks of moorland grass and the track through the moors, and there's the picture. Every stationer's shop in Scarborough used to stock garish postcards of this bit of Harwood Dale Moor. It's famous."

The old inhabitants of Harwood Dale used to call the place *Arrawood Deeal.*

I have known Ravenscar since my boyhood. It was the name that first took me there—a name coupled in my mind with vikings, ravens, cliffs, and the sea—and I travelled on foot along the cliff-tops from Scarborough, playing the bare-faced trespasser at Hayburn Wyke, where the woods are privately owned and one is supposed to pay for the privilege of going down them to the wyke and the waterfall. Ravenscar did not disappoint me, though there were no vikings and no ravens. It is a strange place. The rain-weathered asphalt roads are more than half overgrown with grass, and the building-lots remain vacant. There is a little group of shops near the railway station, and, save for the Raven Hall Hotel, that is all. A little band of sea-anglers meets here once a year in the dark days of winter. They go down to the rocks at dawn, fish all day, return to eat an enormous meal in the evening, swap yarns, and go to bed to dream of shark-sized cod, colossal ling, and "the fish that got away." At the Raven Hall Hotel you stand upon the site of a Roman watch-tower and signal-station, you swim in the open-air pool (I have watched members of the Scarborough Swimming Club revelling here at Christmas), play golf on the private course, knit, gossip, look northward to the red-tiled roofs of Robin Hood's Bay, and speculate upon the grey ruins and scarred cliffs of the Peak, the relics of a vanished industry.

I believe there are still many problems regarding the alum industry of the North Riding coastline that remain to be cleared up by the economic historian. The manufacture of alum seems to have been carried on by "the ancients"—who-ever they were—in the Mediterranean. Arab alchemists jealously guarded its secrets throughout the Dark Ages—

whenever they were—until the predatory Turks obtained a monopoly of manufacture. In 1459 alum-works were started on Italian soil, and the production of alum became a papal monopoly. Various attempts to break this monopoly followed the Reformation. The Germans tried, and the English. Aubrey gives false credit to Sir Thomas Challoner in the reign of Charles the First. A Challoner was certainly implicated. The scene is Belman Bank, Guisborough, on the Challoner estate. The manuscript is Cottonian MS. Julius F.6, folio 456, the author remains unidentified, and the date is uncertain. This, however, is an extract: "Upon Belman bank there is a place conveniente for many houses to worke allome, the myne itself extendinge all long that hill, and exposed in such a sorte to the breathe of the sea and of the sunne and wynde, which are the only ripeners of the stone, that all things consydered a better place cannot be found in this countrye. Your charge will be very great and mount to many thousands, but to comfort you I will not conceale the experyense we have lately made that your allome is as good as the Romishe and is stronger in setlinge or collour." Tradition proceeds to assert the smuggling of an Italian alum-worker aboard ship in a large cask, and with his help Challoner began to work alum at Belman Bank. Thereupon the Pope fulminated majestically, launching comminatory anti-Challoner sentence of excommunication. Walloons, Germans, and French came to Cleveland as the alum industry developed. In 1609 James the First seems to have bought out Challoner and Lord Sheffield, who for two years had held monopoly of manufacture, but under royal control there was nothing but chicanery and inefficiency. One Sir Arthur Ingram, manager of the monopoly, took Templenewsam for himself out of the moneys he appropriated at Guisborough. When Charles the First lost his head, the royal monopoly lapsed and open competition took its place. Sometimes alum-working was profitable. Often the market was glutted, but the manufacture went on along the Yorkshire coast until 1860, when new processes made it unprofitable.

Obviously in this account there are great gaps. They remain to be filled up by the economic historian. Nothing, however, will restore the original profile of the North Riding headlands, including the Peak, or replace the millions of tons of alum shale dug out of the cliffs during three centuries of strenuous labour, or bring back the alum-burners to the old seats of manufacture.

Since even the historian and the economist can now discover nothing on the actual alum-workings, the geologist will make hot-footed for the shoreline of the Peak, for "these three miles constitute the most richly fossiliferous area in England" and there is still the chance of digging out some variety unrepresented on the shelves and in the cases of museums. That obliging fossil *Trigonia literata* is moderately common. Hammer the shale beside it and it will jump out of its bed for you. At least I have known it do so.

He who is neither economic historian nor geologist will be content with one of the finest samples of coast scenery in Yorkshire, with the great sweep of moorland country, the variety of colouring, the peculiarly northern look of the landscape, and as he walks down Stoup Brow to the beach his mind will brim over with unrelated memories of the village he approaches. Stoup Brow was once a test-climb for cars and motor-cycles. A handsome cargo-boat went ashore on the sands not two hundred yards north of the foot of Stoup Brow, and I wouldn't say that her freight was immune from surreptitious salvaging. Beachcombing is a trade along this coast —perhaps the only trade that relies both on individual enterprise and collective security. The local name for a reef is a *steel*. Robin Hood's Bay is something of a misnomer, for despite Robin Hood's Butts and the old ballad of the Robin Hood cycle the earliest mention of Robin Hood in connection with the place is Leland's in 1538. The people who live here call it either Bay Town, or, more simply, Bay. A hundred years ago a windmill dominated the height above the red roofs, but all memory of it is now lost. That does not matter very much. Far more serious is the fact that the fishermen have left Bay, though there were sixteen Storms, all householders, in 1934. Amongst the fisherfolk still remembered in Bay was one Bielby, who wore the sealskin cap and high-heeled boots of an older generation. Besides Storms, there are Ducks and Dukes still lingering in Bay. This was a gathering-ground for artists, too. Phil May worked here as

well as at Whitby. Leo Walmsley's *Turn of the Tide,* a fine
piece of cinema, was made here, and his story of the film may
be read in *So Many Loves.* Tucker, exhibitor at the Royal
Academy, used to live at Bay Hotel, and I report of him this
anecdote. He was painting in Scotland, busy upon a big landscape, when an old drover came along, squatted down beside
him, lighted his pipe, and, without a word, watched the artist
at work until the sun went down and the light began to fail.
Then, as Tucker was putting his gear together, the drover
spoke at last. "I've nobbut seen one other chap like thoo,"
said the drover, "and he came fra Wick and was daft."

There is a track running inland from Bay to the high road
between Pickering and Whitby. The early maps call it "Old
Wife's Trod"—a *trod* is a path—and in the first years of the
nineteenth century it was used by fish-hawkers and flither-
girls. Earlier than that I think it was a salt-road, and I have
heard it described as a smugglers' trail. It passes close by
Lilla Cross and joins the high road north of Saltersgate.

Such are my notes ruminated between the foot of Stoup
Brow and the village of Bay. Interesting, but perhaps not
important. But somewhere along this North Riding coastline
there must be living an ageing student of folklore and custom,
no casual empiricist, who would do well to remind us, before
it is too late, of the why and wherefore of the faded and
dusty garlands hanging in the churches at Bay, Staithes,
Egton, and perhaps elsewhere. I used to know something of
them but am no longer very clear about the details. That it
was a custom is certain, that the garlands commemorate dead
women and girls is also certain, white garlands for the maids
and coloured for the married women; but where, and when,
and why did the custom originate, and what were the cere-
monies associated with it? The year 1873, I am told, saw the
last garland hung in the church at Bay.

CHAPTER III

WHITBY, AND MORE OF THE COAST

THREE things every English girl and boy ought to do. The first is to play some musical instrument; the second is to ride a horse, and the third to sail a boat. There are other things in the world besides atomic engineering and the craft of writing prose. I have been reading an article by J. R. Bagshawe about the Cowes Regatta of 1909, and the reader may well wonder what connection there may be between the Cowes Regatta of 1909 and the North Riding of Yorkshire. The answer lies in one word : Whitby. I shall make, no doubt, a host of enemies, and I hope equally a host of friends, by a dogmatic declaration that there is more of the sea in Whitby's little finger than there is in Scarborough's thigh.

Scarborough's recorded history is packed with complaints to authority that her harbour-works stand sadly in need of repair. So, for that matter, is the history of Whitby, but Whitby has made a better job of her piers and harbour than Scarborough is now ever likely to make. And Scarborough has produced no great seamen like James Cook and the elder Scoresby; she has had no fleet of Greenland whalers, and few Scarborough-built ships engaged in the regular Baltic trade. The truth is that Scarborough harbour silts up. The eighteenth-century gap in the outer pier, called Dowker Hole, was supposed to encourage the tides to wash out the silt. Dredgers have clawed out thousands of tons of mud and dumped them in the middle of the bay, but every tide setting southward lays down its thin deposit of silt to discourage shipping and amuse the gulls. Moreover, boats coming in from the Dogger with heavy loads of fish have an awkward manœuvre to make as they turn from the bay to the gap between the piers, and though I have never seen trawler or drifter, smack or coble, stove in against the masonry, that is a tribute more to the seamanship of the fishermen than to the harbour-works. In a north-easterly gale the manœuvre demands the most precise skill and timing. A south-easter—the best wind for sailing this coast—is safer, but little help to boats coming in from the north. I have known boats compelled to ride out rough seas in the bay. They could never have made the harbour.

Whitby harbour is not safe, either. There is broken water over the bar in any sort of a wind, and to get a boat to sea in rough weather is not a job for amateurs. To fetch it in is equally difficult. Yet Whitby still belongs to the sea in a sense that Scarborough does not, though Whitby, like Scarborough, has turned to exploiting her attractions as a holiday resort. Visitors to Whitby are still interested in what goes on along the staiths. In Scarborough they use the West Pier as a car-park.

Whitby has had a more dramatic history than Scarborough, and has always turned her native intelligence to better account. This little fishing-port has been a focus of the shipbuilding industry, producing colliers and coasters, then barques and brigs for the Baltic trade, transports for the eighteenth-century wars, and Greenland whalers. All these ships were famous for their bluff bows and solid construction, their seaworthy qualities; and not only did Whitby produce the ships, she also found masters and crews to man them. Whitby lads did not then quit the port to work the Cleveland ironstone and Durham coal; they sailed Whitby ships into arctic and tropic waters, wherever their lawful, and sometimes unlawful, occasions called them. When iron ships came, Whitby began to build them, but, unable to compete with the great yards of the north, abandoned shipbuilding and, with the death of the Duke of Wellington, began to develop the jet industry. They buried the great duke not simply with the mourning of a mighty nation but also with Whitby jet. The trade rose to a climax of prosperity with the death of the Prince Consort, after which, though our grandmothers wore them to their last days, jet beads, sequins, bangles, bracelets, and brooches went out of fashion.

Still there remained the fishing—long-line fishing in winter, drift-net fishing in summer, with lobsters and crabs between the two, the harbour in summer crowded with drifters from Cornwall and Skye, Wick, Banff, Montrose, Aberdeen,

Grimsby, and Lowestoft, the great herring-fleet moving slowly southward with the herring-shoals. Along the York- shire coast the long-line fishing was carried out in thirty-foot cobles manned by a crew of three, the herring-fishing in what were called *ploshers*—forty-foot boats also with a crew of three.

Then, north from Hull and south from Sunderland, came the trawler, the otter-trawl replaced the drift-net, and fast boats took the catch direct from the fishing-grounds to the Tyne, Tees, Humber, and Thames. Even though the big inland towns got supplies of fish more quickly and cheaply than before, the coming of the trawler was, in a way, a national calamity. Trawls rake the sea-floor, kill vast num- bers of young fish and destroy the breeding-grounds. In the long run they are a poor investment. "Trawlers is ruinin' us, an' by t'time they ruin theirsens we s'll be finished, mister!" That is what the fishermen said, and they were right. They are now nearly finished; the Dogger isn't the fishing-ground it was when the Silver Pit was discovered, thousands of young men have left the sea, and the men who yet follow the trade are not so chuff with themselves, and they are poorer. To let this grand school of seamanship decline was a tragically myopic waste of first-class human material, and now, I fear, it is too late to do anything about it.

A few families still derive a thin living from the sea. The forty-foot coble still comes into Whitby harbour on the flood, depending now not upon her brown lugsail but upon a petrol engine. She comes in fast, her crew of five grouped motionless round the mast, gazed upon by the little crowd on the staith with eyes that reveal both curiosity and lack of understand- ing. The men on board and the people on shore are not a mere twenty feet of water apart, but a whole world of experi- ence. A few trawlers are tied up above the bridge; Whitby- owned, some of them, and some Lowestoft boats. But they are idle, there are no signs of life aboard them, and to my eyes they look none too prosperous. Most of the east-coast trawling-fleet, however, is still steaming, as I write, through dangerous seas looking for more dangerous things than fish. Next year and in future years, late August and early Septem- ber, Whitby harbour may hold again the fast, heavy Scotch

The Mill, East Ayton

boats, the sturdy Lowestoft boats with their slow-spoken giants aboard, and the native Whitby craft. Time, however, will scarcely bring back the Greenlandmen of Whitby, or the long, graceful Cornish luggers, or the clumsy south-coast boats, or the yawl-rigged Lowestoft drifters, and the working day of the Yorkshire coble is pretty well over.

To touch the mere fringe of Whitby history is, however, no manner of use, and I had better leave it alone. Indeed the deeper I delve into local history the more I am appalled by the truth about it, and the truth about it is that local historians have, for the most part, hardly scratched the surface of their study. And when they have scratched it, the scratchings have proved abominably dull. The combined labours of Lionel Charlton, Dr Young, Canon Atkinson, and Robert Gaskin, for example, are only picturesque preliminary to the authoritative history of Whitby, which is still unwritten and likely to remain so. The local historian gets little encouragement. The world warns him of the labour and expense of publication and the limited number of readers he may expect, publication by subscription is out of date, in this country there are too few university presses and too many university students ambitious only to write themselves doctors of philosophy. When the business of historical research in our universities has been cleaned up and degree-hunting becomes a minor matter, then the historian of Whitby may get his chance. He will be a scholar. He will not confuse lively anecdote and picturesque descriptive with history, nor will he be a mere chronicler. He will know what connections formerly existed between the Greenland whale and linen, leather, umbrellas, corsets, brushes, and mineral oils, and he will know, too, what the probable connection is between the Whitby alum industry and the famous curse in *Tristram Shandy*, and what John Hall Stevenson had to do with it.

The sky darkens overhead and the wind freshens from the north-east, the gulls slant downwind and cry in the dusk over the housetops, reminding me that the gulls are part of the life of Whitby. Their crying is integrated into the noises of the town.

I must get back to the Yorkshire coble.

If a man knows anything of the Norwegian *pram* or *praam*,

he will be able to trace the affinity between the men of the Yorkshire coast and their Continental cousins, for the coble is cousin to the *pram*. It has adapted itself to the troubled shallows and shelving beaches of the Yorkshire coast. The stem is high, for the bow faces the sea in going off and coming in. Aft she is flat-bottomed, and the deep, heavy rudder slopes sharply forward as it goes down into the water. Reaching to midships, the tiller seems enormous. For fun she may still hoist a lugsail, but for serious work she uses an oil engine. Her strakes are broad and, when paint is obtainable, brightly coloured. Scarborough favours white and blue, Staithes may show yellow and green and scarlet, and north of Saltburn black and white are the colours.

A coble without an engine is not particularly easy to handle. They say, for example, that a coble will not "run" with a following sea when heavily freighted with fish, land-lubbers or sand, but, for all that, boat-builders see no reason to modify their specifications, and in general the Yorkshire coble remains the Yorkshire coble. Unless, however, young inland folk on holiday along this coast revolt against pleasures they can so easily enjoy in Bradford or Barnsley, and find interest and enterprise enough to learn how to handle a small boat, the demand for synthetic sunburn is likely still further to increase, and the number of cobles still further to dwindle. It is enormously pleasant to state here that the Whitby, Scarborough, and Bridlington Yacht Clubs are now recovering from their moribundity (if there is such a word) of the war years, and perhaps Whitby Regatta may soon become once more as popular as, for example, Burniston Show in August.

Whitby railway station stands upon the site of an old ship-yard. At the bus station close by, the strata of summer life in Whitby rub surfaces without conglomerating. A London Scot and his wife head the Scarborough bus-queue. Scarborough is a little too garish for their taste; it is spoiled, they say, by a pretence of towny sophistication, and they much prefer Whitby. The Middlesbrough queue is noisier, not so got up for a day at the seaside, much more restless, more avid to scuttle across the road to the fried-fish shop; it is jollier and less critical, and it uses not the North Riding speech but the singing intonation of County Durham. On the seat nearest the river huddle three old women in dark, shabby, shapeless clothes—Clotho, Lachesis, Atropos—the Three Fates, with hard, bleached-blue eyes, withered necks and wrinkled faces. Their harsh, unsympathetic, cackling voices settle the lives and destinies of young and old. Under the steel-grey sky they lean towards each other, breaking into spasms of bronchitic laughter in which there is no amusement. They are old Whitby, native Whitby, born with the bitterness of the sea on their lips and hardened to life and death by the sea. Farther down the harbour by the swing-bridge, at the corner where a hundred years ago master mariners used to stand and talk, there is now in the cold twilight a group of lads, the eldest of them twelve or thirteen years old. They are all blue-guernseyed, bare-legged and bare-footed, rough-haired and not over-clean. The dirt, however, is harbour-side dirt, and their talk is harbour-side talk. One is swinging his legs over the water, making a pretence of fishing. He is not genuinely interested in the little harbour whiting, parr, and billet that even now may be nibbling at his bait, but in the talk of mine-sweeping and trawling.

Their ragged blue guernseys remind me that some years ago the Yorkshire Women's Institutes held an exhibition in Harrogate, and amongst the exhibits was a group of sturdy doll fishermen from the coast in characteristic rig. Each doll's blue guernsey had its individual pattern, and the knitter's note ran to the effect that these patterns were traditional for each fishing-port from Bridlington northwards—Flamborough this pattern, Filey that, and Whitby the other. I make no question that the note is correct, though nowadays the brown jumper, often stained and faded, is usually worn over the guernsey. Lowestoft men wear white jumpers. For rough weather, of course, oilskins of black or yellow.

It is then, during the season of line-fishing, when white waves roll in and spray flies over the housetops, when a ploughman ten miles inland may taste salt on his lips, that the men in oilskins gather in some sheltered spot—in the lee of the outer pier or of the tollhouse by the south entrance to the Marine Drive at Scarborough, for example—and wait there, motionless, apparently unchilled by the cold, the gale blowing in their beards and the spray glistening on their cheeks, for the sky partially to clear and the storm partially to subside. Then, "though it looks nobbut shabby", they make ready to go out on the evening tide. Rough weather or smooth, a man must follow his calling, and many a time, with anxiety tugging at my heart, under a dirty sky full of rain, sleet, wrack, and tumult, and darkening to the four o'clock darkness of a December afternoon, I have watched from my sheltered vantage-point trawler after trawler, greasy smoke blowing away from their black-and-red-ringed smoke-stacks, leave the oily smoothness of harbour to face the crashing seas and freezing spray of a north-easterly gale, watched them rise to the crests and disappear into the troughs until they dwindled to mere specks, until drift and darkness swallowed them up. Equally in similarly filthy weather I have seen them return after daybreak from the fishing-grounds, bucketing through the seas, now with bows buried deep and screws racing, now with the lee rail awash, and have shared the relief with which the white registration letters SH and WY were finally recognized by the keen eyes of the watchers. The lads by the swing-bridge have all this to experience, not as mere onlookers but as participants in the struggle. It will broaden their backs and toughen their muscles. It will develop their powers of endurance and their fortitude.

When I think further of the differences between Scarborough and Whitby I find that Whitby has always, from the time of Cædmon, contrived to act as a catalyst of literary expression, and Scarborough has not. In the beginning there was Cædmon himself. Do not, I beg, pronounce his name as though it were Seedmon. I have no desire to blow the gaff on the Father of English Poetry. I think there was such a person, I believe he was either a Welshman or of Welsh descent, Atkinson is certain that he was no gawky cowhand, and Sievers has brilliantly pointed out that the bulk of the poetry formerly attributed to him owes its origin, and much more than its origin, to the Continental Old Saxon *Heliand*. Bede certainly tells a good story of how the gift of poetry miraculously came to Cædmon, but Bede had the tale by hearsay and the short specimen of Cædmon's work given by the Jarrow monk cannot hold a candle to the poetry of Cynewulf or that

69

of the unknown author of *The Seafarer* and is not what I should call even third-class Old English verse. Yet if Whitby wishes to make much of Cædmon, I may here, on the strength of a single word, attribute the whole of *Beowulf* to this coast and probably to Whitby. The word I have in mind is *hrinde,* an adjective applied to frost. Various editors of *Beowulf* have racked their brains over this strange word. Most of them have accepted the emendation *hrimge* and have translated it *rimy.* The word is the common North Riding *rindy,* still in use. Copying the *Beowulf* manuscript, the West Saxon scribe failed to southernize this word. Further, the *Beowulf* had to be composed somewhere, it smells of the moors and the sea, the local atmosphere is that of the North Riding rather than of the Baltic coastline, I could point out an exact location for Grendel's Mere at Foulsike on Fylingdales Moor (a colony of gulls lives there now, and very shy they are!), and Henry Morley thought the funeral rites of *Beowulf* took place on Boulby Cliff. Yet, remembering Macbeth's crow making wing to the rooky wood, where *rooky* is certainly the North Riding *roky,* pronounced *rooaky,* I must nevertheless be cautious about ascribing *Macbeth* to an obscure Yorkshire playwright of Elizabethan times.

In the eighteenth century Scarborough had some repute as a holiday spa, as witness Sheridan's *Trip to Scarborough.* This was when Whitby was a busy port. Then Sir Walter Scott put Whitby into *Marmion,* and if *Marmion* was improved by his doing so, Whitby was no worse. Scott's eye for the romantic picturesque stimulated subsequent topographers to quote, inevitably, his lines. Myself no topographer, I refer the reader to Scott's poetical works. In the novel called *No Name* Wilkie Collins used the village of Ruswarp. He stayed in Whitby in 1861. *Sylvia's Lovers* by Mrs Gaskell deals with Whitby in the great whaling days. Mary Linskill, Whitby-born, produced *Between the Heather and the Northern Sea* and *The Haven Under the Hill.* Dickens stayed at the White Horse and Griffin in 1844. Gerald du Maurier used Whitby as a setting for quip and jest, Clark Russell found inspiration there, and in our own day Storm Jameson has brought Whitby and Whitby people into a series of novels distinguished by good prose and minute study of local character.

I asked her if she could account for Whitby's thus acting as a catalyst of literature. She said she had no theory to offer, she hadn't thought about it, "but", she admitted, "of course you're right". My list of authors, she was sure, was lamentably incomplete, and we discussed possibilities. All sorts of great men have loved Whitby, or if they haven't loved it they have left it not quite the same people as they were when they went. We were certain Dickens didn't waste his time there, and I reminded her how an anonymous contributor to Horne's *Whitby Gazette* wrote a series of brilliant articles alleging that Whitby and Eskdale were colonized by the Lost Tribes of Israel. We guessed at the identity of the author, a first-rate Hebraist and student of literature who used to spend the long vacation in Whitby.

Without pursuing this subject, I suggest briefly that the impact of Whitby upon the modern writer emerges perfectly from a study of Storm Jameson's prose. If she should insist upon the influence of French prose, I counter that by a reference to the bareness, even the bleakness, the economy, lucidity, directness, and mistrust of embellishment to be found in the native speech of Whitby. Moreover, she is a Whitby woman, and what is bred in the bone will inevitably get itself set down on paper.

So much for Whitby's tribute to literature, so much for Cædmon's Cross.

A superstition, a bit of folklore, or an ancient custom may die in the mere space of a twelvemonth, and I don't know what fragments of the past still linger in the minds of Whitby people. In 1855 *The Times* reported that "until quite recently—and the custom is still secretly maintained—after ill luck the wives of crews and owners assembled at midnight and in deep silence slew a pigeon, whose heart they had extracted and burned or stuck full of pins and burned over a charcoal fire. Then the witch responsible for the spell of ill luck would come to the door and be propitiated." In that day pigs were unlucky beasts, and eggs were unlucky, too. The first fish was burned on the return home. I suppose the Yorkshire coast custom of Raising Herrings is dead, though it was believed to ensure a good fishing season. It was certainly alive at Flamborough in 1894. After the men had put to sea, their womenfolk disguised themselves, often in male garb, and went joyfully about wishing their neighbours well. In the old days fishermen would not put to sea if on their way to the boats they met a woman, a parson, or a hare, and there were, of course, other superstitions like that of Gabriel's Hounds or Gabble Ratchets. The most famous custom still surviving is the planting of the Penny Hedge.

"Everie year the Horngarth service ys to be doone upon Holly Thursday evne.

"Tho. Cockrill being baylyf to the abbot did meete by sonn Rise the Conieres, the Strangwayes, the Eldringtones and Allettson, who were bound to this service, in the Strye-head hard by Lyttell-beck, and the said Cockrill did see every one cutt downe with a knyfe, he appoynting the wood, so muche as should serve. From thence they caym not the nearest way, but brinnging thym upon theyr backe, went a good way before they caym in to the way. So comminge to the water at the town ende they maid the hedg which should stand three tydes, and then the officer did blow owte upon they."

That is the earliest record of the ceremony, and it occurs on the parchment fly-leaf at the beginning of the Abbot's Book or Whitby Register. The writing is sixteenth or early seventeenth century. Since then the ceremony has been broadcast, the horn blown in perhaps a million ears, followed by a stentorian Yorkshire voice crying "Out upon ye ! Out upon ye ! Out upon ye !" It has been photographed for *The Times* newspaper, and yet the mystery has not been solved. Nobody knows the origin of this custom. Atkinson believed that certain tenants of the Abbey lands contested the right of the Abbot to impose upon them the duty of keeping monastic fences in repair, that this compulsion to plant the Penny Hedge was the symbol of their defeat, that the town-end marked the Abbey staith and the shore-limit of the Abbey lands, and that after the Dissolution the ceremony, though then meaningless, was continued.

The place called Thingwal, the site of the Danish folk-moot, cannot now be identified. Green Lane used to be known as the Hearse Road. The great shipbuilding families were those of Barry, Fishburn, Campion, and Chapman. In the Middle Ages Whitby was more interested in the woollen trade than in seafaring. Everyone knows that the early name of Whitby was Streoneshalch, though the derivation of the name is not known. The few houses under the Abbey were once known as Presteby. Whitby is very dubiously the *sinus fari* of Ptolemy's map. Whitby Laithes, Hawsker, Stainsacre, Larpool, Ugglebarnby, Stakesby, Roxby, Saltwick Nab, all speak eloquently of Danish conquest, but I think with Atkinson that the resident Anglian population of the Danelagh finally absorbed the Danes.

Visiting Whitby, the sightseer, however interested he may become in the vivid life of the town, should go into the Museum. It is a fine, well-kept, well-ordered place.

And, of course, the parish church. I recollect trying to drive a car up the church stairs, and having finally to turn in the narrowest of spaces at risk of toppling the car into the harbour. Watching this manœuvre is one of the principal amusements of the dwellers in the fishing-village. I recollect also visiting the church for the first time when Storm Jameson took me there and pointed out how much the interior resembled the interior of one of the old wooden ships of Whitby, and how the master mariners had each his own pew in the gallery—on the bridge, as it were. Visit the abbey, too. Hilda founded it about two years after the Battle of Winwædfield in A.D. 654, and probably had the site from Oswin of Northumbria. There was, it seems, a church there already, dedicated to St Peter (Peter was a fisherman), but under Hilda's able rule the new monastery prospered. The famous Synod of Whitby took place there in A.D. 663 or 664, and this settled once for all the destiny of the northern Church. In 680 Hilda died and was followed by Ælfleda, the next abbess, in 713, after which there is a hiatus of a century and a half in the history of the abbey. The Danes destroyed it about 870, but if they also destroyed the town they subsequently settled there and established their Thing. In the Confessor's time Whitby was assessed for Danegeld at £112. Somewhere about 1078 the monk Reinfrid of Evesham took up residence first at Jarrow, then at Whitby, where he became Prior. Stephen, afterwards first abbot of St Mary's of York, joined Reinfrid at Whitby. Reinfrid was killed while bridge-building at Ormesbrigg on the Derwent, and Stephen, who thought to be next prior, had his nose put out of joint by the Percy family, which took a benefactor's interest in the monastery. Serlo de Percy became the new prior and Stephen went to York.

Under Serlo the priory continued to flourish and became Whitby Abbey under the control of William de Percy, nephew of Serlo, who retired to the Cell of All Saints at York, possibly under compulsion, possibly with good grace. From the Percies came grants of land and wealth for the building of the fabric, and "among the remains of ancient conventual churches with which we may be acquainted there seem to be few that surpass Whitby in symmetry, grace and beauty". This is just the wrong way to write about monastic ruins, but certainly the building programme in the reign of William Rufus was full enough to justify the appointment of a *magister operationum ejusdem loci* named Godefridus. For his work Godfrey had half a century of peace, but then, between 1148 and 1175 (I don't know why the exact date should be doubtful), "the King of Norway entered the port of Whitby with many ships, ransacked the goods of the monks, laid waste everything both within and without, and, though he shed no blood, yet he carried off with him whatever he could find; so that they who by the management of their Abbot had grown very rich now became very poor, the rapacious Norwegians having left them nothing".

About 1220 the first stone of the present building was laid, and building went on energetically until 1235. A second burst of energy followed between 1245 and 1260, and a third between 1310 and 1330 or later. Thus the abbey belongs to the finest periods of English ecclesiastical architecture. From time to time gales damaged the structure, and there were rebuildings in new style—a Perpendicular window, for instance. After the Dissolution the abbey church became a quarry of fine building-stone. The tower, a rather squat tower, fell on a calm day, the 25th of June 1830. It is a miracle it had stood so long.

My envy at leaving the holiday-maker to enjoy his stay in Whitby is tempered by the prospect of travelling northward along the coast. North of Whitby, beyond Sandsend, the fore-shore, mauled by the sea and the old alum-burners, cannot be safely followed, and how Phillips made his geological survey of this part of the coast I do not know. He characterizes it as bold, lofty, and dangerous, and he is right. The boulder clay lies thick all the way to Redcar. Reluctantly the traveller takes to the road from Sandsend, climbs Lythe Bank and finds himself in country less picturesque than perhaps he has any right to expect. The road between Whitby and Saltburn is not easy, and at the same time it is not lovely. The cliff-top journey is long and arduous, and the walker will scarcely, I fear, be recompensed for his labour. At Goldsborough the relics of the Roman signal-station present a wind-swept, grass-grown, neglected site hardly worth the visiting. Here if anywhere Wade's Causeway, the Roman road from Caw-thorn Camps, came to the coast, and here we should expect something more imposing than the other identifiable signal-stations of the North Riding coastline. When I saw it there was only a wilderness of broken ground.

If you go to Runswick for a holiday they will, even in these bleak times, feed you well. The few fishermen still engage in a little long-line fishing, but for the most part they rely upon holiday-makers, crab-pots and lobster-pots. You will not, however, be fed exclusively upon crab and lobster, for though there may not be a hen in sight you will not go without eggs or chickens. Hereabouts the folk have gone back to barter, swapping crabs for eggs and lobsters for chickens, with vegetables thrown in for makeweight.

Years ago I came down into Runswick and thanked my stars that it did not resemble Mousehole, Marazion, Veryan, or St Ives. It has the same things—red-tiled roofs, alleys, whitewashed bulging cottage walls, tiny flower-gardens, polished brass, little square windows, a great sweep of blue-water bay and green tumbling cliffs—but it is still Runswick and no other place. Years later I went again and found summer shacks, tents, bright bathing-huts, motor-cobles in the bay, and a mannequin-show of beach pyjamas. There were pink parasols, and picture-postcards in vast quantity.

Hob Hole in Runswick Bay is where children were cured by the local hob of whooping cough :

75

Hob, hob, my bairn's gett'n t'kink-cough :
Tak't off, tak't off !

That was the cantrip, but no records prove that it worked. I
asked a friend recently returned from holiday at Runswick
if he knew of Hob Hole. He did not. He had spent his time
fishing, climbing Boulby Cliff, and playing ball on the sands.
I told him it was a pity he didn't have whooping cough. He
said Staithes nearly gave him whooping cough.

It was in Staithes that I bought, for five shillings, a salmon
jug. In her white-walled kitchen with little windows facing
seaward, an old woman in a lilac sunbonnet stood shy and
unsmiling. "It's what's called a salmon jug," she said, and
reached up to take it from its nail behind the door. "I don't
know whether it's old or not. My husband got it for me a
long time ago, about two year afore he went down with the
Staithes lifeboat. That was twenty-two years gone by. Ye'd
maybe remember the wreck of the Staithes lifeboat? Ay, it's
a bonny jug. Ye can have it for five shillings."

It had not been planted there by any dealer. I bought it,
and have been ashamed of myself ever since.

Another thing I saw in Staithes. All down the coast from
Saltburn to Filey and beyond, the village folk live in fierce,
detached shyness. Their Viking blood is still strong-running.
They are a silent, dour people, busy among shore-wrack and
sea-junk, nets, crab-pots, boats, tackle, and such. Their eyes
are uncompromising.

At Staithes the village is built on either side of the footbridge spanning the gully, the *hvik* or creek. It is now a concrete bridge, but at the time of which I write it was a wooden
structure, old but stout. Below, nearer the sea, the grey
houses huddled closer; here the view was more open. The
afternoon sun slanted across the gully, kindling all its
northern side, casting into soft shadow the southern. Five
women, all mature, two of them old, brown, and wrinkled,
two middle-aged, unbeautiful, with crows' feet round hard
disillusioned eyes, and one younger though not more handsome, walked in single file across the bridge. Dressed all
alike, in black skirts with cream-white blouses tight-buttoned
up to the chin, black boots and stockings, black gloves and

white sunbonnets, each one wore also a broad black sash diagonally slanting across the breast and tucked into the waist-band. They walked very slowly, in step, with hands folded before them, upon their faces a stoic impassivity. There was something hard and fateful in the sight. It spelled out a bitter resignation, a stern challenge, a silent strength. They were plain women but they walked superbly, with slow grace and pride of spirit. No one spoke to them or turned to watch them, and they did not speak to one another, but held their way without looking to left or right or up or down, on and over the footbridge. They entered the church, Our Lady of the Sea.

An hour later they returned in the same way and order with the same set features, hard and tearless eyes. Do not ask me what they had been doing in the church. I do not know, and I couldn't ask them. But when they came back they wore no sashes.

About thirty years ago Staithes must have been a livelier place than it is now, for fishing-villages were then in fashion among artists, and the Staithes group was an energetic lot, popular, I believe, with the indigenous inhabitants. The number composing the group varied from time to time but the painters did good, original work there. Perhaps one day Dame Laura Knight will write the story in detail. I hope she will. Artists, fisherfolk, the sea, the great winds blowing in, lamplit rooms and good shop-talk, and what more could any reader ask? Besides, there was at least one occasion when the artists, or some of the artists, helped to launch the lifeboat, and more than one of them learned a lot about boats and how to sail them.

Of all the places between Whitby and Saltburn-by-the-Sea Staithes is my favourite. I am sorry, however, about the concrete bridge. Wood is such good, durable stuff, and somehow Staithes and concrete do not mix. Staithes is not the place for tar-spraying but for cobbles, not for pylons and electric power but for oil lamps, not for motor-lorries but for boats.

It is easy to imagine that the road between Staithes and Skinningrove—the road, I mean, which is never more than a mile from the cliffs—is a link between the Roman signal-station on Huntcliff and one that formerly existed near

Staithes or on Boulby Cliff. Upon it there is a tiny place called Street Houses. Skinningrove has ironworks, and at Loftus we reach the fringe of a new population-area whose focal point is Middlesbrough and whose life lies with coal, iron, and steel.

These people are not, believe me, an easy crowd to handle. A more politically minded lot it would be hard to find, and in this they differ altogether from the phlegmatic agricultural workers of the North Riding. In 1928 I stood up in front of a hundred men of the iron and steel trade to explain to them Mussolini's theory of the Corporate State. I thought they ought to realize how first you establish a tyranny and afterwards frame a social philosophy to fit it. I worked the theory out exactly as the fascists had worked it out; I gave my men the same half-baked, half-plausible stuff Mussolini's men were talking. Rapidly I became aware that I had a hostile audience. I saw scowling faces and clenched fists. I heard growlings.

"Carefully! Go carefully!" my chairman muttered.

I nodded, and at the right moment, just before the storm broke, I launched out into a violent denunciation of this stuff masquerading as social philosophy, sneered at its shallowness, cursed its ruthlessness, contrasted it with the syndicalism of the North Italian factories and plainly let it be seen where my sympathies and convictions lay. The ferocity went out of the faces before me. The growlings died away. At the end of the lecture grinning men surrounded me.

"By lad!" they said. "We thowt ye were a fascist! If ye had ha' been, we'd ha' torn ye to bits!"

And they laughed uproariously.

They shoved forward one of their guests, a young Spaniard from Barcelona. We shook hands.

"Are you a communist?" I asked.

"No," he said gravely. "Not a communist."

"Then what?"

"I am an anarchist," he said.

My experiences of Saltburn-by-the-Sea have not all been like that. I have played cricket on the trim little cricket ground there, and hockey on the sands. I once met a man there who demonstrated the principles of economic theory

with a pack of playing-cards, I met miners from South Yorkshire who quoted papal encyclicals at me, weavers from Lan-
cashire who knew all about the *id* and the endo-psychic
censor, housewives with original views upon the medieval
manorial system, and all as keen as a Sheffield whittle. They
were summer-schooling with the Workers' Educational
Association. At the café half-way down the road to the beach
the tutors used to meet between lectures and argue with careless prodigality, but with a mere academic seriousness as
contrasted with the deadly earnestness of the students. This
was before Joad became a Brains Truster and John Edwards
an M.P. One morning the body of a drowned Norwegian
fisherman came in on the flood tide, looking for all the world
as though he were swimming. This was before T. S. Eliot's
drowned sailor and Connolly's drowned helmsman of
Æneas.

The beach was gay with striped bathing-tents, the land-
ladies and shops were not extortionate, the sands were
smooth and firm, the sun actually shone. We walked along
the beach to Marske, along Hunt Cliff where the last
defenders of the signal-station were slaughtered fifteen
hundred years ago, and inland to Skelton Castle. There was
also a tavern in the old fishing-village.

And, I believe, there is an ancient kitchen midden down
there which has some archæological importance.

Why, then, after all this, do I not care more for Saltburn-
by-the-Sea than I do? I think the answer is that always at
Saltburn I have been in a state of intellectual ferment without
a chance to estimate the town at its normal valuation. The
emphasis for me has always been upon people, not upon the
place itself, and after a fortnight's unrelaxing cerebration I
found it blessed to turn inland along the road to Guisborough,
Stokesley, Bilsdale, and Helmsley.

At Saltburn the sea is always cold. As Paignton is to Torquay, so is not Marske-by-the-Sea to either Saltburn or
Redcar. Before 1939 Marske was a quiet, undistinguished
village with interests more agricultural than marine. During
the war it developed an R.A.F. station with all the usual con-
sequences. At Redcar Middlesbrough folk enjoy themselves
in exactly the way Middlesbrough folk enjoy themselves, and

if I do not feel quite at home in Saltburn I feel still more a stranger in Redcar. Redcar has race-meetings.

Without, therefore, saying more than that as Southend is to London so is Redcar to Middlesbrough, I begin to wonder why in the records there is no name for all this area earlier than Clifflond or Cleveland. Another rather surprising thing is that the majority of the place-names carry no indication of Anglian or Danish antiquity : Dormanstown, Wheatlands, Low Farm, Town Farm, Wilton, Thornton Fields, Craggs Hill are commonplace. Saltburn is not marked on Saxton's map and the name has no North Riding form. South of a line drawn from Guisborough to Skinningrove this generalization does not apply, and I am led to conjecture a late development of the whole area north of that line, with extremely sparse Anglian and Danish settlements. In this connection it should be remembered that the Danish termination -by may signify not a village but a single steading.

For the moment I shall not concern myself with Tees-mouth and Middlesbrough, but turn back to cast a glance over the whole length of the North Riding coastline. It may not possess the black wildness of Cornwall or the grandeur of the Shiant Islands, but it has majesty if not sublimity. It is varied, it is beautiful, it is satisfying both to the eye and to the spirit. It has ruggedness, remoteness, and a copious wild life, and for the most part it is unspoiled. As I write, there is a tendency on the part of manufacturers from the West Riding to establish factories in the more populous towns because there is a serious shortage of labour in the West Riding, and the factories must now seek the labour where labour is to be found; but I do not think that this tendency will have a deleterious effect upon the coast towns. It may even do them good. The ravens will not come back to breed along the cliffs any more than the East Riding wolds will go back to sheep-walks or become the haunt of the bustard, but the sea-coast towns and villages will not grow into Ostends or Coney Islands, and there will always be something here for every kind of holiday-maker, the student of nature, the observer of human life, and the passionate recluse.

CHAPTER IV

THE VALE OF PICKERING

A LITTLE group of men and women sat in the lounge of the Queen's Hotel in Leeds. It was early June, and they were discussing holidays.

"We're off to Scarborough next week," said Mr Brown. "By road this time, thank goodness! It'll be grand to get along at sixty on the speedway from York to Malton and Malton to Scarborough. 'Twon't take us long to get to the sea, I can tell you!"

"You go the usual way, I suppose?" said Mrs White.

"Ay. Malton, Rillington, Sherburn, Seamer, Scarborough."

"You've missed out the Heslertons," Mrs Black interpolated, "but it's a good, fast road. Too many accidents on it for my liking, though! Usually I turn off at Malton and go through Old Malton to Pickering, then through the villages Thornton Dale, Allerston, Snainton, Brompton, West Ayton —lying along the southern edge of the moors. It's quieter."

"And I," said Mrs Green, "turn off the main road when I've passed Rillington and go up to your road by way of the high bridge at Yedingham and the hidden bit of old Yedingham Priory."

"A nasty bit of road!" said Mr Brown.

"No accidents, though, because everyone drives so carefully round the sharp bends and over the bridge," Mrs Green insisted. "It's really safer than the main road."

"Give me the main road every time!" said Mr Brown.

Humdrum commonplace, this—exactly the sort of talk you are bound to overhear in the Queen's Hotel lounge—but it has a little importance. It is characteristic of the motoring Browns, Whites, Blacks, and Greens that they all look upon journey's end as the thing of importance, and the journey itself as something to be got over. Vaguely they are aware

Guisborough Priory

that from Malton to Scarborough the rail and road routes
thrust along a level valley floor that narrows towards the
coast, and haphazardly they think of the moors to the north
as browner and more wooded than the bare outline of the
green wolds to the south. Talk to them of the Jurassic limestones and sandstones of the moors, the chalk of the wolds,
and the black lacustrine deposits of the valley floor, and they
remain uninterested. Yedingham may once have been a manor
of the Knights Templars, but of greater importance is the
question, "Can the inn serve ham and eggs?" They miss the
reason for the narrowing of the valley towards the coast and
equally the reason why the Derwent, sluggish and tortuous in
its course through the Vale of Pickering, has carved out a
narrow gorge through the hills about Kirkham Priory. They
would hardly be able to account for the location of the
Pickering–Scarborough villages, or for the sand and gravel
pits behind some of them.

"The villages are dead-alive," they say. "Scarborough's
the place, and even then only in summer!"

Certainly Scarborough is the place. Certainly the villages
are moribund, but there is something to be said of these
villages and still more to be thought about them. The Vale of
Pickering gives rise to speculation and forecast, and in writing
of this region I shall certainly include the wooded digitations,
the dales that thrust northward from the Vale into the moorland plateau. It matters little where I begin, whether at the
Pickering end with the Costa Beck and prehistoric lake-
dwellings, or at the Scarborough end, with the Shap granite
boulder at Seamer railway station and the limestone quarries
precious to fossil-seekers—those same quarries whence, as
lads, my brother and I brought home a pair of young short-
eared owls and reared them to full owlhood on dead mice,
bloody lights, and raw liver. From Oliver's Mount or Seamer
Moor, or from the frescoed walls of Pickering church, from
Gallows Hill at Brompton or King Alfred's Cave at Ebberston, what matters it where I make a beginning?

Off the high road, I think, away from the traffic, following
a vagary, a cirrus of speculation.

On the survey map the Great Moor Road appears as an
unfenced track without economic justification, beginning in

a quiet village, ending nowhere, and valuable now to neither man nor beast. It is, however, one of the green roads of England, and it ranks in my mind second only to the road over Hackpen Hill at the other end of England. No quest of medieval monks' roads took me there on the hottest of summer days; I wanted to be rid of people, and particularly I wanted to find out what the Forestry Commission had been up to in this part of the North Riding. I went by familiar roads, and on the crest of Hutton Bushel Moor I found what I looked for : here was the solitude, here were the conifers, and here, too, was the Great Moor Road.

A treeless landscape is an abominable thing, and a landscape which is all trees is equally abominable. In the presence of trees by the hundred thousand you become too much aware of the unhuman life around you. The lack of birds and little animals is disturbing, and when the trees are all of a kind, ranged, ranked and squared off in rectangular masses, presenting no dappling of sun, no open glades and no variety of form or colour, they intrude a governmental utilitarianism and extrude a timber-factory atmosphere, neither of which is pleasing, both of which are nevertheless tolerable. The timbering hereabouts is called Allerston II, and there is a great deal of it. No restrictions are imposed. The traveller may walk where he likes. The wardens merely warn him of the danger of fire, and in hot, dry weather it is advisable not to smoke and not to leave broken bottles about, for a single spark or a spot of concentrated sunshine may destroy the labour of months and the growth of years. The timber is valuable, though not as a source of æsthetic pleasure.

The ways of the Forestry Commission are hard to understand and irritating when understood. This Allerston II, for instance, has been planned and planted with no regard whatever for the ecology of the district. Game used to be plentiful in this area, but there is no game now, and the only bird I saw on the fringe of a monstrous block of conifers was a jay. Moreover, this moorland was formerly the home of the silent, vanished races; it abounds in camps, dykes, earthworks, tumuli and entrenchments, which now are hidden by regiments of Douglas fir, and which, in time, will vanish as though they had never existed.

83

I went down the Great Moor Road, and after a while struck off in a south-westerly direction. When foresters plant trees they first take tractor or prairie-buster and uproot gorse, birch and thorn; then they go over the site again with a deep-cutting plough which turns in the acid top-soil and breaks up the hard subsoil or pan, so that the roots of their trees may go through to the rock. The result is that the surface of the moor is disastrously rough and uneven, it makes difficult going, and there is always the danger of a wrenched ankle. This was the sort of country I met, and after three-quarters of a mile of it I came to the brow of a griff. A hundred and fifty feet below ran the rocky gorge of Beedale Beck, and since the fifty-foot contour-lines on my map showed less than a millimetre apart it was obvious that the griff was likely to prove difficult. My notion was to cross it. Down into it I went, now checking my descent by clinging to bilberry and ling, now slipping and sliding. Dead birch trees littered the upper slope —the foresters had flung them there—but they proved neither help nor hindrance, for, brittle and rotten as they were from twig-tip to root-stock, all I had to do was to go through them and they crumbled to powder under my feet and my hands. Loose shaly soil gave place to rotten rock, yet still I climbed down into an anarchy of limestone slabs set at all angles, boulders that had crashed into the griff, nettles as tall as myself, rose-bay willow-herb considerably taller, and horrible lyre-strings of bramble lacing up the dead birches into a magnificent mantrap. The bottom of the griff was as dry as a bone : the conifers had drained the water out of the moorland. This was, perhaps, fortunate, for at least I kept my shoes dry. Yet, on the western side, the rocks were sheer, crumbly and covered with the super-wiring of bramble-stems. I couldn't climb out that way, nor could I go forward without terrific expenditure of energy. Down there the heat was tropical. I fought my way down the bed of the griff for twenty yards, then found a possible line of ascent to the headland from which I had come down. I tried it. A bramble-barb caught the fleshy part of my nose, held on, sank in and stuck. I grew impatient, for my footing at this moment was dangerous. I tugged. The barb broke off. Blood poured from the wound. My hands were scratched and bloody, they were tingling with nettle-stings, and then I slipped and fell heavily into the bed of the griff. There I lay, recovering breath and temper, until the bleeding stopped. Combining the skill of a cragsman with the tenacity of a bulldog I tried again, hauled myself to the top, paused, panted, and hoped my troubles were over.

I should have to make more southing than originally I had planned, and felt that I would go a dozen miles out of my way rather than go down again into that corridor of hell. Besides, along the south-eastern skyline I could see a broad field of oats, and where there were oats there was surely a farm-track. I set off southward, slowly edging towards the east.

Then I found out that I had been travelling on a wedge-shaped headland, for shortly I came to the tip of the wedge. Below me lay another horrible descent, with Sitka spruce dwarfed by giant growth of bracken, rose-bay and serpentine brambles. At the bottom I could make out a wilderness of dead birch and thorn. The griff, however, was now a grain, and it stretched away towards the south. Far off, indifferent to blessing or imprecation, lay the bare line of the Yorkshire Wolds. Clinging to the Sitka spruce, into the wilderness I went, a wilderness lit by the rosy flames of the giant willow-herb. Occasionally I was sharply halted, with leafage in my face and bracken-stems round my throat, but at last I reached the tangle of dead birch and thorn. Still farther below lay the bed of an easterly feeder of Beedale Beck, and from where I leaned back against the hillside I saw great clumps of reeds and heard the gurgle of water. Having no mind to go down into the bed of the beck, for fifty yards I crashed through the dead stuff to my right. This took me half an hour. After that the going was easier, for the steep slopes on each side fell away and presently I came to a place where I could cross the beck and reach the foresters' road. First I lay full length on the spongy bank, put my face to the clear water, and drank. Then I washed the dried blood from my nose and hands. A minute or two later I began to travel at a fast rate along the foresters' road with the beck on my left and a great amount of lop and top on my right.

Here in Beedale was a little more wild life. I put up a

noisy cock pheasant, a grey squirrel got casually out of my way, and once I heard the plop of a water-rat as he dived from the bank. There were little rustlings and movements in the willow-herb. On the skyline I saw good tall timber still unfelled, and it put me in mind that somewhere in this vicinity there were flourishing sequoias. Maybe I ought to have turned back to look for them, to find out if they had been spared by the lumbermen, but by this time I was a little tired, anxious to reach inhabited country, more inclined to push on than to linger or turn back. At Beedale Grange there were telephone wires, and presently a metalled road developed. The wilderness lay behind me.

Wykeham has its lych-gate and tower separate from the church, and inside the lych-gate, against the floreated boss where the ribs of the arches met, a swallow had built her nest. Two young birds poked out their heads to look at me; a pleasant, peaceful, domestic scene.

If a water-mill stands by a river and for some reason the river shifts its bed, is it better to move the mill to the river or to force the river back into its ancient bed? At Ayton they had no hesitation in moving the mill, a massive three-story building of good freestone, with small windows, standing about eighty yards north of the bridge on the eastern side of the Derwent. They moved it, lock, stock and barrel, fifty yards, and now, save that at one corner the wall-stones are leaving the structure owing partly to vibration and partly to subsidence, the building is as solid as ever. It is, by repute, the second-oldest mill in England, with a much-weathered coat of arms facing the west. "The river," said Elsworth the miller, "ties us down to an undershot water-wheel," and he took me to look at it, a wheel fifteen feet in diameter made by Harker of Driffield, a firm that went out of business over a hundred and twenty years ago. Occasionally this great wheel has to be shifted away from the inner wall, and this is done by the labour of two pairs of hands, those of the miller and his young son.

In the winter months the mill often produces as much as twelve tons a week of farmer's offal; in summer not so much. "In time, I suppose, we shall have to go," said Elsworth. "We're old-fashioned and we're small-scale, but for myself

I'm not giving up any more than Noble of Hackness is giving up."

We rested our elbows on the polished rail of the wooden footbridge over the millrace and talked about the world. When, however, you happen to be a miller, there are more important things in the world to notice than the fluctuations in the share-market.

"A couple of years ago we had water-ouzels here," he said. "You know the bird?"

"A quick, quiet bird," I said, "with a white breast shading into chestnut, and a dark brown head. It dips and curtsies like a wren."

"That's it. It's pretty scarce in these parts, I believe. We had a pair. For a fortnight they kept on building their nest in the mill-wheel, and time after time it was destroyed. Finally they found a hole in the bank down there and brought up a couple of youngsters. Then they went, and they haven't been back."

"Any kingfishers?"

"In the autumn, plenty. And there's eels in the pond-weed yonder."

It was Canadian pond-weed, the stuff that used to choke canals and quiet watercourses. Here it was well under control and likely to remain so. Inside the mill the air was cool, quiet, and full of the fine scent of meal. The gear-house interested me. The great cog-wheel had cogs of apple-wood and haw-thorn made by a local craftsman. There were four sets of millstones, the pair in actual use being a Derbyshire grey and a French brie.

Millstones are interesting objects even when laid as door-steps to week-end cottages. In the North Riding as elsewhere they are almost always of millstone grit because the coarse-ness of the stone, together with the grooves cut along their surfaces with a claw chisel, prevents the temperature from rising too high and burning the meal. At Ayton the pair with iron rims was French : Montmorency chert set in a matrix of cement. At Robin Hood's Bay they used top-stones of Nieder-mendig lava, but millstone grit is still found to be the best for hard grain.

In odd corners of the gear-house were agricultural implements of a former day : three or four gathering-rakes of wrought iron with three six-inch tines set five inches apart, and an eighteenth-century scythe-shaft with a triangular grip. The blade was missing. Had the whole thing been complete I, who can handle the ordinary scythe with some pretension to skill, would certainly have tried the older pattern. It was ingenious in shape, well balanced and easy to use. In the Castle Museum at York there is nothing quite like it.

The Ayton blacksmith was busy, like all village smiths to-day. Formerly there were two blacksmiths' shops in this village and each employed four men. Now there remains one shop and the smith works alone.

"Old-fashioned gear? Ay," he said, "there's plenty about yet ! It's not everybody that's up-to-date. Wooden harrows and wooden ploughs. Ancient tools of all sorts ! And though I'm up-to-date myself—the furnace runs on electricity—some of the oldest tools in this village are here in this shop. Tools of my own craft. I'm getting on, and I've worked here all my life, but those tools were old when I was a lad, and I use 'em yet."

He took a sample half-dozen down from the rack to the left of the furnace and let me handle them. Obviously they were products of the village smithy itself, specialized instruments for specialized jobs, and like nothing to be found in a modern city forge. They, too, were museum pieces.

Usually the best way of looking at a village is to go round the back of it, and this is true of Ayton. Thousands of people travel through the village by bus, bicycle or car, and how many of them know, I wonder, that a fine fig-tree grows here against a south wall?

Ayton Castle stands on rugged ground. All over the site are signs of foundation-walls under the turf, and either there was a much more spacious castle formerly here or the greater part of Ayton Castle has been used as a quarry. As it stands, the structure to-day is a small ruined peel built to command the village, the river and the road. Obviously it belongs to the late fourteenth or early fifteenth century. The undercroft is in two compartments with ribbed arches, and floor-level is four feet below the modern ground-level. The undercroft, I found, held seventeen head of cattle that had found coolness

88

and shelter from a fierce sun. The ruin is neglected. It is, fortunately, not worth restoring. Primarily a residential peel, its six-foot-thick walls are overgrown with grasses and young quickthorn, and I see no reason why this pleasant little place should ever be cleaned up. Left alone, it will last another hundred years or so.

Not far north of Ayton is a sand and gravel pit. Though the gates were shut and work was not in progress I found an Argus-eyed, shaggy-haired, raw-boned fellow who was familiar with the pit. I waved my arm to include the big wind-rippled dunes of sand visible through the gates.

"How," I asked, "did all this sand get here?"

He set his head on one side and satisfied his mind that I was serious.

"Why, now," he said, "I'm told that this was the mouth of a big river that flowed into the lake that covered all the valley in times past, and," he added, "I reckon it was a devil of a long time ago."

He knew, he knew! The villager isn't as daft as the towns-man thinks he is.

In the dead summer heat I was reminded of Saharan sand-dunes which in my time I have had reason to curse. It was not so much the shapes of the vast piles of sand, or the wind-ripples, as the tiny, stealthy noise of sand-grains sliding over one another in a windless, shimmering heat. Presently I crossed a pasture and walked down a green lane into Hutton Bushel. The Hutton is original; the Bushel, somehow cor-rupted into Buscel, is the name of the family that lived here before the Langleys and the Osbaldestons. I, naturally, was on the trail of George Osbaldeston, the famous squire who complained that he was so busy with hunting, shooting, racing, billiards, cricket, tennis, "ladies etcetera," he had no time to attend the House of Commons, and whose story is summarized in the *Dictionary of National Biography*. When George Osbaldeston's son came of age there was organized revelry at the Old Hall, but something went wrong with the organization and, though the ox was well and truly roasted (a horrible business, whole-ox-roasting!) the Old Hall was burned down. I wanted to know if anyone in Hutton Bushel remembered anything about it. First I asked a couple of schoolboys. Did they know where the Old Hall had formerly stood? No, they did not. They had never heard of the hall, never heard of Squire Osbaldeston. This was not a good beginning. I went up to a pleasant-faced countrywoman standing at her cottage door and asked her the same question. She shook her head, pondered a moment, and then without a word scuttled into the wheelwright's shop four or five yards away. I waited, listening to subdued colloquy within. Then she emerged, followed by the old wheelwright, George Wilkinson, rising ninety but with all his wits about him.

George sat on the little garden seat, the countrywoman brought me a chair from her kitchen. George sat quiet for a moment or two.

"Ay," he began at last, "it all happened afore my time, but I know about it. They roasted an ox between two big elm-trees, and I could show you the very spot. The elms has gone now. I remember 'em, though; I remember 'em. And the hall was burned down. They never built it up again. What was left of it was sold for fower hundred pound and that was the end of it."

"Nothing left of it, then?" I asked.

"Nothing above-ground," he answered, "but when ye're halfway up the churchyard path ye're just over the cellars, and if ye stamp on the path ye'll hear it sound hollow. Ay, and they used some of the stone to build the school."

He got up and rambled off into the cottage. Presently he returned, carrying a tattered North Riding directory of the early nineteenth century. To George Wilkinson this was the most precious of volumes. Broken-spined and dog-eared as it was, I have seen scholars handle the original Old English *Exeter Book* with less care than George bestowed upon this almost worthless volume. What interested him, and what he was anxious to tell me about, was the former existence of a village called Marton in close proximity to the present Hutton Bushel. There was a church at Marton dedicated to St Helen, and this, George thought, would explain the presence of a St Helen's Spring which is either in the vicarage garden at Wykeham or has vanished altogether.

While the old craftsman was talking, a resident of the village called in. He told me of a fourteenth-century grave-slab with a floreated cross and an empty stone coffin, both of which had just been discovered close to the south wall of the church. George listened but said nothing. When, however, his visitor had gone, the old man turned to me with a little high-pitched giggle.

"I recollect the coffin being put there," he said.

For one mad moment I thought the old man was trying to tell me he was alive and conscious in the fourteenth century, but no : "I remember it in another place," he added. "I can't rightly say where, but in another place."

Here, I suspect, is a lesson for the amateur, and maybe sometimes for the professional, digger-up of ancient graves.

When, after leaving George Wilkinson, I arrived at the church, I failed to rouse any hollow echoes from the church-yard path. I found a large araucaria not far from the south door and a seventeenth-century sundial over the porch to remind me that "Time wasted is existence, used is life." Since the craft of clockmaking was well enough known in the seven-teenth century, I suspect that either Hutton Bushel was too poor to buy a church clock or else that there was even then some precious antiquarianism rampant in the North. The church, like the village, is well looked after. It has some good modern oak, two Jacobean chairs in the sacrarium, and, near the south porch, the stone shaft of an old cross with a modern top.

The village carpenter at Ayton, a grey-headed, dour old fellow, looked at me suspiciously over his silver-rimmed spectacles, was not at all anxious to talk, seemed not to be vitally engaged and would not let me into his shop. A char-acter. I peered past his bulk into the gloom and asked questions. "No !" he said, and "Ay !" he said, and I was on point of moving off when I glimpsed a pair of plywood tongs in his little window, labelled "wasp tongs" and priced at two shillings the pair. I went back.

"Those wasp tongs," I said. "What's the notion?"

A gleam of pleasure crossed his face, his forehead lost its furrows and his eyebrows ceased to overhang his eyes.

"I invented 'em myself," said he. "The wasp settles, d'ye see ? Then, without fussing, ye pick him up with the tongs and put him in the fire."

"And does the wasp allow this?" I asked.

"Ay, he does."

"I'll take a pair," said I.

This pleased him so much that he stood away from his door and gave me a chance to run my eye over the interior of his shop. It seemed to hold a lot of smashed kitchen chairs, but there were also three or four miniature yachts, one of them, the biggest, a yard long. His hobby, he explained, was building those yachts.

"Fore-and-afters," I commented.

"Anything you like!" he replied. "And when you pick up the wasp don't squeeze him. It makes a mess of the tongs if you do."

The good man knew his wasps. Arriving home, I found that a gently handled wasp made no protest. Only I never put wasps on the fire, for I've seen wasps in a single day clear an apple-tree of caterpillars that made noises as they chewed. I put my wasp out of the window and he flew away intact.

Back in Hutton Bushel, I watched three men building a new dry wall to enclose a southward extension of the churchyard. Let them say that dry walling is becoming a lost art. I have not seen, in Gloucestershire or elsewhere, a finer sample of dry walling than Dick Vasey was putting up that day in 1945. Dick Vasey is not a Hutton Bushel man; he lives where most of the North Riding Vaseys live, in Ebberston, six miles farther west.

I did not stay in Wykeham nor go out of my way to visit Wykeham Abbey. But in Wykeham I found a bee-keeper—there are too few bee-keepers in the Vale of Pickering—who maintained a single straw skep-hive—a byke—amongst his modern hives. Brompton Church, though it lies off the main road, was too important to pass by. Inside, I explained my errand to a woman dusting and polishing the woodwork.

"Ah," she said, "ye're lucky! Ten minutes more and I should ha' been gone and the vestry locked up as usual. Ye can go in; the door's open."

I went in, looked around, and saw it, hanging on the wall inside the door, framed in a small black frame. The ink was little faded, and one of the signatures—a bold, clear handwriting—I recognized at once. William Wordsworth, described as gentleman, of Grasmere in the County of Westmorland, was here, on the 4th of October 1802, by John Ellis in the presence of three Hutchinson witnesses, married to Mary Hutchinson. The marriage was by licence.

Brompton Church to-day is different from the church Wordsworth saw that day in 1802. The flooring now is parquet, then the paving was composed of rectangular stone slabs. The font then stood near the south door and had a tall cover. The pews were the old oak box-pews high enough to conceal the occupants. The wooden roof had tie-beams and was pitched lower than at present. The east window was much larger than it is now, and was, it would seem, a good piece of work in Perpendicular style. The new window is neither Perpendicular nor is it good.

North of Brompton, Sawdon Moor is a wide area of humped and hillocked heather-plots with isolated firs and birches, and it has, or used to have, a planting of conifers I shall not soon forget. The trees, thickly set, were a uniform twelve feet high. Making across country, and thinking to save time and labour by going through the planting, I climbed the wire, noted the position of the sun and set off. The stiff branches had to be parted at every step I took. I breast-stroked my way, sometimes taking a bristle-brush of green in the face or across the eyes, sometimes doing side-stroke as a change from breast-stroke, and often tacking. Soon my arms ached. Soon I had no idea where I was going. The sun was lost, there was no wind, there was nothing but a density of green that had somehow grown viscous and dangerous. It wanted to keep me and hold me. My movements slowed and became languid. I stopped to consider my position. Then I went on, rather desperately, rather hopelessly. Too busy to suffer the anguish of claustrophobia, I was glad indeed to see daylight six or seven yards directly ahead of me, and did not much care that I got out of the planting three-quarters of a mile west of where I wanted to be, having saved neither time nor labour. Such plantings, even for strong men, are places to keep out of. They have sinister aspects, shutting out the sky, blanketing the familiar world, isolating the individual, and because they are alive they are different from caverns— living densities of green, not densities of dead darkness.

West of the head of Wyedale, between Brompton and
Snainton, there is a pothole only partially explored. It runs
below the face of an old quarry and the entrance is now
blocked by big stones. The antechamber, twelve feet down a
narrow clint, contains only the dusty skeleton of a sheepdog,
and the main caverns, one to the north and one to the south
of the antechamber, are very deep. Stones thrown down them
wake only echoes; you hear no splash and you can by no
means judge when the stones reach bottom. As a boy, by
accident I found the pothole, and by design began to explore
it. My uncle, remembering the fate of the sheepdog, saved my
life by visiting the quarry in the cool of the evening and
dropping a lot of big stones down the clint.

In 1788 Marshall described *ings* as low-lying mowing-
ground, and in 1788 that is what they were. Nowadays the
ings below the road from Scarborough to Pickering are given
up to corn, roots, field peas, potatoes and pasture, with very
little mowing-grass. The alluvium is a black, sandy deposit
full of stones. Even in 1788 the farms were very small—of
thirty to sixty or seventy acres—and to-day the average farm
in the Vale of Pickering is not much bigger. The farming unit
is uneconomic, and though the land is now less starved than it
used to be it still falls short of its potential productivity.
Below the black soil lies a stiff blue clay. Drainage is difficult,
pasturage is poor, the land lacks trees, and in places the ings
become marsh and slack—the haunt of heron and peewit,
where scant willows stand with their roots in water. The
Derwent flows sluggishly between its embankments, and the
by-roads, dusty in summer and muddy in winter, are only
farmers' roads, leading nowhere. Brompton Beck brings
floodwater down in rainy weather, and along its lonely banks
I have seen dabchick, moorhen, kingfisher, heron, reed-
warbler, sedge-warbler, whitethroat.

Winter and summer, it is not an impressive or lovely landscape, but I like its winter aspect better than its summer. The
flat, empty land under grey sky and driving rain seems
inevitably associated in my mind with the sight of a storm-
cock with ruffled feathers singing on the topmost twig of a
wind-swept ash two miles down the lane from Snainton to
Foulbrig. Further, the sky here is neither cut up nor seg-

mented into Laputan patterns by vegetation and by buildings. Blue or grey, bare or cloudy, it is all welkin. Lastly, I find great beauty in a completely flat landscape; its lack of variety is more apparent than real, and I have always liked flat washes of greyish-brown in landscape painting. I am, too, very partial to willows, possibly because the first tree with which I became friendly was an old, gnarled willow in this very locality. The best picture I know of Snainton Ings is an oil-painting by Leonard Greaves.

At first sight there seems to be not much of a future for the ings of the Vale of Pickering, and, if they continue to be farmed as they are farmed now, there is not. But given small-scale mechanization on small holdings, with a preliminary large-scale drainage scheme and a stiffening of the sandy alluvium by plentiful admixture of organic manure, this Vale of Pickering could be made into a second Vale of Evesham. I don't expect this particular half-wilderness to blossom like the rose in my time, but the thing could be done.

I return from the flat lands, called usually "down below," to Snainton village, thought to be the plainest village of all those beads on a string between Scarborough and Pickering. Perhaps it is. Nay, certainly it is. Its plainness, however, will not result in my hurrying through it, for here, if anywhere in this vicinity, linger traces of an older time. The first farm-house as you approach Snainton from the east, past "t'vicar new school," is Manor House Farm. In its granary, scribbled in pencil on the wall, occurs the old farmlad's rhyme :

George Marshall is my name
And wagoner is my station;
Snainton is my dwelling-place
And Heaven my expectation.

In its old tiled kitchen with its plate hearth, rannel-bawk and reckans, I first heard the old folk-play of *St George and the Dragon* at Christmastime, and first tasted frumerty or furmity, and had a wart charmed away by magic spell, and saw my first broadsheet of ballads—new songs to old tunes— and heard the old farmer say, "I've a couple o' sick beeasts; I'll away to see t'wise man aboot 'em !"

"Wise man" was a euphemism for "wizard," and the local

wizard lived in a tumbledown hut a mile below Brompton. Unfortunately he died many years ago, and left no successor.

In that farmhouse people believed in hobgoblins and Hallowe'en witches and ghosts, and their religion was Old Testament, patriarchal, with an open belief that escape from hell's torture was extremely difficult if not impossible. They held that if the butter wouldn't form the devil was in the churn. They said of a confirmed melancholic that "t'black dog was on his back," but the queerest tale of all was that of the man who vanished. He was actually seen to vanish by three witnesses. One moment he was walking in the middle of a pasture, the next he wasn't there, and nobody ever saw him again. The pasture was called Dobbin Hall, and though I have been over every square yard of it I cannot yet make out how that man disappeared. I remember also the story of a murderer who buried his victim by lantern-light and left next day for Klondyke. Nobody was sufficiently interested to dig up the body or inform the police, and to this very hour the bones rest undisturbed. In this instance I cannot identify the field.

"But how!" you say. "Had the villagers, then, no sense of social justice? Didn't they care that a man had been murdered and that his murderer had escaped?"

The answer is that in those romantic days men often disappeared without notice and without trace. Above the village, between the Leys and Nettledale, lies an area of allotments still called Canada, and when, after his day's work was over, a villager announced his intention of "going to Canada," he might equally have been on his way up to the allotments or across the Atlantic, and nobody worried, nobody cared. Those were hungry days in the Vale of Pickering.

I would draw attention, finally, to a short cut through orchards and fields known locally as "t'Duvvocks"—a name whereof I cannot trace the origin. The pound at the west end of the village has not been used within living memory. The twelfth-century doorway of the lych-gate was formerly the south door of the church. The graveyard, by repute, is water-logged. I do not believe this, but I do know that deep graves are not possible; the rock is too near the surface. The family names hereabouts are Dale, Stonehouse, Beswick, Pateman,

Hutton le Hole

Poad, Hardwick, Harland, Lownsborough. The Dales, Hardwicks and Lownsboroughs are red-haired and freckled, the Stonehouses and Beswicks are lithe, dark people. They represent two distinct strains of population.

At sunset I turned my back on Snainton and made north to Cockmoor Hall, Six Dikes and Troutsdale. The road slugged its way uphill between hedges and dry walls to the solidly built farmstead, the belt of pines and the scattered round barrows in the rough ling beyond the last farm gate. When I got to Cockmoor Hall the lamps were lighted and beyond the house the pines were dark against a sky full of cloud, the wind blew cold from the north and the glow of sunset had gone. I climbed a gate and entered the belt of pines. Within a mile, Six Dikes began to heave themselves up among the tree-roots, and I quitted the cart-track, here sunk below the level of the moor, scrambled up the cam-side and began to pick my way along and across the dikes, covered here with tough ling, steep-sided, full of rabbit-burrows and deceptive shadow. Scamridge, Six Dikes and the tumuli on the open moor have always attracted me. Over this ground the archæologists have tramped in vain. Their theory, in which the earthwork system hereabouts is related to a big-scale plan to defend the moors from attack from the west, is nothing. These Six Dikes run closely parallel to one another. Defensively they are worthless. They ask to be outflanked, and, if they were military in origin, the strategy governing their construction was frankly lunatic.

The attraction of Six Dikes was as powerful as ever. The narrow wood was full of moving mist, the upper branches of the pines swayed and whispered. Satisfied that the dike had known no disturbing spade or mattock for years, I went back along the rutted lane and came to the head of Troutsdale. Directly below, the mill, which has not functioned as a mill in my time, lay dark. I stood too high above the valley to catch the sound of the beck. Along the northern side of the dale the road reeled empty into the easterly darkness, and I saw Troutsdale rather as it used to be than as it is now. Forty years ago it was remote, lonely and very beautiful. To-day it lies within tourist grasp of Scarborough, its horizons have closed in, the cultivation-area has spread. Once a gated road,

H 97

Hovingham Hall

the highway is now listed as second-class and the mill as a place for picnic teas. North-west of the mill and the road, however, Upper Troutsdale is neither for city shoes nor for silk stockings, and its level, bare skyline preludes a wild expanse of ling stretching away to Staindale, Adderstone Rigg and the High Bridestones, an expanse without landmarks, without trees, and without more than a single sheeptrack sometimes plain and sometimes lost in the heather. I have, on occasion, crossed this moor at midnight.

Of the High Bridestones, which stand along the eastern scarp of Dovedale Griff, a feeder of Staindale Beck, they explain the origin of the name by a daft legend : after her marriage, a bride on her way home was caught in a thunderstorm and took refuge under the overhang of these rocks. That's the whole story. No names, no dates or details, and so obviously a fiction that it wouldn't deceive a child. With rather more ingenuity I suggest that the word *bride* is the same word as *brede* in Keats's *Ode to a Grecian Urn*—*with brede of men and maidens over-wrought*—and that it means *border* or *edging*; so that these are stones that stand along the edge of the griff. Commonplace, plausible, satisfactory— and probably wrong. I should describe the Bridestones as small-scale Brimham Rocks. Brimham Rocks were carved into their fantastic shapes by wind-erosion when the whole area was a dust-bowl; the Bridestones, capped with hard stone, resulted from the rain-weathering of the softer stone underneath. The Pepperpot has the long neck and brachycephalic head of Queen Nefertiti and cannot be climbed without a ladder or a sturdy pair of shoulders; the Saltcellar is easier but still tricky. Both summits are copiously initialled and dated. The other stones, about half a dozen in number, lack dignity. There is no suggestion of Avebury about them. They do not matter. From Thornton Dale, from Snainton or from Langdale End, the Bridestones make a satisfactory target for a day's trip in rough country.

At the head of Troutsdale I had choice of several ways. I might push westward to Givendale Head, risk the irregular road and the vipers of Dalby Warren, and go down into Thornton Dale by way of Sutherbruff Rigg. I might strike north-west to the Bridestones and then eastward through

Crosscliff and Bickley to Langdale End. I might choose the easy road through Troutsdale to Hackness. In daylight I should have chosen the first or second way. In the darkness and tired as I was, I took the third. Dogs made a disturbance as I went by the mill, and dogs answered from a long way down the dale. An owl, looking like a bit of wind-whirled newspaper, flew across the road in front of me. A nightjar was churring near Rock House. Cock pheasants were restless. Once I heard the bark of an old dog fox on the south slope of the dale.

A timber survey of Troutsdale in 1608 reported that there were only sixty old trees there. Now there are none, and Troutsdale, no longer thick with scrub oak, is good dairy-farming country, a Nidderdale in miniature but with less of an alpine look about it than Nidderdale. And—yes, there are trout in the beck still, as there were years ago when I poached them by tickling.

Troutsdale runs east and west and forms no part of the Vale of Pickering Nexus. Ebberston Dale, I think, is a not very handsome green furrow in the escarpment, but it gives access to King Alfred's Cave, which is not a cave at all but a crude erection of stones with a low hole for entry. A dim legend survives that in Anglo-Saxon times a battle was fought here in which King Alfred—an Alfred of Northumbria—was defeated and crawled here to die. The place has no interest whatever for a grown-up, nor do I find much to detain me on the escarpment between Allerston and Pickering. From Six Dikes and Givendale Head I have on occasion pushed westward across the moors into Dalby Warren, which was laid out as a warren in the mid-eighteenth century, and was moderately new when Marshall wrote his *Rural Economy*. It is now old, but it is still a warren, and its warm, sandy slopes give basking-ground for hagworms or vipers. They are apt to squirm across the track in front of your feet and on a bright day you have to be a wary walker. A mile or so above Thornton Dale the Simpsons of Pexton Moor Farm own a merril-board and still play the Elizabethan game of merrils, which, I believe, is something like nine men's morris but played indoors.

Ebberston is a long, straggling village. As you pass

99

through East and West Ayton, Wykeham, Brompton, Snainton, Ebberston, Allerston and Thornton Dale, you are persuaded that the houses run east and west on each side of the road. In truth they run north and south, and this is particularly true of Ebberston and Thornton Dale. The housing that lies east and west is much more modern, and the old village streets followed the southerly flow of the watercourses. Thus Ebberston, with its cottages of local stone, its varying patterns of domestic architecture, including Georgian, lies quietly off the main road and is untroubled by the traffic stream. Ebberston Hall, standing to the north of the main road, is a small, compact, four-square little building in a curious eighteenth-century style. The place looks remote, detached. Allerston Mill uses Derbyshire greys and makes farmer's offal. The church has what looks like a twelfth-century font and there remains some neat thatch in the village. Thornton Dale preens itself. When a village goes in for the deliberately picturesque it is damned. Thornton Dale is not quite damned. Off the road it is pretty enough, but not on it. What the motorist sees is not lovely. The beck flows through the village, and formerly the central area was the green, with the old market cross, the usual six steps, plinth and column. The old stocks stand at the foot of the cross surrounded by the rotting stumps of ancient trees. One tree still stands, and seats have been set in its shade for the gossips of the village, the old men, and those who wait for buses. In Thornton Dale I saw a number of young women in white boiler suits, but I couldn't discover their occupation, though I asked. I also found a bluetit's nest where the coign-stone of a house-front had broken slightly away. This was precisely at the bus-stop, and one of the parent birds flew into the hole within a foot of my head.

The only famous man produced by Thornton Dale was Richard Rolle of Hampole, a fourteenth-century monk, hermit and mystic, who left behind him a lot of valuable work in the northern dialect. The main body of it is called *The Pricke of Conscience*. It is all about remorse, and is unreadable except by scholars who make notes upon the dialect but not upon the remorse.

Pickering is an old market town, the ancient capital of the

Royal Forest of Pickering, and gives its name to the wapentake of Pickering Lythe. Like Malton, it has old coaching
inns, an old church with mural paintings and a modern
grammar school where Austin Hyde takes care that the
Yorkshire dialect is not snubbed out of existence. Lake-
dwellings have been discovered by the Costa Beck, but they
have small value as compared with those of Glastonbury or
Lake Geneva, and only the feverish enthusiast for pre-history
will ask where they are and in what state they exist. The
market square stands on a slope, and the church with its spire
rises to the immediate north of the square. Pickering Castle is
worth looking at. Some fine wood-carving and cabinet-making
is executed in Pickering, but, apart from the mural paintings,
discovered in the nineteenth century, whitewashed over and
finally cleaned up again, the church held little of interest to
me. There is, of course, a St Christopher. The paintings are
in places dim and patchy, and the little pamphlet in the church
describing them was written for children. It points the moral,
but neglects to state that St George—the original George—
seems to have been an army contractor in Asia Minor who
made a lot of money. The castle took me away from St
George, St Christopher, St Edmund's martyrdom, the
Coronation of the Virgin, Herod's Feast and (naturally) St
Thomas of Canterbury, all very two-dimensional and formal,
and I found it, above the town, of the twelfth century motte
and bailey type.

Pickering is not, as you would expect, a quiet place. I have
always found it busy and bustling, with the shops and the inns
doing good trade. It is an important—almost a self-important
—little place, the focal point of many villages, and yet its life,
the stream of which is eager and strident, seems restricted.
Even in 1788 Marshall took this view of Pickering, and
since his time economic conditions here have not vastly
changed.

Except, of course, for the railway. In Pickering you cannot
shut your eyes or your ears to the railway, for a level crossing
interrupts the traffic flow at the western exit from the town,
and every now and again an engine comes clanking in from
Malton or from Whitby. The line from Pickering to Whitby
is famous in railway history, but the agitation for its construc-

tion came not from the people of Pickering but from those of Whitby. At the end of the eighteenth century Whitby began to feel as isolated from the rest of England as Labrador is from the rest of Canada, and since this was the period when Irishmen were digging canals all over the country, Whitby's first idea was to connect itself to Pickering by canal. In 1793 William Crossley surveyed the route and figured out the cost as £66,447—a curiously detailed estimate. The project fell through and nothing more was done for some years. On 27 December 1830 the Stockton–Darlington Railway extended its lines to a coal-staith at Middlesbrough, where in the preceding April George Chapman had built the first house on the thirty-two acres laid out as the site of the new town projected by the Middlesbrough Owners. While in 1826 the *Whitby Repository* came out in favour of a railway line to Pickering, Robert Campion of Whitby wanted to make Whitby a coal-port by building a line up the Esk Valley to join the Stockton–Darlington Railway. The *Whitby Repository* preached insistently, and Campion's argument came too late.

Now mark the estimates for the construction of the Pickering–Whitby Railway. The first came to £120,000, the second to £226,000. I cannot find out why the second was so nearly double the first, and evidently other folk were just as puzzled, for the next event that took place was the calling in of George Stephenson himself. He worked out the cost at £2,000 a mile, but believed that the carrying of coal, lime, whinstone from the great dyke, freestone, timber and agricultural produce would yield a profit. The act for the construction of the line was passed on 6 May 1833.

John Castillo, the local dialect poet, ought to have hacked out a few verses on the construction and opening of the line, but in *Awd Isaac* he had wrought his masterpiece and any further effort would possibly have shortened his life. He died in 1845 at Pickering.

Many travellers to Whitby by train know the picturesque quality of the line through Newtondale, but they do not experience the thrills of the early journeys. The trains were not drawn by steam locomotives but by horses, which drew the coaches along the levels and hauled them up the inclines,

This line carried no dandy-coaches on which the horses travelled from point to point (the horses grew so clever that they learned to jump aboard the dandy-coaches at the right places and at the right times), and there are, even to-day, relics of the places where the horses were stationed to be hitched to the string of coaches. When the coaches came to a downward run the horses were unharnessed and the train went down by force of gravity. Through Blansby Park, approaching Pickering, it got up a speed of over thirty miles an hour.

The Pickering–Whitby line made still more history, for the first excursion train ran along it. In Grosmont the church wanted money, and that led to the organizing of a bazaar. This was in 1845. The ladies of Grosmont, fearing that they could never raise enough money from the folk of Whitby and district, thought of attracting folk from the Pickering area, and just over a century ago this first excursion train set out from Pickering, the hesitant forerunner of thousands more from that time to (nearly) this.

One last note about this railway. In 1920 I had a mind to holiday at Newton-upon-Rawcliffe, and went by train, booking to Levisham Station and arriving with a brass-bound trunk. I looked about me.

"Where," I said to the stationmaster, "is Newton?"

He pointed up a hill shaggy with pasture and diminutive quickthorn. The hill was high, and a narrow footpath toiled zigzag to its level top.

"Up there," he said. "The path takes you to the backside of the village."

"And how," I asked him, "will this—the brassbound trunk —get up there?"

"Oh," he said lightly, "two o' my lads'll hug it."

They hugged it through the early darkness of an Easter evening. How they got it up the hill I do not know and was afraid to ask, but they reckoned that five shillings was handsome payment. Myself, I wouldn't have hugged it for five pounds.

People are getting to know Newton. It is a village worth knowing. When I first knew it, it was remote, quiet, and hardly touched by modernity. There was not a car in the place, and the only foreigner was Mrs Spring, who talked with a violent cockney twang and had once been in the household of a South African diamond millionaire. She was a superb cook. Newton's village green is still a village green. It is not an asphalted square. It has twin duckponds with ducks, and the little cottages edge the green, which is not level but slopes southward and rollicks as it goes. Now, however, change has come, and in the proper place I shall note the change, for Newton-upon-Rawcliffe is a village of the moors, not of the Vale of Pickering. The five miles of road between Pickering and Newton separate the two places in time as well as in space.

Before I leave Pickering for Helmsley, however, I have much to record, and this seems to be the place for it.

Below the road from Newton to Cawthorn there used to be a little wilderness, twenty or thirty acres of ling, birch, bramble and bracken. Wartime necessity brought the prairie-buster, stump-jumper and gyro-tiller to this wilderness, and, cleared of all surface vegetation, the brown soil, levelled and copiously marled, was ready for its first sowing down. Above Stape, by Mauley Cross (not Manley Cross, as the Survey map gives the name), it was not the rich variety in colouring and contour that took my eye but a southward-falling intake on the slope of the moor; a square of dry walling and a carpet of dull green inside the walls. The intake was on the 800-foot contour line, and the dull green was the healthy foliage of potatoes. Farther up, on the level moor, another intake held another crop of potatoes. Their flourishing at the moorland level seemed to me an extraordinary thing, for this was the level of birch, pine and thorn, of ling, bilberry and bracken. How, then, potatoes? And if potatoes, why not pasture, roots and corn?

People argue that William the Norman, finding the North York Moors waste, left them waste, waste it is now and waste it shall remain. "Why spoil the beauty?" they demand. "Burning cannot wither it nor afforestation stale its infinite variety. Wordsworth would have condemned the rectilinear acreages of Douglas fir and Sitka spruce, but the blue horizons would still have induced a flow of poetry, there is beauty here, and may the time be far distant when this beauty shall vanish. Besides," they add thoughtfully, "isn't it unlucky to plough up the heather?"

"Granted that love of the wilderness is latent in man, woman and child," comes the answer, "we cannot in these days be neglectful of economic necessity, delight in the wilderness does not go at all with a hungry belly, and human beings are not moorland sheep to feed on uncooked heather-shoots and bracken-tips. This country must grow all the food it can, and the North York Moors and the Cleveland Hills together embrace 172,000 acres, much of which could be turned into good grazing land and some of it into good arable."

When the man of science speaks his mind, we must perforce be silent and attentive.

"No, sentimentalizing won't do!" he declares emphatically. "About bracken, for example! Stuff for the artist, no doubt, with its curious unfurling in spring, its deep green in summer and its glorious autumn gold. Makes good bedding for cattle, no doubt! All right! Well, now, I denounce bracken as nothing but the crawling pest of neglected hill-farms and derelict woodlands. We can't afford to grow bracken. And mark this! Bracken and clover will grow in company, and this means that where bracken now grows clover can be grown and clover ought to be grown."

With one sweeping gesture he eliminates all the bracken in the Riding. Then he kicks scornfully at a tussock of grey moorland grass.

"And this beastly mat grass!" he snorts. "Wherever it grows the soil proclaims its poverty, peatiness and acidity. After early summer the leaves are nothing but tough cellulose and even moorland sheep won't eat it. And it flourishes, it proliferates, and it ought not to be here. Now," he continues, "do you remember that strip of the Pickering–Whitby road by the Hole of Horcum, and the strip beyond the inn at Saltersgate? Do you remember the closely bitten, thymy grass by the sides of the road at those points, and how the black-faced sheep never stray far away from it? You do! Now how do you imagine that that sweet grass got there? I'll tell you. I remember that road long before it was tar-sprayed, when it ran like a narrow ribbon over the moors, muddy in winter and confoundedly dusty in summer. Both sides of the road, that is, got a continuous spreading of lime. This discouraged the heather and encouraged the grasses and herbs, and once the grasses and herbs were there the sheep attended to their permanence. You see? What has been done by nature near the road can be done by man over whole square miles of moorland. Burn off the heather, set the gyro-tiller to work, lime copiously, spread artificials and sow fescue grasses which give healthy but rather scant grazing. Then, after a year or two, plough up the fescues and sow wild white clover with Yorkshire fog, crested dogstail, cocksfoot, rough-stalked meadow-grass and perennial ryegrass. The result will be pasture with a good long grazing season for both sheep and cattle."

This is your modern agricultural man of science, but as long ago as 1788 Marshall's *Rural Economy of Yorkshire* discussed the possibility of transforming heavy slack and barren moor into productive grassland, and described at length the experiments carried through by Sir Charles Turner in Kildale. The experimental routine consisted in paring and burning, in breaking up, in fallowing for two years. After that, the fallow was still left as fallow but was stirred thoroughly, and in the fourth year was cropped. Turner's experiments were costly and not altogether successful, and Marshall grew rather to believe in a mixture of timber and pasture for the North York Moors and the Cleveland Hills, recommending Scotch fir, birch, Norway spruce, larch and perhaps oak for the timber; he knew the value of liming and spreading the ash from the burnings; he was no fool about the fertilizing capacity of vetch and clover, and approved of attempts to grow turnips and rape in addition to grasses.

With a keen eye for husbandry, Marshall had a North Riding tongue. He knew and used the local terms, and here, because those terms still appear upon the maps, is perhaps the place to explain at least a few of them. A *swang*, for example, is a low, long, grassy place covered with water; a *slack* is a little shallow dale; a *skufe* is a precipice; a *rigg* is what I have called a headland, a long, level-topped hogsback; a *griff* is a deep valley with a rocky chasm at the bottom; a *mar* is a mere; a *holl* is a deep and narrow valley; and where-as a *car* or *carr* is a low-lying marshy pasture-land, an *ing* is low-lying meadow or mowing-ground; a *grain*, finally, is a little dale which merges into a bigger dale as a branch merges into the trunk of a tree.

I leave Marshall to the curious reader and come back to our own day. During the summer of 1945 I had occasion to spend an afternoon in a Georgian grange with two acres of garden and orchard, a couple of good country Adam fireplaces and a great deal of scrub oak timbering. The house stood at the foot of the southward-facing tilt of the moors, at Snainton in the Vale of Pickering. I went there to put questions to my brother, who has spent a lifetime of research into the agricultural problems of the West Indies, Brazil, Peru, Russia and the world in general. Some of my questions were upon topics in which he has every right to hold opinions and I none : questions, naturally, bearing upon agriculture in the moorland area and in the Vale of Pickering.

I found him, dressed in a huge suede jacket with a plaid lining, bending over a little walnut window-table covered with a sheet of newspaper; he was crumbling faded brown flowers between his fingers and sorting out the seed.

"Wild white clover-seed," he explained without looking up, "from Hardwick's hundred-year-old pasture up beyond the Croft. It's for experimental purposes. I'm taking it to my place in the foothills of the Andes and there I'll see what'll come of it."

"I've come to talk to you," I said, "on problems of local agriculture."

"My dear fellow," he said, "this locality will always present more problems than the devil himself could solve until people develop a mentality rather superior in calibre to that of the larger anthropoids. The place holds nothing but problems. They're all over the show. They pull faces at me when I stop to look at them."

"About the work of the Forestry Commission," I began.

"Good so far as it goes," he said. "The acid soil of the moors suits conifers but the conifers don't suit the moors : they're foreign, and they don't blend into the landscape like our native trees. The trouble is that nobody's thought of establishing a research station for British forest trees, or if anyone has thought about it there's been no practical result as yet. There's a lot of work to be done in that direction, and until it is done the problem of afforestation won't be scientifically solved."

He went on sorting clover seed.

"As far as I can make out," he continued, "the result of covering the moorland with coniferous timber will be to lower the water-table in the Vale of Pickering here. That might or might not be a good thing. The drainage at the moment is totally inadequate, and the planting of osiers and cricket-bat willows in the ings and carrs would do something to absorb a lot of superfluous water in the neighbourhood of Malton and the Marishes. Pending an adequate drainage scheme, of course. Then there's this about timber. You've been into Beedale lately?"

"I have."

"Then you'll have seen the bracken."

"I have."

"And the rose-bay willow-herb?"

"Acres of it."

He nodded.

"The bracken, of course, is an unmitigated curse. I'm not so sure about the willow-herb. It provides humus, but often it's hard to tell where usefulness ends and nuisance begins. Anyhow I'm not so inclined to curse the willow-herb as I am to damn the bracken. Next?"

"About the transforming of moorland into pasture," I said.

"Every moorland intake proves that heather-bracken-gorse land can be made into good pasture," he told me, "but I think it would be better to make a start by improving the potentially good but neglected pasture."

"Neglected?" I asked. "Neglected, when the North Riding Agricultural Executive Committee's been active for so long?"

"Neglected!" he affirmed. "The new ley-farming system needs a vast amount of propaganda-work putting in."

"But——"

"Oh, I know! You're going to tell me there's some good new pasture between here and Seamer. So there is, but there is a lot of old and neglected pasture, too. Wherever you see tussocks of coarse grass in a field, that field needs ploughing

up and resowing. Coarse grass has no food-value for stock.
All the nutrition lies in the young and tender growth. What
you do is this : you sow the mixture of grass seed recommended by the Aberystwith folk; one or two or more of the
varieties become dominant in your pasture, and after that you
know what grasses suit your soil. Next, you divide your new
meadow into small units wired off with electric fencing, and
you mow in rotation, monthly, so that the grass available for
your cattle is always sweet and highly nutritious. In that way
you double the size of your dairy herds."

He blew lightly upon his minute seeds to dispose of the
chaff.

"Ay," he said thoughtfully, "and you'll not see many absolutely first-class dairy cattle between here and Scarborough,
either ! Most of the stock seems to be of Holstein blood, but
it's all very mixed and unsatisfactory."

"Roots?" I asked.

"Likely to decline in importance all over the country," he
said promptly. "Roots involve a desperate amount of labour
both in summer and in winter. Silage will take their place, I
guess, and there's a queer-looking, olive-coloured grass
powder on the market—rather highly priced at the moment,
I'll admit—that has a higher nutritive value than the best
cotton-seed cake. I'm not overfond of roots."

He began to slide his clover seed into an envelope, and,
completing the job, sealed the envelope and made a note on
the outside of the date, the contents and their origin. "Of
course," he went on, "this has always been an area of small-
scale farming. I think you'll find that, a hundred years ago as
to-day, a hundred-acre farm was considered big. Now I'm all
in favour of the small farm hereabouts, always provided that
small-scale mechanization goes with it."

"What do you mean by small-scale mechanization?"

"Little implements."

"I see."

"Oh, and about fruit-growing. Apart from the risk of late
frosts, the Vale of Pickering is potentially an excellent fruit-
growing district, but you'll find that ancient orchards full of
neglected trees still serve the area. It's possible, of course, to
have the trees sprayed for pest control, but few people take

advantage of the possibility, and so far as I can make out they allow nature to do the thinning of the fruit. By inherited knowledge and experience the old inhabitants know what varieties suit this region, and they're mostly old varieties. Those old varieties, through the neglect of nurserymen, are dying out. You can't blame the nurserymen, who try to satisfy a popular clamour for new varieties which may or may not suit this particular region."

"So what?" I asked.

"Well, for my part, if I were to settle here, I should get myself some material for experiment: stocks of the new Canadian varieties of apple, for example, and certainly the new Russian varieties with Siberian blood in them."

"And then?"

"Even then I shouldn't be doing myself much good. The clue to the whole unsatisfactory position in the North of England is that in this direction the universities are not right up to their job. In the North of England there isn't a single professor of genetics, or even a lecturer, and certainly there's no research geneticist. A thoroughly scientific soil survey is also necessary, soil temperatures ought to be properly studied, and micro-climatology needs attention."

"Micro-climatology?"

"The climate of a locality is based upon its weather. Weather reports are framed to cover about a fifth of Great Britain, whereas the Vale of Pickering in the course of a single twenty-four hours may produce a dozen sorts of weather in a dozen different areas: frost in the marshes, absence of frost a mile to the north; a cold sea-roke extending only four miles inland, and sunshine beyond that; snow on Sawdon Moor, rain at Sawdon Ings. Thus, micro-climatology."

"Good! You'll need an army of workers."

"I'll come to that in a minute. Meanwhile I'd like to tell you that in the United States of America there exist county agents, very lively and well-qualified fellows whose business is not simply to offer advice but mainly to inspire experiment, to cultivate the research spirit amongst the agriculturists of their individual areas. They do first-class work, and a few like them in the North Riding wouldn't do any harm. Now as to this army of workers, I'll let myself go. I see from the newspapers that Bradford is very anxious to give its technical college university status, and, I suppose, to develop a new Bradford University upon precisely similar lines to those along which Leeds, Manchester, Sheffield and Birmingham have already developed. Now I think that's all wrong. The policy is radically short-sighted, and I say so with all the emphasis of which, in polite conversation, I am capable. Yorkshire doesn't need another glorified technical institute, it needs an Oxford, a Cambridge, a Yale, a Harvard : a university of residential colleges with first-class libraries, laboratories, equipment and men. Yorkshire could afford a place like that, and Yorkshire ought to have it. That is my studied opinion."

From that point we drifted into a discussion too ambitious for the scope of this book, and I am not going to follow its course here. Nor do I purpose to comment upon the views of my brother, which I have recorded here, but am content to accept the position of reporter. Perhaps, however, the reader will have gathered the truth that, given his head, the man of science could, and would, in a few short years, jolt whole areas of the North Riding out of their traditional ways of life into ways both strange and new. One of the biggest obstacles in this way, however, is that in the North Riding there are no fewer than 175,705 acres of common land. In 1873, there were 247,409 acres. It is mostly rough land, and it has been nobody's business to improve it. Furthermore, the Common, Open Spaces and Footpaths Preservation Society exists to keep this common land pretty well as it is. The man of science is not likely to have things all his own way.

CHAPTER V

THE NORTH YORK MOORS AND THE CLEVELAND HILLS

TRAVELLERS to Whitby by road from Pickering, Scarborough and Guisborough accept the North York Moors and the Cleveland Hills as they accept an acknowledged masterpiece of painting, music, sculpture or poetry. The moorland country between Pickering and Whitby they call either the Pickering Moors or the Whitby Moors; that between Guisborough and Whitby once more the Whitby Moors. This, I suppose, is because Whitby forms a focal point of the moorlands, but you never hear the indigenous population speak of their land in such general terms. They speak of Silpho Moor, Allerston Moor, Danby Low Moor, Castleton Moor, and so forth, naming each limited area after the nearest village or centre of habitation. If there is no village, then the name is often that of a farmstead or of the people occupying that farmstead. If there is no farmstead, then there is a general name like Howl Moor or Wheeldale Moor. The point is that there are roughly a thousand square miles of the North York Moors and Cleveland, and Dartmoor and Exmoor would go into one corner of the area and hardly be noticed. Size, however, is not everything. The Sahara is big, and so is the Pacific Ocean. Something else beside extension is needful to make a country interesting.

Let me say a word first about the structure of this area. The rock substance varies, though it is all of the Jurassic Age. There are limestones, sandstones, shales and clays, patterned by frost, rain and rapidly flowing rivers into great variety. All along the western escarpment no less than along the coast this is Cliff-land or Cleveland. Sometimes, as from Lastingham to Pickering, the hills run north and south in riggs or ridges; farther east, between Pickering and Scarborough, they are tabular in formation, and here and there, as at Langdale End, Blakey Topping and Rosebery Topping, there are isolated cone-shaped hills produced by outliers of hard grit protecting the softer rocks below them from erosion. The Rye, Leven, Seph, Derwent, Esk and the Costa Beck drain the whole area, but they have each a vast number of feeders, noisy little becks like Bloody Beck, considerable streams like Wheeldale Beck. From the Vale of Pickering the moorland shelf slants northward not too steeply; the slope, in other words, falls towards the sun. Then comes an escarpment, steep in places, with a depression running east and west. North of this the plateau slants upward again towards the highest elevation of the moorland country, then it slips down into Eskdale, and, crossing it, climbs slowly once more to the sharp ridge overlooking Stokesley and Guisborough and the levels of Teesmouth.

Indigenous to the soil are ling, bell-heather, bilberry, birch, furze, thorn and pine, but there exist numerous intakes and cultivation areas dry-walled and ditch-drained, or, alternatively, with hedges that look like Wordsworth's "little lines of sportive wood run wild." Now as to why the whole area is mostly unenclosed waste, without fences, hedges, walls or steadings, most people will tell you that William the Bastard's Harrying of the North was so thorough that the land has even yet not recovered from it. This, obviously, is inaccurate. My own theory is this : somewhere about 1500 B.C. there was in northern Europe a sharp change in climate. Before that time the weather was comparatively dry and favourable to human habitation. It was the period during which Neolithic man inhabited this area, made his pit-villages, put up his monoliths and stone circles, and used the trackways which are in existence to this day. After 1500 B.C. Iceland began to export depressions, the climate turned cold, it rained almost every day in the year, and the wet, cold conditions proved favourable only to the formation of peat-hags, mosses, marishes and moors. In such conditions, pit-dwellings in Jurassic or another limestone and sandstone became untenable, and the pit-dwellers left the region, crossed the Vale of Pickering and set up housekeeping on the drier chalk of the Yorkshire Wolds. When the Brigantes arrived they found an empty land, and, save for the coastal strip and the dale-ends, they left it empty. The Romans drove a road through it from the camps at Cawthorn to the signal station at Goldsborough, but these moors were not their sort of country, and obviously they feared no attack from tribesmen, outlaws or rebels. There is no evidence that they policed this wild area.

When the Angles came, and later the Danes, they found exactly the sort of country they had always been used to, and, building wooden shacks for themselves and their families, they settled down to wring a living from the bitter sea and the inhospitable land. Very likely there was fighting between Brigantes and Angles, Angles and Danes, but between Angles and Danes I think not much, for Anglian *tons* and Danish *bys* exist pretty well side by side. Certainly, too, William's harrying of this area was as thorough as elsewhere, but there was never much to harry. This is proved by his returning south through Bilsdale. In the feudal age the manorial system hardly penetrated the moorland country. The Forest of Pickering was a royal forest, a hunting area, very wild and desolate. The coastal villages look to the sea for a living. Elsewhere, villages ring the escarpment and penetrate into the green recesses of Eskdale. In the interior the land is still almost empty.

When I was a small child there came a day when the family to which I belonged crowded into a farm wagon and had itself driven up to the moors for a whole summer day. That was my first experience of the moors, and I thought I had never seen anything so mysterious and wonderful as the great stretches of ling in bloom, the wind-blown pines and the golden-yellow sand-streams threading the clumps of ling and bilberry. In later years I roved these moors in all seasons and at all times of day and night. Later still I was drawn by the place-names and would set out to visit 'Blue Man i' t' Moss or follow Bloody Beck to its source. I grew familiar with this country and its people, talked its language, recognized its moods and knew its ways, and finally realized that it had a history that has never found its way into the books. This history, I believe, will not be written down; it is not factual enough. I have mentioned the pit-villages, the stone circles and monoliths and prehistoric trackways. Now I come to the howes, barrows, tumuli. You will find them in abun-

dance on the Cleveland Hills and on the moors. Many of
them have names such as Lilla Howe, Jugger Howe, Pen
Howe, Sil Howe; where they stand in groups they are called
Two Howes, or Three Howes, as the case may be. They
have always appealed to the antiquarian sides of my interests.
Unknown to the owners of this or that howe, I have sweated
and dug in the vain hope of finding a cinerary urn containing
charred bones or some relic of Bronze Age times. A vain
hope, because the bearded antiquarian of Victorian days, a
Mortimer or an Atkinson, had already done his stuff (the
phrase is sixteenth-century). Every obvious howe in the North
Riding of Yorkshire has been opened, and what is left on the
moorland shelf is what the Victorian antiquarian ransacked.
Dig if you like in any of these howes; you will find not a
potsherd, not a bone, not a bead.

In this region there are no long barrows. There is nothing
to parallel the great long barrows of Wiltshire, of the Cotswolds, of the East Riding. The North Riding barrows are all
round barrows, belonging to the Bronze Age and to the
period of transition between the Bronze Age and the Iron
Age. I do not know why there are no long barrows. The
Neolithic people lived here, but they set up no great monuments, no great memorials to their dead, and they left little
trace of their occupation of the country.

In addition to the tumuli there are dikes and entrenchments
everywhere. Nobody knows who constructed them and
nobody knows why. You may, for example, survey the whole
region of Scamridge Dikes and compose a learned mono-
graph upon the military situation which dictated their
construction, but every word you set down is no more than
conjecture and not very convincing conjecture at that. These
dikes, earthworks, entrenchments, have no history; they are
merely there. This is one of the places in the story of the
North Riding where there is a hiatus in the manuscript, and I
do not think it will ever be filled in. I am glad of this, for it
gives a little scope to the imagination of topographers.

Next, the moorland crosses. Everyone is taken by them,
everyone is curious about them—Mauley Cross, Ana Cross,
Redman Cross, Lilla Cross, Ralph Crosses, White Cross, the
cross that once stood at Brown Howe a mile north-east of

Mauley Cross—and tries to make out who set them there, and why, and when, and why there are few indeed in the western hills of the North Riding, so many in the eastern. Not very much is known about crosses. We know that a cross was often set up at the entering of a town. Sharow Cross just north of Ripon is one of these. Then of course there are market crosses. Scarborough used to have an old butter cross, and market crosses are common enough. Everyone takes them for granted. Then there are churchyard crosses. Most of these were smashed either during the Reformation or during the Civil War. I can tell you very little about Paulinus Crosses; their story lies in pages I have never explored. Next, there is a curious set of Manx crosses, Scandinavian in origin, which march through the Lake District into the North Riding, cross the Vale of Mowbray and penetrate the Howardian Hills, with a fine example inside the church at Stonegrave. Nobody knows much about these crosses, and nobody knows much, either, about moorland crosses. I used to say they were set up for no religious purposes, that they stood on high places and at crossways to serve as landmarks and direction-posts. Mauley Cross, for instance, stands a few yards to the right of Wade's Causeway north of Stape, where a moorland track branches off to Brown Howe and thence into Newtondale. Ana Cross and Redman Cross stand in high place three miles north of the holy shrine of Lastingham, while Lilla Cross is a landmark for travellers crossing the open moor from the neighbourhood of Saltersgate to Robin Hood's Bay or from Whitby to the plains. Ralph Cross and White Cross a mile to the east show where the old northward-thrusting track along Blakey Rigg sent out branches to Westerdale, Castleton and Danby.

Unfortunately, however, Mauley Cross is not visible from Wade's Causeway. And why should there be two crosses rather close together above Lastingham and again on Castleton Rigg? Lilla Cross has to be looked for if you follow the moor-track from Saltersgate, and again the old cross on Brown Howe was not far away. How, moreover, did these crosses get their names? The Mauleys were a famous North Riding family in the Middle Ages, but who was Redman, who was Ana, who was Ralph? Was White of White Cross a

person, and what was Botn of Botn Cross? Lilla Cross on
Lilla Howe may have marked the site of a beacon-fire—I
have heard it suggested—but certainly it stands at the junction of the townships of Fylingdales, Allerston, Goathland
and Levisham, and is evidently, then, a boundary cross.
When they served one purpose, they probably served more
than one; they were direction-posts, boundary stones, praying
crosses, landmarks in featureless land. I do not think they
are of vast antiquity. They are not Ruthwell Crosses, they
have no runic inscriptions, they are merely picturesque and
rather puzzling survivals. Ana Cross is broken, the Brown
Howe Cross has gone, and the last time I visited Lilla Cross
louts had done what they could to push it over. Probably it is
straight again now.

Next there are the "killing-pits." Ah! "Here," writes the
credulous traveller, "the ancient Druids performed their
ghastly rites, and we can but dimly guess what scenes of barbaric slaughter have taken place in these long-abandoned
haunts." Wilson of Farndale could not pass them by without
a dramatic shudder-in-print, yet, I am sure, these "killing-
pits" are no more than kiln-pits, the sites of old lime-burnings,
probably no older than the eighteenth century, when men like
Turner of Kildale were trying the effect of copious liming on
acid moorland soil and when every peasant shaping a new
intake needed lime to sweeten the surface of his enclosure.

Not far below the surface of the North York Moors lie
thin seams of coal, and you will find old coal-workings—they
cannot be called pits—on Egton Moor, Wheeldale Moor,
Westerdale Moor, Farndale Moor and on Danby Low Moor
north of Eskdale. There is a thin outcrop of this coal at
Cloughton Wyke, an outcrop worked within the limits of
my memory. For the most part, however, the moorsmen—
they call them "moorpouts" or "moorpoots," and the
feminine is "Margerie Moorpoot"—burn turf or peat. The
slices they cut are much thinner than those cut in the western
peat-hags. From the high moor they bring their loads down
into the gills and dales on sleds. Tradition affirms that some
of the peat fires in these moorland habitations—the inns in
particular—have been burning for a matter of a couple of
centuries without being allowed to go out. Visit the inn

kitchen at Saltersgate and verify the tradition if you can; at least you will be staggered by the kitchen range.

Some of the old coal-workings suspiciously resemble tumuli and should not be mistaken for Bronze Age antiquities.

Next there are the alum-workings, now abandoned, with which I have dealt elsewhere. You will find them not only along the coast, where the sea-breezes were thought to mellow the alum, but also inland. Finally, there are the old ironstone mines in Rosedale and the abandoned railway-line which conveyed the ore to the furnaces lying to the north. There was ironstone elsewhere, of course, in Cleveland, and the silhouette of Rosebery Topping is not quite as it was before they began digging ore out of the great hill. The furnaces at Skinningrove are still active, but do not use the local ironstone. Ore is imported from Sweden. Add the dead jet-workings, and you have almost come to the end of the attempts to industrialize the North York Moors and Cleveland apart from the Middlesbrough area. Occasionally a gang of workers invades this or that solitude and bores for oil, but so far without success. The latest boring, as I write, was at Aislaby, where they discovered not oil but natural gas. Dr. G. M. Lees reported the discovery in *Nature*, 12 May 1945 : "The reservoir rock is a Permian limestone. Short tests have indicated that the gas may be present in sufficient quantity to justify commercial exploitation. A by-product of the search for oil has been the discovery of potash salts of Permian age in Eskdale. Both sylvite and polyhalite are present, and this result shows that the potash deposits of the Zechstein Sea, which have such economic importance in north-west Germany, extend also into north-eastern England. The potash-beds in Eskdale are at a depth of 3,650 to 4,775 feet, and, while this may exceed easy mining depth, there is a possibility that the deposits may extend farther north towards the Tees valley and rise to a lesser depth." My latest information is that the deposits are of great economic value.

One very recent move of industry in the North Riding is the establishment of Imperial Chemical Industries at Wilton Castle, which thus becomes a fortress of scientific research.

In the past, therefore, from time to time industry has sought to exploit the Cleveland Hills and the North York

Moors, but without either vast or continuous success, and obviously the cultivation of crops cannot be carried on as intensively as it is, for example, in the East Riding. The alternative is stock-breeding, and everyone knows that Cleveland, in former days at least, was famous for its horses. Sheep-rearing is not neglected, and the whole area produces its own breed, called generally the moorjock, an active and hardy brute, inquisitive and stubborn, the commando trooper of the ovine battalions. He is the sheep of the moors, the cropper of heather shoots and the little sheep's fescue that grows in the moorland districts. In the valleys, the dales and gills, you find the usual cross-bred sheep. Of game there has been, of late years, not very much, and the moors have known more of the explosion of grenades and twenty-pounders than of the noises made by partridge and grouse shooters. The shoots are not so carefully preserved as they used to be, gamekeepers not so thick on the ground. Yet, while these moors provide an excellent training area for soldiers, I don't want to see the day when W.D. warnings confront me wherever I go, and I don't want to see the red flag warning me of the risk of being blown to bits if I try to cross Allerston High Moor from Ellerbeck to Barnscliff by way of Little Ark, Brecken Howe and Lun Rigg. The soldiers at the moment have captured Fylingdales Moor as a training area.

If you are tough, go into this country. If you are not, survey it from the few roads that thread it. Visit it in August when the leagues of ling are in full glory, visit it also in the depth of winter with a north-easterly gale blowing in from the sea; and if you want a secluded life, ask the North Riding Education Committee to keep the school at Bickley open for you, and become the schoolmaster or schoolmistress there.

I ought to say something of the Whinstone Dyke. It is an alien intruder, but important. In Devonian times—I speak geologically—Yorkshire went through a period of terrifying plutonic activity, which I shall deal with when I come to the north-western limits of the North Riding. Then the volcanoes subsided, to be followed in Tertiary times by a spell of violent earthquakes, volcanic activity, and, far away from the epicentre, by shattering of the rocks and fissuring of the ground. These fissures filled up with lava, and the biggest and widest of them is the Cleveland Dyke. If you want to find its eastern end, go first to Robin Hood's Bay, and strike westward by the road that leaves the shore at Mill Beck, follow it to the Scarborough road, and look for the farm track that joins the moorland trail for Lilla Cross. Cross Jugger Howe Beck—Jugger is *Jaeger*, the huntsman—and north of the path you will find two holes in the ground near a swampy patch of moor. Here the thin feather-edge of the whinstone is visible, dark bluish-grey, metallic, hard, with tiny points and sparkles of light in it. Farther west and a trifle north, a thirty-foot trench near Cock Lake Sike shows where the whinstone has been dug out for road-metal. Its general direction is east-south-east and west-north-west. You see it near Goathland. "Near Egton Bridge," wrote Phillips, "it stands up in a lofty wall, over the waters of the Esk; and beyond Lilhoue Cross it ranges along the moors like an ancient military road." That, however, was in 1829, and the Whinstone Dyke is different to-day. At Cliff Rigg Wood by Rosebery Topping, for example, the quarrymen have gouged out a chasm twenty feet wide at the surface and eighty feet wide over three hundred feet down. From Cliff Rigg Wood it makes for County Durham and vanishes at last beyond Cockfield Fell.

For myself I care little at what time of year I go into the moorland country. In rain, snow and sleet, on misty evenings in late autumn and in the pallid sunshine of early spring, it has its attraction always, but it was during the second week in August, with the ling in full glow, that I took the road northward from Pickering to Newton on Rawcliff. This is still a lonely road, and where the gradient rises sharply the tarmac weathers, revealing below it the white limestone track of an older day. As I left Pickering I saw that the water-mill is still working and still prosperous, but I did not linger there. Newton had, I found, changed since last I stayed at the White Swan. The blacksmith, famous for his diurnal thirst, had gone. His forge had been converted into a cottage. The old-fashioned, dark kitchen of the White Swan, from which the villagers formerly refused to be excluded, had become a pleasant little dining-room with modern furniture. Outwardly the place wears its old, quiet aspect. You might suppose that nothing ever happens here, that nobody comes and nobody

Helmsley Castle
Kirkdale Church

goes. You would be mistaken. Newton is so quiet that large numbers of quiet people want to live there. The White Swan is always busy with guests, and property changes hands here at remarkably high prices. Quiet, in these times, has to be paid for.

North of the village the road turns westward. Tall broom was in dry pod to the right, and to the left a parcel of land had been rescued from the moor. Gorse, heather and birch had been rooted out, the ground ploughed and cross-ploughed, and as I went by men were spreading lime and superphosphates over the dry, brown, peaty soil. After that, they would sow down to wild white perennial clover.

Presently the road dipped down Rawcliff Bank and I headed northward to Stape, where the old inn now sells teas and refreshments only. Here were good intake meadows, and oats, and potatoes. Lean, nondescript cattle grazed the open moor. A single-storied cottage, low to the ground, on the south-western slope of the hill, maintained contact with the world through its wireless set. Farther up the road to the moor, Mauley Cross seemed less imposing than it used to be, and not a furlong north of it, almost buried in the ling, was the stone trough full of spring water, inscribed, in crude capitals, NATTLE FOUNTEIN. At the first ford, where the Roman road begins, a couple of broad-spoken North Riding men were fixing a newly painted Ministry of Works notice. For permission to roam the open moor, apply to the fourth house for a free permit. Eastward from this ford, a mile away over the heather, stands Brown Howe, with tumuli and the site of a stone circle, but it makes no great landmark and the best way to find it is to follow the rough track from Mauley Cross.

Familiar with Stonehenge and Avebury, the traveller will think little of the stone circles of the North Riding of Yorkshire, but I suppose them of interest to the archæologist, who will look intelligently for similarities and differences.

The Roman road is, or rather was, Wade's Causeway. Of Wade the Teutonic culture-hero I shall here say nothing, but I will repeat the local legend which is kept alive only by topographers and antiquarians. In the countryside it is completely dead. Wade was a giant. He made this road so that

Kirbymoorside—the Black Swan
Mount Grace Priory

his wife might have an easy journey when she went to milk their cow, which grazed on the moor a long way from home. Carrying stones for him in her apron, she neglected to see to her apron-strings, which broke. The great heap of stones on the moor is the burden she let fall, and that the story is in every detail true is proved by the rib of Wade's Cow, which was once on view at Mulgrave. It was a pretty piece of whale-bone. This shows how a twisted sense of humour perpetrates accretions to ancient legend; the whalebone was obvious to all but children.

Wade's Causeway was never a first-class Roman road any more than the four camps at Cawthorn were first-class Roman camps. It was, I think, always a rough road, built in unquiet times, when Rome was loosening her grip upon Britain. The field kitchen near this first ford is no great piece of archi-tectural construction. The two footways over the water are also rather primitive, but, in its day, the road no doubt served its purpose well enough. It is now eighteen inches below the level of the moor, and was neglected during the years of war. I found heather growing upon it, and, in spite of the frequent warnings posted to stave off military traffic, one of the infantry crossings had been smashed. Clumps of stiff reeds grow in the peaty soil on each side of the road, but there are signs that the authorities do not intend that the care and labour expended on excavating this ruin of Rome shall be wasted. Let me, finally, warn the traveller that if he thinks to discover Roman coins, bits, lynch-pins and shoe-buckles along the line of the road he will waste his time. Nothing of impor-tance was discovered during the excavation. There is nothing to find, and the traveller must be content to set his feet where, long ago, the legionaries marched.

After three straight, steady miles, the road ended at a field-gate, beyond which there was pasture and a slope down to the peaty waters of Wheeldale Beck overhung with willows. I crossed the beck by a footbridge hidden among trees, then again by a concrete tank-track, and climbed to the good road that runs from Hunt House to Goathland. This road ran along the western slope of Howl Moor to join the Egmont Bridge road, and less than half an hour's walking brought me to the Mallyon Spout Hotel and Goathland Church.

Goathland, once upon a time, was Godeland, then Goad-land. In 1117, King Henry I granted a hermitage here to one Osmund, a priest, and a few brethren. They, I suspect, endured the solitude as long as they could, but finally went to Whitby. Nowadays Goathland is flourishing with guest-houses and retired leisure. It is a very pleasant place, a green jewel in the moorland waste, and I enjoyed coming down into the village. Already before I left the heather I had seen several cars parked close to the road, and people were wandering here and there on the moor. In Goathland itself there is much fine, closely bitten turf, and more people were sitting on its slopes enjoying the hot sun and the breeze blow-ing in from the sea. As I left the place the sunshine was suddenly cut off, the afternoon grew dark, a sea-roke drove in from the east and the warmth went out of the day. This is always liable to happen on or near the North Riding coast even on the most brilliant of summer days. The colour faded from the ling as well as from the sky, and the chill proximity of the sea could be felt particularly upon the hands. The gradients between Goathland and Sleights are stiff and rather perilous; one in five is more than common; it is, indeed, usual, and if you are not climbing a hill then you are descend-ing a hill. Blue Bank took me into Sleights and Ruswarp Bank took me up into Whitby West Cliff.

I have no fondness for either Sleights or for Ruswarp, and I do not care very much for the road running parallel to the Esk. Herbert Hopkins, the architect living at Bay, aptly described Sleights as "neither nowt nor summat." It was, he said, all bits and pieces. Ruswarp remains in my memory because I once saw a monkey, of all living creatures, clutching a postman's head there. "Ah was fair capped!" said the post-man to me afterwards. The joiner's shop in Ruswarp, as in Hawsker, is in itself a museum of antiquity.

Night closed in, the darkness grew more sinister, and as I walked into Whitby Town the gulls were mewing and crying over the housetops.

The ling that grows on the Jurassic sandstones is often high-deep for a grown man. For little people it is difficult to get through. Even so, the North York Moors have this advantage over the western fells, that they are drier and less cut up on the surface. There is no vast depth of peat and bog, the water gets through to the sandstone, and though there exist patches of slack and marish ground these can always be detected from a distance and avoided. Moreover, sheep-tracks thread the moors, and though they meander and by no means take one direct from place to place they can be followed, abandoned and picked up again with a fair amount of ease. Further, the surface is level, for the glaciers of the Fourth Ice Age islanded these moors and refrained from grinding and scooping out deep and steep-sided valleys. This, of course, on the actual tops. The going, therefore, is not so bitter as perhaps might be expected, and is more tiring to the muscles of the thighs than to the soles of the feet. There are no mountain birds. I do not think I have ever seen curlew, and stonechat and whinchat are rare. Larks nest here, and peewits. There is too little woodland for hawks and owls. Rabbits do not thrive, and there are no hares. Carrion crows are scarce. In fact, there is singularly little wild life, feathered or furred, on these moors. Sometimes, in June, you will find huge hairy caterpillars—brown beasts with a row of red dots along their sides and an appearance of pugnacity in their demeanour.

From Whitby West Cliff a moorland motor-road runs through to Guisborough without impinging upon a single village or providing memorable landscapes; a straight road with glimpses of rather harsh pastoral country slanting down towards the sea and the drab villages between the road and the coast. Guisborough is a little market town of red brick and tile, pleasant and not without dignity, but yet a dis-appointed town, for while the Cleveland ironstone was being mined, Guisborough looked forward to becoming populous and prosperous. Nowadays on their way to the sea or to Red-car races people may stop to bait there and to look at the relics of the Priory and the handsome Bruce Memorial, but mostly they pass north of the town and touch only its outer fringe. Like Malton, Guisborough is a transit centre. South of it is Belmont Mine—ironstone—and at Belmont or Belman Bank is the residuum of Chaloner's ancient alum-works. You may cross the railway south of Guisborough and make over the hills into Sleddale, and thence, crossing

Sleddale Beck, arrive at Kildale, a good little village where once stood a hermitage and a house of the Percies. Kildale is a stock-breeding area, and there is a good deal of heather there. Thence you may turn east along the high road into Commondale, not so attractive, to me at least, as Kildale; thence to the drab and rugged village of Castleton, and so to Danby, once more important than it is now. Formerly there existed a Forest of Danby, but like the silk-mill at Castleton it has gone, evidenced only by a few names to prove the location of clearings in the scrub oak—Danby Lawns, Leal-holm Lawns and Glaisdale Lawns. *Lawns* is probably for *laundes*. Formerly, too, there was an inhabited castle at Danby, of the late fourteenth and early fifteenth centuries, concerning which guide-book print relates how Henry VIII was overtaken by a storm on his way to visit Katherine Parr there, and took refuge at Stormy Hall. This is a legend deserving no credit. A farmstead is parasitic upon Danby Castle, but the place merits mention, a visit and a photo-graph. You reach the ruin by way of the hump-backed structure called Duck Bridge. It dates from the fourteenth century, but derives its name from George Duck, who restored it in the eighteenth century.

No one could fail to admire Eskdale from Sleights to Kildale, and especially the wooded area between Egton Bridge and Glaisdale. There, approaching Glaisdale, you will find Beggar's Bridge, and from Glaisdale you may cross the Esk and strike north and west for Danby Beacon. Wherever you go in Eskdale you cannot go wrong, and if you follow the by-roads up Glaisdale Side, up Fryup Beck and into Wester-dale you will certainly go right. All the better if you fish. The Esk is not so good a salmon river as it used to be, but it has its fishing, its beauty and its water-bailiff who can tell more tales about the river, its spates and its poachers, than I. West of Glaisdale the valley provides little woodland until you reach Kildale, and Kildale is the gateway from the west into the Esk Valley. There is moorland and pasture, with some arable, and the whole countryside is famous for the breeding of horses, cattle and sheep, Westerdale particularly. You reach Westerdale from Castleton—a modern village, though there was a castle at Castleton before ever Danby Castle was built—and all this region, from Baysdale Head to Burton Howe, the highest point in north-east Yorkshire, Baysdale Moor, Westerdale Moor, Rosedale Head, Blakey Howe, Danby High Moor and Danby Rigg, is as wild, waste and empty as any civilized townsman could desire. It is fine but rather difficult land. The traveller coming north from Hutton-le-Hole to Ralph Cross is in the middle of it. If then he journeys on foot from Ralph Cross to the sources of the Esk he will experience the best and the worst of it—the best of the scenery, the worst of the going.

At Westerdale there is a ribbed medieval bridge over the beck. North of Westerdale, in the area called Kempswidden, Turner did his best in the eighteenth century to bring open moor under the plough. He spent much money for very little result. Near Baysdale Head, Baysdale Abbey stands upon the site of a priory, and this reminds me that Eskdale was the savage haunt of the North Riding hermits who retired from the world to share the company of wolves. There they lived, and there often they died. I ascribe the popularity of hermitry to the over-sanctity of Whitby Abbey; the anchorite could make his own disciplinary rules and was not compelled to get up and pray at two o'clock in the morning unless he felt that way. But perhaps I err.

I think Danby is the focus of interest in Eskdale, and if anyone wishes to know what life in Danby was like in the nineteenth century he should read Atkinson's minor classic, *Forty Years in a Moorland Parish*. There is also Bishop's *My Moorland Patients*, another good piece of work.

The place-names show how Danes and Angles maintained their own settlements in the Whitby and Eskdale area. I suppose *Esk*, like *Usk* and *Wiske*, is Celtic, but side by side with the *tons* and *thorpes* there are plenty of *bys, holms* and *wicks*. *Grosmont* is Norman-French. There are *garths, yats, carrs, waths, riggs, fosses, kelds, swangs, lawns, mires* and *mosses*. *Beulah Hill* and *Doubting Castle* show the influence of Bunyan—very strong in north-east Yorkshire; *America House* and *Quebec* that of history. *Boggle Hole, Hob Hole, Hob on t'Hill* and *Hobbin Head* that of superstition. I once knew an Irishman who told me that fairies could not and would not live where people didn't believe in them; he said

126

that was the reason they had left England and migrated to Ireland. He believed this, and gave it as his explanation of the scarcity of fairies and hobgoblins in Eskdale to-day. Recently I talked with a friend who had lately returned from a holiday at Ruswarp, where he had enjoyed himself greatly.

"Did you," I asked, "explore Eskdale and the moors?"

"No," he answered. "I hadn't the time."

He had been too busy making holiday, and his experience is that of the majority of summer visitors to Whitby. After months of routine in factory, workshop, office or school they seek leisure rather than strenuous change, and it is certainly true of the North Riding that exploration demands energy. Rosebery Topping, for example, is not a mountain, but merely a high point in the Cleveland Hills. The mountaineer may well laugh at Rosebery, yet, if he would learn how the spring tides of industry may reach a place only to ebb from it, he might do worse than climb Rosebery Topping. It has even a few treacherous places and the rock is mostly rotten.

I have, on occasion, visited Cook's Monument on Easby Moor, and on each occasion have borne in mind that the storming of the Heights of Abraham and the spectacular capture of Quebec owed much of their success to the navigational survey of the St Lawrence carried through by James Cook. At the cinema, being shown the marvels of the Great Barrier Reef photographed in Technicolor, I have remembered Cook. I remember also how he recommended a cure for scurvy to the Admiralty, and how he finally met his death. Cook was a great man, and there is a whole library of books about him.

Another man was not so great. By way of Skelton and Skelton Castle you may, from Guisborough, reach Saltburn by the Sea, though travellers usually take the road through Upleatham. Eighteenth-century people knew Skelton Castle as Crazy Castle. That was the name its owner, John Hall Stevenson, gave it. He was a lewd eccentric, and I suspect him to have been the leading spirit in a kind of North Riding Hellfire Club, with Crazy Castle as the scene of its orgies. His sequel to Sterne's *Sentimental Journey* is witlessly obscene. In vain he tried to capture his master's manner and mannerisms.

Because, however, he exerted a bad influence on Sterne, some-one ought to explore his life in detail.

I have said that Loftus and Skinningrove are sad, unlovely places. Loftus, in the nineteenth century, used to have boiling-houses, presumably for whale-oil. I know very little about Easington. At Skinningrove they tip slag into the sea, and it makes its way southward, so that you may find lumps of it in Bridlington Bay. At night you may see from miles inland an orange glare in the sky above the ironworks, but since you may observe the same phenomenon at Rotherham or Low Moor perhaps it is not worth while remarking it.

"Anything more," you ask, "about this Cleveland area?" Why, yes, though much of the matter is historical. The Bruce Cenotaph in Guisborough Church, for instance, came from the Augustinian Priory of St Mary after the dissolution of the monasteries, and it was originally in the Priory because the Bruces—the famous Bruces—were a great North Riding family in the Middle Ages. They commonly wrote themselves Brus or de Brus. The Challoners settled here in 1550. There is a Chaloner Pit (the spelling of Chaloner or Challoner is optional) north-west of Guisborough, and a Belmont Mine to the south. There is also a Chaloner's Hospital, founded in 1865. I have often wondered if the Guy of the Robin Hood ballad of *Guy of Gisborne* was the original Guy of Guis-borough, but I do not think there is any answer to that question. So much for Guisborough. When we cross the moors into Eskdale, we find that had there been no ironstone there would have been no Glaisdale village. Grosmont, like Glaisdale, has seen the rout of the iron-miner. In 1836 the first cargo of ironstone from Grosmont was dispatched by the Whitby Stone Company to the Birtley Iron Company. In 1839 the Wylam Iron Company began operations at Gros-mont and the mines were still open in 1874. They are now closed, and the men of Grosmont quarry building-stone. As for the antiquities of Grosmont, there was once a priory on the left bank of the Esk.

Liverton has a mill. Lealholm once had a paper-mill. Stonegate has a water-mill, and Egton the old Mass House. Now look for Roxby Church, but look for no congregation, no choir, no parson there. The church is disused. Survey the abandoned iron-mines of Rosedale. They employed three hundred and fifty men and two boys in 1874, and sent fifty thousand tons of ore a year to Jarrow. Do not forget the ruins—what is left of them—of Rosedale Abbey. Go to Kirk-leatham, that had salt-pits in the Middle Ages, and look at the seventeenth-century hall, the pseudo-Gothic there, the eighteenth-century gateway and the leaden urns of the same period; look also at Turner's Hospital and admire its eighteenth-century style. Hinderwell? A dull, straggling village, rather neglected, rather poor. It is hardly obvious how Hinderwell people make a living.

John Phillips kept his eye not only upon the Whinstone Dyke but also upon industry as it existed in north-east York-shire in his day. He noted alum shale lying a hundred and eighty feet thick in the coastal strata, the jet at Lythe and Hawsker Bottoms, the coal-workings at Cloughton Wyke, Maybecks, Goathland, Glaisdale, Danby, Blakehoe and on Rudland Moor. He knew of the ironworks near Rievaulx Abbey, in Bilsdale and the Vale of Hackness, but, says he regretfully, "the ironstone is at present of no value except as ballast." He had, however, no eye for the flora and fauna of Cleveland and the North York Moors, and, so far as I know, no single field naturalist has yet been so hardy as to cover the ground exhaustively and fill the gaps that certainly exist. The nineteenth-century records need much overhauling, and nobody has yet tackled the problem of vegetation slowly extending its grip on the ice-sheared slopes after the glacia-tions of long ago. If Dr Gregor of Edinburgh ever comes this way he will find some fascinating material ready to his hand in this respect, and I recommend it to him. I myself am but a poor observer, knowing little of botany and even less of the former wild life of the area. Witherby may speak with authority on the birds of the coast and the moors, of the species that have been utterly wiped out, and of the rare vagrants that visit here. I know only that, should a strange bird wander into the vicinity, some fellow with a fowling-piece will shoot it and boast thereafter of his prowess, for in this part of Britain there is still little respect for wild life and a good deal of gull-shooting still goes on. I know that the Hole of Horcum near the Devil's Elbow on the Pickering—

The Mill, Thirkleby

Whitby road is a paradise of rare plants, but though I have more than once been right down into the Hole all I ever found there was the picked carcass of a sheep. I have seen peregrine and sparrow-hawk, several varieties of owl (I once picked up a long-eared owl in the middle of a ploughed field); guillemot, puffin, cormorant, herring-gull, razorbill and such along the coast; warblers, finches, buntings and tits in the wooded and marshy areas, and once a nightingale nested at Brompton in the Vale of Pickering. But the records sadly need collecting and collating. There are huge gaps in our knowledge of the wild life of the North York Moors and Cleveland that ought to be filled up as quickly as possible. Meanwhile there is room here for a National Park, and something ought to be done, now that industry has relinquished its hold, to extend the range of profitable agriculture and to preserve the wild life. Though Great Ayton may have lost its three tanyards, its comb and horn factory, its brewery and oil mill, its tallow-chandlery and brick-and-tile works, it could still become a centre for field-naturalist research and holiday-making. There is, apart from the coastal resorts, great need of such a centre, and Great Ayton, with its air of Quaker scholasticism, is, I think, the place for it.

Back again at Newton on Rawcliff, I said to myself, "I will not, this time, take the breakneck dog-leg down Rawcliff Bank; I'll take this westerly route, half road and half track, and look at the Four Camps." For a mile I followed that pleasant route with a dry wall on my right hand and open moor with bracken on my left, and when I judged I had gone far enough I went over the wall and melted cautiously into a plantation of pines. I found the Four Camps. Pines grew up within their bounds, from fosse and vallum, but the lines were traceable, and I, pacing them out and scrabbling round rabbit-burrows, enjoyed the spongy feel of dead pine-needles under my feet. Had I been equipped for trenching I should still have found nothing. The Yorkshire Archæological Society has been over the ground, has published its findings and recorded its discoveries. The discoveries came to little, for these camps were never important in the story of Roman Britain. Whatever cohorts halted here, they scattered no coin and buried no treasure. But what a view they got to northward! From the crest of a sandstone scarp they looked out to Black Rigg and Raven Stones over miles of empty moorland. I stood where the Roman sentinels, in this bleak outpost, kept watch, and, clear of the shadow of the pines, I saw more than they saw. I looked into the foreground, covering the immediate mile below. It might have been a bit of Warwickshire or Gloucestershire. An ornamental lake, deciduous woodland, open parkland, these provided the environment of Elleron Lodge. To the north stood Keldy Castle. These were not shooting-boxes but country houses, their grounds carved out of the moor by windbreaks and contrived plantings, controlled water-supply and careful tending. Four square miles rescued from marsh and moor has become a small game-preserve, a pleasant place in the wilderness kept at bay by rectangular guardian pine-plantings on Wrelton Moor.

From the escarpment my road took me first to Cawthorn, set amongst fields of roots and pasture—little meadow, and that not good—then to Cropton, where the elder Scoresby was born—a largish village of stone cottages and steadings on the hill above the dales of the River Seven and Little Beck. Again the land was pasture and arable. The corn—mostly oats—grew to no great height, and the fields lay open to all the winds. Not particularly good ground.

From Cropton I might have struck north into Rosedale, but Rosedale and Rosedale Abbey have never exerted much pull on my mind. Trudging the road above the brown river and along the eastern slope of the riggs, past the old smelting-mills and the abandoned mines as far as the desolation of miners' cottages, I have never loved that walk. I did not, therefore, go north but westward across the beck and the river into Lastingham.

Like Hutton-le-Hole, Lastingham is not of the moors and not of the levels, and for that reason is attractive. If I so wished, I could now follow the track north from Lastingham to the stump of Ana Cross or go south through Spaunton to Appleton-le-Moors. But it was a day for leisurely movement, and I spent some time in Lastingham itself; not a big village, not small either; very trim, well kept, with neat walling and clipped hedges, solid houses and a look of quiet prosperity. Lastingham has had ample time to mature, and though the thatched cottages or hovels of hermitage days have gone and the Saxon saints are no longer there, the tradition of habitation is strong. If to-morrow every house in the village were pulled down and new houses were put up the day after, one would still say, "This is not a new place, not Silkinesque."

The church is big. It is apsidal. I went into it, and down the steps into the Norman crypt, which is another complete church. Paying my devoirs to the church, I did so not in the usual style.

May I give you a specimen of the usual style?

"A more lovely spot could not well have been chosen by St Cedd on which to found his monastery, and in this place it is easier to imagine the monastic, or religious, life, than in most of our villages. Thoroughly secluded from the busy world, with purple moors stretching to the north, and to the south wooded hills, where on a bold knoll stands a massive cross of stone, clearly defined against the sky; this cross is modern, but is said to have replaced an ancient one." The old vicar's syntax was a trifle crazy, but you can appreciate his enthusiasm.

St Cedd "chose himself a place to build a monastery among crags and distant mountains, which looked more like lurking-places for robbers and retreats for wild beasts than habitations for men." So in better style but with more imagination wrote Bede, giving the date of foundation as 660 and the spelling of the place-name as Lastingaeu. Cedd, the bishop of the East Saxons, was the first abbot, and, after the Synod of Whitby, went to Lastingham during an outbreak of plague (the yellow plague), died and was buried there. The monastery grew, the old wooden church was replaced by a stone building, the monks learned to sing and to illuminate, and Lastingham became an important cultural centre. Then the place decayed and fell all to ruin. In 1078 Stephen of Whitby became Abbot of Lastingham and began building in the massive Norman style, but the district proved such a haunt of rascals and robbers that he stood it for only ten years before he fled to York and founded St Mary's Abbey. As a monastic establishment Lastingham failed, but it came within an ace of being another Rievaulx, another St Mary's Abbey, another Whitby.

There were no more abbots, but James Torre gives a list of vicars and assistant priests. It included one Jeremiah Carter, resident priest in the eighteenth century. He had £25 a year, about half the amount that would have made him "passing rich," and he had a wife and thirteen children to keep. He fed them mostly on trout from the becks, and, since his wife ran the village alehouse, on ale. The result of an episcopal inquiry was that he was allowed to continue running the inn but his stipend was not increased.

About 1770 much of the monastic stonework went to build field walls. The church as it stands is a mass of restorations. The apsidal plan of the eastern end is Norman; the roof of the apse is modern; the lintel of the south-west porch seemed to me to be an old grave-slab; the old door-handle is fixed to a modern door. The Early English nave and choir were once the choir of the abbey. The murals that once adorned the walls have disappeared. Several windows are in Perpendicular, one in Decorated style; Saxon stonework exists in the fabric of the tower. Formerly the descent into the crypt was by trapdoor; I went down an open flight of steps and found a three-bay nave with aisles and an apse. The piers were massive, and each capital is designed differently from the others. The altar-stone was that of the old abbey. When I examined the roof, I made out that the roofing of the crypt was once lined out with wood, and I think the woodwork was probably painted. Relics? Yes, there are relics here : two bits of wood, each about four feet long, carved to represent a serpent and a wyvern; four old crosses, one the churchyard cross discovered in 1838, one the original Ainhowe Cross from the moors near Rosedale, one a Saxon cross with characteristic knotwork.

Lastingham remembers John Jackson, born there on 31 May 1778, the son of an itinerant tailor, a North Riding Andrea del Sarto. Schooled at Kirbymoorside, like Fra Lippo Lippi he

> drew a string of pictures of the world
> Betwixt the ins and outs of noun and verb.

Wordsworth's Sir George Beaumont set him to study at the Royal Academy, in 1817 he was elected R.A., travelled in

Italy in 1819, and became a famous portrait-painter and equally a famous copyist of old masters. For Lastingham Church he made a copy of Correggio's *Agony in the Garden* and had it placed over the altar with a lantern of amber glass over it. This meant altering the roofing of the apse, and to complete the design a loo-table with drawers took the place of the altar-stone.

I suspect Ainhowe Cross to be Ana Cross. You will remember I have reported it broken.

The Victorian apostles of sweetness and light, could they now be set down in Hutton-le-Hole, might burst with spleen. "Here," they would shout, "is a village damned. Once it was inhabited by a simple peasantry that knew nothing of commerce and politics, that tended sheep and cattle without wondering what was happening on the Stock Exchange, that drew water from the moorland stream that foams through the village, that had learned self-reliance from the conditions of their life and strength of body from the occupations they followed. And now the humble cottager is ousted from his home to make room for a stranger who fills the low-beamed chambers with sham antiques and demands the installation of a telephone, a garage and an electric supply. And the guest-house-keeper has arrived to fill the village with vulgar holiday-makers, disturbing the quiet and upsetting the balanced economy of this rural paradise." Ruskin wouldn't have written it as badly as that, but that is what he would have meant. And with real tears he would have deplored the tar-spraying of the road that soars up from the village to the level of Hutton Rigg and leads the speeding motorist to Castleton and Eskdale.

I am not a Victorian apostle of culture, and I see what is to be said in favour of the changes that, within my experience, have come to Hutton-le-Hole. Here is the other point of view : "We don't like, and we cannot afford, pools of stagnant population in this country. Men and women of this village, having seen the world, prefer not to be cut off from it. Older folk sense a fertilizing agency in the presence of newcomers. Money, another fertilizing agent, jingles into the village. Without becoming feverish, the tempo of life quickens. Whoever stands at midnight on the village green and sings the

Red Flag (I remember this event, but in Ambleside, not in Hutton-le-Hole) acts rather as a bumper of champagne than as a beaker of soporific Burgundy. Thirty years ago the children here were the shy, serious children of Wordsworth's poetry. Nowadays the people of Hutton-le-Hole prolong their youth into a cheerful sixth decade, and that is all to the good. Therefore let the week-end cottagers bring their colour, music and Harris tweed to this village. Let the chara-bancs roll up over the southern shoulder, halt in the village, spill their loads for a few minutes, and then grind away up the bank of Hutton Rigg, into the green recesses of Farndale and over the purple splendour of Castleton Moor. Let the guesthouse thrive. All this is summer work. But summer passes, the light dies out of the ling, the migrants depart, and Hutton-le-Hole has a long winter."

My friend Edward Colston Williams says that this country cannot call itself civilized until every household in the land is within the orbit of a first-rate health service, and if he is right then there are many parts of the North Riding that are far from being civilized. It is, he insists, foolish to admire the remote and inaccessible at the expense of the human beings who live in wild and inaccessible places. Hutton is neither very wild nor inaccessible, but there are two opinions about its having been spoiled, and both should be put on record.

There is still another thing I want to say about places like Hutton and Lastingham and Newton. When I look at the road-map of Britain I note how the vast majority of our villages are strung out along the highways of the country. One passes through them on the way to some other place, but one cannot do that with villages like Hutton and Lasting-ham. The roads reach them, and there they stop, or used to stop. Hutton and Lastingham and Newton were destinations, not posting-stations. I find the same phenomenon around Old Byland, Cold Kirby and Scawton, and again on the western fells, but it is rare enough to be worth noting. It implies a settled way of life that doesn't hold good any more.

By way of Hutton-le-Hole down the long road past the big quarry overlooking the lowest, wooded stretch of Farndale I went down to Keldholm and turned eastward along the high road from Kirbymoorside to Pickering. Along this road stand four villages, the most famous and finest of which is Sinnington. The village lies north and south, the green is still a spacious green, the place, like Lastingham, is quiet and prosperous. There is, as hunting men know, a Sinnington pack. Wrelton, Aislaby and Middleton stand along the high road, but they will not soon change their quiet, self-sufficient, solid appearance. There is one interesting building. Tuke's *View of the Agriculture of the North Riding*, published in 1800, states that North Riding farmhouses of some importance often contained only a parlour, usually with a bed in it, a living-room called a *house*, a back kitchen, "and some very ordinary chambers open to the roof." Middleton post office seems to be a survival of this sort of building, and of this sort there are very few now left. The roof is supported on heavy curved principals carried down to the floor and evidently originally open to the roof-ridge. I quote here the *Victoria County History*. Middleton Church has a pre-Conquest tower, and Wrelton, if I recollect rightly, has some thatch. All four villages are wealthier than those lying along the Vale of Pickering farther to the east, and this is because the land is better drained and more fertile. The floodlands and the waterlogged patches lie to the south nearer the Derwent. I think this is good orchard country, in which Rogers of Pickering may take considerable pride.

CHAPTER VI

MALTON AND THE VICINAL WAY

I HAVE not yet finished with the moorland country, but before I once more take the road into it I think it best to turn southward for a while into country more various and not less interesting. Malton is the starting-point, and for a description of Malton I turn to a biologist friend of the sort familiar with genes, chromosomes and problems of heredity. "Malton," he once said to me, "is a triploid town." Loose biology that may be; it is still accurate, for there is Norton, Old Malton and New Malton, a triple centre of human activity, the three villages interdependent. With Norton I have nothing to do, for it lies in the East Riding, is dull, looks raw, and yet is older and more mellow than it looks. As for New Malton, I do not think I have ever seen it on a fine day. Invariably the wind has been cold, the sky overcast. That hardly matters. Adverse conditions have not blurred my impressions of Malton. In my time I have seen a number of English and Continental market towns; they have been busy, quaint, full of individuality, picturesque and interesting. Counting Malton as amongst market towns, I risk criticism by describing Malton as a failure. It is busy without the appearance of business, it is neither quaint nor picturesque, it is interesting no more than other little towns are interesting and it has lost a great deal of its individuality. I am going to give you the reasons for all these things.

When you enter Malton market-place you ought at once to be impressed by the size of the bank on the northern side of the square. This clearly implies the transaction of a considerable amount of business, yet not the buying-and-selling business you associate with a market town. This implies not marketing but finance, and I should describe Malton rather as a little money-market than as a cattle-market or produce-market, as the financial focus of a big agricultural area whereof the stock and produce drain away towards York, not particularly into Malton. Further, within the last half-century Malton has tried, though without vast success, to change its status from that of a country market town to that of a small industrial centre. It reminds me somewhat of Stroud. It has flung away what picturesque quality it might have had, and the market-place reveals the town as a transit-camp. People and goods pass through Malton. It is a metabolic agent, a gut, and I do not think it possesses the organic unity it once had. It presents the cold comfort of a junction, and has about as much individuality. If Malton has anything to be proud of, all that lies in the past, not in the present and not in the future. The future of Malton will not be vastly different from its present, for the stimulus to growth is not there.

All this is to say the worst of Malton, and you might suppose, quite wrongly, that I despise the place. By no means. Malton has, for one thing, never pretended to be other than it is. It has had the sense to see that a transit-camp cannot shape itself into a beauty-spot, and the industries of the place, frankly utilitarian—a gasworks, the railway, the road, flour-mills and breweries—make no material for picture-postcard work. If farmers drive into Malton they are on business, and business can be as well transacted in a modern office as in a half-timbered tithe-barn. When farmers' wives shop in Malton, they are not so much concerned with the appearance of the shops as with the quality of the goods they buy, and I incline to the view that they prefer an old-fashioned Manchester House to a modern departmental store. As for a river-front laid out like the lakeside at Como, it would be incongruous and absurd. Even the Derwent has to justify its existence by working.

No, it would not be any use pretending that Malton is one of the beauty-spots of the North Riding, yet I am justified in asking a cogent question: if Malton is a little workaday place, half urbanized, half rural, what can it show as a result of its labours? Well, for one thing, race-horses. There isn't a racing-man in England who hasn't heard of the Malton stables and the winners that come out of them. He would rate the breeding and training of race-horses as the chief industry of Malton. The connoisseur of ale would jerk his finger towards the breweries, for Malton ales are first-quality stuff, and the hunting man would insist that there are no riding-breeches like those made by Malton tailors, who maintain extraordinarily high standards of craftsmanship. The flour-millers, too, would have several words to say for their products, and not without justification. Small-scale industry as it exists in Malton to-day has no need to be ashamed of itself, and Malton need fear no comparisons. The work it does may be a survival, but it is not a superannuated vermi-form appendix in the body of the state.

You may be tired of hearing how places come into existence, but, though you find economic history lacking in sparkle, I still have to explain that the town originated at a ford across the Derwent on a spur of hill above flood-level. As a natural centre of communications it developed a Roman camp, probably a transit-camp, with three or four military roads converging upon the ford, and I should guess that, though the Anglian town stood away from the Roman camp, Malton has been a small population-centre and transit-camp ever since, and perhaps before, Roman times. The books, moreover, insist that "in former times, the Derwent was navigable as far as Malton and that ships were built there." I should have to have indisputable documentary evidence of that. What happened to the river traffic when it reached the monks' weir and the shallows at Kirkham, and the manorial mill at Stamford Bridge? Moreover, the Derwent has always been a capricious river. North of Malton it picks up the waters of the Costa Beck, the Rye and the Leven, and is liable to sudden spates and widespread floodings not even yet under control. As a waterway, the Derwent is satisfactory for skiffs and punts, by no means for barges.

Obviously Malton has always had importance as a baiting-place for man and beast, man and motor-car. Its spacious inns prove that. Nowadays traffic flows through it, if it can. In summer Yorkersgate is an important focus of congestion, bad temper, impatience and inflamed language, even though much traffic is now diverted down Railway Street to the level crossing and the road to Scarborough and Filey. The roads north of the town show that the land thereabouts was not enclosed until the end of the eighteenth century, and the drains and ditches show that land to have been unproductive marish and moor. Even now it is not first-rate agricultural land, and the rural population is thinly distributed between Malton and Pickering. The fields are flat, the hedges scrubby, the soil is not seldom spongy, the labourers are few.

When, on the road from Malton to Pickering and Whitby, I come to Old Malton, invariably I pick up the ghost of William Cobbett—not the tiresome fellow of the *Political Register* but that other Cobbett of the *Rural Rides*. From him I get a dig in the ribs, and "Look!" says he. "Look at Old Malton Church!" Not much use replying to Cobbett that I know exactly what he's going to say, that I've heard it before. "Here is a church," says he, "big enough to hold three or four hundred folk—they stood to worship, they had no cushioned pews or chairs—obviously built to hold that number, and standing now in a tiny hamlet. Hence the population of medieval England was far bigger than it is now." Old Malton Church is one of Cobbett's churches, though nowhere in *Rural Rides* does he mention it. But of course the church grew up from Old Malton Priory, and in former days Old Malton had as great importance as Malton itself, which owes a good deal of its growth to the railway. Old Malton has no railway; there are only some noble old trees by the roadside.

I took a West Riding man to look at Old Malton Church. He flung a casual glance at it, then he stared.

"Extraordinary!" he muttered. "Quite extraordinary!"

I waited.

"Don't you see?" he asked. "This church makes me feel at home! It's built of millstone grit!"

There's no mistaking this dark, pitted freestone. Millstone grit beyond a doubt, fetched all the way from Pennine quarries, went to build this church. And there are others in the North Riding. The circumstance is not so extraordinary as my friend thought it was.

Twenty years ago, when Old Malton was mostly thatched, I knew the schoolmaster there. I asked him how he, a townsman, proved so popular with the village lads.

"Whya noo!" he explained. "Ah gans inti t' skeeal garth an' Ah laiks at taws wi' 'em!"

"And what," I asked him, "is the function of Old Malton in the economy of the state?"

"It is," he replied, "a producer of that most valuable of all commodities, skilled labour for field and farmhouse, and such is Old Malton's sole prospering industry."

I reminded him of the amateur theatricals in which he had played the part of Rip van Winkle.

"Ay," he said. "But now I'm not acting!"

"Would you consider a town job?"

"I would not!"

From the west three roads enter Malton. One is the main highway from York, one is the road from Castle Howard, and the third you may call the Vicinal Way. I myself call it the Road of the Saxon Towers. It ought to run through from Malton to Aldborough near Boroughbridge, but it founders, long before it gets there, somewhere near a tiny place called Coldharbour west of Hovingham High Woods. I do not propose to bore myself by eulogizing this road as a road Roman or modern, but whenever I go westward along it from Malton I have to admire the nice reasons why the Romans made it run along the northern slope of the ridge and not on the summit. South of the ridge is the gorge of the Derwent, a tactical barrier to forces moving north. North of the ridge lie level carrs seven miles wide, so that the least observant of legionaries could sweep it with easy eyes.

Broughton and Swinton, the first villages out of Malton, are Anglian in origin, and therefore they stand not on the road but below it, at the foot of the spur where the springs break. The Danes built Amotherby, the next village, in similar fashion. Then comes Appleton-le-Street, this time built along the road, and it has the first of the Saxon towers. As I look at it, I picture this road coming across the green wolds of the East Riding, and how there, too, it is beaded with Saxon towers—towers rather cruder in build than these of the North Riding. This is no Earl's Barton, however, and what surprises me about the North Riding Saxon towers is their comparative slightness. They are tall but slender. They have no bulk, no massive strength, and they would never have held more than a few refugees at most. Still they have style and they look what they are. I like them better than Early

English or Decorated or Perpendicular. At least I like them better as village work. They have grown where they stand, and they belong there. When I came to Barton-le-Street I found a difference. The Normans were not genuinely fond of architectural simplicity and they hadn't any taste for village work. Here they fetched millstone grit to build their church, and were not happy until they got a skilled carver to gouge out the fantastic carvings of a round-arched doorway facing north, tympanum and all. The worst of this Norman door is that it demands imperatively to be photographed as a show-piece. Those are your Normans!

Slingsby Castle, next along the road, was, I believe, a rather late erection with a brief, inglorious existence. It is the only castle in the North Riding that has ever made me lift my eyebrows. I came to it first in the days when I had some reverence for antiquity, when I expected castles to behave like castles. Slingsby did not. It was a warm summer's day when I left the road and went down to the ivy-clad ruin and found myself, almost at once, in a cowhouse. Slingsby Castle was a cowhouse! Nowadays I should not blink if I found a castle used as a branch of Woolworth's, for I have now come to realize that the English are one and all as mad as Dick's hatband.

At Hovingham, about three miles farther west, stands another Saxon tower, and a beauty at that, and here in Hovingham I have a declaration to make. Very often I turn over the pages of *Country Life* and look at the pictures of spectacular landscapes and magnificent country houses, quaint inn-signs, wrought ironwork, intriguing signposts and the like, and I am tempted to say, "There's nothing in the North Riding to compare with this!"

Then I remember Hovingham. Hovingham has every-thing. It stands in an ancient forest region, and though I would not say that the beeches in Hovingham High Wood form part of the woodland of 1086, I am sure that there are no nobler trees in the North Riding than these. The village is clean beauty all through. It has a proud community life, it has some Roman remains, and I'm pretty sure that more, and more startling, remains await discovery; it has given up its silly ambition to be a spa, and it stands in lovely country.

Hovingham Hall, facing westward, is good mid-eighteenth-century building, its windows looking across the park towards the high woods. The Vicinal Way runs through the wood, and the last time I went through, not very long ago, a red squirrel chattered at me from a green-mossed fence. The terrific group of statuary on the lawn of Hovingham Hall was one of the marvels of the Riding. The man who hacked it out, John of Bologna, ought to have been one of Browning's heroes. The men who brought it here were also heroes. George III presented it to Thomas Worsley, surveyor-general to the Board of Works in 1750, but how it was transported from wherever it was to the grounds of Hovingham Hall I cannot imagine. Unless, of course, as Yorkshiremen say, it comes from together.

Hovingham is a centre of cricket. I think that should be noted.

Motorists, so far as I have observed them, have the good manners to picnic away from the hall; they choose a site by the ford and the little lake.

The eighteenth-century nabobs were fond of the Howardian Hills; they liked park rather than moorland, a soft air rather than a keen wind, broadleaf trees rather than pines. Two miles south of Hovingham, Wiganthorpe Hall stands secluded in park and woodland, and from there you may move south to Terrington, not far west of the Castle Howard estate. There ought to be deer in these woodlands, but for many reasons there are none.

From Hovingham town end I did not, this time, walk through the High Woods to Coldharbour. The road here is narrow and winding, with high hedges, and there are no prospects. Instead, I went north to Stonegrave, where rustic antiquity beckons from the hillside elbow in the main road. I forget if Stonegrave church tower is Saxon—I don't think it is—but, if it is not, at least it must be early twelfth century. A *grave* here is not a hole in the ground but a march or boundary-line, and the *stone* is probably the very fine Manx cross standing in the church close to the south door—the last cross, I believe, of a series that, no one knows why, runs through from Cumberland. This cross is in splendid state—a wheelhead, and, as I think, a boundary-cross.

To see the Anglian fragments at Edston I went a few
miles out of my way. The old sundial here is much simpler
than that of St Gregory's Minster at Kirkdale, and its
inscription is a mere *Lothan me wrohte*. Somehow I missed
the ruins of Dolemaid House, where there is still another
ancient sundial; and of the villages of Harome, Salton,
Nunnington and Muscoates I can tell you nothing. They are
the indecipherable characters in the palimpsest of the landscape which lies between Kirbymoorside and the Vicinal
Way. Of Wombleton, which I admire for its name, I can say
only that old Harker Summersgill, farmer of sixty acres in
the Vale of Pickering, was very proud to let it be known that
he was born there.

Of the country I passed through between Malton and
Hovingham, and again between Hovingham and Kirbymoorside, I have always been particularly fond. The rural economy
is satisfying, and I like well-farmed country, flat or rolling,
arable, meadow and pasture. This area is mostly cornland
and good meadow. It is well watered, but the water is under
control. There is plenty of woodland, though perhaps not
enough in the trough of land between Stonegrave and Kirbymoorside. Small farmers may plant windbreaks but not
woodlands, which are long-term investments demanding
capital and an interest in posterity. The deciduous woodland
hereabouts is the work of the old squirearchy, and for this
woodland in all seasons I owe the squirearchy my gratitude.
Next, the villages are moderately neat and yet not in their
Sunday-best. I don't suppose they are enormously prosperous,
and the cottagers ought to put up a better show of flowers
and vegetables in their gardens. It is time that the old notion
that good farmers are bad gardeners died. Of all deciduous
trees I like best beech and oak. Elm I mistrust, and with
reason, and my recollection of all this area tells me that it is
a land of fine beeches and massive oaks. The contours,
especially from Slingsby through Hovingham to Stonegrave
and Edston, are diverse enough to provoke that sort of suspended pleasure that led Stevenson to say it was better to
travel hopefully than to arrive. The population is neither too
scanty nor too thick on the ground, and, save in Hovingham,
it is a natural growth. It belongs here and remains unspoiled.

What do I mean by *unspoiled*? I mean that their outlook from day to day remains uninfluenced by the popular press; they don't seem to take much pleasure in football pools, though they follow county cricket with great keenness and their own league matches with greater; Hovingham Ladies have a famous eleven, and also play hockey with verve and skill. The knowledge of the people is the deep, satisfying knowledge of their environment, and their wisdom, their powers of judgment, are exercised upon that environment. Discontent is far to seek. We used to say that discontent led to agitation, action and progress. Nowadays we are not convinced of the validity of progress, and, consequently, of the validity of discontent divine or other.

Some day I shall strike westward from Coldharbour—there has been no digging at Coldharbour yet—and try to trace the foundered Vicinal Way as far as Aldborough, the Roman Isurium.

Coxwold

Chapter VII

THE HELMSLEY DISTRICT

I AM in Helmsley, sitting on the plinth of the Feversham Memorial in the middle of the market-place, and I am looking about me, thinking of many things. Having known Helmsley for over thirty years, I picture it as it was those thirty years ago, as it was long before that time, and as it is likely to be thirty years hence. My thoughts are troubled. Before my time this spacious square was green with grass; cobbled, no doubt, round a broken market cross. I am sure a big old tree with spreading branches stood where the Feversham family put up its monument. With reasonable certitude I can say that half-ruinous, half-timbered cottages stood round the square and a half-timbered inn stood round the corner by the church. The roads leading in from Thirsk, York and Scarborough were soft roads; the Stokesley road through Bilsdale was no better and perhaps worse. And nobody cared about Helmsley Castle, nobody looked after Rievaulx Abbey, and the Fevershams, remote and grand, ruled in their spacious park and Vanbrugh house. And there were no antiquarians coming and going, no men and women in country tweeds driving into the market square, and the coffined dead of Helmsley were wheeled to the churchyard on a bogie with the mourners holding ribbons attached to it.

Things have changed in Helmsley. The Ministry of Works and Buildings has taken charge of Helmsley Castle and Rievaulx Abbey, the Ryedale Anglers have taken over the fishing reaches of the river, Trust Houses has taken over the Black Swan. Cars, tractors, ice-cream carts, come and go. Charabancs drive in from Whitby and Scarborough. Buses from Ripon, buses from Stokesley, buses from Scarborough, cyclists, youth-hostellers, middle-aged people with rucksacks, pass through the square, and within the hotels sit the "residents" in deep, comfortable armchairs and settees, discussing Clark Gable, Eisenstein, *Forever Amber* and the

146

Quantum Theory. Shrinking from imagining what Helmsley will look like on a fine summer day in 1980, I get up and walk into the grounds of Helmsley Castle by the wrong gateway, make my way along the outer ditch and so over the first bridge, through the barbican, over the second bridge spanning the second ditch into the inner ward of the castle. Six people are already there. The two little girls are excited and romantically moved by this relic, and their mother is pleased this should be so. The man, his wife and grown-up daughter, move around with the help of the twopenny guide and its plan of the ruins.

I talk to the warden.

"Not many castles," I say, "with twin moats like Helmsley."

"Ditches!" he jerks out.

"Dry moats," I say, "like Scarborough."

"Ditches!" he repeats.

"The walls," I comment, "have been grouted."

"Eh?"

"Grouted."

"Ay."

We follow him to the domestic quarters, he pointing haphazardly to his right.

"Chapel," he informs us, "and well."

The chapel was foundation-wall only, the well a small turfed hump in the greensward. Nobody troubled to look at either. He mounted the wooden steps to the hall, unlocked the door and went in. We followed. What most interested him was a series of mangonel balls ranged along the wall. He had two words for the panelling—original, Elizabethan. It was not bad panelling, but I have seen better. The oak beams were in poor state.

"Any beetle?" I asked.

"Beetle?"

"Death-watch, furniture or powder-post," I said.

"Dry rot. No beetle."

There were fragments of the original plaster, handsome stuff of the sixteenth century. That dead-white plaster. The laths were decrepit, the fireplaces wrecked. This had been a rambling Elizabethan house with barrel-vaulted cellars and a warren of domestic offices, a fairly comfortable residence rather dark but not draughty. The fate of the bulk of the panelling, the ironwork and the furniture remains unknown. The Office of Works found the place in bad shape, and the architects, archæologists and masons have made the best of a poor job. The narrow keep must have been a cramped unhappy place to live in at the best of times. The plaster in the domestic buildings set me wondering if the butter-moulds of the nineteenth-century farmhouse owed their elaborate designing to Elizabethan plasterers.

Two local men were grubbing saplings and wartime weeds from their upper lodgments. The saplings came away easily. The workmen had taken over one big room with decrepit oak and broken flooring as their workshop, and its wide fireplace held a Victorian kitchen range thick with rust and dust.

That was all I saw and cared to see of the stronghold of Roos and the hunting-lodge of George Villiers. From there I walked on through the Polish commando camp to Duncombe House, so much like Hovingham Hall, so little like Castle Howard. Here the architect had subjected his ebullience to discipline, and the house is shapely and not too big. Its stone-work, however, is rather dingy. It ought to gleam against those dark woods, as Hackness Hall gleams, but it doesn't. The residence of Duncombe, financial tycoon of the early eighteenth century, is now a preparatory school. The pseudo-Greek temple, half-hidden in summer leafage, was never worth its building, and were it broken down or carted away, nobody would miss or regret it.

The Poles were playing football.

Through the woods I went down to the banks of the Rye, picking my way along pathways overgrown, broken away and slippery from recent rains. Now the Rye here is a clear and copious water. It ought to be a good trout-stream, but I saw no trout. For the first two miles the path kept me close to the river, for the hanging woods fell right down to the bank—neglected broadleaf trees with convoluted roots bared by floodwater, and the whole woodland very rank. From a distance hanging wood looks superb, but only from a distance. Here the landscape was a small-scale Wye Valley, and all the better for being small-scale. There was no road through it and faint indication of a footpath, with broken wire at intervals and deep holes in the rough ground. The water talked, and sometimes made noises as though cattle were wading in it. I put up a heron, then a pair of dabchicks, then whole platoons of rabbits. The path drove me up the wood, but I came down again to a footbridge, and, across it, to water-meadows full of tall thistles, seaves and springs, very boggy, very treacherous, with meadowsweet in flower and black steers grazing, and then to split chestnut palings, which I had to climb, and crossbred sheep. Artillery practice on Ample-forth Moor wakened no echoes in the valley. The river ran its rapid course, now making little green islands, now between steep banks of reddish sandy clay. Then there were men mowing the thistles, and, finally, the road. From the foot of Ingleby Howl Bank I followed the road to the two-span stone bridge, with Rievaulx Abbey on my right, crossed the bridge and so arrived in the spacious twelfth century upon the site that Walter l'Espec gave to the Cistercian monks.

I have great admiration for Rievaulx Abbey. I was once there when a West Riding chapel choir straggled down into the nave of the church, assembled under its choirmaster in drizzling rain and sang "Abide with Me." Having sung, the choristers straggled back the way they had come, off went their charabanc up Rievaulx Bank and the sound of its grinding gears died away amongst the trees. There was something very West Riding about that gesture.

I used to visit Rievaulx before Ancient Monuments took it over, when its walls were overgrown and all to-fallen, with vast nettle-beds and immense docks, and nobody romanticized the big, rambling place. That was before the diggers, from under one of the nettle-beds and the wreckage of a wall, got out the pigs of lead with the royal Tudor stamp upon them which, after 1918, went to relead the Five Sisters Window in York Minster. After Ancient Monuments took Rievaulx into its care, I talked to a couple of masons busy on restoration. These experts restored, wherever it was possible, every fallen stone to its original position. To their patient and knowledg-able work the modern visitor to Rievaulx owes much of his pleasure. From Rievaulx, I understood, these two masons would go to Cyprus on much the same sort of work.

"Paphos?" I asked. But they did not know.

I found excavation and restoration going forward near the infirmary block. It had begun only a fortnight before I got there in mid-August 1946, and its object was the uncovering of the site of the infirmary chapel. The work lay under a green tarpaulin and I did not see it, nor shall I here describe the history and the present layout of this great Cistercian mission-house. Castles as a rule restore better than abbeys, but I take Rievaulx as an exception. It is magnificently restored and very well kept; but, large and beautiful as it is, it is no more admirable than Jervaulx Abbey, restored and maintained by private hands and private purse.

One swift note. I have a neighbour who calls Jervaulx *Jarvis*, and in Helmsley market square stands a shop calling itself *Rivis*. For Rievaulx I have heard the pronunciations *Reevo, Rivis* and *Rivers*. I see no reason why the French pronunciation should not be valid, and I fear *Jarvis* and *Rivis* are a trifle pedantic.

Rievaulx was swarming with visitors, arriving in chara-bancs, private cars and Rolls Royce taxis, arriving by bicycle, arriving on foot. I suppose that everyone was intelligently interested, but I have some suspicion that a twopenny pamphlet and a plan of the ruins for many folk do not replace the spoken word and the touch of impromptu of a human guide. Pamphlets and plans do not answer questions and they assume foreknowledge.

The tiny hamlet of Rievaulx is not growing, and it still has its thatch, some of it in sad need of repair. The thatcher was actually at work when I went by. Three or four village lads were playing french cricket close to the abbey entrance, and from them I heard plain, undiluted North Riding dialect—very different from the young woman at Thirsk who was on her way to Scawbro. From Rievaulx I had choice of ways. I could go back to Helmsley by way of Rievaulx Bank or Ingle-by Howl Bank, or I could return by my outward route. I climbed Rievaulx Bank to the Stokesley road, was not attracted to the terrace walk and the frescoes, though both are worth a visit, and at the top of the bank I stopped irresolute. Then I turned and went down to the Rye again.

In Thomas Gent's *History of York*, 1730, the author

wrote of Roch Abbey, "not far from Rivaux," as follows :
"In the year 1236 there was seen at several times near Roch
Abbey a wonderful Prodigy as of Men compleatly arm'd on
horseback ascending out of the Earth into the air, where
separating themselves into parties, they seemed afterwards
to come to a fierce engagement and at last to sink in the Earth
whence they came." Now I looked in vain for Roch Abbey
near Rivaux, or for sign or trace of it, and for "fierce, fiery
warriors" fighting in the clouds. I knew Old Byland, more
than a mile west of where I stood—Old Byland with its green,
stocks and Norman font, its air of cold, detached walled-in
solidity, and I knew that the first site of Byland Abbey stood
not far from the bridge over the Rye. What I did not know
was the site of any Roch Abbey near Rivaux, and still I do
not know it. There is no Roch Abbey near Rivaux, and never
was. Thus, road or no road, path or trackless wood, I faced
north along the eastern bank of the Rye—here beyond doubt
a fishing stream—followed it to the confluence of Seph and
Rye and found myself beyond Shaken Bridge. The Seph is
Bilsdale water. Here at the confluence lay lush wet pasture,
but, the hanging wood having come to an end three miles
above Rievaulx, I was satisfied to set my feet upon the road
to Hawnby and New Hall.

New Hall is like Hawnby, old, small, unpretentious, dating
from the first years of the seventeenth century and standing
in lonely, wooded hill-country. Another mile brought me to
Arden Hall, also seventeenth-century and built upon the site
of an ancient nunnery. Here is good panelling, and here also
a fine yew hedge. From Hawnby I struck east. I climbed to
the inn, went down to a swift little beck and climbed once
more, skirting the shaggy shoulder of a great bluff, crossing
(with great trouble) the Seph, and with Bilsdale West Moor
in full August glory at my back I went up the steep hillside to
Rievaulx Moor—conifers, ling, marish ground and great
expanse of wilderness. Northward the moor climbed to a
high horizon, to the south it fell away towards the plainland.
Honestly I do not recommend this journey from Hawnby
to any but the hardy and reckless. At last I turned south and
came down rapidly into Helmsley by the track that slides into
the market square by the Black Swan.

The villages of the moorland, Cold Kirby, Scawton, Old Byland and Hawnby, remind me strongly of the villages on the western fells, stone-built, remote, compact and independent of spirit, in the midst of a little, lost land of their own. Here life is necessarily puritan or quaker-hearted, simple, stern, without the warmth that emerges when conditions are easier, communities larger, amenities more ample. I always suspect the inhabitants of such villages of pagan practices or at least of a pagan outlook.

In a book of this sort I must be truthful or nothing. Let me here record, then, that though it wasn't yet five by the church clock, which, by the way, was dumb that day, I could get no tea. The little café refused me, one of the inns was packed out, the other was serving tea only to residents, and I might go thirsty and hungry. So indeed I did, yet lost none of my affection for Helmsley. I went along to the bridge over the Rye and contemplated the darkening water, surrendering myself to the gentle hypnosis of the noises it made. I remembered as in a dream the spring woodland of Bransdale, not many miles from where I leaned with my elbows on the cool grey parapet. I remembered a day when I stood away from the path that runs along the high fringe of the trees, and, at my feet, a spread carpet of lilies of the valley, and, farther down the hillside, Lent lilies, or, if you like, wild daffodils. For nearly thirty years I had kept the secret of their flowering in Bransdale, and yet I had not, even then, found them for myself. Mrs Crosthwaite, who in those far-off days kept the Black Swan, had told me where to find them. Now the secret is out, but I feel that vandals will look in vain for the flowers. Bransdale is not easy to get at, one has to know the locality, and this is not motoring country. Running north from the high road, the dales begin as grass-grown, shallow troughs like samples of park. One expects to see the Old Hall with its balustraded terrace, and tall elms, with rooks. But there is no hall in Bransdale, the dale narrows to a gill, the woodlands thicken, the beck begins to chatter, and finally there is open moor, with a fresh wind blowing. That's how it is and that's how I hope it will continue to be.

Car-traffic slid along the dull road between Helmsley and Kirbymoorside, a road too long for me to travel after the day

I'd had. Back in Helmsley market square, I waited for the bus that would take me into Harrogate. No room at the inn. It wasn't like that in the old days.

But I had not finished with Helmsley, I had to go back, and it was not more than a day or two before I saw the place again—identically the same picture, almost the same folk. From Helmsley, through Nawton, I came to Kirkdale. The new high road from Helmsley to Kirbymoorside avoids Kirkdale, but the traveller will do well to seek it in the first place for its seclusion and beauty, in the second place for Kirkdale Church, and in the third for the famous bone-cave. Many people have a deep-rooted horror of caves, and no reasoning, no psycho-analytical explanation, can rid them of it. Without being of their number, I visited Kirkdale Cave badly equipped for cavern-crawling, and a poor job I made of it. Climbing the fence, I pushed through the undergrowth that menaces the path, looked up at the face of the quarry, contemplated the yawning jaws of the cave some few feet above ground-level, and, standing in oozing mud, took stock of my mental, physical and moral equipment for the task of creeping into that hole. I was not properly dressed for it, I had no electric torch, matches had a scarcity value, I was recovering from an attack of lumbago, I was older, taller and stiffer in the spine than the ideal cavern-creeper, and I knew next to nothing of the interior. Was there, within, a great chamber where a man could stand up? Or was there nothing but belly-crawling? Climbing up the stiff clay incline, I reached the mouth of the cave and peered inside. There was a tunnel, its floor worn smooth by previous knees and forearms. So far as I could see, it went straight into the rock. Having arrived thus far, was I to turn a craven back? Down I went on my knees and paddled forward on my forearms. Within two minutes my hands, trouser-knees, arms and shoes were stiff with wet clay. My knees slid into little pools of water, and there were little hills of clay into which they bumped. I pushed forward. The passage divided. I chose the branch that seemed to penetrate direct into the limestone, pausing at intervals to strike precious matches. Another division of the passage occurred six or seven yards farther on. Reaching it, I found I could stand up, lean against the wet rock and get my breath. The air was cold and still, and the fumes of the matches I struck thickened it more than you would believe. Surveying my position, I saw I should have to get down on hands and knees again if I were still to go forward. By this time, however, I had had almost enough of a mode of progression which, tolerable in the nursery, is undignified in the eyes of the adult world. Nevertheless I assumed this bestial posture once more, plunged into the most promising tunnel and came to a place where, upon a slab of wet limestone, stood the final fortieth of an inch of candle with a curved, blackened fragment of wick. When I put a match to it, it burned, and from my hands and knees I stared at it with foolish joy. Then, like a broken colossus, I leaned with sagging spine against the wall of the cave.

Usually in a big cavern there is almost always a drift of air. Here the air was perfectly still. I waited. When the candle had burned smokily for forty seconds the wick collapsed and the light went out. The darkness was prodigiously thick. Was there, I demanded of myself, any point in going on? And, if I went on, what should I achieve, what profit or merit should I earn, and, above all, how should I get out? I hadn't many matches left. I remembered, too, that the bone-cave had been thoroughly opened out and described in Buckland's time. Why, then, should I penetrate deeper into this viscous darkness? This had been a hyena den.

"If hyenas lived in this cave," said I solemnly, "I don't know what they found to laugh at."

At this crudity I myself laughed, and to my appalled ears the laughter sounded gruesomely like that of a hyena. Or, maybe, a jackass.

Briefly, then, I cursed my way back towards the light of day and found myself jammed into a tunnel once, no doubt, used solely by hyena puppies. There for some time I stuck. Then, contriving with peril to my spine to back out of the hole, I came head first into dazzling sunlight. From head to heels I was thick with clinging clay. Edging round the quarry face to another hole in the rock I found it an object uninviting and even repellent. I abandoned the whole business, climbed back over the barbed wire fence and went down to the beck to wash.

That was not Kirkdale Cave, but my experience of Kirkdale Cave—a very different thing. As I contaminated the water of the beck with yellow clay, I tried to remember things about the famous cavern, but for the life of me I could recollect only the vague outline of the story. First, a young man on his holiday from London had seen the quarrymen turning out quantities of bones. He had collected some and submitted them to the Royal College of Surgeons. Buckland examined them. In his opinion they bore signs of having been gnawed by hyenas. He took fresh bones to the Zoo and got modern hyenas to gnaw them. His theory was completely verified. Travelling north, he went through Kirkdale Cave with a fine-tooth comb. Hundreds of bones of goodness knows how many animals, some now extinct, some still with us, resulted from his labours, bones that nowadays repose in undisturbed order upon the shelves and in the glass cases of museums.

"If," I said to myself, "I had the courage and pertinacity, the cold heroism of Norbert Casteret, I should now go back into the cave, and, matches or no matches, explore every nook, cranny and cramped chamber of the place with a view to supplementing the discoveries of Professor Buckland. But I shall do no such thing. I possess no such courage, no such enthusiasm. Norbert Casteret was a speleologist in a million, and I am not even one of the million."

Nevertheless I had been interested in the cave.

When I had washed the clay from my shoes, hands and face and out of my hair, I looked at Kirkdale Beck and found it as of old except that a layer of concrete has been plastered over the shallow bed of the stream to smooth out the crossing of the ford for motor vehicles. There are still swallow-holes and clints in the limestone down which the water vanishes, and probably not far below ground-level there exist caverns not yet measured by man where age-long dribblings of lime-impregnated water have created the wild phantasmata of a mysterious underworld.

Kirkdale Church is very different from the cavern, although any building, come to think of it, is an artificial cavern. I do not know and I have never seen a church and churchyard more remote from the modern world. When I looked over the dry wall into the churchyard and along the path to the church porch, I thought (covered with clay as I was), "How many miles to Babylon!" I won't say that Kirkdale Church as it stands to-day is quite a thousand years old, for it has been restored. But the tower is good Saxon, and two very ancient grave-slabs (one of them the grave-slab of a king) have been built into the walls of the church. There is Saxon strapwork in the east wall, and another grave-slab in the west wall. Further, there is the famous sundial over the doorway, with its Saxon inscription.

The upright rails of the porch doorway were a trifle too closely set together to permit of an easy reading of the inscription, so with a bit of wire I eased open the padlock, entered the porch and translated into reasonable English: "Orm, son of Gamal, bought St Gregory's Minster when it was all ruined and broken down, and he caused it to be made new from the ground . . . in the days of Edward and in the days of Tosti the Earl." And, over the dial, "This is the day's sun-marker at each hour." *At ilcum tide*. Beneath the dial, "Haworth made me, and Brand, priests."

When, in April 1927, I visited Kirkdale, I made a pen-and-ink drawing of the three panels of the sundial and of the doorway below them. Since then, something has happened to the upright stones on each side of the doorway. My drawing shows a large X on a huge upright stone by the door-sneck, but now there was nothing but a dim something-or-other which some amateur antiquarian will take for a mason's mark. And the rough blocks that supported the stones of the arch had been smoothed, fashioned new, made less rude. Further, in 1927 I made a note that immediately south of the church below the turf there seemed to be the foundations of a monastic building of considerable size. This, I suggested, might have been the original St Gregory's Minster "when it was all to-broken and to-fallen," and my note reminded me that the tomb-slab in the east wall is supposedly that of King Æthelwulf, who has left no mark upon my memory. I do, however, clearly recollect that in 1927 there was a nest of wild bees in the Saxon tower. I looked. The jagged hole by which the bees came and went was still there, but the bees had gone.

In the graveyard not far from the church porch I cleaned the moss and lichen from this inscription :

> Remember, Man, as Thou Goest By,
> As Thou art Now So once Was I,
> As I am Now So must Thou Be,
> Remember, Man, that Thou must Die.

On the other side of the grave-slab is the blunt inscription :

Here lieth the body of Iohn the son of Robert Barker who departed this life February 25th 1767.

Up the dale beyond the church a big marquee promised great doings in Kirkdale that day, but there were no signs of human activity.

Since the new road from Helmsley to Kirbymoorside bypasses Kirkdale, and the Pickering road bypasses Kirby, Kirby may one day become as quiet as Kirkdale, so easy is it for the motorist, at any rate, to miss the pleasant village. If there is anything for which I praise Kirby it is for the rich quality of its tiling. Moreover I praise the layout of the village as it slopes down the side of its hill, and I must put it amongst the most popular of North Riding villages. Helmsley has lost its industries : it used to be a linen-weaving centre and focus of handloom weaving; Kirby is busier nowadays than Helmsley, for it has its orthopædic hospital for children, and, particularly, its glider factory. I must also put in a word for the Black Swan. The wicked Duke of Buckingham, poor George Villiers, did not die at the Black Swan. The house in which he expired is no longer there; it stood next to the King's Head. "1687, April 17th, George Vilaus, Lord Dooke of Bookingam." Thus the parish register. But about the Black Swan . . .

Pleasant things happen to me in Black Swans. At the Black Swan in Helmsley, in the days before it became a Trust House, I met there three men of Ancient Monuments. Paterson had come down from Edinburgh, a London official met him there, and there was the local man who looked after Rievaulx, Byland and Helmsley Castle. Then there was an ex-officer of the Indian Army who knew of an ice-cold current in the tropic waters of the Arabian Sea and used to persuade people to bathe in it. He spoke, too, of the most poisonous snakes in the world, the sea-snakes of the Indian Ocean. There was a man who played Beethoven sonatas with, it seemed to me, the touch of a Schnabel. In the Black Swan at Kirby, late one autumn evening between the two wars, the parlour was dimly lit, and there, miraculously, was Hazlitt's "gentleman in the parlour," trim-bearded, quiet in demeanour, politely anonymous, gravely communicative. Somehow we began talking of the Saharan oases—of Baharia, Kharga, Khufra. He knew them all. He knew people, too, explorers and adventurers of this day. We talked a long time. In the early hours of the following morning I took the road again. The picturesque outside of the inn was on that occasion but a mask of event.

Now Kirby seemed quieter than usual as I walked up the village and set off for Gillamoor. The road was as long and empty as the roads that lead from the line of Northumberland villages to Hadrian's Wall, or the road from Pickering to Newton. In Gillamoor, however, the long road gets rid of its monotonous quality. Gillamoor is one of Milton's upland hamlets, neat and quakerish. The thatched cottages are in decay, the other houses seem well-kept and prosperous. I took the Farndale road, and within a couple of minutes Farndale opened out before me.

If, or when, you stand where I stood that day, you will think, "I am glad I made this journey; I shouldn't like to be dead without having seen this." If you don't, you are mighty dull of soul, for this is one of the famous views in Yorkshire. I recollect coming to it one afternoon when the northern sky was a huge drift of black cloud, the green hollow of Farndale was filled with sunshine, and a vast rainbow spanned the valley from the height of Harland on the left to the sharp skyline of Hutton Rigg on the right. To-day there was sunshine of a mellow autumn quality skeined through the standing corn on the eastern slope of the dale. Down below, the steady clicking of a reaper blended with the hum of a tractor, and I sat on the seat or leaned on the railing talking to a bronzed, lean-jawed chap in a dark blue pullover. His name was Todd. A native of Gillamoor, he was a dentist's mechanic, his mother was the oldest inhabitant of the village

—"a real old Yorkshirewoman and a treasury of local know-ledge"—and he himself was home for a few days' holiday.

"You don't talk like a North Riding man," I said.

"Been out and about in my time," he explained. "In the army, as you might expect. Anyhow the old dialect's dying."

"In this area?"

"Ay, even here. The youngsters in Fadmoor, Gillamoor and Farndale are better spoken than they used to be."

"A pity?" I asked.

"In some ways, maybe."

We talked about the view.

"A grand prospect," he agreed, "but rather spoiled just now by the young trees growing up in the waste of the hill-side. There's talk at Gillamoor of cutting them down or trimming them back. One public-spirited gentleman has offered to buy the whole hillside and keep it tidy for the benefit of those who come to look at the view."

I didn't argue this point but passed on to something of personal importance.

"My name's Harland," I told him, "and over yonder to the north lies the original home of the family. One of them was hanged in August 1588, the month and year of the Armada, for stealing a few yards of fencing at Kirbymoor-side."

He looked me up and down, grinned, and said he wasn't surprised to hear it. "But," he said, "there have been no Harlands at Harland for over a century. I don't know who's got the place now, but my mother used to go there when she was a lass, and there were no Harlands there then."

"No," I said. "They've swarmed like bees—some into the Vale of Pickering, some into York and the Vale of York, some into the Middle West of the United States, and else-where. The nearest Harlands to this place are at Hutton-le-Hole. They've not moved far."

"They've left nothing but the name behind them," he said.

We were silent for a while, watching the play of light and shadow on the slope of Hutton Rigg, and the motor-cars, very like small beetles, moving along the Castleton Road on the summit of the great headland. I picked out the top of Rosedale Chimney just above the skyline, Todd picked out

for me the old Quaker burying-ground away to the north-east,
and told me that the fifty bright green hives on the pasture
opposite were brought from Hull to catch the heather-honey
flow.

Presently, "There's a famous ghost story about Farndale,"
I said.

"Not famous!" he replied. "Hardly that! You mean the
tale of Sarkless Kitty!" He pointed down into the dale.
"That's the haunted mill straight down below us!"

"Haunted mill? There isn't a haunted mill in the story as
I know it," I said. "But I had it from Minnesota, by way of
Trinidad to me in England, and maybe it suffered from dis-
tortion on the way."

This is the story as I know it.

Kitty was a Farndale lass who loved well but without wisdom. The young man, son of a wealthy farmer, refused all
responsibility for the bairn shortly to be born. Neither tears
nor prayers had any effect on him. Kitty succeeded, however,
in making a last appointment with him. It was the wildest of
winter nights, with a cloudburst in the hills to the north, and
the young man did not appear at the trysting-place. Learning
that he had galloped hell-for-leather down the dale towards
Kirbymoorside, and now assured that she was both betrayed
and abandoned, Kitty tore off her garments, sark and all, and
plunged into the raging waters of the Dove.

Next morning they found her body in the shallow water of
the ford, and, by her, the body of her drowned lover. It
seemed that his jaded horse had stumbled in the swollen
waters of the river, flung him off and drowned him. In his
waistcoat pocket they found a brand-new wedding-ring. Since
Kitty had clearly committed suicide, they buried her at the
nearest crossroads, the young man in the churchyard.

She did not rest. Many times they saw her, a naked, flitting
figure haunting the ford. She was seen even in broad daylight.
Demented laughter troubled the dark hours, and once a year
to the very day the ford took its toll of life—a wandering
packman, a shepherd, a young lad on his way home from
courting. No one laid these drownings to the account of Sarkless Kitty until one starless night, in dream, an old Farndale
Quaker saw himself at the crossroads with spade and lantern.

160

Waking his wife, he told her what he must do. She, brave soul, got up too, and in the dead darkness they went to the crossroads. There by lantern-light the old Quaker and his wife dug up the remains of Sarkless Kitty and before dawn laid her in a shallow grave within the churchyard as near as might be to the grave of her lover. Thereafter no man ever saw Kitty's ghost, naked, like a wreath of mist by the ford across the Dove, and nobody save the old Quaker and his wife knew why she lay quiet at last in her grave. The Quaker died in Farndale and was buried in the Quaker graveyard there. His sons and his sons' sons live to-day in the Middle West of the United States.

There is another, lighter story of the supernatural centred on Farndale. A farmer was so pestered by a hob that he, in desperation, finally made up his mind to leave his house and take another farm in the vicinity. He had loaded up his household gear on a wagon, and set out for his new home. On the way he met a neighbour.

Said the neighbour, "Weel, George, Ah see thoo's flittin'!"

A stentorian voice bellowed from inside the churn.

"Ay, lad, we're flittin'!"

And the farmer, in a mood compounded of amusement and despair, turned his horses and went back to his old homestead, furniture, hobgoblin and all.

Presently I left Todd and went down into Farndale, but, instead of taking the fork back to Hutton-le-Hole as most travellers do, I swung away to the left and began the long, slow climb to Harland. There the ling was in full bloom, the air was heavy with the murmuring of bees and as I walked through the ling the pollen rose in clouds. The August honey-flow was at its height, the wild thyme at the close-cropped verge of the road gave out its clean fragrance, and the afternoon sunlight mingled gold with the colourings of this empty world. Here there was nothing to look for, nothing to comment upon, nothing within the penumbra of expectation, nothing to philosophize about.

Then I found a spider's rope. Then I found another and still another. They flamed bright green in the sunlight. Each was a foot or sixteen inches long, and they were both tough and elastic, drawing the clumps of ling together when I pulled

M   161

on them. These ropes used to be important. In the City of York there is a world-famous firm of lens-makers—Cooke's. This firm used to employ a man who came and went pretty well as he pleased. His job was to wander the North Riding moorlands in search of these ropes. He collected them, took them to his workshop, untwisted the cables into their separate strands, and fitted them into Cooke lenses for gunsights, bomb-sights, binoculars, microscopes and what not. But nowadays another device is adopted. The spiders' ropes are out of date.

At Olive House I came to a halt. To the left of the road rose a steep bank overgrown by immense fronds of bracken, and this bank rose five hundred feet from the road—a gradient of one in two—to level itself out at the crest, and roll westward in an immense stretch of purple ling. "On that headland," I said to myself, "is the thing called Obtrusch, or, by the folk of Farndale, Obtrusch Roque. I will go up and look at it."

Unless the reader is young, agile and fond of matching his strength against the waste, he will not go up that hillside. The bracken-fronds were seven feet high, there were big stone walls completely hidden amongst the bracken, there were sikes and marish ground. I climbed laboriously, slanting up the hill, clinging to clumps of ling and to bracken-stems, hauling myself up into a great amphitheatre of broken rock in which stood the ruin of a cottage built of huge masoned stones. From there to the crest of the headland was a moderately easy climb.

Naked on the headland, here in groups and there singly, stood heaps of grey shale about thirty feet across. Tumuli? They are often so described, but the truth about them is rather different. Not far below the surface of the moor lies a narrow seam of coal and these are the outcrop workings, long abandoned by the Farndale people, and that is all. The ling will not grow upon the shale.

I looked for Obtrusch Roque. "Obtrusch," of course, is all my eye. It looks wrong, and is as wrong as it looks. "Obtrusch" is Hob Thrush, and "Obtrusch Roque" is the haunt of a hob, a goblin. In 1910 it was a huge heap of stones. Phillips the geologist was the first to make a survey of it. In his day there were two circles of stones, the outer ring about fifty yards round. Each ring had twenty-six stones, those of the inner ring being smaller than those of the outer. Inside the two circles was a pit, a depression in the ground, which at one time, they say, contained a rectangular stone chest.

The shale-heaps, stretching away towards the skyline towards the west and north, broke up the view. I could see little but the immediate foreground and nothing at all of Obtrusch. If, however, I struck north-west, I ought to come upon the thing close by a moor-track 1100 feet above datum-line. After a strenuous spell of heather-walking I glimpsed the track over the moor and had a clear view of everything lying between the track and the spot I occupied. One solitary landmark stood out on the headland. Precisely where Obtrusch ought to have been, stood, of all things, a Churchill tank that had been used as an artillery target. Fragments of old iron lay all round it. I did not find Obtrusch. Taking the moorland track, I followed it down to its junction with the track that came in from West Gill, and then turned east, following a road the soldiers had cut through the moor. Presently it headed for Keysbeck or Scarth Nick. It was time to take to the bracken again. Inevitably I chose the steepest bank to scramble down, and inevitably I landed, after all, at Keysbeck.

Keysbeck is the most primitive of moorland hamlets. It has no road and precious little semblance of a track. Two middle-aged daleswomen were swapping gossip by a cottage door which, open, disclosed a tiny stone-flagged kitchen, a glowing turf fire, a plate hearth, rannel-bawk and reckens— what fifteenth-century Yorkshire wills call "pot-hingils." Had I gone through the doorway I should have walked straight into the eighteenth century. There is one house here built round leaning baulks of timber. The children in this part of the North Riding were the shyest I have known anywhere. I met two little girls and a little boy and wished them good afternoon, but they stared with strangely blank faces and said not a word in answer. At last Obtrusch faded from my mind, that queer stone tumulus; I got down to the road, followed it north to the junction of West Gill and the Dove, crossed the

Dove at Low Mill and turned south down the other side of
Farndale, climbing slowly up the hillside along a grass-grown
and sometimes leafy lane, the easterly thoroughfare into
Farndale from the world, past Thunder Heads to join the
main road from Hutton to Castleton, with Gillamoor hidden behind the massive headland that thrusts north at this
point.

Farndale merits more than this bald account of my
journey, if only for the wild daffodils that grow in profusion
by the banks of the Dove—daffodils that are surely and
swiftly dwindling in number as cars, motor-cycles and chara-
bancs penetrate the upper reaches of this once-secluded dale;
if only for the fact that as a trout-stream the Dove is not what
it used to be; if only because the Farndale men still bring turf
down from the moor in sleds, and wooden ploughs were in
use until yesterday. The stone for the great house in Duncombe Park at Helmsley came from the Farndale quarries.
Mrs. Baillie Reynolds used Farndale in *The Man Who Won*,
and other authors might do worse than pitch a romantic yarn
about Farndale before progress and the great reservoir
change the place, the people and their way of life. Gone even
now is the day when Alfred P. Wilson, in 1910, could walk
the Farndale moors with ghosts and hobgoblins dogging his
steps, when he could lament the decline of religious ortho-
doxy, and conjecture that Bilsdale, farther to the west, was
so called because William the Conqueror, "or some other
Bill," once passed that way.

If William the Conqueror returned from the Harrying of
the North by way of Bilsdale, it stands to reason that the
Bilsdale road from Helmsley to Stokesley is an old road, a
thoroughfare from the fat lands to the south to the flat lands
to the north. It still has the look of a horse-road though
nowadays it offers a good surface for motor-cars. Clear of
Helmsley market-place, I started on the long, slow climb up
towards Rievaulx Bank, noting as I went the rather thin
pasture on the hillside and passing a great lorryload of timber
out of the Rievaulx woods. The lorry bore not only timber;
astride the huge trunks eight youth-hostellers were riding into
Helmsley with triumph and hilarity. They were in an extraordinarily good humour, and sang as they rumbled down the

hill. I knew this road when nobody but farming folk used it, when it was white and dusty and narrow. I knew also that fork to the left, two miles north of Rievaulx Bank, that goes down through the woods to the Rye at Shaken Bridge and so to Hawnby and the digitate gills, grains and griffs, whose rapid becks feed the Rye as it comes rushing down from its gathering-grounds on Snilesworth Moor to Blow Gill and south to Hazel Bank and Hazel Heads. Up Ryedale itself, as I remember, there is nothing that can be called a road, much tangled woodland and bracken impede progress, the dale-sides are steep, the views are fine though restricted by the bends in the stream, and the dale makes ten miles of rough going and primitive living conditions. There are farms and steadings, but the population is very thin on the ground, and, when at last you emerge from the narrowing dale and cross the rough track that leads across the waste to Osmotherley, there is no population at all. The land is empty and the desolation complete, here is nothing but a vast stretch of ling with sheep-tracks threading it, the bright yellow of thin sand-streams in the ling, the rich black-brown of peaty pools, and occasionally a narrow ribbon of bright silver sand. Here are hagworms, and, sometimes, buzzards. Here are peewits and grouse, but, so far as I remember, no curlews and certainly no eagles. Black-faced moorjocks wander at will through the heather, cropping the bright green of young heather-shoots. You are very unlikely to meet human beings on this most desolate part of the North York Moors, though you will find old shooting-butts, no doubt, with the turf cut in long, thin strips like stair-carpet. I will admit to having carried away a six-foot strip of this turf to burn on my drawing-room fire at home. It burns well, with a hot glow and an occasional crackle of flame when a tough heather-stem catches fire. It makes a lot of dirt, rich in potash for the garden. The contours of this land are irregular and there is much marsh ground. You may have the luck to find the track that wanders across the moor in a north-easterly direction towards the Bilsdale Road south of Chop Yat, but, when you have found it, you are just as likely to lose it again and find yourself in the wet ground near Arnsgill Rigg. It is a track not to be blindly trusted by the young and innocent, and, whatever you do, avoid this land when snow is thick on the ground. You will not have fun.

Beyond Rievaulx Bank, the road runs along the high eastern crest of the steep bank that plunges down into Ryedale, and I halted to see what I could, in the bright sunlight, of this part of the land. The woods were broadleaf trees, dense and umbrous, and though it would have been possible to descend the bank to the waterside I did not go. Here I felt myself on the heights with a keen wind blowing freshly from the west, a wave of ploughed land rising above the road on my right, and larks singing in the rather watery blue of the sky. I love this country best with great white clouds crossing the lift, but at any time it is good to be there. The soil is dryish, porous and not soggy, a pastel shade of brown; the prevalent weed is ragwort, and, pest though it is, it is not devoid of beauty. The hedges are trimmed high, not close-cut to the ground, and there is much hazel and a fair amount of hedge-maple in with the quickthorn. The cattle in pasture were mostly Friesian, Noah's Ark cows with the paint still bright on their angular bodies. Then the road took me through a belt of coniferous woodland, with tits larking in the branches, and so slanting down to the waters of the Seph I came into a pastoral dale subtly different from the dales of the Lake District. Subtly different, of course, by reason of the differences in the underlying rock. Here in Bilsdale there is sandstone, shale, limestone, all Jurassic, and they soften the contours of the land, round off the upward curves of the slopes, making a green trough of dairy-farming country with hedges and not dry walls.

I saw thin plantings of conifers on the upper slopes, and farmsteads isolated on either side of the dale. Then I met a Bilsdale man.

"How's life?" I asked him. "How's life up this way?"

"Why," he said, "middling! We've nowt to grumble about."

He meant that buses now run through from Stokesley to Helmsley, and that if he wanted to see a bit of life he was able to do so. The kids could go to the pictures now and then; the wife could get herself down to Helmsley on a market day; a special bus took the children to school and brought them home again. There was nothing to grumble about. Even before buses threaded Bilsdale there was nothing to grumble about. People were satisfied with their living conditions because they had never known anything better or different. Their life was work; an alternation of work, evening lamplight and sleep. A good life, I think.

The road ran close to the water in the valley bottom. I found myself in a peaceful solitude. Nothing, I thought, could ever happen here. Then, suddenly, I recollected travelling through Bilsdale from Stokesley towards the end of a fine August day, and, as dusk was falling, seeing on the newspaper placards in Scarborough the two words, BILSDALE MURDER. I experienced a distinct heart-tremor. Then I solved the mystery. Bilsdale was the name of a little pleasure-steamer plying out of Scarborough Harbour. I was reassured. Nothing ever happened in Bilsdale after all.

Beyond Low Mill the slopes grew wilder and more rugged, with occasional outcroppings of rock and great stretches of bracken, mingled thorn and ling. Here the Norman William probably sighed for the tame lands and orchards of Normandy and wondered what harrying could render such a desolation more desolate. This was the portion of Bilsdale that motorists travel long distances to look at : this, and Chop Yat, and the level headland at the southern end of the silent dale. You note the gash of rust-red in the rock to the right of the road, you know thereby that the ironstone is here at the surface, rich and somehow melodramatic in its appearance.

Bilsdale Head was now not far away, and I nursed a suspicion that the land was growing a little conscious of its beauty and that the ancient simplicity was being lost. It was, I think, an unworthy suspicion. I dare say the time is far away when Bilsdale will be floodlit and men invent fancy names for its beauty-spots. If what passes for civilization has indeed penetrated here, and tractors and lorries and petrol-wagons now rumble along the high road, the new veneer is thin and below it the old life goes on. A word here about legends and superstitions. I have said elsewhere that in all parts of the North Riding they are now dead. In Bilsdale I put the matter to the test, asking questions at a farm-gate. I got my answer.

"Neeabody thinks owt o' that sooart noo. Lads an' lasses hez mair sense. Bud Ah'll tell thoo summat. Deead or nut, t'awd teeals get thersens telled ti t'bairns. Ah wadn't say t'bairns believes 'em, mindstya, bud that maks ni matter!" So the old stories of ghosts and bargasts and hobs are still told for their picturesqueness if not for their veracity, and everybody will be pleased, I hope, that this is so.

You know how the green valleys of the moorland country narrow and grow steeper-sided as they mount towards the hills and the open moor. So it is with Bilsdale. Bilsdale Head lies to the east of the main road beyond Chop Yat, and the moorland plateau impinges on the slopes of the dale. On the top there are old coal-workings, sheep, a line of barrows along the eastward-facing crest, a few gaunt pines, a silver birch or two, delicately grouped. There is nothing else. Precipitous gills with brown beckwater flashing down their runnelled sides, and tiny intakes, green velvet in the rough turbulence of bracken, with stone-built laithes on the high hillsides, characterize the country round Ellermire. Ironstone comes near the land-surface hereabouts, and the monks of Rievaulx used it. You may ask, "How did medieval metal-workers contrive to extract the iron from the ore?" I think I can tell you. A lot of those shallow pits on the moor-top were probably used for lime-burnings. Many were certainly used for iron-smelting. The process needed the most exposed position it was possible to find, a place where the prevailing wind could blow with gale force across the site. Then the iron-smelters dug a shallow hole, and in this hole they built a fire of peats and turves that roared to a hot red glow. Then they fed the fire with lumps of iron ore. The iron did not melt and run, but it grew soft enough to be malleable. Then they took their tongs and brought out the lumps. They gave them a good hammering on some sort of anvil, and as they hammered most of the impurities vanished, leaving an ingot of iron shaped like a bar. These pits were called bloomeries, and that was the method of getting iron, in primitive times, in this neighbourhood. Elsewhere there may have been plenty of timber to take the place of peat and turf, but the trouble was that it took a whole acre of timber to produce a couple of tons of bloomed iron and the process was not economical. Hence the denuding and stripping of the native timber roused a sense of responsibility during the reign of Elizabeth, and restrictions were imposed, though rather late in the day.

I went on, climbing the narrowing dale, considering the diminished and noisier waters of the beck, and at length found myself skirting the western slope of Hasty Bank, a bald eminence of the Cleveland Hills, and then descending the broad road down into dull country and the large, dingy, red-brick village of Broughton two miles south of Stokesley. I somehow resent Broughton. It looks as though it ought to be an industrial, not an agricultural, village. It reminds me of Garforth and Micklefield in the West Riding. The little houses are terraced, the little shops come straight out of side-streets in Leeds or Bradford, and the whole place seems morose if not completely squalid. I came down into the flat land with a sense of disillusion, as though I were entering another and a less happy country. Perhaps I was not deceived.

The stay-at-home traveller can get a fair idea of this flat land by looking at the map. He will then see how the road-system proliferates, with Stokesley as an important nexus and Middlesbrough standing apart from the main road-plan because the road-plan existed before Middlesbrough had any importance. The main road, for instance, that runs from Yarm to Redcar avoids Middlesbrough, whose roads have to join it at right angles. Map-reading will also reveal a denser population in all the agricultural area whose business it is to feed greenstuffs, milk, eggs and poultry into Stockton, Thornaby, Middlesbrough, Eston, South Bank and Grange-town. Although from Yarm, Crathorne, Hilton, Hutton Rudby, Stokesley and Great Ayton no observable signs of industrial Tees-side intrude themselves, I somehow sense that industrialism is not far distant. Perhaps the nostrils are sensitive to a different kind of air, or perhaps the sky loses its clarity and crystalline transparency. Further, with reluctance I confess that the folk of this area are not quite my kind of folk; I take them as cousins—second cousins and quarter-cousins—liking them well enough but not loving them. They speak differently and behave differently. They do not give the right reactions. The agricultural land seems no longer quite wholesome. It strikes me as harsh and not kind to growing things. There are too many roads and crossroads, and through the flat fields runs that whacking great highway from Yarm to Redcar, pioneered through Normanby and Eston by the labour of the unemployed in a time of industrial depression, with South Bank and Grangetown a couple of miles to the north. All this area of Teesmouth has known prosperity and dire depression. It is extraordinarily sensitive to economic changes, and knows, or has known in the past, no real security. Naturally the farming country south of Stockton, Thornaby and Middlesbrough with its satellite towns is not unprosperous, stands in little danger of going derelict, and owes to the proximity of an industrial population a stability it might not otherwise know.

To Teesmouth I shall return, if only to write a note upon its genius for association football. Meanwhile, something very different.

I went back towards the south not across the uninhabited wastes of the Cleveland Hills but by way of that good road which makes south-west from Stokesley across the bridge over the Leven and, avoiding Great Busby, Carlton, Whorlton and Swainby, joins the main road from Thirsk to Stockton. This may be an interesting road for the motorist, but not for the pedestrian. It is broad, flat, straight and unexciting, its sole virtue that it never loses sight of the massive escarpment of the Cleveland Hills. As for this escarpment, it lacks the bold beauty of the western-facing scarp, and has nothing like Roulston Scar to show the traveller. The steep slopes are green to the top, like Roseberry Topping itself. But then, seven miles from Stokesley, I came to Ingleby Arncliffe, Ingleby Cross and the hanging slopes of Arncliffe Wood. It was there I began to feel at home again, for this little place, not of the hills and not of the plain, has a good deal of the sort of thing I like : a pleasant little beck, a worthy little inn, a quiet crossroads, a dignified though small church, good trees and good shelter. Then, moreover, a little to the south, I came to Mount Grace Priory.

At least once in a lifetime every traveller in Yorkshire should visit Mount Grace Priory. You leave the highway and follow an unfenced road by way of a white gate. This road takes you straight to the home of the Bells—you have certainly heard of Gertrude Bell and this old North Riding family—and you skirt the house to the ruins of the Priory. You won't find them like Bolton Priory in Wharfedale or Kirkham Priory in Derwentdale. First, may I describe them generally? They stand at the foot of the steep escarpment with an old fish-stew in front of them and the dense woods behind them. They stand on a site levelled by copious labour. They stand round two irregular four-sided courts, each court on a different level. There is an outer court with buildings on its north, west and south sides. To the north of this lies the cloister court, with nineteen monks' cells or little houses with gardens behind them. Between the two courts is the monastic church, and a second group of six cells and gardens breaks in upon the area of the outer court. The whole structure dates from about 1400, and by that time monastic building had passed its noblest period. But this place was never meant to be noble, and it certainly is not noble. Still, it is the best example in this country of a medieval Carthusian monastery. There is no magnificence in the ruin and it has no vast size. The church does not aspire to heaven. All these Carthusians were anxious to do was to shut out the world. Beside Fountains, Rievaulx, Jervaulx, it is cheap austerity, and it shows with appalling clarity how logical thinking leads to the very extreme of human behaviour. The logic is dreadfully simple. If the whole universe was created by God for man, man's physical frame was merely intended as the house of the soul, and the human soul was the most precious object in the universe. God and the Devil in all ages contend, and the object of their contention is the individual human soul. Therefore, if you were a Christian, it was your plain duty to save your soul from the wiles of the Devil, and since the Devil uses the body in order to seduce the soul it was legitimate to flog, torture, flay and mortify the flesh to and beyond the limit of human endurance. But the Devil also uses the World as one of his instruments of seduction, and particularly the world of womenfolk. The voices of the world are whisperings of the Devil. Woman first led man astray. Therefore, said these Carthusians, it was well to isolate the soul as much as possible from all manner of temptations, and to isolate the soul it was clearly necessary to isolate the body. A single whisper might bring damnation, a moment's contact a perpetuity of hell's tortures. Solitude, then, and silence. Each monk should live alone in his own cell, issuing from it only at the sound of the church bell calling him, in company with his fellows, to the worship of God. In that act of worship he might mingle his voice with those of his fellows; at other times it should be heard by no human ear other than his own.

That was the theory. How did it work out at Mount Grace Priory? Look at this cloister-court, at the nineteen solid doors, the windowless wall, the nineteen dog-leg apertures some four feet from the ground. From each door at the call of the bell, whether in the small hours of a winter's morning or at sunset of a summer day, a single monk came out, fell into line and step with his silent brethren and shuffled along to the church. The service over, he shuffled back to his cell. His food and other requirements came to him from a kitchen run by lay brothers. They were pushed into the hole in the wall by his door; he could take them into his cell without making any sort of contact with the pusher-in. He had no need to use his voice. Within his cell he had a little living-room, a workshop, an oratory, a fragment of sunless garden and a whole lot of austerity. He could wear a hair shirt if he liked; he could go naked, though he never did (on principle) if he wanted to; he had no fuel, no ease, and the grace he sought had nothing to do with the grace of this earthly world. So he lived, so he died, and so was his soul saved for ever-lasting bliss.

This sort of thing is so alien to my mind that I have never visited Mount Grace Priory without suffering a darkening of the spirit. When people talk to me, as sometimes they do, of the colour and splendour of Merrie England, I remember Mount Grace Priory, and I never go there for the amusement I derive from its rather mean architecture, its deliberately contrived dampness, its institutional monotony and its logical lunacy.

Yes, I think all travellers in the North Riding ought to visit Mount Grace Priory. It is, in the words of George Crabbe, "a prison with a milder name."

The house called Mount Grace? In 1654 Thomas Lascelles adapted part of the western range of the outer court as a dwelling-house, and the Bells have added to the existing structure.

CHAPTER VIII

PLEASAUNCE OF LORD AND CLERIC

BECAUSE the Plain of York and the Vale of Mowbray together make one huge structural unit I shall not deal with it in any way but piecemeal, showing you, I hope, not only what is in it but also how to get out of it. As, for instance : from York in a north-westerly direction runs a long road, a weary road, towards Boroughbridge. I shall say at once that it is a motorist's road, no road for the walker. It is as flat as a table-top, there is almost no woodland, and the road avoids villages. From York it passes by way of Clifton and the County Mental Hospital, where a bend of the Ouse passes within a quarter of a mile of the road, it skirts Skelton and Skelton Hall, reaches Shipton, which, lying more than a mile and a half from the Ouse, has obviously nothing to do with ships but used to have much to do with sheep, and then on the left of the road there are—or were—bomber-stations. There is still an aerodrome at Shipton with new jet-propelled aircraft; there is another at Linton-upon-Ouse, four miles away, beyond Beningbrough and Beningbrough Park. It was from these and from nearer aerodromes that the people of Wetherby used to mark the preliminary warming-up of the four-engined Lancasters and Halifaxes, and then, at dusk, watch the broad ribbon, almost a river, of bombers, pass overhead on their way to hazards and heroisms. Between Shipton and Newton-upon-Ouse lies a spacious area marked on the map as the Old Deer Park, but the deer vanished a long time ago for the same reason that they vanished in Wensleydale. I turn to the massive folio volumes of Whitaker's *History of Richmondshire* for his recording of that reason : "It was not without regret," he wrote, "that in traversing a country abounding with every mode of elegance about the mansions of the principal families, and even where so many parks, as they continue to be called, remain, herds of deer, whether red or fallow, the first of all elegances, the greatest ornament of an adorned domain, should appear to have been almost universally banished. The systematic destruction of these noble animals is another fruit of that wretched system of economy, that minute attention to agricultural profit, which has arisen out of extravagance. The estates of great families are racked to meet the expenses of their owners; the calculating and computing spirit is set at work to extract from every inch of ground the utmost which it will produce, and it is ascertained to a farthing how many pounds per annum are thrown away on a herd of deer and a keeper, while it is forgotten how many thousands are needlessly lavished on the turf or at the gaming-table."

Whitaker's grammar and sentiments were alike those of a gentleman, and he may have been reading Estimate Brown. Elsewhere in the same ponderous volumes he ascribes the extermination of the deer in Swaledale and Wensleydale to the felling of the forests and the encroaching of the lead-mines and smelt-mills, but of these things more when I come to write of the Swale and the Ure. The matter to bear in mind is that a park on the map was formerly a deer-park, and that the deer have been systematically destroyed. And so from Shipton towards Tollerton, a village in warm red brick, and to Alne, which has a hall, a demesne and a church. At Tollerton a road comes in from the east, where Sutton-on-the-Forest reminds the traveller of Laurence Sterne. All this area was formerly within the purlieus of the Forest of Galtres, that huge and famous acreage of wood and wilderness which people still talk of with some show of ingenious learning. I am cautious of etymology, but now and then I find some delightful conjecture (remember Bilsdale!) that forthwith I adopt because of its ingenuity and because it is just as likely to be right as that of the most learned scholar, with whose painful guesses I am seldom in concord. *Galtres* looks very French or Norman French, does it not? But remember that the principal tree of this Forest was the oak. Now how about *Gall-trees*?

North of Sutton-on-the-Forest there remain traces of the old strip system. The road running north to Stillington, for example, is still called Wandell Balk because it used to separate the north field from the middle field. Middle Field and West Field are marked on the Survey map, and between Middle Field and the village is Diana Field, which seems not to belong to medieval England but is unmistakably Yorkshire because *Diana* has no genitive inflexion. The North Riding man will speak of *John Metcalf bull* or *Mary Metcalf dog.* South of Sutton lies Southfield House, and wood and waste are indicated by East Moor. Further, the common lies in an angle of the road that leads to St John's Well—St John because he took over from pagan deities the rites of well-worship and well-dressing and associated them with himself and with his Eve. St John's Eve is the time you paddle and splash in well-water anywhere between southern Sicily and northern England.

Apart from the records and stories of Sterne's tenure of the vicarage from 1741 onwards, during which time he planted cherry trees, an espalier hedge of apples, nectarines and peaches, failed to make his dairy-farm pay, and made some of the local people very angry by guying them in his books, I find the village interesting because a family of Harlands lived at the hall for a couple of hundred years. I have no notion whether they are collaterals of mine, or whether I am a collateral of theirs, or whether they bear no blood-relationship to me. The great man of the Sutton Harlands was Richard, who recovered the hall from Lilburne's men and died, aged ninety-seven, in 1689. His grandson, Philip Harland, did not get on well with Sterne. No more should I have got on with him. In 1863 or thereabouts, the estate passed out of the Harland family. The arms of Harland—this is quite irrelevant—are argent a bend sable cotised azure with three harts' heads caboshed on the bend and a scallop gules in the cantle. I think that is a noble coat, and some day I shall set the College of Heralds to find out if I am entitled to wear it.

Nearly four miles beyond Alne the traveller may look for the confluence of Ouse and Swale. It lies west and a trifle south of Myton upon Swale, where the great Roger de Mowbray's bones lie at rest. They were brought here from Byland Abbey in 1820. There is nothing spectacular in the meeting of the two great North Riding rivers—nothing like the meeting of the Arve and the Rhone—for the Ure has by this time forgotten Aysgarth Falls and Hack Fall, nor does Swale remember his early turbulence. This point of junction is a long way from keld heads—the springs of the rivers—and the two streams wind tortuously between steep banks of soft reddish alluvium, looping and meandering deviously over the great plain. In the angle between the two rivers, in Ellenthorpe Ings, lies an old battlefield, and a mile away across the Ure runs the Roman road from York to Aldborough. The modern road divagates from the straight Roman line, but a fieldway, the genuine road, links up with the road from Lower Dunsforth, and the Roman road is plain once more. But that is a West Riding road and out of my syllabus.

The more I consider the whole of this flat land with its warm red brick villages from Helperby to Brafferton, Raskelf to Aldwark, Tollerton to Wigginton, the more I am persuaded that antiquity survives not in the dwellings or habits of the people, but in the old names. I think I know where the red brick comes from, the stiff blue clay dug out of the huge pits at Boroughbridge—tough, laminated stuff; it is not earlier than the seventeenth century, and probably not as old as that; but here are moors, commons, granges, thorpes, thwaites and parks; between Shipton and Sutton are laundes, and two miles south of Easingwold, near Ox Moor, lie the Hawkhills. This is, in general, a peasants' country; originally wet mounds in the glaciated tundra, then isolated clearings in a wilderness of scrub and marsh, then the fields, commons, wood and waste of medieval England, and, following that, the slow, sporadic enclosure of forest, leaving the old system of tillage, fallow, pasture and common almost untouched. The Forest of Galtres is an economic unit with only an economic history. It has had no spectacular outlaw like Robin Hood or William of Cloudesley; it has now no oak like the Cowthorpe Oak, which was reaching maturity when Alfred the Great was winning prizes for reading, or translating Orosius into West Saxon; it has no glades, no deer, no vistas, no forest; and of the population I will say that it is dour, not volatile, not given to excesses of joy or grief, but stubborn, old-fashioned, rather grim and silent. It matches the workaday landscape, and when I walk through this landscape, growing tired of the circle of the horizon, the

Coverham Bridge

Dutch barns, the brick villages, the scattered trees, I have to look to the sky for brief respite. The sky is the real charm of all this flat land—the sky and the reflections it throws on the surfaces of ponds.

Travelling steadily northwards, at last I reach the jumping-off point for the Coxwold–Gilling Gap. It is, for me, at Boroughbridge. Across the Swale the Great North Road swerves a few yards and then takes up once more its direct march to the Wall, and soon the traveller is moving along a slight ridge from which he looks to the left and sees the blue hills of Richmondshire, from which also he looks to the right and sees the dun ruggedness of the Hambledons closing in upon the road. But, for my part, I turn right and take the Stockton road, keeping to it for something less than half a mile and then pursuing a minor road, a narrow by-way, first between high hedges, then through miry, open country. In this heavy land I walk stolidly through its villages and along the straight fringe of its single pinewood. Rooks and peewits are the noticeable birds. Joining the main Thirsk road, I quit it at once for Husthwaite, where I begin to reap the reward of plodding perseverance.

Husthwaite is both a terminal and a starting-point. It marks the eastern limit of the levels and the beginning of the Coxwold–Gilling Gap. Consequently it ought to have something about it, and so it has. The villages of the plain are doggedly functional. The brickwork is uniform, the house-fronts often abut upon the pavement, and sunlight can hardly bring grace to them. In Husthwaite the cottages have variety, the village street is wide, airy, and set upon a westerly slope, the gardens are tended, rose-red and cream with hollyhocks and ramblers, smoke-green with simple topiary, the inn is old, the church dignified on its hill. Best of all, I now stand upon the crest of the first low roll of land above the patch-work plain and look north to the white tower of Coxwold Church, Tom Taylor's Kilburn Horse and a southerly escarpment of the Hambledon Hills. The prospect opens out, is wooded like a park; the trough of the valley is bright, and in late autumn sunshine, is peculiarly attractive.

Knowing that the Coxwold–Gilling Gap owes its existence to a faulting between the tabular Hambledons and the rounded, wooded Howardian Hills, and that it is full of Kimeridge clay, you rather expect to find it flat and uninteresting. From Husthwaite the road runs along the hillside eastwards, then turns north, winds, and brings you into Coxwold. I have heard it said that the *wold* in Coxwold ought to be *wood*—that the real name of the village is Coxwood. But this spelling business is complicated. In the eleventh century occurs *Cucvalt*, the thirteenth gives *Cukewald*, the sixteenth has the unfortunate *Cuckold* and the seventeenth *Cuckwold*. Evidently *Coxwood* is not authoritative. Coxwold was formerly a market town, and even to-day it has more than the dignity of a village, a certain stateliness, a knowledge of its own importance. For not merely did Sterne live here for seven years, appointed to the curacy by Lord Fauconberg in 1760, and not only did he give great content to his parishioners. Here in Coxwold was the famous grammar school founded by Sir John Hart in 1603. Here, overlooking the church, is Colville Hall, of the early seventeenth century. Shandy Hall, probably of about the same date, was remodelled in the eighteenth century. The church is full of Fauconberg memorials. These, perhaps, are things to be forgotten, but what will remain in mind is the spacious dignity of the little place, its very English charm.

Leaving Coxwold I made for Byland Abbey, and the road was now level, now steep, with sudden sharp rises and not many dips. Road engineers had been at work; they had concreted a motor-way across the ford just beyond the village school in Coxwold, and here and there they have straightened out the old, crooked road. Taking by preference the old road, I noted in how few years vegetation will cover and conceal neglected tar macadam. Thus I entered the Gap, rather rough hillside with bracken and coarse pasture to my left, a series of low, wooded hills to my right, and the grid running through the middle. Oak and ash are the chief trees hereabouts, and Friesian cattle are common. Friendly country, all this. The low hills, I should say, are rock overlaid with the Kimeridge clay, and hence their roundness. The soil is dark chocolate in colour, and seems rich. The fields are mostly pasture, with cornland away to the south. Unlike Rievaulx, Byland Abbey is architecturally all of a piece, dating from the late twelfth and early thirteenth centuries, whereas Rievaulx was in building from 1131 to about 1230. The ruins of Byland are imposing enough, but the situation is not naturally favourable except to ascetically inclined monks. The best view of it is that from the Oldstead road, or from the windows of the inn, but the monks who built the place took the site because they had to move away from their original site down towards the Rye from Old Byland. Tradition declares that the Rievaulx monks were annoyed by the Old Byland bells competing with their own, and were the more influential body. Had they been Mahommedan monks the question would not have arisen. Mahommedans have no bells.

Not far away there is a battlefield which never finds mention in the histories. It took place at Stocking, in narrow glen country, where Robert Bruce fought and won. Then he made a temporary headquarters at Byland Abbey and, I suppose, ravaged the district pretty thoroughly. Here also at Byland Abbey was buried the great Mowbray. "Roger de Mowbray, who dy'd in the Holy Land, founded this Abbey, A.D. 1134, for Monks of ye Cistercian Order. And in the 9th of King Richard 2nd A.D. 1385 Tho., Earl Marshal, Earl of Nottingham, Lord Mowbray and Segrave, did Deed, recite, ratify and confirm, this his said Progenitor's Foundation." This appears in Sam Buck's engraving of the North Prospect of the Ruins of Byland Abbey near Thirsk in Yorkshire, 1721. The situation of Byland is damp. Springs break from the ground at the foot of the hanging woods.

Wass lies at the foot of Wass Bank, a one-in-five route to Helmsley alternative to the Sutton Bank road, and to the right as you climb you will find an old box-tree more than big enough to conceal a dozen Toby Belches. Wass is not old. The inn is the Wombwell Arms. All the inns in this region favour the county families, except in Thirsk, which has the usual Red Bears, Three Tuns, Golden Fleeces and Crowns. The inn-sign at Wass bears the Wombwell device with the motto *In Well Beware*. Wass, however, has still another sign : THE SHOP, WASS.

Between Wass and Ampleforth the undulating road runs above the floor of the Gap, picturesque but not magnificent, interesting because the traveller is aware that on the summit of the moor above him stand the stumuli and double dikes of prehistory, an ancient settlement of flint-workers explored by the monks of Ampleforth College. College and monastery, Ampleforth stands below road-level and is built mainly in French style, like the châteaux of the Orleans district. There is, however, some castellated building and some in modern style. The place looks wealthy, well kept, up-to-date, and one thinks with envy of the boys who spend their schooldays in such handsome surroundings under the care of learned Benedictines. The village of Ampleforth, however, is not impressive, and the children I saw there were not clean. At Oswaldkirk the Gap widens and ends, for Gilling lies two miles south across the levels. I wonder if James Tankerley, once rector of Kirbymoorside, used to walk this way from Byland Abbey to Kirby, "and one night he blew out the eye of his concubine there." His body found repose in the dark waters of Lake Gormire; his ghost walked.

John Dryden used to say, at Wills's coffee-house, that he learned to write English prose by reading Tillotson, and any student of prose-writing will testify to the ease, grace, clarity and simplicity of Tillotson's sermons. He preached his first sermon in the little old church here at Oswaldkirk. The inn —the Malt Shovel—is a late seventeenth-century building, rather big for so small a village, and I hope Tillotson was familiar with its fine staircase, which in his day was new. Oswaldkirk Hall is, I think, later in date. Certainly the oldest building in this old village is the tiny church. Ampleforth has a youth hostel, and I noted youth arriving, youth departing, but not particularly youth walking. From Oswaldkirk the road runs to join the York–Helmsley road and climbs the steep of Caulkley Bank, from the summit of which I looked out over many square miles of rich agricultural country towards Malton and the East Riding Wolds. Across this land comes the Vicinal Way, perhaps taking the Gap. Of the present road through the Gap I will say that it is a second-best way of reaching Helmsley from Thirsk. Better, I insist, either to climb Sutton Bank or to face the less sophisticated road up Wass Bank. On the summit of Wass Moor, edging the road, grow wild raspberries. Sutton Bank gives access to Lake Gormire, caused by a vast subsidence of cliff long ago.

This lake has no outlet, and hence, of course, it is reputed fathomless. It is a gloomy pool, edged with hazels. In certain lights the shadows on the crag take on the appearance of a huge, lean stockbroker in top-hat and clawhammer coat taking a gigantic leap from one pinnacle to another. At the top of Sutton Bank you will often find a number of cars parked on the closely bitten grass. This is a very pleasant though exposed spot. Over the moor to the south gliders take the air from the edge of Roulston Scar. There are afforestation schemes here, to the north of the road to Helmsley, but much woodland has been cut down. Bleak land, yet not too bleak. Neglected dry walling. Open moor. Stony land. That is how I remember this part of the country, and, from the summit of Sutton Bank, the western hills and the great expanse of plain, seen best at sunset.

To different people towns mean different things. To a farmer, Thirsk means agricultural machinery and a market. To a race-goer the place is a vestigial appendix to its race-course. To medieval kings and barons, monks and merchants, it represented a stage on the journey to or from Scotland and the North. To a stage-coach driver it meant a change of horses, and to a modern lorry-driver it means one more little town in a string of little towns along the road from point of departure to point of arrival. To me, Thirsk has always been something of a problem. Not interested in horse-racing and far more interested in the hills to the east than in the plains to the west, I have, perhaps, been a little impatient with and a little unjust to Thirsk. I might have displayed interest in the castle, but the castle disappeared long ago. The Chapel of St James might have fascinated me, but there is now no Chapel of St James. There used to stand thatched buildings in the middle of the market square, but they too have gone, and though no doubt there remains much of interest in Thirsk to-day, I must acknowledge that what, on occasion, has kept me from lingering for more than a couple of hours in the cobbled market square, or looking out equally long from the windows of the Golden Fleece, has been the spectacle of a continuous flow of commercial motor-traffic through the heart of the town. Thirsk grew up between two important medieval roads, one to the east of the Cod Beck, the other to the west. The first runs from York to Yarm, the second from Topcliff to Northallerton and Scotland. At Thirsk they converge and all but meet, and the miracle of modern Thirsk is that the place does not develop into the motoring counterpart of Crewe.

Old Thirsk lies on the eastern bank of the Cod Beck, and the oldest houses stand about Long Street and about St James's Green, the *Oldemerkat Sted*, where until 1859 the cattle-market was held. The Three Tuns is the quaintest inn in the town, and the Fleece is the noblest. If the Three Tuns has a stairway with twisted balusters, the Fleece has an early eighteenth-century atmosphere, stabling for forty horses (in the coaching days), some first-class Hepplewhite, and rooms with individual names, like Falstaff's Boar's Head in Eastcheap. Thirsk Hall lies beyond the town up Kirkgate. It has a country Adam dining-room, and the library is in a still earlier style. The old market cross stands in its grounds.

In 1723 Robert Harley passed this way. On the Northallerton road is Spa House. "Half a mile from the town," wrote Harley, "passed by the Spa, which is covered by a thatched house, built by the Corporation, who have placed a poor old woman who makes what little profit she can from those who resort thither. It is said to have wrought many cures on lame and rickety people." By 1859 the well ran dry and not even the prayers of the lame and the rickety could stimulate a renewal of the flow.

There was little in Thirsk to delay me, and, strolling down Vinkle Street into Old Thirsk, I took the road to Easingwold. An unimpressive mile brought me to a farm-road, a rutted track that, provided I kept my wits about me, would bring me to Bagby. The farmsteads hereabouts ought, I think, to be called granges. They look exactly as a grange should look. They were, though, mostly built during the period of agricultural expansion at the end of the eighteenth and in the first years of the nineteenth centuries, and barns, granaries, stables and wagon-sheds have the spaciousness and solidity and shapeliness of that period. The farms are big and handsome, and the cottages have a thoroughness in their building which, though a trifle Benthamite, is still handsome. Dutch barns add to the dignity of these farms, and mechanization has come to stay. Arable and pasture share the landscape fairly evenly.

Bagby was a small place. First I came to the church, but the door was locked and I had to peer through the windows. The interior had been wantonly restored, I thought; yews fifteen feet high were growing out of some of the graves. Down below, tough roots were twining between yellow ribs and feeling their way into eye-sockets, no doubt, but the spectacle was a mere flash of morbid picturing and I did not dwell upon it. Many of the tomb-slabs were of the early nineteenth century, but in the soft stone—sandstone—the inscriptions were indecipherable. Bagby was a quiet, secluded spot. Bagby Hall was a farm, looking out on to the road with prosperous complacency. It had an interesting chimney-stack.

The villages in this area are brick and tile. There is no thatch and no cob walling. The bricks are narrow, and mellowed to a rosy hue. So, too, are the tiles. They blend into the landscape, and when in company with simple topiary work, the rectangular buildings with rectangular windows, up-and-down palings, square garden gates and low brick walls, they make a good pattern, in which eighteenth-century formality finds room for a splash of quaintness and colour in the inn-signs. The Greyhound at Bagby had a recognizable greyhound in pale grey against a sombre background.

Beyond Bagby the road dipped and swerved, and across the dip from north-west to south-east the pylons marched majestically into a distance pale violet or dove-grey. Brought up on H. G. Wells, I am not repelled by pylons. I much admire the way they range the country, and how they encourage the growth of buttercups at their iron feet.

At Balk I found a three-story water-mill now derelict and emptied of its machinery. The millrace had the merest trickle of water amongst choking pond-weeds, and the ground floor of the mill was full of rubbish. In the village the thatch had vanished, and there was little life and less beauty. Not quite sure of my direction, I went to talk to two lads playing by the beck. I pointed down the beck.

"Is Thirkleby that way?" I asked.

They nodded.

"Is there a mill at Thirkleby?"

They nodded.

"Is it derelict?"

They stared at me.

"Is it abandoned?"

They went on staring.

"Is it working?" I asked.

"Oh, ay! Ye follow t'beck, mister! Keep to this side till ye come to t'bridge! Then cross and go on and ye'll come to Pollard's Mill."

I left the road and followed the beck—Thirkleby Beck—Fishing for York Tradesmen—had some trouble with the bridge, which was dense with dead thorn, more trouble with a herd of steers, but at last came to Pollard's Mill. The miller was getting ready to go to a meeting at Thirsk, but delayed himself to show me round. He was a big man, straight-backed, with huge bones, swarthy and active-eyed, a long-headed Nordic, and the Miller of Thirkleby, I said to myself, ought to be just like that. The mill showed a blending of very old and very new. The old water-wheel had gone, though the dark stain on the old wall showed where it had formerly threshed round. The mill was turbine-driven, and water-power activated the turbines. Pollard showed me a huge ranking of accumulators, but they were out of commission. A hundred yards south of the mill the grid stalked across country, and when restrictions were removed he would bring in the Electricity Board to help him run the place. In spring, particularly in May, the volume of water coming down the beck fell off. At intervals he had to close the sluice and wait until the water rose.

The dim interior was filled with the sound of machinery and everything was covered with fine, mealy dust. The overhead baulks were stout oak, the walls were old stone. His Derbyshire greys were spinning in a circular framework of oak, and a sack of barley was slowly feeding the mill. One of the millstones had come out of an old windmill that Pollard himself had helped to dismantle.

"The thing was derelict," he said, "and a blot on the landscape."

I didn't realize that an old windmill could be a blot on the landscape—didn't people even buy windmills and set up housekeeping in them?—but I was ready to take his word for the fact.

The rest of the first floor was new—no oak—and filled with sacks of meal. Down below, leaning against the wall, were two more millstones, blues this time. There were wheelbarrows made of solid oak. Indeed everything about Pollard's Mill was very solid, very English. He himself, the miller, was a bowdlerized Chaucerian miller, and about him I need say no more than that.

Crossing the footbridge over the beck I went northwards across the fields towards the Kilburn road. The last field took me to High Osgodby Grange, and had a couple of magnificent grey horses pastured in it. They were not the first greys I had seen that day, and when the farmer pulled up his car at his own gate just as I got there, I took occasion to ask him about the greys.

"I've three myself," he said, "and they're popular, as you've found out, in this district. Why? Well, I reckon it's on account of the association with the Kilburn White Horse. There was a time when a grey would fetch five pounds more than a horse of another colour, but nowadays there's too many of 'em about for that. We've had grey stallions walking the district. Ay. But"—and he added this regretfully—"machinery's replacing horses. A man has to keep pace with the times. I've three tractors on the go myself."

Three grey horses, three tractors. No mistaking which were the more beautiful, but a man, unfortunately, has to keep pace with the times even though he lives at High Osgodby.

I was now clear of the plain and in the hill country—not the wild heights of Black Hambledon, but the steep and tumbled foothills, and I was approaching Kilburn from the west. The road ran through bracken, rough grazing and hanging wood—broadleaf trees with a good deal of scrub oak. The shout of the cuckoo and the murmur of woodpigeons blended into the hum of a timber-saw. Three men and a landgirl were busy with timber in a clearing to my left. They regarded me with half-hostile curiosity, as though saying, "And what the deuce might he want? Why does he stare? How, moreover, does he come to be here, and on foot, and why does he not go away?" I went, and so reached the last hill-crest above Kilburn, where the broken hills were bright with yellow broom and two shades of pink hawthorn blossom. There I leaned on a gate, looked at the fine landscape, and thought hard about nothing at all. I had, you understand, found the ideal spot for doing these things. If I, however, was idle, other folk were not, for all the way from Thirsk, wherever there were root-crops, men were busy with the hoe.

It was above Kilburn that I saw a cuckoo perched on the dead bough of an isolated oak. Then I went down into the village and asked for Robert Thompson.

Robert Thompson is a famous man. He has become famous in his own despite, and is in consequence a living paradox. Nowadays the great majority of famous (and notorious) people achieve their fame (or notoriety) not by what they do but by what they say, shout or print. Thompson is no talker and no writer. He is a craftsman, a wood-carver. He is skilled with his hands, and his hands do his thinking and talking. The very first thing he said to me was : "Don't expect me to talk!"

I found his place at the top end of the village, and Robert Thompson completely absorbed in his job. I looked at him, and below the quiet exterior of this middle-aged, greying artist-craftsman I saw the fires burning. A quiet man, almost in Quaker Woolman's sense : "He studied to be quiet." The quietness is eloquent of an inner harmony. Thompson of Kilburn is a man all of a piece. Looking at him, studying him as he worked, I realized something about myself. I have a disconcerting habit of presenting to the world a largish number of different selves : I can, in turn, present the philosopher, the politician, the writer, the clown. Whichever way you turn Robert Thompson and from whatever angle you look at him, he is the same unified personality, the same concentrated individuality.

Many thousands of people in this and in other countries know of Robert Thompson and his work, and more have admired the work than know the man. Nevertheless I have to say my say about him and his work, and I shall try to be discriminating. Thompson is a master-craftsman in hand-carved oak. He has been at his job for over twenty-five years. Before 1939 he was training up a whole school of wood-carvers to match the famous Ripon carvers of medieval days, and in his workshop he employed thirty-three men and boys, local fellows every one. He would have no specialization in his workshop. Specialization would have nullified his protest against the mechanical production of goods, against the twentieth-century machine-made, glue-and-sawdust furniture in cheap materials and of uniform pattern. The oak he uses comes from trees south of the village. No foreign wood is tolerated. The tools he uses were made to his own specifications, and their designs are based upon the patterns of wood-carving implements used by the medieval carvers. His work-shop now reminds me of William Morris's *News from Nowhere*, and now of an Italian, German or Dutch Renaissance school of artistry. The sightseers bring in an alien, almost hostile atmosphere. They come from the world of machines into a world where the adze is still a monarch amongst tools. There is no hurry here, no working against the clock, no split-second timing of the job, no worry about waste. You will find plenty of rejected fragments, spoiled pieces, rough drawings : on the wall a crude caricature of Adolf Hitler, with darts sticking into it, and, above the head, an inscribed aureole : "He has had it!" An atmosphere of industry, of industry in a quiet place.

That is what the Mouse symbolizes—the Mouse carved on every piece of work sent out from the Kilburn workshops, the Mouse that is Thompson's sign-manual. Industry in a quiet place. That mouse may be found in three hundred English churches. It lurks in the library wing of Leeds Girls' High School, in the Catterick Bridge Hotel, in the Memorial Dining Hall at Haileybury. It tells its silent story in the United States Naval Academy at Annapolis in Maryland. The five-foot memorial candlesticks of H.M.S. *Barham* in Westminster Abbey carry it. For twenty-six years Thompson has worked for Ampleforth Abbey. The sign of the George Inn at Piercebridge carries the emblem of the mouse, too, and a good deal of carved woodwork in York Minster. I cannot, however, pause to complete the catalogue of Thompson's achievements; I hope that he himself will one day do this. For the moment I am occupied by another problem—the problem of hand-work and machine labour.

I have some awe of machines and the things they do. A machine is a super-tool of miraculous precision, regularity and power of production, yet, in operation, the machine, not the stuff with which the machine is dealing, is the controlling agent. The pattern is imposed by the machine, and often I fear the machine patterns not only things but also human life. Now on the other hand the manual worker knows the potentialities of his material. He has a grasp of what it will and will not do, and the tooling is guided by the material. Consequently a man like Robert Thompson has much to teach the man of machines. I suspect also that the man of machines has something to teach the handicraftsman. Somewhere between the mass-producer and the individual craftsman there is a place for one who will make the best use of both tools and super-tools.

I spent a long time in Thompson's two-story wooden workshops. I watched Thompson designing. I watched his men at work. I tried to handle the adze and went in fear of cutting off one foot at least. I went through the records of his achievements. I admired the furniture of his office. Most of all I enjoyed the smell of wood and the fact that Thompson left me entirely to my own devices. I wasn't there to report; I was there to get an impression of the man and his work, and I think I shall remember the man longer than I remember his work, fine though the work is. That, I consider, is proof that that day I met an artist.

Kilburn village is in reality Low Kilburn, a quiet, pleasant place with a stream running alongside its cottage gardens and an air of being in the hills. Sheltered, secluded and yet famous, its name presupposes the existence of another village —High Kilburn, on the hill above Low Kilburn. I climbed that hill and found High Kilburn. The red-faced, rather pear-shaped gentleman pushing a lawn-mower over an irregular patch of grass, not a lawn, in front of his house thought High Kilburn with its village green a finer place than Low Kilburn, but then he lived in High Kilburn. Low Kilburn has older houses and a more clothed appearance. High Kilburn has an aloof dignity and a Quaker quietness.

Beyond High Kilburn I missed the overgrown by-road that would have taken me through Kilburn Thicket and Fox Folly to the main Coxwold road. Thus, with my shadow lengthening rapidly, I pushed on to Oldstead—there is no Newstead here—with hanging wood to my right and alpine meadow-slope to my left. At the inn I went forward to fetch an irregular arc towards Coxwold, and behind me, rosy in the late afternoon sunlight, Byland Abbey against its green background seemed poised to take wing for the upper air.

Royal MS. 15, A.xx. in the British Museum once belonged to Byland Abbey, and a monk of Byland filled the blank pages at the end of the volume with ghost stories. Dr M. R. James translated and edited them, and the Yorkshire Archæological Society published them. They make fascinating reading.

The ghost that appeared to Snowball the tailor in the time of Richard II took the shape of a raven, then of a peat-stack, of a dog with a chain, then of a man whose "inner parts could be seen through his mouth, and he formed his words in his entrails and did not speak with his tongue—a man of great stature, horrible and thin, and like one of the dead kings in pictures." Another allowed itself to be caught by a woman, who carried him on her back into a certain house in the presence of some men, "one of whom reported that he saw the hands of the woman sink deeply into the flesh of the ghost as though the flesh were rotten and not solid but phantom flesh."

What, however, of this? As I came near the village of Coxwold I encountered two men as it seemed in altercation. One of them held a small bundle of brown feathers in his hand.

"'Tis living," said one.

"An't please your honour," said the other, "the bird is dead."

"It is not dead," said the first.

"Alack a day, it will never fly again," said the second.

"It shall fly," said the first vehemently.

"Alas, it cannot fly," replied the other.

I saw they were talking of a bird they had found upon the road, a poor thing that had lain motionless, with blood upon its ruffled feathers, and dust all besprinkled upon the blood, and its eyes filmed over and dull.

"'Tis some wretch with a stick," said my Uncle Toby, flourishing his own silver-mounted cane.

"An't please your honour," said Trim, standing very straight, "I think 'tis some motorist."

"'Tis a shame," said my Uncle Toby.

Trim wiped away a tear.

"Murder," said my Uncle Toby, and stamped his foot so that he winced with the pain of it. "At Steenkirk and Landen our soldiers did their duty, but they did no murder."

"True," said Corporal Trim. "And as your honour knows, in Mackay's regiment——"

My Uncle Toby whistled "Lillibulero."

"What kind of bird is it?" he asked at length.

"A sparrow, an't please your honour. I have heard them called winged rats. And now 'tis dead."

"But this morning," said my Uncle Toby, "it was full of joy and gladness. It greeted the sun with a chirrup and fluttered its wings cheerfully against the dawn. It chattered to its mate and fed its young ones, scattering morning dew upon its breast plumage. You shall bury it, Trim."

"Indeed I will," said Trim.

"You shall bury it," said my Uncle Toby, "at the foot of the glacis, where is the little kind of esplanade where you and I confer and hold councils of war upon."

"Near the sentry-box, your honour?"

"Near the sentry-box, Trim." My Uncle Toby paused. Then he nodded.

Trim picked the dead bird up out of the hand that held it, and wrapped it carefully in his handkerchief.

"'Tis life one moment and death the next. Down goes Dick and down goes Joseph. We stand," said Trim, "like oak trees, and then there comes a wind and down we go."

"All of us," said my Uncle Toby. "'Tis life."

"And death," said Trim, near to weeping.

"Why, as to that," said my Uncle Toby, "it was God's child and God will take care of its poor soul, as, I hope, He will take care of yours, Trim, and mine."

"Amen," said the corporal.

They turned aside along a little path I had not seen. It ran diagonally across a meadow towards the houses, and they went along it, talking as they went.

Easingwold, as it stands to-day, looks maybe two hundred years old, maybe less. It is as though, in the Napoleonic era, when the farming community enjoyed several prosperous decades, the old market town in the Vale of York was almost entirely rebuilt of red brick and slate or tiles. Then Easingwold turned over and went to sleep for a century. Nowadays there are, on the fringes of the town, a few modern houses, but nothing yet disturbs the unself-conscious serenity of the older part of the town. On a Saturday morning in June 1945 I looked in vain for the population of Easingwold. A tabby cat asleep in a shop window did not even lift its head as I went by, and I saw no dogs, no children, no grown-ups in the silent street. No doubt I was deceived by the impression I got, no doubt Easingwold is really a go-ahead place aware of the latest developments in science and the latest movements in literature and the arts, and no doubt there was somebody somewhere in the town who would be able to show me the parish coffin and unlock the church door for me. Since, however, I could ask no questions because there was nobody to answer, and because I can revisit Easingwold whenever I please, I set off out of the town on the northern road to nowhere.

Before I was clear of the edges of habitation I saw a row of old thatched houses and a man. Said I to the man, "How old are those houses? Jacobean, by the look of their brickwork."

"Much too old," he said. "I know nowt about Jacobean, but I do know this, that they've stood condemned a devil of a time. They ought to be pulled down."

He stared at them, vindictively demonstrating that Easingwold contained at least one spirit scornful of decayed thatch, rotten timber and Jacobean brickwork. I too stared at the cottages. They had sunk below the level of the picturesque into squalor.

"You're right," I said. "It's time for them to go."

"More than time!" he corrected me angrily. "Why

192

haven't they been pulled down? Why hasn't anybody done anything about 'em? Lousy, that's what they are!"

"Certainly disreputable," I said.

"Dynamite!" he barked. "They'd be all the better for a stick or two of dynamite!"

I left him still barking and went my way. North of the town the countryside had more pasture and meadow than the farming-land near Thirsk, and the Herefords, Jerseys, Lincolns and Holsteins seemed in excellent shape. Good dairy-farming country. Prospects for the hay harvest looked excellent, and small flax fields of five or six acres diversified the greens of the landscape. About flax and linen, though this has nothing to do with Easingwold, my doctor tells me that the sheets at present on his bed were hand-woven at Guisborough a generation or two ago from local grown flax. The linen, he says, is rather coarse in texture but is stout enough to last a generation or two longer.

From a long way off I saw Crayke Castle among trees on the last outlier of the Hambledon Hills. Had there been no castle there I should have been surprised, for medieval strategy if nothing else demanded that there should be one, and the eighteenth century, anyhow, would certainly have built a ruin there. There is little doubt, however, that a castle of Crayke existed in the time of Hugh Pudsey, who supped at Crayke in 1195 as he was travelling south from Durham. This was the bishop's last journey, for, riding on to Howden, he died there. Crayke and castellation existed in natural concord, and so, too, did Crayke and religion, Crayke and commerce. St Cuthbert had set his mark upon the church and an anchoress named Etha lived tranquil and died happy there in 767. Crayke, moreover, stood upon the medieval road that ran from York through Coxwold and Thirsk to Northallerton and the north, and this explains the association of the place with medieval royalty. John Lackland stayed here, and, each in his turn, the first three Edwards. As for the castle of Crayke, it was built by a fighting bishop "of harde stone, the walles wherof v fote thicke; the same is all vaughted underneth throughout and is thre storie height above the vaught."

By order of the Commons of England it was dismantled

o 193

in 1646 and 1647, no garrison thereafter to be maintained in that stronghold.

When I got there I found the castle still a stronghold, and still stoutly garrisoned. In the castle grounds I came face to face with a robust land-girl. She looked at me for a moment and then fetched Mrs Barlow. Mrs Barlow was the châtelaine, and the garrison consisted of twenty-three land-girls in permanent occupation, together with a fluctuating number of volunteers who settled in for a week or more at a time. Crayke had been thus garrisoned for three years.

This building they occupied, however, was not the castle Hugh Pudsey supped in. Only the merest trace of the old castle is left, and I was looking at the Great Chamber which, before 1939, had been a big, old, draughty, chilly, inconvenient and expensive private residence, a nightmare to every domestic worker that looked at it. Picturesque, certainly, and not lacking in nobility, but hardly built for comfort.

Mrs Barlow showed me what dog-hearted officialdom had done to the interior. It had stained some of the original oak flooring a dull and awful brown. It had knocked extra flooring together and put in cheap staircasing. It had stuck a villainous Victorian firegrate into a vast arched fireplace, and had painted the arch itself, of good freestone, a smoky red. Then Austrian prisoners of war had walked in and added a little Continental artistry to the wall-plaster of one room— a repeated pattern of callipers and saw-edging in pale blue and pink. The effect, Mrs Barlow thought, was singularly hard on the eye. Much of the original oak, however, was still *in situ*, and the great beams across the lounge had carved rosettes. The fireplaces throughout were repulsive. Then we came to the "vaught"—a massive bit of barrel-vaulting of stone full of gas cookers, women helpers and hot air, the best-equipped and most comfortable room in the whole hostel. Two-tier sleeping-bunks are bad enough in ships' cabins. In a W.L.A. hostel they are intolerable.

I ought to quote Mrs Barlow's acrid words about the water supply, which had a careless habit of failing altogether. Certain officials had visited the place without giving warning of their intention, and Mrs Barlow had provided them with tea. When they had drunk it, she asked them, "How did you enjoy your tea?"

"Very well," they said.

"I'm glad!" she told them. "The water with which I brewed it was nice, green, stagnant rainwater. It was all I had."

The village of Crayke stands on a hillside, with no memorials of antiquity except a half-timbered cottage, an ancient crowned shield built into the front of the Methodist chapel, and the church. The roof of the church is good fifteenth-century work—a tie-beam roof in three bays with curved supports springing from moulded wooden corbels. The pews, plainly panelled, with moulded knobs to the bench-ends, are, I think, Restoration work. The pulpit is Jacobean. I found two mutilated figures, effigies of the late sixteenth century, the male figure in armour, the lady in a ruff and a Mary Queen of Scots cap. On the floor of the bell-tower I discovered three oak chests. The biggest, six feet long, is carved out of one solid block of oak, the second is similar but smaller, the third is seventeenth-century work. The north side of the chancel has an ancient altar-stone found in the basement of the castle—whether actually in the "vaught" or not I do not know. It bears two small crosses, one central, one towards the top right-hand corner. In the sacrarium stood two chairs, dating about 1650, with winged angels at the back. An attempt is being made to preserve the embroidery.

So much for Crayke. Crayke Manor lies at some distance from the village and is a fine example of a Jacobean manor-house in this part of Yorkshire. As it stands, the house has been almost doubled in size, the newer portion in keeping with the old. The hall panelling is not original to the house but was brought from Howley Hall near Morley in the West Riding. The wainscoting, or some of it, is original, and there is a fine staircase and gallery.

At Brandsby I expected to find the water-mill working at full pressure, but the millpond was a weedy mire, the millrace was dry, the millwheel had gone and the mill itself was occupied by a farmer's car and three fine pigs. Brandsby Mill was, in the sixteenth century, a mill. It has possibly fallen on evil days because the village of Brandsby has prospered. I found several prettily designed houses, largish, with spacious and well-tended gardens. Yew hedges five feet high bore witness to the tastes and status of the owners, and whether Mr Cholmely of Swarth Gill designed them, caused them to be built, or merely knew all about them, these houses are well matched with their environment. I did not, however, altogether like the look of Brandsby Hall as I saw it from the road. It is the seat of the Cholmelys, and was designed by the architect who designed Hackness Hall near Scarborough, Thomas Atkinson of York. He set it well away from the village in a dingle, built it of dark stone and gave it a background of deciduous trees. When I saw it there was no graciousness of sunlight upon it. From Brandsby the land rolls upward in a long, steep climb with woods on each side of the road. Near the summit I looked for the old race-course on Black Moor, which nowadays is neither black nor moor. The outlines of the race-track are still fairly clear, and as I came to the summit of my climb to an area devastated by foresters I fell to thinking about the abandoned race-courses of England, how some were overwhelmed by the nineteenth-century growth of towns, and how race-courses without railway stations near them failed to attract either the public or the owners, and finally how the racing racket (and it was a racket) succeeded in centralizing its activities in profitable places close to thickly populated areas. When there were race-meetings on Black Moor and Black Hambledon the commercial exploitation of leisure had not begun. In the eighteenth century, for example, a heavy-weight squireen would bet that his horse could beat the horse of another heavy-weight squireen, and the public would flock to see the fun.

I came to the lodge of Gilling Park, now a stronghold of the Forestry Commission, and obtained entry despite the notice, NO ADMITTANCE WITHOUT A WRITTEN PERMIT. Within, I had on the one hand a vast plantation of larch and on the other a similar plantation of spruce. Growing rampant amongst both groups of conifers I found sapling silver birch in great quantity, but the birch will not survive. The foresters will destroy it. A few magnificent rhododendrons in pink and crimson blossom had survived the regimentation of coniferous woodland, but utility had blasted all the former artistry of Gilling Park.

Farther on, I grew doubtful (for once) of my road and climbed a little hill to look about me.

As I looked back I saw spacious hillsides all newly planted by the Forestry Commission and in front of me a long open patch of country with fifty or sixty wagon-roof, corrugated iron huts and a few Italian prisoners of war in attitudes remotely suggestive of work. I went back and ran into two forest wardens. They took me back to the open patch. One of them pointed.

"This," he said, "was the famous avenue."

"The beeches are gone," I said in dismay.

Here, in former days, had been one of the finest avenues of beeches in the north.

"Ay," said the warden. "Private felling, and not very well cleaned up. Things were vastly different in the old days. My father was a gamekeeper here and I was brought up in the middle of the estate when the drives were well kept, the rhododendrons were properly cut back and everything was in top-class order. But now—well, you see!"

He wouldn't say any more. I walked down the avenue, or what was left of it. The prisoners of war made a show of working with sickles, scythes and motor-scythes of a pattern new to me, and then I came into view of Gilling Castle. There was no sign of life about the place and I wandered about at will. Occasionally an army lorry came thundering past and vanished round a curve in the road. Presently I crossed the gravel and found someone alive. He was mending a leaded window in his workshop, and as he leaned over his doorway I talked to him—a lecture, in fact.

"The glory of Gilling," I said, "was Gilling Castle, with its entrance drive opposite the church. The castle stands on a hill west of the village and the ground falls away steeply on the other three sides. The castle," I continued, "has two frontages, one belonging to the sixteenth century and earlier, the other a remodelling of the early eighteenth century. William Wakefield added the two wings, though the design, everyone hopes, was that of Vanbrugh."

"Ah!" he said. "Vanbrugh!" And he smiled.

"Vanbrugh's work," I suggested, "was beautifully fitted into the landscape."

"What then of Gilling?" he asked.

"I'm not sure," I said. "I looked at it carefully as I came down the avenue and past the cricket field, but I couldn't make up my mind."

"Nor can I," he admitted, "nor anyone else."

"And the tower-house?" I asked.

"Built by Thomas de Etton or his father, reconstructed in 1585 by Sir William Fairfax," he said promptly. "The Lord General Fairfax used to address his letters 'from my poor house at Gilling.'"

"I remember. And there was a great chamber with precious oak panelling and wonderful stained glass."

"Ay. They've gone," he said rather sadly. "Gilling Castle is now the preparatory school for Ampleforth College, the great chamber is now the refectory and nothing is left of the splendour but the flooring and the ceiling. The stained glass? I don't know what's become of it. The panelling was bought by an American millionaire and it may be in America or it may not."

"So," I said, "there's nothing to look at but the exterior."

"Nothing," he said. "I knew it as it used to be. The stained glass had four hundred and fifty shields of arms of the resident gentry of Yorkshire, and the heraldic glass was the work of Baernard Dinickhoff. You'll read all about it in the *Journal of the Yorkshire Archæological Society*, volume nineteen. John Bilson covered the subject pretty thoroughly."

And that was all. The old man seemed glad to have been able to talk about the house as he remembered it in former days, but there was still a shadow in his eyes as I left him, and he turned back to his releading of the broken window as if the energy had temporarily quitted his thin, clever fingers.

Did I, on this occasion, enter Gilling Church? I am almost sure I did, and yet somehow occasion is superimposed upon occasion, impression upon impression, until little is left in my mind of Gilling Church but a vague, edgeless blur.

The modern highway from York to Scarborough lies almost entirely within the limits of the North Riding, and, because it has a good surface and the kinks in the old road have been straightened out, it may be reckoned a fine piece of road-engineering. It is, however, so consistently utilitarian that it tempts to careless driving, and, worse still it has left the old inn at Spitalbeck, of which travellers still speak with nostalgic affection, off the main traffic-line. What Spitalbeck has lost, the Four Alls may have gained.

By the time I had, along this highway, reached the fork for Welburn, I had had enough of wheeled traffic and dropped off the bus. The Howardian Hills—their modern name—lay before me. What I know of their geological structure will pack into few words. They belong to the Hambledon Hill system but are divided from it by the Coxwold–Gilling Gap. They are of Estuarine sandstone, which weathers gently. They carry no moorland, the soil is fertile but not over-fertile, there are acres of good broadleaf trees, and the variety of undulating scene is the result of irregular, wide-spread faulting and shattering of the rock. Possibly Wegener's disciples would know the cause of the faulting, but I do not.

Welburn is much of a muchness with other villages of the North Riding plainland. Its water supply is communal, the church stands well back from the village street. I found nothing to detain me there, and, passing through the military camp where even the marigolds stood to attention, I turned towards Castle Howard and at once recognized that I was moving through carefully planned scenery. Nature was nature still, but nature methodized. There was nothing fortuitous in the grouping of the great trees on each side of the carriage-way. The beeches and horse-chestnuts stood in companies of nine or a dozen, regularly spaced, equidistant, within limits, from the road, and though a few were blasted and a few had fallen, they made as noble a company as those in Hovingham High Wood. I was thankful that the timber merchant had left them alone, and, in swirling drizzle and a high wind, walked along Charles Howard's great avenue to the boundary-wall of the Castle Howard domain. Of dark red sandstone, its castellated Gothic was all of a piece with Pope's *Imitations of Chaucer*. It was Augustan virtuosity amusing itself. Nearly half a mile farther on I came to the Guest House, a long, low, neo-classic building with the avenue passing clean through the middle of it, the old gateposts devilled by name-carvers and scribblers of casual *graffiti*—

soldiers, girls and sight-seers. I believe the L.N.E.R. ran
this Guest House, and the demand for accommodation always
exceeded the supply. Above the archway :

CAROLUS HOWARD, COMES CARLIOLENSIS, HOC
CONDIDIT ANNO MDCCXIX

with a weathered coat of arms and three swallows' nests, the
parent birds feeding their young.

I came to the Obelisk, standing at a crossroads of some
importance on the crest of a long, low ridge. Here Charles
Howard had let himself modestly go in heroic couplets :

If to perfection these plantations rise,
If they agreeably my heirs surprise,
This faithful pillar will their age declare
As long as time these characters will spare.
Here then with kind remembrance read his name
Who for posterity performed the same.

CHARLES THE III EARL OF CARLISLE
OF THE FAMILY OF THE HOWARDS
ERECTED A CASTLE WHERE THE OLD CASTLE OF
HENDERSKELF STOOD, AND CALLED IT CASTLE HOWARD.
HE LIKEWISE MADE THE PLANTATIONS IN THIS PARK
AND ALL THE OUTWORKS, MONUMENTS AND OTHER
PLANTATIONS BELONGING TO THE SAID SEAT.
HE BEGAN THESE WORKS
IN THE YEAR MDCCII
AND SET UP THIS INSCRIPTION
ANNO MDCCXXX

On the other side of the Obelisk is a tablet set up in gratitude
to John, Duke of Marlborough, for his famous victories,
then so fresh in memory that the great soldier's genius shone
undimmed even by Jonathan Swift's attack.

The spacious stabling, with its accommodation for coaches
and six, grooms, coachmen, stable-lads, in classic style, was
occupied by lads from Hartlepool camping in bell tents not
far away. They all looked as though they knew a great deal
more than they were willing to speak. Apart from them there
was nobody to talk to, and I went on from the stabling to the

main Vanbrugh erection. In his own day, Vanbrugh's notions of architecture were ridiculed by the wits, but Castle Howard pleased Charles Howard mightily. Charles seems to have had a similar sort of mind, working on big-scale projects and perhaps never quite sure how they would turn out in the end. Now I do not care what I am expected to think of Castle Howard; I shall set down what I honestly believe. First, there is, to my mind, something wrong with the ground-plan. A classic or neo-classic building ought to be graspable by the eye and the understanding at the first glance, like Como Cathedral. Castle Howard is not. The ground-plan is full of ingenuous afterthoughts: "Let's stick on a bit here, a bit there," and "More weight, a greater degree of massiveness!" and "Good Lord, we've forgotten the coal-palace and the bell-tower over the usual offices!" Secondly, there was something not quite normal about Vanbrugh, something aberrant, megalomaniac. Suppose Caligula had spent a year at Versailles, then had come to England and resolved to build a country residence, Castle Howard is the kind of building he might have evolved. It is not indigenous, it is theatrical, and it takes a lot of puzzling out.

Within the huge place there were flitting ghosts dressed in modern style, but they were soundless and elusive. I made no contact with them only because I couldn't bring myself to do so. By this time it was raining fiercely and the wind had risen to a gale, but though the main door of the house yielded to the turn of a handle, and though the brass bars and bolts within offered no defence, I did not go in. Through the glass I saw the ponderous marble and the heavy gilding, the monumental solidity, the great staircase, the gallery, the dome, the vast fireplace with a comfortable sofa at an angle in front of it, and I lamented within my heart that this place had nothing to offer me that I wanted. I am not a romantic. I love Congreve, Pope, Swift, Gay, Arbuthnot, Addison and Steele; I have a sneaking fondness also for Robert Harley and Henry St John, for the members of the 'Brothers' Club and the Scriblerus Club. But this was not Augustan. It lacked restraint and genuine power. It was, in brief, cinema stuff. It led me to think what a film director, Hollywood style, Vanbrugh would have made. Still, his work pleased Charles

Howard, third Earl of Carlisle, and it has pleased many people since Charles Howard's time.

The Howards have gone from Castle Howard, and now as I write the place is a boarding-school for girls. Reconnoitring the exterior, I found the gymnasium—wall-bars, vaulting-horse, scales, ropes and all—but the girls were on holiday and the place was empty. Through another window I caught a glimpse of pictures in gilt frames, and then I turned away. I had not been good-mannered in my approach to this build-ing, but was I to blame, or was the building? My memory tells me that famous men have visited Castle Howard, and reminds me how vastly they appreciated the noble house, the park, the hospitality. Did not Sidney Smith pay tribute to this grandeur? I forget. But well I know that when I was young and the Howards still lived at Castle Howard the mansion was famous for its collection of old masters and its *grande dame*.

By way of a field-track I went down to the lake, passed a terrace of cottages with neglected gardens, and got into muddy ways where timber-men had been busy. Then I found my way back to the Obelisk, passed a fine herd of Ayrshires on the right of the road and retraced my steps to Welburn. The gale was beating through the beeches, and they looked none too safe in that wild weather. Back on the great highway I struggled westward against the wind for a mile and then turned downhill towards the gorge of the Derwent, Kirkham Priory and the hamlet of Crambe, which the villagers call *Crawm*. Kirkham Priory—what is left of it—stands on the East Riding bank of the river, and travellers by rail between York and the coast see it pretty plainly. They catch glimpses also of the winding, wooded gorge. What they miss is the peace and solitary beauty of this river valley. It is known to anglers, but to few others. From the road above Crambe I saw the quiet reach of the Derwent by Kirkham, with a wide belt of fireweed on the hillside above the woods, and then I went down to Crambe. Not more than a mile from the busy highroad, Crambe is one of the few quiet places that people looking for quiet have not yet discovered. A few cottages, a few country folk, a lean and amiable vicar, a church with a good fifteenth-century tower, a font of the Transition period, a handsome Jacobean pulpit and a very wide Norman chancel-arch, a Norman doorway, a couple of high-placed Norman windows and some evidence of pre-Conquest work, and that is Crambe. From there I went along an unfenced road through pasture, and stayed for a while by the weir which marks the navigational terminus of the Derwent. On the opposite bank stood an imposing mill with a fine active millrace, and the river itself, much swollen since leaving its gathering-grounds below Lilla Howe far to the north-east, was here about thirty yards wide, swift and noisy over its shallow bed.

At Bossall, on the road to Stamford Bridge, stands a very handsome modern house of red brick in Queen Anne style. The church has a good Norman door. Beyond Bossall the road forks south to Sand Hutton, and here I entered a timber belt and wilder country. On the south side of the road there used to be masses of rhododendron, but they appear to have gone. Miraculously the giant red-barked Scots pines have been left. They like a light soil, and here had reached full growth. This was no neat afforestation scheme under government control, for self-sown birch grew rampant amongst the conifers, and briars, brambles, bracken, honeysuckle, hedge-maple and thorn dominated the fringes. Where the woodland had been cleared there was heath, and now and again a track opened up into the woods. A detailed survey of this area might prove scientifically valuable.

Thus at last I crossed the border into the East Riding at Stamford Bridge with its weir, motor yachts, mill and quiet centre. Fishermen joined me at the bus-stop. They had had a poor day.

I think, though I am not sure, that the road by which I reached Stamford Bridge was, in medieval days, much more important than it is now. It keeps to the Derwent gorge, it does not miss a single village on the way, and it makes for Malton. By way of Leavening, it also makes for the remote villages of the Yorkshire Wolds, and by unfrequented roads one may reach Beverley. I recommend the journey to all who prefer quiet roads and pleasant landscapes.

Gate Helmsley, on the main road between Stamford Bridge and York, offers nothing of vivid interest, and with

that note I settled back in my seat and looked for the towers
of York Minster across the strip of plain between the road—
Harold Godwinsson's road, no doubt—and the city.

Following the northward line of the River Foss out of
York, I found Earswick a pleasant enough dormitory village
in the midst of the flat plain. Strensall Camp and Strensall
Common are difficult of access to the ordinary traveller, and
I left them both alone with the single remark that Strensall
Common is as near an approach to the medieval Forest of
Galtres as this generation is likely to see. From Strensall,
which has nothing remarkable to recommend it, I went almost
directly northward, and as I went I noted that though the
water-table hereabouts is never more than a dozen feet below
the rich alluvium of the surface, the land is well enough
drained for the flourishing of good broadleaf trees. Lom-
bardy poplar is scarce, ash and sycamore are more common,
and grow very well. Beech trees are not numerous, for this is
not the sort of soil they like. Oaks abound, and wherever the
land is wet there are willows. The few Spanish chestnuts had
been deliberately planted and were of no great age. Rushes
flourished in the drainage dykes, and at intervals I came to
little patches of rough woodland which seemed to prove that,
left untilled and untended, this area would slip back into
waste and forest in half a century or less. The alluvial soil is
naturally fertile. It grows potatoes, corn, roots, and the
meadows are good.

Approaching Sheriff Hutton, I found myself climbing : a
mere hundred feet, it is true, from the 100-foot contour-line,
yet in the flatness of the plain a veritable climb. Sheriff
Hutton at its crossroads was busy and talkative. There was a
lot of motor traffic, and the vicar was out on his bicycle. More
than a mile south of the village I had sighted the ruins of
Sheriff Hutton Castle and now I made their nearer acquaintance. The ground upon which they stand has been artificially
licked into shape with some attempt at a ditch and a mound,
and the detached bits of walling and tower stand some seventy
or eighty feet above the motte.

Below the alluvium of the Plain of York lie beds of
Permian and Triassic sandstones and marls, and of these
rocks—mainly sandstone with curious glints in it—the castle

was built in the late fourteenth century. Ruined by 1618, nobody has since then taken any care of it, and farm buildings and silage tanks, a dutch barn and a penthouse with a desolation of smashed tiles, a dry wall, pits full of bottery trees and an L.D.V. hut occupied the layout between the high towers. The fragmentary masonry cannot be climbed, but from its summit no doubt superb views could be obtained of the huge plain to the south and of the broken country of the Howardian Hills to the north and east. I was glad to see Sheriff Hutton Castle neglected. It was a genuine ruin.

I regret that I neglected to look at Sheriff Hutton church, which other travellers should see if only because its architecture ranges in date from the early twelfth century through the thirteenth, fourteenth and fifteenth to modern times. The market-place, I believe, used to be grass-grown, but motor traffic has altered all that, and Sheriff Hutton is a lively little village.

From there I went westward along the low ridge towards Farlington, and, at Mount Pleasant and Cornbrough Farm, saw gracious examples of North Riding farmsteads. For dignity and efficiency they would be hard to match anywhere. The southward-facing slope and equally the northward were rich with some of the finest meadows I have ever seen, the grasses a mixture, the fields big and handsome. This was farming on the generous scale, and I was glad to look at it. Ten miles to the south the towers of York Minster and the huge gasometer squatted on the skyline, and to the north I had broken wooded hills with some wet land in the bottoms. The district produces fine cattle of various breeds, but there seemed to be few sheep, and those Leicester crosses.

Marton Church, between Farlington and Stillington, is good twelfth-century work carefully restored. It has a curious barrel-vaulted chancel, an old font and some good bench-ends. So I came at length to Stillington which, I had always understood, was dull and a trifle arid. I found it pleasing enough, though I don't think I should ever want to live there. It speaks well for the eighteenth-century inhabitants that Sterne was unpopular there, and that when the ice broke under him on one of the Stillington ponds they fished him out only when he was on point of drowning. In 1766, however, he managed to get an Enclosure Act through Parliament for fourteen hundred acres of land in the neighbourhood, and Stephen Croft, then of Stillington Hall, had the honour of rescuing the manuscript of *Tristram Shandy* from the flames when Sterne flung it into the fire in a fury of disappointment because the local gentry couldn't, after a heavy meal, appraise it at its true literary worth. Nowadays Stillington has no enormous importance except that it stands upon the highroad between York and Helmsley. The bus service is not good.

CHAPTER IX

WENSLEYDALE

WHY should I waste my reader's time by telling him that Wensleydale is one of the finest valleys in the country? He knows this already. Why should I catalogue the names of the villages of Wensleydale from Hawes to West Tanfield? He knows them already, and, if he cannot remember them all in their proper sequence, he has only to look at a map. Why, moreover, should I here list the names of the notable books that have been written about Wensleydale when the card-index of the nearest reference library will furnish such a list? I will, however, tell the reader one fact about these books, and, indeed, about almost all the books wherein the North Riding of Yorkshire is described and praised. It is that I have found the majority of them valueless, and I must explain why. First, the nineteenth-century topographers were entirely vague in their descriptive matter. They tell me that a superb view is to be had from such or such a vantage-point but they never describe it in detail. Secondly, they are romantic in their vocabulary. Masham, for instance, "nestles in the green bosom of Wensleydale," and Richmond Castle is "perilously perched on the height of a precipitous crag that frowns sternly over the foaming torrent of the Swale." That kind of writing displeases me. Thirdly, these writers were completely blind to the rural economy of the country they describe, but had eyes like hawks for armorial bearings and ancient pedigrees; they know all about the squirearchy but nothing of the carriers and tradesmen and workers on the land. In brief, they seem never to have heard of the French Revolution, or, if they have, they wish they hadn't. And, lastly, they will give two or three pages to a silly story of how a parson tried to conduct a religious service with wasps in his breeches, and to picturesque superstitions forgotten before the writers were born. If I want to know anything about lead-mining in Swaledale and Wensleydale, or coal-mining in Colsterdale, it is not to the old topographers I turn.

My first business is to clear away one or two popular misconceptions about Wensleydale; misconceptions that owe their origin largely to the books and their propagation to town-dwellers relying upon the books. First, that the weather conditions in Wensleydale are bleak and inhospitable, particularly in winter. On occasion, whole areas are snowbound and villages cut off from the world. That, indeed, is the case as I write these very words. Stalling Busk, for instance, has been cut off for a fortnight. So has Keld in Swaledale and many other hamlets. Drifts are twenty or thirty feet deep, and thousands of sheep have been lost in the hard weather. Farms are isolated. Only journalists and postmen seem to get through, and main roads have had to be cleared time after time. But no travellers are reported missing, and no indigenes, and there have been similar conditions in the Midlands, in Lincolnshire and Devonshire during the last three weeks. On rare occasions people have died of exposure, or have reached home to be thawed out of their ice-casing in front of the fire, but the truth is that the climate, apart from the weather, of Wensleydale is mild rather than severe, there are few days in the year when a foot-traveller, car, motor-van or bus cannot follow the dale from end to end, and still fewer when the whole area is snowbound and inaccessible. Then the stranger is led to believe that the principal industries of Wensleydale are cheese-making and offering hospitality to weary travellers. This is no more true than that Stilton cheese is made at Stilton and that there is a spare bed in every flat in London. The recipe for making Wensleydale cheese is not lost—I shall give it in its place—but there are few farms indeed that have not turned over to milk production and abandoned the cheese-press as a redundant bit of farmhouse machinery. Next, the inquiring spirit is led to think of the Yorkshire dalesman as a broad-spoken, steel-muscled, shrewd-minded fellow whose natural habitat lies about fifteen hundred feet above sea-level and who is never thoroughly happy until he has dug a couple of hundred sheep out of the snowdrift in which they have been buried for over a fortnight. Now there is some truth in such a picture, but it is

208

a journalist's and topographer's picture. It distorts. It emphasizes the wrong things. The truth is that the Yorkshire dalesman is a prodigious worker, he has to turn his hand to a variety of jobs, he knows a lot about his own particular bit of fell country, but he is happier in his own fields and intakes than striding through peat-hags and over the tops that don't belong to him. He does not go for a Sunday afternoon stroll over Penhill for the fun of the thing.

I know how dangerous it is to generalize, but I'm going to risk one or two generalizations. The indigenous population of Lower Wensleydale is of Saxon origin. There is a Scandinavian strain higher up towards the western watershed. The two strains are pretty well mixed. Thus Wensleydale men are not usually tall, loose-limbed and wiry. They are broad-shouldered, dour, strong, and not at all given to exhibitionism. The womenfolk are often dumpy. Wensleydale men are not much given to the townsman's conception of sport. They have shotguns but no football boots or hockey sticks, and their wives are not crazy on dancing.

From end to end Wensleydale is pastoral country. It stands for sheep and cattle, not so much nowadays for horses, though Jervaulx horses were once very famous, and certainly not for goats. There isn't a vast amount of woodland, and there is not much crag. The valley is a wide, glaciated trough, and the pastures climb to the very summits. The villages stand in the dale on both sides of the Ure. Some are attractive, others are dull, and few have any claim to architectural antiquity. For the holiday-maker and investigator, however, the villages afford plenty of accommodation, and that, from the outsider's point of view, is the chief justification for their existence. The attractions lie outside the villages, and I shall not boast of the beauty of Hawes, Carperby, Redmire and Leyburn. Moreover the Wensleydale highroads have their dull sections. The only people whom they do not weary are the saloon-car motorists.

The well-made motor-roads of 1950 were formerly pack-horse roads and sled-trails, drovers' roads and wagon-tracks, and although the economist's word for the Yorkshire dales is *wool,* the word is not comprehensive enough for Wensleydale. North of Preston under Scar, Preston Moor is dense

Hawes in Wensleydale

with abandoned coal-pits. Bolton Moor has old lead-workings. So has Carlton Moor, so has Braithwaite Moor, and you have to realize that Wensleydale villages were formerly, even in the nineteenth century, more thickly populated than they are to-day, that Wensleydale was what Phillips called it, a great mining valley, and that rain, hail, snow or lightning, snowdrift or spate, the mines went on working and the trains of jagger ponies got through. In those days Wensleydale was not a pastoral quietude, for the miners were rough, uncultured fellows much given to drink and primitive living. I suspect that as lead and coal went down the dale gin came up, and it would be interesting to learn the whole history of crimes of violence in Wensleydale. I know that the neighbourhood of Haworth in the West Riding is proud of its tales of orgies of gin-drinking and desperate cloggings, and what is true of Haworth is probably equally true of Wensleydale and Swaledale. This is the country of which Macaulay recorded that in the eighteenth century no traveller ventured there without first making his will. No traveller through this country has, however, spread himself in eyewitness accounts, though Whitaker thought the miners and their families a rude and barbaric race.

Now they have gone. No use, I fear, asking where they went as one by one the coal-pits and lead-mines and smelt-mills closed down. Speight in 1892 records that many of the lead-miners went to Spain, but he offers no details. Wensleydale is now given over to dairy-farming and sheep-raising, to the boarding of holiday-makers, to the training of race-horses and to grouse-shooting. During the war much of the fell-country was used for purposes of military training. Wherever tracked vehicles tore up the fell-slopes, the grouse vanished. The Ure and its tributaries are good trout-streams. Lastly, Wensleydale is full of scenery, and so much by way of preliminary. Now for details.

The motor road from West Tanfield to Masham lies along the northern slope of Lower Wensleydale, with spacious views of a landscape pleasant without nobility, a delectable land in the midst of which rises the spire of Masham Church dwarfed by distance. Crossing the Ure, the road mounts the hill into the big market-place. Nowadays there is no market

at Masham, but the cross with its five worn steps and slender
upright of dark stone is still there, with the ball on top and
four fenced-in trees planted round it, just as it was when,
many years ago, I first went to Masham. The trees, curiously,
do not seem to have grown at all. In this market square, on
most days in the year, there is solitude without privacy, for
the silent houses stand solidly gazing at one another across
a cobbled emptiness. The variety of the houses is characteristic of Lower Wensleydale. The King's Head is tall and
has a slated roof. Next door has a lower-pitched roof of
broad stone tiles but with chimneys taller than those of the
hotel. Then comes a small cottage with three windows. Its
roof is still lower, and, of course, its chimneys are much
longer. An old virginia creeper covers the wall of the
chemist's shop on the other side of the square, and at the
south-west corner of the square two or three small but dignified houses seem to draw back from public gaze. Yet, away
from the market-place, there are houses which have the
uniformity of twentieth-century domestic architecture; they
could be matched anywhere between Sandersteads and
Swansea. The older part of the little town has a gratifying
solidity.

In mid-September there is still in Masham a great rallying
and buying and selling of sheep, but in these days it is an
auction and not a fair. Times have changed since Masham
kept open house during the fair for shepherds, farmers and
buyers, but the auction is still important because it is one of
the earliest, if not the earliest, in the country, and the prices
that rule at Masham sheep-auction exercise guidance and
control over the sales that follow it. The sheep here are
mostly the Swaledale breed.

By the south door of Masham Church stands a broken
pillar. It may be a Paulinus Cross or it may not—I will not
pretend to know. As it stands, the pre-Conquest or early
Norman carvings are all but weathered away, and what, in
the lowest group, I took to be a man with either a very large
greyhound or a very small horse might well have represented
some ingenious torture of the damned. The topmost ring of
carvings on this six-foot shaft supposedly represents Christ
and the Twelve, in seven panels. Demons are chained and

mastered in the lowest ring, and in the middle come subjects
from Scripture, of which only the offering of gifts by the
Three Kings of the East can be dimly made out. Fragments
of modern stained glass in their leading lay by the west door;
I remembered that Masham suffered from bombing during
the war. The head of a Burne-Jones lady took my eye; I
could have walked away with it quite easily. Within the
church—I am tempted to call it the Church of Banners—I
found a Breeches Bible in a new oak case, and a lot of old
stonework at the foot of the tower. Some of it was Saxon,
some Norman or Early English. The old, disused font held a
stirrup-pump, the stirrup-pump also part of ancient history.
The picture at the eastern end of the nave is part of a
Reynolds. Nobody knows how it reached Masham, but it
brings grace and colour into the building.

And next, by the Grewelthorpe Road, I went to Hack Fall,
officially closed, as I write this, to the public, "but," said the
lady of Hack Fall House, "people go." I went. I went over
the wall a little higher up the hill, and through an overgrowth
of willow-herb, brambles, bracken and nettles, down the path
to the Falls. It was not a difficult wilderness to thread. Given
a capable man with a sharp billhook the track down to the
water could be cleared within a week. But the king-thistles
and the willow-herb will seed, and next year the job will be
more difficult. Hack Fall Woods could soon lapse into the
primal savagery. Over these woods, though now rather
lightly, lies the hand of the eighteenth-century landscape
artist. Lancelot Brown himself might have arranged the
vistas, saying, "Here should be a pleasaunce, here a classic
temple, here a Gothick ruin." Not far from the Fall, indeed,
there is a Gothick—a sham and tawdry Gothick—summer-
house, with a freestone lintel over the door inscribed *W.A.
1750*. From this point, by a series of wrecked steps, the path
leads to the Fall. You may scramble over the big, slippery
rocks to the river's edge.

I found the current moving at about fifteen miles an hour.
The water was a dark, peaty brown, bright bronze where the
sun fell on it, pale amber where the light shone through the
thin curtains of water. The surface was translucent olive-
green with swift rushes of foam and bubbles over the flat sills

in the bed of the river. There is much shallow, but there are also very deep pools. At this point the gorge is about two hundred feet deep, and only the geologists know how it was scooped out and what energy went into its making. The sight-seer will be more occupied with the voices of the water, with the huge water-worn boulders, the willows with their feet in the river and the moth-like flies, pale grey of wing and long of body, that dart over the surface of the water. He will be concerned not with geological problems but with the gnarled roots exposed in the laminated shales above the Yoredale stone, and with the westering sunlight upon the stream.

There was a bird—I couldn't tell what sort of bird—busy between the river-bank and a mid-stream boulder, a mere flitting shadow against the shadows. There were the fossils I turned up in the shale and the limestone. The afternoon was warm, yet, most curious of happenings, my breath condensed as I stood at the water's edge.

Hack Fall was deserted. Two people wandered up the woods, three stayed by the Fall. When I left, the river had the gorge all to itself and the sky was rapidly darkening. Here one of my phantasies came into play, a habit of my imagination. I pictured Hack Fall in the dead vast and middle of the night, the river roaring to nobody's ears, and, in that deep gorge, no light upon the moving water. I pause to recommend this loop of the Ure to those who are either too stiff in the joints or too sluggish of mind to go fell-walking. It is green, park-like country, rich and pleasant. For myself, from Hack Fall I went on to Middleham.

My knowledge of the turf and of the breeding of blood-stock is both loose and little. If it were accurate and compre-hensive I should have much to tell about Middleham and Matt Peacock's training establishment. I shall regret my lack of education in this matter, acknowledge that horse-racing and the breeding of racehorses fulfil a useful purpose, and pass on to other matters. In the early hours of a summer afternoon I walked into Middleham remembering another Peacock—Robert Neville, Lord of Middleham, called The Peacock of the North, slain in battle at Berwick—and remem-bering, too, how in 1823 Whitaker lamented the decay and neglect that in his time had overtaken Middleham. In mine,

I regret to note that the general spread of better conditions and higher standards of life seems hardly to have reached this place. Leyburn has grown into a holiday resort and traffic centre, Masham has its sheep auction and a great deal of fertile land round it, but at Middleham the high fells are never far away, the land above the village is poor, the fields in the valley are not rich and are, I think, sometimes subject to flooding, and the training of race-horses seems to be so limited and specialized an affair that the general life of Middleham has remained unaffected. It may be, however, that the village lies still under the spell of Middleham Castle, grim stronghold of the Nevilles.

Now Whitaker was entitled to call Middleham Castle "the noblest work of man in the whole County of Richmondshire" if he thought it was, but even he admits that it is not a happy work. I went up to the ruins, paid my sixpence, walked into the bailey and looked at the broken stonework. It compelled my respect, but I withheld my admiration. In truth I have never liked Middleham Castle. I may study it from the antiquarian standpoint and develop interest in the Prince's Tower, the huge keep with walls ten to a dozen feet thick, the relics of the thirteenth century chapel, the wreck of the horse-mill, the bakehouse and the oven, but Middleham Castle is full of cold shadows, and the rolled turf seems dank and loth to thrive. I am always glad to leave this stronghold of the Nevilles. There is no sunshine in it, the stone does not reflect the light, and it is not much visited. It was, I believe, a favourite haunt of Richard Crookback.

After a final glimpse of the empty market-place I took the road over Middleham Moor, facing a cold wind from the north-west. I did not survey the roll of earthwork on the high site of the old motte-and-bailey castle that existed before the Nevilles settled at Middleham, but the four race-horses high-stepping towards the pond at the stud-farm drew my eyes as inevitably as a slow-motion cinema film. So, too, did the great bulk of Penhill over towards Leyburn. Thus I crossed the shoulder of moor and went down into Coverdale.

Any reader in search of the picturesque might do much worse than explore the recesses of Coverdale. He will, I hope, think as I do, that it is very lovely, all this dale. It is

green, sequestered and various. The road through it is, however, an old coaching road, and used to be much busier than
it is now. At Coverham Abbey I found medieval blending
with seventeenth century, and seventeenth century with
modern. I went down a farm-track towards the abbey and on
the way I met first a man walking, then a small girl on a
bicycle. The man answered my questions : yes, I might look
at the ruins, but they weren't anything extraordinary, there
wasn't much of them, and the church, in his opinion, was more
interesting than the fragments of the monastic ruin. I asked
the small girl about the two mailed effigies, but though she
lived on the spot she had never heard of them, knew nothing
at all about them, and was not interested. I think this is typical
of North Riding farming folk living in historic areas. For my
part, I found Coverham Abbey very interesting indeed—
more interesting, I daresay, than the monks who lived there
in the Middle Ages, and more interesting than they proved to
Whitaker in 1823. I shall tell you why.

When the Ministry of Works takes charge of a ruined
abbey or decrepit castle it proceeds to document the place. It
provides a plan. It gives you the whole layout from bakehouse to garderobe, and summarizes the history of the ruins,
telling you who built them, and when, and why. You are
guided round the place by printer's ink. When, however, as
at Coverham, you come across a bit of dogtooth, the face of
a gargoyle, a fragment of pier or arch built into workaday
farm walls, when you find thirteenth century pillars and
arches in the lawns of a seventeenth century manor house,
when you look over a garden wall to examine the grave-slabs
of medieval prelates and find the gardener's bicycle leaning
against a couple of hauberked effigies in stone standing side
by side against the courtyard wall, then you are possibly more
taken by such relics of the past than by the carefully surveyed
ruins of a place like Middleham. Next door to this ruined
abbey they carry on the busy life of a modern farm. Next
door also stands in dignified silence the seventeenth century
manor house. Betwixt them, and rambling into them, the
thirteenth century abbey.

The gardener took me to look at the effigies and talked
briefly about the house. "A queer old spot," he said. "Full

of holes and corners, bits and pieces, nooks and crannies, ups and downs."

Let me now quite Whitaker. "The situation of this house (he means the abbey) has been treated with injustice, and its remains very indistinctly described. It stands indeed in a deep and not very cheerful bottom, surrounded by mountains, which approach too near to admit a sufficient portion of sunshine; and the site, especially as it has been neglected since the Dissolution, is not free from damp and its concomitants. But the outline of Whernside and Penhill, as seen from the south windows, is the most majestic in Richmondshire, and the brisk trout stream of Cover, which washes a fertile meadow under the walls of the house, once, no doubt, conveyed away the superfluous springs which now stagnate about it."

In this account I find some exaggeration. The bottom is not deep and it does not lack cheerfulness. The mountains do not beetle over Coverham, the view is hardly the most majestic in Richmondshire, and nowadays the superfluous springs are under control. Whitaker goes on. "The outline of the whole church and choir may still be traced, as well as that of the cloister quadrangle." Without doubting my learned author's word, I fear it would take a vast amount of digging and careful investigation to trace them now, except perhaps by aerial photography. He proceeds. "There are three remnants of the earliest period of the abbey, and of Middleham Castle, the seat of its founder and patrons. These are two complete statues in hauberks, and the torso of a third; all which having been removed from the chapter house, the two former have been built perpendicularly into a wall adjoining to the principal dwelling-house, while the third is thrown out at random near the place of its disinterment." One of them, says my author, shows three dogs, "one playfully biting the scabbard of his master's sword, while the two others are keenly pursuing a stag into the recesses of a thick wood." The statues have been brought out of the wall. The dogs, I fear, have vanished down the gloomy corridor of time, though I have seen reprints of the statues, from Whitaker, which purport to represent the carvings as they now stand. No, the dogs have weathered away and the skill

of the carver is lost. But, quitting Coverham, I found four
lively foxhound puppies in the merest strip of an intake by
the roadside.

The graveyard of Coverham Church lies on a steep hill-
slope, and some of the gravestones have foundered. The
place is none the worse for that. Passing beneath a stone
Gothic arch, once the approach to the abbey, I turned left
and came to a halt on the bridge over the Cover. Like so
many North Riding bridges, it is a narrow, single-span affair,
steeply hump-backed and more suitable for foot-traffic, horse-
men, packhorse trains and light wagons than for copious
motor traffic. When progress comes to Coverham this bridge
will no doubt be replaced by a wide affair of stone and steel.
Meanwhile it stands. The North Riding County Council
takes immense care of its bridges, and keeps a watchful eye
upon them all. I leaned over the parapet to study the water.
Certainly a trout-stream still, and still rapid as in Whitaker's
time, the water a pale golden-brown, at the moment it was
placid and harmless, but the width between the banks, the
tumbled boulders and the bared roots of the overhanging
trees showed that, in spate, the Cover may be a terrible little
water.

Over the bridge I went to the left, making for Braithwaite
Hall. I looked across the lower vale of Coverham and
thought I had seldom seen such calm, pastoral beauty. A tiny
scarlet beetle came slowly down over Middleham Moor—the
post-van on its round. There were Shorthorns and Friesians,
and the road I followed had not long ago been gated. The
sheep here were crossbreeds, the lambs still sucking their
mothers though old enough to know better. Then Braithwaite
Hall came into view on the hillside to my right, and, because
the National Trust purchased the great house about two
years ago, I had to climb the rugged farm-track to the level
plat of ground upon which this house was built. The Trust
purchases not only property of startling architectural beauty
but also property typical of its period and its environment.
Braithwaite Hall, I suppose, is not to be compared with certain other properties owned or administered by the Trust,
and I hardly know whether to call it a glorified farmhouse or
a Wensleydale manor house. Upon one of the coign-stones is

a twelfth-century date, and incorporated into the present structure may be some twelfth century work. The expert archæologist would know, but I do not. The chimney nearest this coign-stone was rural Queen Anne, and curious in its irregularity. The interior had everything an old Wensleydale farmhouse ought to have—wine-cellar, game-cellar, creamery, cheese-making room; a hall paved with Hawes flagstone and a platform of stone raised perhaps six inches above the general floor-level. The purpose of this platform? I couldn't say. Miss Lord, the farmer-tenant's daughter, had had it from an old farmer in the vicinity that this platform used to have a long table on it where the jockeys took their meals. I pushed inquiry concerning these jockeys, but legend is silent about them and their exploits. The story didn't strike me as being authentic, but you never know. I looked at the oak-panelled rooms, used not long since as store-rooms. The panelling was plain and unpolished, mostly sound, but here and there splintered and knocked about where rats had lived behind the wainscoting and where heavy boots had kicked in the woodwork to get at the rats. Or, maybe, gavelock and chisel had played their part, and what happened to the oak mattered less than the death of the rats. The plaster ceilings were plain. There was no decoration, no butter-moulding. In most of the rooms the original oak flooring had been replaced by level deal planking, and where it remained it was scrub-oak—wide boards of seven or eight feet in length fitted together and subject to sag in the middle of the room. The fireplaces were late in date except for one handsome bit of Jacobean. They were not, on the whole, impressive. The staircase was good, wide, of sound oak, and it will polish finely. Its newel-posts were rather plain work though in pretty good state. In the kichen the oak panelling had been painted brown, and there the flooring was of stone. The dairy, of course, faced north, and there was some tradition that originally it contained a fountain. From other observations I think the seventeenth century made small distinction between fountain and spring, and I see nothing unlikely in the idea that this dairy contained a spring, for cheese-making demands a copious flow of cold water at even temperature, and nothing would be easier on this hillside than to fetch in spring water by means of a lead conduit and, having used it, to lead it out again in a similar way.

The National Trust has done well to take responsibility for this property. "Now," I said, "it will be cared for without losing its character, it will remain a farm, but it will never again fall upon such evil days as it has known within the last century. It will be lived in and used, but used by people who know its worth to the nation." And with that I went on my way to East Witton, one of the prettiest villages in Wensleydale, fine and clean, standing on the slope of the hill falling towards the main road between Masham and Leyburn. Here the cottages stand round a roughly ellipsoidal green, and the villagers are friendly and helpful—the little girls particularly. Here is none of the shyness of the moorpouts of North-East Yorkshire. There were two of these little girls, and they knew the times of all the buses from dawn till dark. One of them, later in the evening, was catching the bus into Leyburn. These villagers, even the smallest villagers, are used to travelling. "Next week," said the other little girl, wide-eyed and breath-less, "I'm going to Morecambe with our school treat!" The Women's Institute at Middleham had selected Whitby for the day's outing. These brief notes, mark you, are to be taken as important. They are of greater import than the life-history of Robert Neville, Peacock of the North, for they are the abstract and brief chronicle of the times we live in.

Now I shall tell you something about Wensleydale cheese, which some day you may be able to buy once more. There are two sorts of Wensleydale cheese, the blue-veined and the white, the blue-veined being older in origin than the white. Until recently, Wensleydale cheese was little known outside the county, but now that its beauty is more widely appreciated it is made in other parts of England as well as in Wensleydale. A good blue Wensleydale weighs anywhere between ten and twelve pounds, spreads like butter and is sweet, rich and creamy. It has no acidity, no bitterness. This is how to make it. You strain the evening milk into the vat and cool it to 65° Fahrenheit. Next morning, you skim off the cream, mix the evening milk with new morning milk, heat it to 90° Fahren-heit, return it to the vat and add the starter, which is intended to produce acid steadily and vigorously throughout the whole cheese-making process, and which must be free from yeasts, moulds and coliform bacteria. You put in anywhere between one ounce and three ounces to every twelve gallons of milk. The amount depends upon the time of year. Then you heat the whole to 84° Fahrenheit until 0.18 per cent or 0.19 per cent of acidity has developed. Then the milk is ready for renneting. You don't over-rennet. One dram to four gallons of milk is usually enough. The curds form by stirring the diluted rennet into the milk. Then you cut the curd lengthways and across the vat with a widely set American knife, you let it settle for ten minutes, then you cut it lengthways with the horizontal knife. This is to encourage draining, but not rapid draining. You never stir the curds much, but you slowly raise the temperature to 86° Fahrenheit during this draining process until 0.14 per cent of acidity has developed. Then you turn on the draining-tap and draw off the whey.

Next you scoop the curd into cloths on a draining-rack, enough curd for one cheese in each cloth, and you try not to bruise the curd as you do this. Bundle up the curds by the corners, cover the bundles with cloths and leave them on the rack for twenty minutes. Untie them, cut the curd into blocks four inches square, turn these blocks, wrap them up again. Repeat this process every twenty minutes. Test the drainings for acidity until they show 0.28 per cent to 0.3 per cent. By this time the curds are flaky and soft. Three hours have gone by since you started the draining-process, but you can't hurry it, for it is the most important part of the whole making. Next you weigh the curd, and next you break it up by hand into lumps the size of walnuts. Then you gently mix in an ounce of salt to every four pounds of curd.

Have you finished? By no means. Next you take your moulds. In the bottom you distribute a handful of the smallest curds, then you fill the moulds loosely and put a handful of small curds on the top. The drainings now show 0.3 per cent to 0.35 per cent of acidity. Leave the cheese to drain without pressure for two hours, remove it then from the moulds, turn it, return it to the moulds in cloths, and leave it overnight at 65° Fahrenheit.

All this, you will admit, is a day's work. Next morning you turn the cheese, put it in a dry cloth and put it to press with

6 cwt. pressure for a couple of hours. Then you take your
cheese out of the mould again, sew a calico bandage on it,
using lock-stitch, and return it to press for another two hours.
By this time it ought to be evenly pressed. Carry your cheese
(or cheeses) now to the cellar for ripening, and set on the
floor. Turn every day for six weeks and then every other day.
In six months the cheese will be fit for human consumption.

That is how blue Wensleydale is made. White Wensleydale has many sub-varieties, and you find them in Cleveland,
in Swaledale and elsewhere. They are small cheeses, firm but
not dry, and the process of making is almost as complicated
as that for blue Wensleydale, but not so lengthy.

Nowadays cheese-making is not much practised in farmhouse economy. It demands time, and farmers' wives have no
time to spare. It demands a high degree of skill and of
patience, adequate room and a good deal of equipment.
Moreover, cheese-making only pays when the milk can't be
got to market. It is more profitable and less trouble to send
milk to centralized dairy firms. Commercialized cheese-
making is now carried on at Northallerton and elsewhere,
and the old domestic skill is being lost. War-time necessity, as
well as economic pressure, has contributed to this giving up
of an old skill.

Between East Witton and Masham lie the ruins of Jervaulx Abbey, still in private hands. Somehow I have always
gone to Jervaulx when spring was in its prime, when the sun
was shining and the wallflowers and forget-me-nots were in
bloom on the silver-grey walls, so that my recollections of the
place are all of sunshine on the smooth lawns, birds singing,
and the richness of the year. It is a lovely ruin. I am not sure
that it isn't the very pick of the ruined abbeys of Yorkshire,
though it is not the most popular. Here the monks of Jervaulx bred the finest horses in the kingdom, and here was a
focus of resistance to the new order that would dispense with
all monks and monkishness. There is plenty of light here, and
the wind blows freely through the ruins. There are no hanging woods, there is no gloom and there is just enough
sequestration from the Wensleydale traffic-stream. Over the
way is a fine nursery-garden with as imposing a herbaceous
border as I have found in the North Riding.

Either the traveller into Wensleydale moves along the highroad that traverses it from end to end, or he breaks into the dale from over the hills. The second way is the more exciting. Wharfedale in the West Riding is the principal stamping-ground of the motorist, cyclist and walker from Leeds and Bradford. Buses trade up Wharfedale from Skipton to Grassington, and, rather late in the forenoon, to Kettlewell, Starbotton and Buckden. They are peopled by farming folk and by weather-browned young men and women with nailed boots and heavy rucksacks. The lusty walkers seem to confine themselves almost exclusively to Wharfedale, but I use Wharfedale and Langstrothdale as ways of breaking into Wensleydale over the fells. From Buckden in Upper Wharfedale to Leyburn in Middle Wensleydale a metalled highway crosses Kidstones Pass and makes down Bishopdale. Right and left of this road, and even upon the road itself, lie outcrop masses of silvery Yoredale limestone. Beyond Cray the timber belt ends, with sporadic thorn and scrub oak. Then, with Middle Pasture on the left and the high slopes of Buckden Pike and Bishopdale Gavel on the right, comes the open crest of Kidstones Pass. Here, where the gradient at last flattens out at nearly fourteen hundred feet, the stonechat population is fairly dense, peewits are scarce, curlews not so scarce, and gulls are on the increase. A shepherd and his dog move along the skyline, a few cyclists rush madly down the pass to Buckden, and burdened trampers in sparse groups straggle in the same direction. Less than a quarter of a mile ahead the boundary between the two Ridings crosses the summit and marches along the heights to east and west. A strong south-westerly wind fetches masses of storm-cloud up over the green obscurities below. They move across a uniform canopy of pewtery-coppery grey, and the austere landscape wears a grim and frowning expression. A few heavy drops of rain bespatter the ground.

To the left a grass-grown track zigzags up through Middle Pasture to High Pasture and the desolation of Kidstones Fell and Stake Moss. This track is not, at present, a motor road. Its surface is loose, rugged, deeply runnelled and stony. Towards the summit of Stake Fell it grows worse. Unrelentingly steep gradients climb to the boundary, but there is

neither landmark nor boundary-stone to tell where the West
Riding ends and the North Riding begins. Wherever you
stand upon a crest, there is the boundary, and that is the only
rule to go by. At great speed a pair of hill farmers follow the
course of a dry wall down to Kidstones, giving you no chance
to pass the time of day with them, and they are probably the
last people you will meet before reaching the green pastures
of Wensleydale. The wind is stronger and keener up here in
the desolation of Stake Moss. The westerly skyline rises to
the summit of Yockenthwaite up the spongy peat-hags of
Cray Moss. On either side of the track the sweet pasture is
closely bitten by the black-faced Swaledale sheep which, seem-
ingly resentful of human presence, stand, stare, bleat and
clear unwillingly out of the way. Farther off, tough old ling,
hoary mat-grass and sponges of bright green moss offer
sparse nutriment to even this hardy breed of sheep. Patches
of reedy ground bid the traveller beware of quitting the track
particularly when sudden curtains of heavy rain and driving
mist rush down over the fell and reduce visibility to a few
yards. This is the sort of ground where, at twilight and later,
even those familiar with every square yard of the fells take
care not to lose contact with landmarks. Here the traveller
crosses a green sike into which somebody has puddled a lot of
absorbent peat without reducing the sponginess of the surface.
Next comes a dry wall, and, after that, unenclosed fell, with
the immense downward sweep of Cragdale invisible to the
left and the grains and griffs of Bishopdale equally invisible
to the right. At eighteen hundred feet above datum-line there
looms into view a dry wall with a gap in it, and here the fell-
walker may leave the track and take to a sheep-trod. On the
map it is clearly marked as a footpath edging along the wet
slope of Cragdale Allotments, but it degenerates and disappears into the waste. Risking the mosses and mires proves
worth the effort since, half a mile or more to northward, the
green track begins again at the crossing of a nameless gill
where there is a crudely constructed sheep-wash. Then it
skirts the side of Stake Fell. Across to the west the belt of
woodland fringing Cragdale Water is now a lumberjack's
wilderness of lop and top with never a sign of either bracken
or willow-herb. Far down in the valley as it seems to be, it is

yet above the bracken-line and is merely a rich brown stain on the grey-green slope of the moor.

In Cragdale Bottom the pasture is at its best, and up on the fell-side, at the junction of the track with the Bainbridge road two hundred feet below the highest point of Stake Moss, Shorthorn heifers congregate near the stile. If at this point the traveller says to himself, "This is Shorthorn country!" he will not be far wrong.

The curving shoulder of Stake leads to a sight of the little grey hamlet of Stalling Busk. It lies on a shelf above the green valley bottom where the land levels out into pasture and marsh, with the beginnings of Semmerwater as a number of converging becks flowing down the slopes of Baysdale. The southern end of the lake comes into view and is again obscured. Semmerwater is a glacial lake. Its lateral moraine is still clearly distinguishable. An old overflow channel runs below the shoulder of Addlebrough, the crag-edged giant dark under the stormy sky to the north. Slowly the little lake reveals its full extent, not very imposing and not very lovely. It used to be bigger than it is now, for its level has been lowered a couple of feet. Even Gormire, at the foot of White-stonecliff east of Thirsk, is more impressive, and Semmer-water, despite its familiar legend versified by William Watson, is merely a sheet of water set in pastoral country with a boat tied up to a mooring-post and a big stone, the Carlow Stone, a vestigial remainder of the ice age, at its northern end. "Disappointing!" says the traveller, and passes along towards Bainbridge. At a distance, however, let him look back to see Semmerwater, a silver shield, set in its amphitheatre of gigantic hills, with the late afternoon light breaking up the cloud-masses above, and he will then delight all the more in Turner's rendering of this scene. A side-road swerves downhill here towards lake-foot and crosses the little river to the western side. The traveller may follow the winding course of the Bain first through pasture, then through a narrowing gorge, down to Bainbridge. Or he may keep to the higher road as I did, watch the rounding-up of ewes and lambs, make a note of the first dogroses of June, catch sight of Askrigg as a grey blotch in the northern distance, small and unimpressive in the wide expanse of Wensleydale, and

224

Swaledale sheep

finally go down the steep descent into Bainbridge, where the river comes down in a series of shallow limestone terracings to the bridge and the watermill. There on the bridge he may at last come to a stand, rest his elbows on the parapet, watch the clear water and listen to the water-wheel's faint threshing within the tall fortress of the mill.

The first people I met in Bainbridge in June 1946 were not genuine dalesfolk, for they had lived in the village only a quarter of a century, and though no doubt they understood the dialect they did not speak it, and they belonged, if they did belong, merely by adoption. The young man at the garage was certainly born and bred in Wensleydale; the innkeeper's wife, just as certainly, was not. There were traders' vans out of Northallerton and Ripon, too, and subtle indications, such as the presence of crazy paving, to prove that the villages of Wensleydale are in closer touch with the great world than they were only twenty years ago. In Hawes, Leyburn, Askrigg, Aysgarth, the stranger is within the gates. An atrocious punster would say that every hamlet has its Osrics —miniature enclaves of leisured, literary or artistic folk withdrawn from the big cities. Well, there is ample room for them all in the Yorkshire dales, and perhaps they bring with them the leaven of generous living. Yet, for myself, I vow that I will never buy a country cottage, have it done up with oak beams and a fireside settle, crazy-pave the path and plant Russell lupins between the house door and the gate.

Nevertheless I find Bainbridge little altered. The irregularly shaped village green is exactly as it used to be, the farming is carried on in the same old style, the Roman camp on Brough Hill has remained untouched for many a long year, the drumlins in the Ure valley have not been levelled and spread, the Rose and Crown still boasts of a fireplace which, it declares, is thirteenth-century, though I should put it much later, and the horn is still blown to bring travellers and shepherds down from the high fells. Bainbridge is a good place to look at, and the stone-built sturdy little houses with small white-painted windows and stone tiles yield their architectural secrets willingly. Before the Elizabethan building boom, the usual building materials for dwelling-houses in the Pennines were scrub oak for the timber framework and small

Castle Bolton, Wensleydale

stones and daub for the walling. Then, perhaps because oak ran short, the Elizabethans built of stone and roofed their houses with fine-grained slabs of fissile gritstone. Millstone grit is dark in colour and grimly utilitarian, but it weathers well and evenly. Small windows keep out the cold. Picturesque gabling, earthenware tiling and built-on sun-parlours would never stand fast against the blizzards of the upper dale-country, and the houses have to be squarely and sturdily built. They offer little indication of the century to which they belong because the building style is traditional and the masons are local men. For them, anything different, like half-timbering, red brick and pebbledash, would offend the eye. As things are, the houses seem like outcroppings of rock.

These dale villages are tidy places. You do not see bits of torn newspaper blowing about, or refuse strewn in odd corners. Because the rock lies so near the surface there is little dust or mud, and the close-cropped uniformity of green slope, the comparative absence of woodland, the copious dry-walling and the bare outline of the high fells produce an austerity of patern absent from blowsier landscapes. This is the country for the puritan artist.

Though in the valley bottoms a few old pastures have been ploughed and re-seeded, the economic conditions around Hawes, Askrigg and Bainbridge are all against sweeping change. The soil is thin, and the scope of mechanized agriculture is very limited, though the small farmers are buying tractors as general utility implements. Forestry has, I think, no future in Upper Wensleydale, nor is there any scope for mixed farming. There are no big-scale landowner-farmers to conduct expensive and probably unremunerative experiments, and the small men know exactly what they are about and how far they can go in the making of innovations. As things are, my impression is that the less these small farmers are interfered with the better for the countryside as a whole.

From Bainbridge to Askrigg the road is neither long nor difficult. It crosses the Ure by the ancient site of Jervaulx; the monks deserted it for a more favourable situation farther down the dale. Then the road runs along the northern side of the dale, climbing with a sharp turn to Askrigg market cross. At Askrigg railway station there are more drumlins.

Drumlins? They are elliptical mounds of boulder clay on the flat floor of the valley and their axes are always parallel to the flow of the glacier that made a great U of this dale. Their origin is obscure, but the geologists think they were once masses of ice containing a large amount of heavy material which tended to remain at rest while the bulk of the ice flowed to lower levels of the dale. Then, when the ice melted, these masses remained. They are, in any case, a curious feature of this part of Wensleydale.

Just by the market cross in Askrigg the traveller will see a triangular cobbled patch which, they say, marks the site of the old bear-pit. In the churchyard near the south porch stands a tombstone erected to the memory of an honest lawyer. This is one of the curiosities of the neighbourhood. The inn, formerly a fine Jacobean manor-house, has vanished without leaving a trace of its dignified existence. It was burned to the ground not so very long ago. For the rest, Askrigg seems untouched by change.

Twenty years ago, in this village, I lived through a little Wordsworth poem. About the old lady pacing up and down the churchyard path there was certainly a touch of the un- canny. Small, wrinkled, with a grey shawl over her shoulders, she lived in the cottage by the church tower—had lived there many years, though she had been born as far away as Ifra- combe and had lived long in Bradford. It was quiet, she said, in the village, for one who had lived in a big city, but she was happy. Her son kept the temperance hotel over the way, and on winter nights the journey from the hotel to her own cottage was something of an ordeal for her. Once she had slipped on the wet stones and had fallen down among the graves. She had well earned her rest and retirement, for during her active life she had seen two hundred babies into this world. She expressed simple pride in the church. They had had to keep it locked up in the summer months because motorists and cyclists went inside to eat their food. They made a mess of the place, she said. Yes, there was a tomb- stone erected to the memory of an honest attorney, and near the southern path, a gravestone in memory of an old dame, Betty Webster, who, born in 1790, had lived to be a hundred and six years old without losing any of her faculties. She herself remembered seeing her. She had come to Askrigg with a church choir from Bradford. They had asked her if they might sing to her, and she had asked for "Abide with me" and "Sun of my Soul," and they had sung to her, and gone away.

Before going down Wensleydale I turned back to Bainbridge. I wanted to see the Roman camp again. Parallel to the stream a narrow path brought me to the foot of a smooth green hill whose summit was not high above the level of the valley, yet high enough to place this hill among the hills. From its summit the eye passed over Bainbridge with swift acknowledgment of its quiet beauty, and ranged outward to command the flats of the Ure and the empty hills sweeping down to them. The green mound upon which I stood made the centre of a circular sweep of horizon. It was once a Roman camp. Ground-ridges marked its lines, rounded corners, broken turrets, buried prætorium and external hump of earthwork. Pegs driven into the ground marked the sites of gateways. Some scrabbling had been done, and there was a small, wired-in enclosure with masonry round a scummy pond. The edges were crumbling clay and loose stone, and when in my turn I did some scrabbling I turned up a coarsely fashioned, rust-eaten something which had once been a lynchpin, a bit of genuine antiquity. In the dim rubbish of the north-western angle a meadow-pipit had built her nest. This bit of Rome was hers, not mine. I stood to reflect that, neglected though it was, this Roman camp had given Bainbridge its existence, and I thought that more thorough excavation might reveal more traces of Roman occupation. I promised myself I would one day take again the Old Cam Road, the Roman road from Bainbridge to the south-west, and with that I went my way.

In medieval times, Bainbridge was the most important place in the whole dale country. It was the capital of a big cattle-ranching area. The ranches were known as vaccaries, and they were a matter of concern to the Norman barons who owned them.

Now, I think, a word about Hawes. As a market centre, Hawes in Upper Wensleydale is more important than Rich-

mond in Lower Swaledale because, obviously, it lies in the
heart of the area given over to the only sort of farming
possible in a land of fell and mountain. It is a grey place. All
the books insist upon the picturesque quality of the dale villages, but I, who am used to places like Kirbymoorside,
Helmsley, Coxwold, Whitby, do not find them very attractive. I do not very much like millstone grit as a building-stone.
It looks, to my eye, too much like the delta mud of which it
was originally compounded, and it offers no variety of texture
or colour. Any effect of height or dignity is lost, and square
corners remain very square, devoid of irregularities pleasing
to the eye. But the villages are well enough, for they suit the
scene. As you enter Hawes from Askrigg you note the twists
and turns in the very narrow road. The houses and shops
huddle together for shelter, and the market square is neither
big nor imposing; there isn't enough room for it in the narrow
flat of the dale floor. Were it not for its people, Hawes would
be dull. It reminds me of a lesser Otley without Otley's partial
industrialization, and the last time I was there the whole
place sadly lacked a lick of paint. True, it was tidy enough,
but it seemed to be living upon its guests, and living not tre-
mendously well. At the fag-end of July Hawes was full of
tweeded middle age and young folk in flannels or corduroys
and summer frocks. There were too many scholarly gentlemen about, and it was impossible to establish relations with
them or with the native population. I went up through the
market square to the abrupt ending of the village and there
contemplated the signposts. First, that which pointed out the
road over Fleet Moss into Wharfedale; secondly, that which
indicated the long road to Sedbergh on the one hand, and to
Ribble Head on the other. I know the road to Ribble Head
as well as I know Fleet Street and the Strand, and the Sedbergh Road was not my choice, either. Nor, for that matter,
was the road over Fleet Moss. At its junction I stood for no
more than twenty seconds. Then, in the strong wind, I hitched
my raincoat close about me and set off up the road to Gayle,
where Sleddale Beck comes down over its clints and ledges to
join the Ure three-quarters of a mile north of Hawes. I could
have stayed there a long time watching the water, but my
journey called me, and, once through Gayle, I left the metalled

road and set my feet on the turf with my face turned to the summit of Wether Fell, marked on the Survey map as 2015 feet above datum-line. First there was rough pasture with shorthorn cattle, and little streams and spongy places with reeds and peaty water; then the climb grew steeper and wetter, with Swaledale sheep grazing busily. I came up to adits in the fellside leading into the old coal-workings, and here I would issue a warning which the traveller will disregard at his own risk. Do not be tempted to explore either the old coal-workings or the old lead-mines in Wensleydale. They are not safe. Indeed they are dangerous, and, to my mind, there is no fun inside them. I have tried them, and I know.

Farther up towards the summit the slope levelled out into a wide area of peat-hag, black pools of water and big tussocks of mat-grass and bilberry. The rich brown peat deposits were four feet thick. Water ran amongst them. The tussocks were unkind to my ankles, and I had a lot of jumping to do. Once I put up a pair of red grouse, and once a pair of peewits. A few gulls were crying overhead, but there was precious little wild life of any sort. Slowly I climbed to the last dry wall, went over it in a great squall of rain and crouched in its shelter until the sky cleared. Then I looked northwards and westwards.

Across Wensleydale stood the great ridge of Stags Fell rising to the height of Lovely Seat. West of Lovely Seat, Shunner Fell was a grim hump on the skyline, and far away over and beyond Shunner Fell I saw the heights of Black Fell Moss. Through the Sedbergh Gap, dimly visible in the cloud-drift there, the mountains of the Lake District towered even higher than the great fells near at hand. It was magnificent, and it was exactly as I had hoped it would be, with masses of swiftly piling cloud, slant fringes of rain, the fell slopes dappled with shadow and sunlight, and the distances veiled or half-veiled. To the south-east lay Semmerwater, to the south-west the slope of Dodd Fell with minute white dots two-thirds of the way up towards its summit. I could not be sure they were sheep; they might well have been cattle. Of one thing I was sure, that they were not spectacled gentlemen in tweeds or young men in flannels or corduroys. I saw the green, thinly wooded lower slopes of Wensleydale in which Hawes is set, and then I faced the broken peat-hags that lay between me and the old man—the cairn—marking the summit of Wether Fell. The ground was unfenced wilderness and the going was not easy. Here and there the peat had been swilled away from the bare rock. There was much water. I did not linger at the cairn, but added a stone and climbed down to the Old Cam Road which runs just below the crest of the fell.

On the Survey map of Roman Britain this road is marked as travelling the country from the camp on Brough Hill at Bainbridge in a more or less westerly direction towards Lancaster, but it doesn't get through—it founders half-way there.

When in the company of historians I have talked about the Old Cam Road as a Roman road, I have been asked, "How do you know it isn't just an old drove-road? When it's called Roman, how do you know the wish isn't father to the thought?"

The subject of the drove-roads in the Yorkshire dale-country is now being carefully opened up, and the tendency is to lay some stress upon them at the expense of other roads. The Old Cam Road has the right width for a Roman road, it has the forthrightness of a Roman road, it skirts the boggy crest of Wether Fell in exactly the Roman way, and the stone is just below the thin covering of grass. I myself have no doubt of its Roman origin. Equally I am sure it has been used from the time of its making as a packhorse road and a drove-road. It is easy to walk along it at a sheep's pace; that is, at two miles an hour. The declivities are nowhere very steep. On its southern side it is walled, on its northern open, and sheep find better grazing on it than upon the fell. Over the wall the fell sloped steeply into the green of Bardale, and I knew I was not far from the boundary between the North and West Ridings. Presently I came down to the narrow metalled road to Wharfedale and began to climb up it. Behind a dry wall two cyclists ate their sandwiches—the only human beings I had encountered since leaving Hawes, and they stared hard as I went by but said nothing. At the top of the rise I stood facing westwards. Here the Old Cam Road began again, still as a green road, making over the shoulder of Kidhow towards Ingle. In something less than a mile it quitted the North Riding and ran out of my province, and so I did not follow it. Instead, I stared like Cortés straight ahead, for there, unmistakably solid and equally unmistakably recognizable by its shape, stood the mountain Ingleborough.

From Wethercote in the West Riding Ingleborough makes a magnificent picture, but this aspect of the mountain from Bardale Head is, I think, much finer. I looked for Whernside to the left of Ingleborough and found its indigo bulk against the skyline—not all of it, a mere fragment against the heavy sky—there to be greeted as an old friend and enemy. Below me the road swung away downhill towards Oughtershaw and Beckermonds, and presently the two cyclists, grinning widely, swooped down it. I looked to my left along the boundary line into the waste of Fleet Moss, the dangerous areas fenced off by the hill farmers not for my sake but for the sake of their sheep, and I knew that, instead of going down the road, I should keep to the tops and follow the boundary line past Oughtershaw Tarn, Middle Tongue Tarn, the crest of Yockenthwaite Moor and the southward-facing crags, and so, scrambling down through Cray Moss to Cray Tarn, to the Stake and down past Cray to Buckden.

That was the way I went, now above the 2,000-foot contour line, now slightly below it, through bog, seavy slack, peat-hag, brown and thwarted ling, stony ground, mat-grass, bilberry and blue-grass, through hot sunshine and driving rainstorm. I acknowledge that when in the late afternoon I reached Buckden I was tired. My muscles ached, my feet felt that they had been soundly hammered, my mind lay far within myself. At the bus-stop I found a score of people waiting for the southbound bus. They regarded the tatterdemalion who joined them with curious and rather hostile looks, yet he remained indifferent, for his mind was set not upon them but upon the hills. He was beginning to sort out the elements that made them so terrific in aspect. First there was light, the light upon the fells, varied in brilliance, emphasized by shadow, full of changes unsequential and capricious; light that revealed, and light that veiled. Then he added the element of vastness—vastness of size, distance and duration, fold upon fold of the hills rising to the doorsill of heaven, remote and inaccessible. Upon this remoteness, the alien nature of mountain country, its distance from human affairs, its aloofness and indifference. Vagueness and obscurity added their quota, and then there was the contrast between the prettiness of the daisies on the Old Cam Road, and the mole-hill beside them, contrasting powerfully with the grandeur of the landscape. Finally came the notion of force, the passive strength, held in reserve, of the hills; not the power of lightning and gale, which is active power, but power motion-less and silent. And he had to consider the nature of silence, too. For while the wind blew about him and made noises in the mat-grass at his feet the farther hills were silent. In his mind lurked no fear. Fear changes the aspect of the grand and makes it terrible, withdrawing the beauty from it. No, the mind rests in fearless passivity, in contemplation, and then there follows a burst of exaltation, a soaring and exhilaration of mind.

Waiting for the bus, I resolved at last that this wild country has grandeur but not quite sublimity. It does not tower high enough to the clouds. The sublime stuns by its size and incomprehensibility, staggers the mind and stills the tongue. Not even Ingleborough, that noble mountain, quite does that.

More than once, you see, I have had an urge to travel along the boundary line between the West and the North Ridings, but for vast distances there is no road and the fell-walking is treacherous and arduous. I shall say something of one more such journey, and leave the reader to follow my track at his own risk. This time I went up through Nidder-dale, through green alpine country as far as Lofthouse, and from that grey little village I took the fell-road which, had I pursued it to its end, would have brought me into Masham. Let no motorist, no cyclist, be persuaded to take this road. It is not, at first, a road. On the day I travelled it, volumes of clear mountain water were rushing down its deep runnels. It was a beck, a sike. The road—there had formerly been a road—had completely foundered. I am told that, in fell-climbing, one should be able to whistle all the way to the summits; by the time I reached the crest of the fell I was moderately breathless. Whistling would have been out of my

compass. The scenery was good, the road took on a reasonable gradient, it wound as it climbed, and I reached the crest
at last. To my right a road went off to nowhere, the road to
Masham lay in front of me, the border ran away across the
moor to my left. I went to the left.

Now whether through malice or through good intent I
have no means of knowing, but the boundary of Mashamshire
is marked hereabouts by a fosse and a vallum. There is, in
brief, a deep draining-ditch with an irregular, overgrown
ridge of earth, peat, rock and mud stretching away for miles
across the moor towards Little Haw, Great Haw and Little
Whernside, and if a man is to make along the border between
the two Ridings he must walk either in the ditch or alongside
it on the ridge. The ditch is, in places, much below the level
of the moor, and the moor is not level, but dips to sikes and
mosses, rises to stony heights, spreads itself out in beds of
rushes and gathering-grounds of becks. There is ling in great
quantity, and there are huge tussocks of white grass, there is
barbed wire fencing, and there are miles and miles of nothing
else but these things. Once the draining-ditch forked, and,
having carelessly taken to the southern fork, I had to make
direct across the moor to the north. On the way across I
scared a little bunch of Swaledale sheep. They looked at me,
then they ran. In truth, they were wild. With some trouble I
found the proper route and thereafter kept my eye, as best I
could, upon Little Haw, the first landmark. By the map it is
a short journey. In reality it is very long and not without risk,
for a careless step may mean a sprained or smashed ankle.
Once I tripped and fell headlong into peaty mud. I splashed
through bogwater, for miles on end I leaped from one tussock
to another. Between the tussocks there was black slime. For
half a mile of this journey I dropped back into the West
Riding and followed a green track along a southward-falling
slope. It was there I saw a buzzard—a common buzzard, not
a rough-legged buzzard—hovering for a minute or two
before he went off towards the south-east in a long, effortless
glide. Then I went back to the border. Here I found a couple
of shooting-butts, not in the middle of nowhere but conveni-
ently placed so that the sportsmen could find their way back
to civilization without a map. I put up a few grouse—not, I

think, more than a dozen all told, but enough to tell me that this was certainly a grouse-moor.

Little Haw was a paltry nipple on the skyline. I reached it, and from its summit I looked northward down the green length of Bishopdale. A very wonderful view. Had the horizons been clear of haze and slants of rain, I suppose I might have seen Beulah, the Delectable Mountains and perhaps the Cleveland Hills. I looked for Great Haw, and there it was. Between me and Great Haw, I regretted to observe, there stretched a league of precisely the same sort of moor I had already traversed, and, in addition, a couple of what cannot be described as lakes yet may not be described as ponds. They were not my notion of tarns, either. My notion of tarns is based upon memories of Welsh tarns. These were something out of "Childe Roland," where the land breaks out into substances like boils. Ugly, black, forbidding, and between them lay reedy, marshy ground.

I had of my own volition set myself to this journey, and I would go on. I did so in no spirit of gaiety. Now and again, over the shoulder of the moor, I caught sight of Little Whernside. It looked huge, dark and grim. My track would take me to the cairn on the summit of Little Whernside, and it looked very far away.

Cloud gathered round me, not dense but damp and moving erratically. Soon it thickened. I had no option but to go on, and go on I did. It was then that I came to the abandoned hut. Obviously it had been used by a small body of troops in training. Within, it was dry. There were pegs for caps and overcoats. There was a smashed stove, a table with empty drawers. There were two overtoppled chairs, and there was nothing else. No road led to this hut, and no road led away from it. I continued to follow the ditch, the wire, the low ridge, and, almost exhausted, reached the crest of Great Haw. My route still lay along the high ground. In general, visibility was restricted to a few yards, but occasionally the grim shape of Little Whernside loomed through the mist. It came into view now on the southern quarter, now directly to the west. It was a tough, dense indigo in colour, and I did not like the look of it.

I believe in going on beyond the point of ordinary weariness, because only then do I reach the mental state of hallucinated vision, which is the state at which poetry takes shape in the mind. Therefore I went on, but the poetry was not of the sort that can get itself written down. I remember vaguely that it concerned itself with "huge forms that do not live like living men," and then I found myself climbing the wet slopes, the rocks, the sliding screes of Little Whernside. Then I remember the blackness above me, the stumbling of my feet, the unsure grip of my hands, and finally, the heavy rain. The rough going had skinned my feet, my muscles ached intolerably, and I had reached that beastly stage of weariness when a man begins talking to himself. I knew something of Little Whernside, I knew that the darkness above me and the darkness in my spirit were not going to lift, and I realized, fortunately, that it would be idiocy to go on climbing that black mountain. Not that day should I look down from the mountain-top into Coverdale towards Bradley and Horsehouses. I turned my back on the summit and went down towards Scar and the West Riding. Of my journey on foot from Scar back to Lofthouse I shall write nothing, nor of my state when at last I reached my base very late that night. I have, I think, written enough to prove that this border-country between the two Ridings is only for the tough and determined. It is not merely lonely, not simply wilderness. It is also liable to break the spirit of a man. I do not admit that it broke mine, but the fight through the six-foot bracken on the lower slopes of the mountain brought me dazed and trembling, wet through and with darkened mind, to the reservoir and the road at last.

Looking back on this trip, I know now that I thoroughly enjoyed every yard of it. You will not, after that, expect me to describe in detail every journey I have made across the fells between Wensleydale and Swaledale, Wensleydale and Wharfedale, Swaledale and Teesdale. They have mostly been like that : wind, rain, wilderness; solitude, sheep, stone and crag; black tarns, spongy peat, and always that grey-haired, tough mat-grass which is no good to either man or beast. Walking in the fells is very different from walking in the North York Moors. It is all the difference between Jurassic limestone and Carboniferous limestone with cappings or boulders of millstone grit on the tops. I will say this, however, that in the North Riding fells there are few sink-holes, clints, swallow-holes and pot-holes, and in very few places is the Carboniferous limestone stripped of its cover of vegetation to make what are often called *pavements*. The thing to do, if you go fell-walking (and I hope you will), is always to allow yourself an hour or two extra, more than you think you will need. I myself am a fool when I go fell-walking. Invariably I find myself walking against the clock, I travel too fast and too far, and I don't get the fun out of the business that perhaps I ought to get. Another thing is that I always go alone, and on reflection I do not think that this is altogether wise. Still, I do not set off to climb the fells when snow is deep on the ground, and I give two reasons for this : first, that I do not know the fells well enough to take liberties with them; secondly, that the dead whiteness of the landscape would prove intolerable. I have something of the horror of whiteness that Melville wrote about in *Moby Dick*. I travel in light shoes, by the way—never in hobnailed boots. I agree with the man on his walking tour in Cornwall who flung his boots over the cliff into the sea at Hell Mouth and went on in slippers to the end of his day's journey. Boots are not the wear, though everyone else may say they are essential to good fell-walking.

Now I abandon personal reminiscence to record much miscellaneous information regarding Wensleydale. When Phillips the geologist went through this area on foot his expeditions took him to those places where the strata were exposed—to the coal-mines and open-cast workings, "the widely-wrought collieries of Colsterdale," Brown Beck colliery, Witton Fell collieries and the collieries of Leyburn Plain where coal-seams twelve to eighteen inches thick ran about a hundred and twenty feet above the main limestone. At Tan Hill the seam ran to a thickness of four feet and the mining was only very slowly abandoned. Even in 1906 Kirk Gill coal-mines near Masham were still being worked. Nevertheless, says Whitaker in 1823, "in the upper parts of Wensleydale, though less civilized than those of the lower country, the inhabitants, even yet, are simple and pastoral in their habits, but the spinsters and the knitters in the sun, thanks to mechanical improvements, are seen no more."

Whitaker was much against industrialization in this area. "In my progress through this district," he wrote, "I beheld many ruins with pleasure, but none, perhaps, with equal satisfaction to that which I experienced in the sight of a ruined cotton mill, which had once obtruded itself upon this beautiful and sequestered scene. I beheld it not only as the removal of a single nuisance, but as a fortunate presage that the tide was receding, and that an evil (the greatest that ever befell this country) is gradually declining." He wrote that about Aysgarth, the local pronunciation of which he gave as *Escar* or *Ayscar*.

So much, apart from lead-mining, concerning industry in Wensleydale. Now for other notes. Semmerwater, said Whitaker, has trout, bream, roach, minnow, loach, bullhead, and, probably, pike. Birds noted there included osprey, water ouzel, kingfisher, red sparrow, heron, bittern, curlew, whimbrel, snipe, godwit, greenshank, redshank, red sandpiper, dotterel, oyster-catcher and crested grebe. Some of these are no longer found anywhere in England; others are rare vagrants. In 1609, at Bainbridge, memory remained of a forest-law obliging travellers to pay three farthings "to some guyde to gyde them through the forrest." The forest-horn of Bainbridge is blown at ten o'clock at night from Holyrood to Shrovetide. At Coverham Abbey "there was good singing." Leyburn Shawl was laid out in 1841. Redmire Church, the south door particularly, is worth notice. Wensley Church has the famous Flemish brass of Simon of Wensley, rector from 1361 to 1394. The first establishment of Jervaulx was at Fors near Aysgarth. There is hardly a stone left there now. The Cistercian monks removed to Jervaulx in 1156. In 1537 the eighteenth abbot was executed in London for his share in the Pilgrimage of Grace, and in his cell left behind him the inscription *Adam Sedbar Abbas Joreval* 1537. In the same year, dated 8th June, comes a letter by Arthur Darcy: "for surely the breed of Gervaix for hors was the trydd [he means *tried*] breed in the north. Ye stallions and mares well sortyd : I thinke in no other realme shold be found the lyke to them."

Obviously Wensleydale in the long centuries of the Middle Ages was not wholly deer-forest, for neither cattle-ranching nor horse-breeding could be well carried on in forest-land. No doubt there was forest with extensive glades for deer and wild boar, but also much fertile grazing-ground.

I find a note that the rood-loft of Jervaulx after the Dissolution was preserved at Aysgarth, but of ecclesiastical wood-carving there is still more to tell—a curious story.

The grounds of Jervaulx Abbey were laid out, much as they are to-day, by the Earl of Ailesbury in 1806 and 1807.

Of Bolton Castle, "exposed to storms and tempests without and to darkness and discomforts within," Whitaker says that it stands out against the slope of the dale with "blank and melancholy distinctness." So indeed it does. He gives it, moreover, a very majestic and feudal aspect and reports that after the Civil War it was abandoned for the great country house called Bolton Hall, finished in 1678, in the midst of its wooded park in the levels of the dale. Mary Queen of Scots was imprisoned in Bolton Castle from July 1568 to January 1569, and, it seems, endeavour was made to provide her with good hunting and domestic comfort. Tradition reports that in spite of the amenities with which she was provided she tried unsuccessfully to escape. Her residence here gave material for a play acted within the walls of the castle not long ago. When I looked round the place I found the situation very exposed and the building grim. It is one of the best examples in England of a fortified house of the fourteenth century. Built between 1378 and 1399, its four grey towers do not overlook a space of flowers, and, though the arch and gallery at the west end of the chapel are admirable, the custodian will show you a dungeon which really was a dungeon and not a primitive wine-cellar. Apparently prisoners were hurled headlong into its black pit and there remained till famine and the ague ate them up. While Bolton Castle was still a fortified dwelling-house, William Bulteflour and Thomas Wren were credited with having caught a hundred and sixty fish in a day, mostly trout.

Farther up Wensleydale, in and about Askrigg, the commonest surname is Metcalfe. Nobody knows the derivation or origin of the name, but churchyard and dwelling-house alike are still inhabited by Metcalfes dead and alive. The living Metcalfes are proud of their name, for this was formerly a distinguished clan or sept. James Metcalfe of Bear Park fought what is reputed to be the last private war in England against the Robinsons at Semmerwater. I have been through the legal documents bearing upon this furious incident. Like most legal documents they are complicated, but, as far as I remember, Metcalfe of Nappa, hard pressed for money, leased the property at Semmerwater to one Robinson of York, and when he wanted the property back Robinson, on legal grounds, refused to budge. Sir Thomas Metcalfe marched against the place with his armed tenantry, surrounded it, demanded the evacuation of the garrison and, being denied, laid regular siege to it with his musketeers. There was a good deal of shooting, a lot of bad language, and a fair amount of risk for both attackers and defenders. There were woundings, and one or two men were seriously damaged. The whole episode finished in the law-courts and the Robinsons were confirmed in possession.

The last of the Metcalfes of Nappa Hall, now a farm-house that still looks like a fortified dwelling, was Thomas Metcalfe, who died on 25 April 1756, aged 69, and who was buried at Askrigg. Metcalfes were vulgarly called *Mecca*.

So, slowly, the traveller makes his way up the floor of the dale to Hawes, and there, though not at dale-head, he finds the contours promptly growing steeper and the green country giving place to wilder scenes. "From Meerbeck upward the appearances of fertility and verdure gradually diminish: there is little alluvial land, ling and sweeping surfaces of mountain pasture range from the immediate vicinity of the Ure to the foot of the highest fells; the river diminishes to a beck and the beck to a sike. The collateral features shrink in proportion, and the traveller finds himself on a level peat-moss, suddenly appalled by a dreadful and perpendicular disruption in the rock, where a stream is heard to murmur at a vast depth beneath." But do not let this description deter you from visiting Hell Gill, the Stygian rivulet described by Camden, who, careful observer, noted the presence of wolves in Wensleydale.

William Morris declared the Pennine highlands "the pick of all England for beauty," and many of those who concur find much of their delight in cascades and waterfalls. Wensleydale is rich in the possession of falling water, but you have to go out of your way, off the main roads, to find it. This is the origin of the cascades. First, on the very tops of the fells is millstone grit. Below that lies a narrow scar of chert, and below that again about seventy feet of perpendicular limestone scar, followed by a flat or concave slope; below this slope, which is mingled pasture and scree, there is another scar made by a thinner band of limestone. Then comes a long slope of grits and shales, a third limestone scar, thick at Addlebrough and Penhill, thin above Hawes, followed by a steep slope down to the level terrace of Simonside Limestone, then another drop over the edge of the Hardraw Scar Limestone, and so by a steep slope to the valley floor. Hardraw Force gives a fall of 96 feet. Mill Gill, with Upper Mill Gill Force and Lower Mill Gill Force, shows a drop of 80 feet and 40 feet. Aysgarth Falls drop 100 feet in just over a mile and a half of the main course of the Ure. At Hardraw you may easily work your way behind the fall to note the shales sandwiched between the limestone bands. Upstream at Mill Gill, which you reach from Askrigg churchyard, is a sawmill where hay-rakes are made. Here in Mill Gill the geologist may collect lamellibranchs in the shale-beds, and trilobites, and cephalopods if he is lucky. There is also a little coal-seam with a rootlet-bed below it. If the traveller by this time is not weary of falling water he should look for Cotter Force and Moss Gill Force, or go up the dale in rainy weather, when water spouts from every fellside.

Force in the western dales, *foss* in the north-eastern moors, you will note.

In Hawes there linger still two or three old drovers who in past years used to cross the fells from Wensleydale with cattle and sheep for Leeds. Their regular route took them over Fleet Moss. Of them it may be quoted: "We old men are old chronicles, and when our tongues go they are not clocks to tell only the time present, but large books unclasped; and our speeches, like leaves turned over and over, discover wonders that are long since past."

You begin to see that an exhaustive account of Wensleydale, bursting the bounds of this volume, would flow into another just as big. I have tried to write with economy, but

Aysgarth Falls

still there is a little more detail to give. This for those who
do not know the dale and have no access to maps. Wensleydale is between twenty-five and thirty miles long. It has a
broad, flat floor now covered with rich pasture. From this
floor the fell-slopes, walled to the top, rise in a series of
terraces selvidged by crag or scar. These scars are always
potentially there. Between northern and southern scar the
distance across the dale varies, but Middle Wensleydale is
between four and five miles wide, Upper Wensleydale
between two and three. The fall of the Ure in Middle
Wensleydale, between Aysgarth and Jervaulx, is about 150
feet every three miles. After that, it is much less. The Middle
Ure is not a turbulent river. If you picture the whole dale full
of ice you will understand at once the width of the valley, its
sloping sides, the sliced-off scars. To understand the complete
story of the Wensleydale Glacier is yet impossible. The
geologists, though they know much about the final glaciation,
do not know everything. They are not, for instance, sure
whether Stake Fell was wholly overridden by ice or whether
it was a nunatak; they have not yet solved all the problems
associated with the formation of glacial lakes in Coverdale,
Bishopdale, Cragdale and Bardale; and they do not yet know
a great deal about the glaciation of the fells between Swaledale and Wensleydale. All we others can do, therefore, is to
keep our eyes open for terminal and lateral moraines, nunataks and drumlins. As to the vegetation of the fells up beyond
the pasture-line, the thing to remember is that, in spite of its
ancient appearance and the depth of the peat-hags, the clothing of the fells is geologically recent, there is no depth of soil,
and the plants and mosses that flourish are tundra-growths
aided by a rather heavy rainfall. The mat-grass that tussocks
on the fells is no good. Heather is edible in its second year
after burning. The high pastures are chiefly of *Ovina festuca*,
sheep's fescue. Down below, the only harvest is the hay
harvest, and that may last from June to October. Towards
Masham, Jervaulx and Tanfield mixed farming begins, and
Friesian cattle are as popular as Shorthorns farther up the
dale.

The fells are a "negative area," mainly uncultivated and
almost uninhabited, but they have their uses.

The villages are either on the floor of the valley or on the lowest terrace above the water. The road system is simple, and the road surfaces good in the dale itself and on the main roads crossing the fells. Relics of ancient occupation are rare. Middleham has the hypocaust of a Roman villa, but Neolithic Man kept clear of this district. Penhill shows signs of Celtic nomenclature, but the majority of the place-names are Anglian with a scattering of Danish. The Vikings hardly penetrated Wensleydale. They came down into Swaledale from the north-west. In 1909, Aysgarth had thirteen farmers. Yore Mills employed three millers. Bishopdale had seventeen farmers and a gentleman, West Burton boasted a cheese-factor and Harmby a watchmaker. Leyburn had two printers, W. Horne and Son were watchmakers and dealers in antiquities, the gasworks employed a manager and a gasmaker. Now, I believe, there is a single Lord High Gasman. Middleham had six innkeepers, three sporting correspondents, four coachbuilders, a shoeing-smith, a bootmaker, a jockey, a woodcutter, a watchmaker, a butter-factor and M. D. Peacock, trainer and district councillor. Since 1909 the economic situation has not changed enormously. Beyond Bolton Hall there is no resident squirearchy and the population consists chiefly of farmers, shepherds, quarrymen, innkeepers, shopkeepers, garage-men and such. Watchmaking and clockmaking no longer flourish, and cheese-factors have gone out of business. There are still sporting correspondents at Middleham, and Leyburn keeps its dealer in antiques.

In summer Wensleydale is thick with holiday-makers. Even so, the villagers lead their own lives. At West Witton they still burn Old Bartle, and Redmire and Castle Bolton run a group of players. Florence Bone, Watson Dyke, Muriel Smith and George Jackson write plays in their own dialect, rehearse them in Bolton Castle, and, as likely as not, produce them there or in Redmire Town Hall. Castle Bolton has also a group of artists, of whom I suppose Fred Lawson is the best-known. The villages are lively with the modern spirit, but I have yet to find a dalesman passionately addicted to football pools.

CHAPTER X

SWALEDALE

ABOUT Richmond I have never been able to make up my mind, and I do not think that, finally and dogmatically, Richmond has ever been able to make up its own mind about itself. Most of our English towns know both why they are where they are and what they are doing there. Some have existed in the same locality since the days of Cunobeline and Cartimandua, some were built by the Romans as new towns, and when the Romans built a town, as for example they built York, they knew how they fixed its position. They had commercial, hygienic or strategic reasons. The Normans did not build towns but fortresses, and towns grew up round the fortresses. Richmond Castle justified the growth of Richmond. But why Alain le Roux, Alan Rufus, son of Odo, Count of Ponthièvre, built Richmond Castle on the height of the rock overlooking the Swale is not so clear. Alan the Red, valuable ally of William the Conqueror, received as a reward for his services five wapentakes in the North Riding of Yorkshire, or roughly a third of the whole area covered in this book, and I suppose that as a rational overlord he had his manors thoroughly surveyed. He was a soldier, and the territories granted to him were peopled by rude and barbarous Anglo-Danes acquainted with the whole technique of murder, rapine, looting and burning. The history of the City of York proves that conclusively. Alan the Red chose to build his castle on the crag above the Swale. Obviously his new fortress commanded the river-crossings. It put a check on Swaledale barbarians contemplating a raid into the fertile Vale of Mowbray. From Richmond Alan could keep an eye upon the road, if there was a road, to Bowes and Barnard Castle. But to what purpose? If I know anything about Swaledale in 1071, when Alan built his castle, it was thinly populated and presented no real menace to the security of the plainlands. The river-crossings north and south led into wild, unpeopled fell-country, and between Richmond and Bowes, Richmond and Leyburn, there was nothing in need of powerful protection. Was Alan Rufus as great a huntsman as his king, and did he build Richmond Castle as his abode so that he might ride out on hunting expeditions into the Swaledale deer-forests? If so, he was over-ambitious in his building plans, and the Percies were wiser than he. They built hunting-lodges, not massive fortresses, for their amusements.

I am convinced that Red Alan made a mistake. He built Richmond Castle because he allowed a nostalgia for his native Breton landscapes to overcome his military judgment. Had he looked at his newly granted manors with the eye of a soldier he would, I think, have built at Catterick. But he wanted Richmond to look like something out of Brittany. He had emotional and artistic reasons, and Richmond Castle justified his choice. Richmond, the town, grew up round the castle, and the result is that the whole place, even to-day, strikes the observer as not quite English. It is a fairy-tale town depicted by a French artist.

Not fully realizing this truth, Richmond has never been quite sure whether it exists in symbiotic partnership with the castle or whether it justifies itself as market town, traffic centre and capital of the Honour of Richmond, or whether it is merely there because there is nowhere else for it to go, or whether it really is an important military post.

In a sense, the symbiotic partnership between town and castle still exists, although the castle has now no organic existence of its own. It is in the care of the Ministry of Works, and during the summer of a normal year about four thousand people a month visit the castle to survey the barbican, climb to the top of the Norman keep to view the spacious landscapes of Swaledale, stroll round the ruins of Scolland's Hall and sit on bits of broken walling overlooking the valley and the river. These four thousand people bring money into Richmond. They arrive by bus, train, private car and on foot from places where money is, notably from Darlington and County Durham. Such people like shops, and Richmond's shops are exactly what they want. They have a passion for the red and gilt of Woolworth's, and therefore Richmond has a Woolworth's. They like multiple stores, and Richmond has them. They like country scenery, and Richmond has it. They can breathe the good, untainted air, picnic by the river-bank, take a day off in a place not too distant from their homes.

Moreover, Richmond has its soldiery, and Catterick Camp, the strategic centre of this part of England, is not far away. Soldiers grow restless and discontented when isolated from the civilian community, and therefore a good service of buses runs between Richmond market-place and the huge military focus of Northern Command. But Richmond itself has no great military value. The opposing forces in the Wars of the Roses and the Civil War neglected to lay siege to the place; they could afford to ignore it as having no importance. Nowadays it may provide a jumping-off place for commando training and military manœuvres in the hill country, but that is not the full extent of its importance for the training of troops. It gives them cinemas and dancing.

As a market town, Richmond is not so important as Hawes. I do not think I have ever seen a single sheep in Richmond, but no doubt that is because I have chosen the wrong times and seasons for visiting the town. Hawes, however, is a famous market, and Richmond is not. Up Wensleydale there is a railway and a passable bus service. Swaledale is not so well served. It has no railway and the bus service is indifferent. Wensleydale folk, it is true, come over the hills from Leyburn, but not in droves. Swaledale folk, certainly, come down the dale from as far away as Keld, but, again, not in droves. The people who come into Richmond arrive from the north-east and from the camps at Catterick, from the more populous and sophisticated, though less civilized, industrial areas. That is why Richmond is more suburban than Hawes. A case of economic necessity.

Do not suppose, however, that I fail to give this capital of the Honour of Richmond praise for its beauty. Set Richmond on the coast of Brittany or above the Rhone Valley and it would be melodramatic, but here its northern colourings neither shock the eye nor dazzle the mind. The stonework is silver tarnished by time, the tiled roofs burn red without hurting the retina, and the Swale sparkles without blinding. Richmond is an illuminated manuscript, the work of an Eng-

lish artist trained in the monastic schools of Northern France.
It is a fragment of the Middle Ages at their twelfth-century
zenith of achievement, dignified without pomposity, lovely
without garishness.

It is more than this. There are fragments of seventeenth-
century and eighteenth-century Richmond. The visitor may
stroll away from the market-place into cobbled squares with
quiet Georgian houses, and grass growing between the
cobbles, or admire the quality of Ryder's Wynd, with its
billboards of Reeth Agricultural Show and of Ruth and Her
Rhythmists. He may penetrate into the amusement park laid
out for children, or sit amongst the lawns and flower-beds
around Grey Friars Tower, or post his picture-postcards at
the neat and modern post-office. At the same time, his companion may be searching out the vantage-points from which
J. M. W. Turner executed his lovely drawings of Richmond
and Richmond Castle. He will have no great difficulty in
locating them, and, having done so, he will see Richmond
pretty well as Turner saw it, though, I dare say, he will miss
Turner's specious handling of the planes of the landscape.

From the height of the castle keep the eye looks down to
the goods yard of the railway, to the modern bus station, to
the market-place, to Woolworth's, the King's Head, the
rather ugly market cross, to the sight of navvies digging for
gas or water-mains; he will look across the river to the horizontal scar of the military barracks. There is a man fishing
from the weir, there are picnic parties down by the river.
Lorries come crawling up the hill towards Frenchgate and the
market-place. And the eye, moreover, surveys the wide
horizons of Swaledale.

When the traveller descends from the summit of the keep
he will necessarily pause to look at the multitudinous
scribbled or carved *graffiti*, the names, the dates, the pierced
hearts, on the walls within the keep. There are names from
Auckland, Warsaw, Quebec, Washington, Wellington,
Birmingham, Bradford—from all over the civilized and un-
civilized world. I have no dislike of such records, though
many people think them silly. Did not Wells's time-traveller
scribble his name upon the nose of a statue which will come
into being some thousands of years hence? He obeyed what

Wells calls "an irresistible impulse," and you may, if you will, condemn him as too much the philistine to resist the irresistible.

I have been thinking of something which strikes me as natural but worth noting. Jervaulx Abbey and Coverham Abbey lie within easy riding distance of Middleham Castle, Byland Abbey and Rievaulx Abbey are not far from Helmsley Castle, and Easby Abbey is a bare half-hour's walk from Richmond Castle. It is clear, I think, in this part of the world that castle and monastic establishment could not afford to be too far apart. Each had something to contribute to the wellbeing of the other. I shall come to Easby Abbey in a moment. Facts concerning Richmond still obtrude themselves.

Originally Richmond Castle contained five acres of ground, but even now, despite the vigilance of the wardens, bits have a tendency to slip away. The building stands on a hill a mere hundred feet above the Swale; you would imagine it more. The keep is a hundred feet high and its walls are eleven feet thick. The population of Richmond is something over four thousand. Richmond, Yorkshire, gave its name to Richmond, Surrey. The Lass of Richmond Hill lived here in Yorkshire. There are many Richmonds in the world, but how they came to be named I do not know : Richmond, the suburb of Melbourne; Richmond in Wayne County, Indiana; Richmond in Madison County, Kentucky; and, of course, Richmond, Virginia, where the tobacco comes from. And certainly these are not the only Richmonds in the Anglo-Saxon world.

In the reign of Henry VII, who was Harry Richmond, the Honour of Richmond became Crown land, and thereafter seems to have been conferred upon the bastard sons of royalty. Nevertheless, or perhaps therefore, in the eighteenth century it produced that astute and dangerous philosopher Conyers Middleton, for whose work we ought to express more admiration and respect. J. Pye, for Whitaker's *History of Richmondshire* (in two volumes, each of which weighs nearly a stone), produced an engraving of Grey Friars Tower —a dull business—and, admiring the architectural features of the place, young Hazlewood and Henry Bertram in riding-boots, stovepipe hats and clawhammer coats escort Julia Mannering and Lucy Bertram in mantillas and late eighteenth-century furbelows. In 1817 Thomas Bradley's plan of Richmond shows the strip-system of agriculture still functioning. West Field has six strips, with the rest either fallow or waste; Gallow Field lies to the north of the town and with Bolton Croft shows many strips; the old raceground lies north of Gallow Field; then there are High East Field and Low East Field, both also in strips; the cockpit is shown west of the castle garth; there are Friary Closes and Nun's Closes, and Richmond School Lands lie to the north of High East Field. Whitaker in 1823 found sheep grazing in the castle garth.

You may feel some urge to consult Whitaker's *History of Richmondshire*, and I should advise consulting it where it lies. The two volumes are difficult to transport in anything less than a handcart, and they are full of genealogical tables and manorial records largely in Latin. Whitaker is not history but the rawest material of history—rawer by much than Stubbs and Prothero combined. He has no genius, this Whitaker. Speight later condemned his work as slipshod and inaccurate. Not that Speight is very much better himself.

The finest phrase concerning this neighbourhood comes from Phillips the geologist, who remarks how "the long digitations of the mountains come boldly to the Swale." That is almost poetry, and, moreover, it is accurate in its observation.

Most people nowadays take large and lively interest in town planning. They concern themselves about linear cities on the Russian plan, about green belts and the relationship between town and country. Within the area of the North Riding of Yorkshire they will find little to perturb them. In Scarborough they may dislike the class segregation of the Barrowcliff Estate, but they will have far to go before they find further justification for criticism. In Richmond they will find a town, an organic unity complete. Richmond must be a good place to live in.

From Richmond market-place I walked down Frenchgate to the Swale and followed the footpath on the right bank of the river. It took me by way of a market garden to Easby Abbey, a Præmonstratensian house with very picturesque surroundings and the most curious layout I have ever seen in monastic architecture. The plan of the ruins provided by the Ministry of Works shows that there is hardly a single right-angle in the whole structure. Rievaulx Abbey was purposely misorientated north and south, but how Easby came to be planned as it was I do not know and I have come across no explanation. No matter how long you stay there you will hardly grow used to its craziness. "Everything," reported Bradley, "is anomalous and disproportioned." He did not pretend to understand why. The situation, picturesque as it is, is not very good, and except for the abbot's solarium the buildings must have been dank, dark and cold. The church— the abbey church—was built first. The primary necessity for the monks was the worshipping of God, and after that the rest might follow. The abbey church has pretty well gone, and of monuments to the monastic dead there are, I think, only two. Turner sketched Easby with the weir in the background, densely wooded, rounded hills—Phillips's digitations— descending to the stream, a waterfowl just alighting on the water and a milkmaid milking a cow in the ruins. Farm buildings impinged upon the crumbling walls. Nowadays the ruins are fenced off from the farm and the milkmaid's place in the sun is occupied by a group of well-informed ladies who can probably make better sense of the ruins than I can. There is good fishing—trout-fishing—in the Swale here. The water-flow is rapid in places, the surface is limpid elsewhere, and a group of common gulls and a pair of pochard are perfectly mirrored in the stream. For the visitor, the trouble is that he is as apt to be interested in the setting as academically intrigued by the medieval architecture, and if he knows Turner's drawing as well as Ruskin knew it he may be even more interested in the drawing than in the reality. I recommend going to Easby Abbey in murky weather with the Swale in full spate. It is then that the Early English chapel, the Decorated gateway, the fragments of the church and the general plan of the ruins can be taken at their full value.

Hard by Easby Abbey stands Easby Church, which, like the Abbey, is dedicated to St Agatha. I found the little church as interesting as the monastic ruin. The abbey vicinage is ruined by the custodian's ugly house, which obtrudes upon the eye. Though I do not vastly admire medieval wall-paintings

—they are insufficiently rich in colouring and always remind me of cheap distemper—the paintings on the walls of Easby Church merit reproduction as throwing light upon medieval rustic life. In 1897 Speight recorded that their subjects were difficult to trace. Now they are not. Here is a man of the Middle Ages broadcasting seed from a wooden bowl slung round his neck. Then there is a horseman with falcon on wrist —I could not identify the species of falcon—and there is Adam, there is Eve, both in handsome though two-dimensional nudity; there is the Tree of the Knowledge of Good and Evil, and there is a singularly cheerful Serpent. All this is on the north wall. On the south wall the painter has spread himself in episodes from the Life of Christ. The colours are more vivid than those of the murals in Pickering Church, and they pleased me.

Finally, there is the seventh-century Northumbrian cross. Speight, curiously, does not mention it. Vale states that the original is in the Victoria and Albert Museum. The notes in the church imply that the visitor is looking at part of the original cross, the other part being in the Victoria and Albert. Cast or original, there is evidence of fine culture in this Easby Cross, and it is justly famous.

Here, when you walk down to the edge of the river, you realize that the Swale, within the length of a mere mile, has ceased to be a hill stream. It has now finished with swelling turbulences, tumultuous foamings and spumings, and has become a river of the peneplane, quitting the beauty of Swaledale for flat arable and pasture, for a slow, unstimulating tortuosity. From this point it gains only one feeder of importance, the Wiske; and the Wiske (the name is probably cognate with Usk and Esk) is a river of marish ground even more than the plainland Swale.

I went back to Richmond and thought about Swaledale. What, in fact, had I to say about Swaledale?

"On eche side of Suadale be greate hilles where they digge lead. Little corne groweth in Suadale."

"Sualedale, litle corne and much gresse, no wodd but linge, and sum nutte trees."

The first statement is not in all respects now accurate. They no longer dig lead in the great hills, though if you look at the

Encyclopedia Britannica you will be persuaded that they do. The abandoning of the lead-workings would have delighted Whitaker, who despised every form of human toil except charitable, agricultural and clerical, and who lamented the brutish and ungentlemanly conduct of the Swaledale miners. I, too, am glad, though for a different reason. I know one old lead-miner. All his comrades died young, of lead-poisoning. He, the survivor, is dead-alive; he has been moribund, paralysed, full of poison, for many years. Lead-mining is not a healthy occupation, and the abandoned adits, the deep holes, the wrecked smelt-mills, represent an increase in the general health of the Swaledale and Arkengarthdale population. The great hills remain, the grass and ling remain, and the nut-trees.

Swaledale has few antiquities, and this is to be expected, for in ancient and medieval days and well into modern times Swaledale was deer-forest and lead-mines, heavily wooded and sparsely inhabited. In writing about Swaledale, therefore, my difficulty is that the area is all of a piece. There is variety in the scenery, but no economic variety and little temporal variety. Little corn and much grass; no wood but ling, and some nut-trees. That is Swaledale.

I sat on the steps of Richmond market cross and thought about the Whartons—the Earls of Wharton who formerly owned great areas of Swaledale, and I wished I had before me the Wharton Papers. I wished, too, I could at that moment read through Swift's *Character of the Earl of Wharton*, perhaps the most savage indictment of one man by another in the whole of English pamphleteering. When I reached home I read it through.

"He is without the sense of shame or glory, as some men are without the sense of smelling; and therefore a good name to him is no more than a precious ointment would be to those. . . . He seems to be but an ill dissembler and an ill liar, though they are the two talents he most practises, and most values himself upon. The ends he has gained by lying appear to be more owing to the frequency than the art of them; his lies being sometimes detected in an hour, often in a day, and always in a week. He tells them freely in mixed companies, though he knows half of those that hear him to be his enemies, and is sure they will discover them the moment they leave him. He swears solemnly he loves and will serve you, and your back is no sooner turned but he tells those about him you are a dog and a rascal. . . . He is a Presbyterian in politics and an atheist in religion."

This *Character of Thomas Earl of Wharton* (1645?–1715) is not to be regarded as typical of the Swaledale population of the late seventeenth century and the early eighteenth. Wharton was a man of affairs, a Whig politician, not a Swaledale recluse, though the royalties from the Swaledale lead-mines formed part of his wealth. As for the lead-mining, tradition and archæology are positive that the Romans began it. Pigs of lead have been found with the stamps upon them of Domitian, Nero, Hadrian and Vespasian. For myself, I should set its beginnings even earlier, upon evidence that the Brigantes worked in metals and that their capital city was not far from Swaledale. King John's reign certainly saw lead-mining in Swaledale, Arkengarthdale, and principally on the Yorkshire side of the Tees, over thirty square miles of rough country in the vicinity of Maize Beck and the Lune. In 1609 the London Lead Company began thorough mining operations in Teesdale and Lunedale, and the work went on until, owing to Spanish competition, only twenty tons of ore were mined in 1913. Nowadays, if a stranger to the Yorkshire dales visits Pateley Bridge, Grinton or Leyburn and professes himself interested in lead it will not be long before someone offers to sell him a mine. He will be well advised to decline the offer, for though the twentieth century has seen shafts sunk and galleries opened out the workings in general have been casual and superficial, the veins of galena unreliable and the profits non-existent. One owner in Wensleydale threw away £800 with no return whatever for his outlay.

It is time I wrote something about the groovers or lead-miners, "exhibiting in their language, customs and manners strong traces of aboriginal descent or something like it." Companies ran the mines—the Hurst Mining Company, the Surrender Mining Company, the Old Gang Lead Mining Company. There was also a good deal of private enterprise. Small men worked small mines. David Harker of Muker worked the Muker Edge or Providence Mine and "made such a lot of money he was nicknamed 'the Rothschilde.' " His mine was closed about 1860 and no plans are now available.

Sometimes lead-mining was easy. Moles discovered or uncovered a rich vein on the Bolton Estate. At Ballowfield the ore came right up to the sod. Yet rich veins, sometimes six feet wide, brought in a rapid accession of wealth to the companies and royalty-owners and then mysteriously and capriciously petered out. The rich veins had special names : Watersikes Vein, Friarfold Vein, Kinning Vein. Nobody knew why the lead was there. Nowadays it is believed that the veins were squeezed into the limestone during periods of intense volcanic activity, but this is still theory and not yet verifiable fact. Most of the lead-workings closed down between 1870 and 1890. The names of the mines are not enormously impressive or romantic : Old Gang, Beldi Hill, Barbara Level, Cat Shaft, Craw Level, Copperthwaite, Hard Level, Sir Francis Level, Pryes Level, Beezy Mines, Alsop's Shaft, Applegarth Mine, Ashpot Level, Allmaker's Shaft.

Up Cogden Beck I found the old Grinton smelt-mills, and, all along the bare hill-slopes, the low-level and high-level adits and the shafts and spoil-heaps; little hemispherical archways of stone showing just enough darkness to swallow up a stooping man. Within, rusty broken rails, rotted sleepers, pools of stagnant water. Where the miners sank shafts they were shaped just like wells, lined out with stone. I dropped stones into the darkness. Five seconds was a long time to wait for the splash. Many of these mines are now flooded. They are all without exception wet.

Often the miners resorted to "hushing." They dammed a mountain runnel until they were satisfied with the volume of water collected, then they broke the dam, the water rushed down the slope of the fell, tore away the surface vegetation and soil, and exposed the veins of galena. If the veins held prospect of profitable working, they made adits and burrowed inwards. None of these old lead-workings is safe.

To-day the only active industry dependent upon the earth's crust and not the earth's surface is the quarrying of chert. This chert comes out in blocks of tough siliceous material and it goes to the Potteries. There they make millstones of it for grinding calcined flints used in the manufacture of hard china-ware. The earliest chert-workings were between Reeth and Richmond. Now the industry is also carried on at Leyburn and elsewhere in Wensleydale.

Examining the looping of the Swale round the castle crag at Richmond, you may be tempted to imagine that it was deliberately so designed by nature to perfect the picture. This is not quite the case. Formerly the Swale ran through the hollow north of the market-place. This was in the years before the Ice Age. Then, during the Ice Age, the Teesdale glacier pushed its snout over the hills and dammed the river, which, rising until it became a lake, finally "hushed" its way round the snout of the glacier and cut the gorge it follows to-day. There are traces of laminated clay in the castle crag, and these relics of the former lake are responsible for the occasional slipping of the castle walls. The story of the Ice Age in Swaledale, however, is not yet complete.

The beauty of Swaledale is not that of Wensleydale. The fell-slopes are precipitous and craggy, and the head of the dale, except for Buttertubs Pass, is closed. The road up Swaledale is the road to nowhere. The scenery is wild, and, in Whitaker's time, the population was equally wild, very isolated, almost immune from civilizing influences. The medieval church showed little interest in Swaledale, more-over, and Marrick Priory stands as almost its sole relic. Though Rievaulx Abbey owned much land hereaway, the monks exerted no civilizing influence. They owned the land for what they could wring out of it, not what they could put into it. The Anglican Church has never done much mission-work in Swaledale, for the population turned early, under the Wharton influence, to nonconformity. Personally I think religion throughout the bulk of the North Riding is something that veneers the surface of conduct and speech but hides a deep-rooted paganism that has no gods but those of nature, worshipped not in name and not consciously but yet held in awe and reverence. In Swaledale remains a good deal that has perished elsewhere in the Riding—old ways of life, old ways of speech and old customs. There are, I believe, quilting-patterns peculiar to Swaledale. Hill farmers call themselves statesmen. The cairns on the fells are known as curracks. The sleds they use in Swaledale are called coup carts, straight from the Old Norse. Within living memory the Celtic numerals for counting sheep were in use, as they were also in the Vale of Pickering and in the north-eastern moorlands. White cats are curiously common. So are brass bands. And Swaledale is full of "they says."

They say that Old Gang Lead Mine was worked two thousand years ago. They say that fugitives from Culloden took refuge in Swaledale. They say that Swinnergill Kirk was used as a secret place of worship during times of religious persecution. It is now hardly possible to verify many of these traditions.

The economic history of Swaledale presents a series of shifts. In medieval days, the almost unpopulated deer-forest and its verdurers. Concomitantly, lead-mining. Concomitantly, monastic or conventual establishments. Then sheep, probably very small sheep, for the wool was always worth a good deal more than the carcass. Knitting seamen's woollen caps and stockings, largely for export through Richmond to the Low Countries. Pauper children and the children of hinds and carters were apprenticed to this knitting industry. Lead-mining still, and men, women and boys engaged in it; men and boys in the mines, women earning a shilling a day for an eight-hour day and thinking themselves lucky to be married to miners rather than to farmers. In those days the population of Swaledale was roughly double what it is now, and the mining communities demanded double or more than double the number of taverns that now exist. The miners always formed an economic segregation. Often they built their own villages, which have since gone derelict or disappeared into dry walls and laithes. They were a strange folk. Often they had no knowledge of the names they had been christened by (when they were christened at all), and the muster-roll of the Loyal Dales Volunteers in 1804 makes curious reading. There were, for instance, eight Thomas Aldersons, and to distinguish them from one another they were called Grain Tom, Glowermore Tom, Screamer Tom, Poddish Tom, Tarry Tom, Tish Tom, Tripy Tom and Trooper Tom. Then there was Angry Jack, Nettlebed Anty, Katy Tom Alick and Rive Rags. The last name is still, in the moors, applied to mis-

chievous lads : *a proper raav-rags*. This system of nomenclature—it really is a system—has now died out in Swaledale,
and in 1909 the mining community had all but vanished.
There remained eleven miners in Arkengarthdale; in Low
Row, one; in Feetham, one. In Feetham Anthony Waters and
a man called Calvert combined mining with farming; in
Fremington William Hird and Chris Hird were coal-miners,
though Chris Hird was also a farmer; in Grinton, Frankland
was farmer and miner. And that, I think, made up the full
tally of the mining community in Swaledale in 1909. Farming
was not then profitable, for many Swaledale farmers followed
other occupations in addition—shoemaking, joinering and
shepherding chiefly. The dale had its gamekeepers, game-
watchers, graziers, woodmen, foresters, wood-hewers,
quarrymen, masons, smiths, joiners, shepherds, hinds, carters
and carriers. Close of Gunnerside was chapel-keeper and
gamewatcher; George Alderson was clock-dresser and stone-
mason.

Wells's *Tono-Bungay* portrays the country house system
yet unvanquished in 1910. It existed then in Swaledale,
though the proportion of grooms, coachmen, chauffeurs,
valets, lady's maids, kennelmen and gardeners to farmers and
craftsmen was small. The gang of squires which ran the
Tono-Bungay system in Swaledale was also an economic
segregation as queer in its ways as the mining segregation.
Hutton of Marske who died in 1783 remembered that at
Richmond Races it was considered advisable to drink a bottle
of sherry out of a tankard at a single draught. At Newton
Hall in Sir Henry Liddell's time six bottles of wine were
laid on the floor beside each guest. When every bottle was
emptied the horses were brought in and the riders, if they
could, rode upstairs to bed. Voltaire and Rousseau were the
favourite authors of these pot-valiant fellows. All that, of
course, was a long time ago.

How to penetrate into Swaledale? The railway will take
you to Richmond, the good road will take you up the dale.
Or, better, you may cross the fells from Wensleydale. The
road from Leyburn, for example, is a good road, forthright
and interesting. Following it, you have a fair cross-section of
the fells. The worst of this road is that you may not, after all,

Easby Abbey

reach Swaledale. It has so many tempting by-roads branching off towards remote hamlets and wild places. Leaving Leyburn, it is not at first very interesting. The outskirts of Leyburn have an Edwardian hardness upon the eye, their stonework is cold, their frontages are unattractive, their terracing is repellent. Then, climbing, the road threads hill-country all tamed for sheep and cattle. Swaledale sheep and Shorthorn cattle. You greet the outcroppings of Yoredale limestone and find mute witness that in Napoleonic times or in the forties of the nineteenth century some of this thin grazing land was ploughed and baulked for corn-growing. Once this turf has been disturbed it cannot regain in a whole century the fine smooth quality it develops in ages of close grazing. Foreign grasses and noisome weeds, securing root-hold, refuse to be ousted and thereafter the pasture has a shaggy, unkempt appearance.

As usual in this region the villages are difficult to date, but here and there I came upon a handsome Jacobean manor house or farm that told me plainly enough that in the seventeenth century big-scale sheep-farming was profitable if the owners did not worry overmuch how their shepherds were housed. The shepherds' homes, the mud and timber hovels, have vanished under stress of time and economic blizzardry. The hamlets I saw belonged to the late years of the eighteenth century and to the nineteenth, with some cottages of the usual modern sort, red brick, slate, and steel-framed windows.

The fells are green, but greyish-green. The grass lacks nitrogenous manure but is good enough for Swaledale sheep and store cattle. There is little corn, much craggy outcropping, with gorse and sparse patches of ling. When I went through in late August I found men, women, girls and boys hay-making, taking advantage of a spell of brief sunshine. Elsewhere some of the meadows stood unscythed.

"A bad summer!" I said.

They agreed it had been a bad summer, but, good summer or bad, there is inevitably a vast difference between the hay-crop in the hills and that in the lowlands. Large-scale mechanization here would pay no dividend.

From the spacious hill country the road makes down into

Lower Swaledale. I remarked the masses of deciduous woodland on each side of the river, but the massing, though seem-
ingly heavy, was more apparent than real. There were no
noble trees. This was scrub-stuff whose function was to prevent subsidence of the steep slopes into the valley of the
Swale. Now a good deal of it had been cleared. Beauty had
been destroyed.

So I came down from the hills into Swaledale and looked
through the screen of hazels to the turbid river, the water
leaping, like liquid silver slightly tarnished, over the rocks in
the bed of the stream. The gorge was narrow, filled with
shadow dappled by sunshine. It lacked no element of the
picturesque. I stood four miles from Richmond, and presently
turned up the dale, my road running pleasantly alongside the
river. As I went by the relics of Ellerton Priory, the dale still
narrow and its sides precipitous, with plantations of woodland
on the lower slopes, I saw the hamlet of Marrick above the
northern bank of the Swale, and, lower down to the river and
a mile farther upstream, the ruined tower of Marrick Priory
upon which the newer church is parasitic. Turner made a fine
drawing of Marrick Priory and historians have dealt exhaustively with the community of nuns once living there, and how
much the property was worth at the Dissolution. Those days
wake in my mind no echoes louder than those of the horns of
elfland.

Grinton parish holds 49,000 acres; 30,000 of them consist
of grouse-moor and mountain. Swaledale widens here, perhaps to hold Grinton Church, which is bigger than you would
expect. They talk of the green road south of the river, running
westward along the hillside, as the old corpseway, along
which the dead were carried in wicker baskets to be buried in
the churchyard at Grinton. There is a Maiden Castle about a
couple of miles west of Grinton. Reeth, a small grey village,
is the capital of Swaledale, but now lacks importance. Its
market and its fairs have dwindled; its agricultural show has
still value, but when I look at a place like Reeth I am inclined
to fear that what has been lost on the swings is not always
made up on the roundabouts. Life even in the villages does
not remain static; it changes for better or worse, and though
agricultural prosperity and depression show themselves pretty

quickly in the Vale of York and the Vale of Mowbray and one can see with one's own eyes the seesaw of values, that is not so easy in places like Swaledale. Anyhow Reeth is a worthy place. Swaledale is at its widest here, with a flat valley bottom, green and rich where the Arkle Beck joins the Swale. And still the dale is wide and green up to Healaugh, and then the hills close in upon the river towards Feetham and Low Row. Harkerside Moor and Whitaside Moor rise to the south, and an old trail crosses the tops towards the abandoned Apedale mines, towards Redmire Moor and Castle Bolton in Wensleydale. Feetham and Low Row were both famous mining villages. Arkengarthdale, with Arkle Town, Langthwaite and Whaw, is as famous for its pastures as Swaledale itself, and Fremington Edge, along its northeastern side, is as brant a scar as exists in the whole area. There is woodland in Arkengarthdale, and here I would remark the occurrence in Swaledale and Arkengarthdale of yew and juniper. Juniper I have always thought of in association with the chalk of Wiltshire, but here it is indigenous to Swaledale.

Calver Hill (pronounced Cawver) is south of Arkle, and has quarries of chert. A mile beyond Langthwaite a road toiling north over Arkengarthdale Moor to Barnard Castle shows one of the routes taken by the jagger ponies with their loads of lead, which were driven finally to Stockton for London, the Low Countries and the Baltic ports. Often these trains of jagger ponies were driven by women.

On this road there is vast isolation. There are precipitous descents, sudden mosses, difficult fords, holes in the moor where the clints have widened and deepened, gathering-grounds for Eller Beck, Thwaite Beck, Brignall Beck. The prevailing impression is one of immense, silent, primitive, greyish-brown, brutish moorland. Hope Moor, with the crag of Hope Edge lit slantingly by the westering sun, gives an amphitheatrical view to the north and is worth the climb to 1700 feet above datum line. When I crossed these moors between Swaledale and Teesdale I met rain, driving mist and darkness.

From the heights south of Hawes I looked across Upper Wensleydale and saw the long trail of Buttertubs Pass doglegging upward through the brown hills over into Swaledale, and presently I found myself on that road. It is a good road for motor-cars, though the water in the radiator is apt to boil before the crest is reached. It is a long road for pedestrians, yet still a good road. Into Swaledale I do not know a better. The Buttertubs themselves are holes in the limestone rock, their sides go almost perpendicularly down, with little ledges where ferns grow, and rich green in the bottoms, which vary in depth from shallow to very deep. They are the work of acidified water enlarging original clints, and they attract sightseers as surely as buddleias attract butterflies. They are not dangerous to survey except in darkness or snow.

I came down to Keld on its sloping terrace above the gorge of the Swale, and from Keld I might have caught the bus to Richmond. Instead, I stayed to look at the place after an interval of ten years. It hadn't changed, though I suspect it grows more familiar with holiday-makers in the summer. The Swale was low when I looked into its bed, but I have seen it angry and turbid here, dangerous and powerful after a quick thaw. The word *Keld* means *spring*, and hereabouts are the gathering-grounds of the Swale. There is a village band, as there is at Stape above Pickering; Keld numbers in its population a professional dry-waller who knows all the secrets of the craft, and Keld sports make June important in the locality. Men fling quoits here.

When I took up a vantage-point from which I could look down Swaledale, I found something to puzzle me. Like the Ure, the Swale carves its way through the Yoredale Limestone; like Wensleydale, Swaledale was subjected to intense glaciation; yet Swaledale is narrower and deeper than Wensleydale and its steeper slopes are not terraced like those of Wensleydale. I cannot give any reason for the differences.

From Keld I went to look at Kisdon Force as a matter of duty. It is the finest cascade in Swaledale, but I preferred the walk to the waterfall. Keld is a magnificent centre for walking. You may follow, as I did later, the young Swale from Keld to Muker, or pursue the track along the north bank of the Swale to Gunnerside, Feetham and Reeth, or ascend Sleddale to Hell Gill, or make a beeline over Shunner Fell to nowhere in especial. But choose your day! You must certainly visit the inn at Tan Hill to find out when coal-mining was abandoned here and what conditions were like at the inn during February 1947. You may try to establish the evidences of secret religious worship in the cavern called Swinnergill Kirk (it is not a very imposing cavern), find out what proof exists that fugitives from Culloden settled in the recesses of the dale, what remains of the traditional quilting-patterns— fern, star, bellows and star, twist and plate; whether the Celtic numerals for counting sheep are anywhere remembered, how many members of the Swaledale Sheep Breeders' Society there are in Keld, Muker, Reeth and Gunnerside; who remembers Richard and Cherry Kearton in Thwaite; what connection there is between the saeters of Norway and the Seats of Swaledale, and what further evidences there are of a Viking penetration and settlement of Swaledale from the north-west.

All this locality around Keld passed into Wharton hands after the Dissolution. Philip Lord Wharton built Gang Hall, and Thomas Earl of Wharton built Park Hall at Healaugh. They drew royalties from the coal and lead workings and preserved the forest in its wild state. Wild deer roamed there as late as 1725, and in the same year the Whartons, much to the astonishment of the natives, introduced shooting flying. The farmers of Swaledale and Wensleydale are pretty handy with shotguns. They shoot foxes without any remorse of conscience. For myself, I have never seen a fox in either Upper Wensleydale or in Swaledale. They must be secretive beasts or else they are rare.

The woodlands of Swaledale are necessary to prevent the stripping of the steep hill slopes. Some damage has already been done, and there is one place on the road from Richmond to Reeth where you were formerly asked to beware of falling rock. Last time I went that way the notice was not there.

Swaledale as a whole has moved little since the mining community went away. The bridges have not been widened to any extent, and though the roads have been improved the road system has not been extended. There is indeed no call to extend it, for Swaledale is not a development area and is not likely to become one. It has few potentialities for expansion.

CHAPTER XI

TEESDALE

ROUGHLY a century and a half ago, the craving for romantic landscape drove leisured ladies and gentlemen into the wild areas of Britain to make sketches in pencil or water-colour and to compose emotional impressions in the fine Italianate calligraphy of their journals. Yet they seem largely to have neglected the ninety square miles of Upper Teesdale. The springs of Tees on the slopes of Cross Fell, of Maize Beck on Murton Fell, of Lune water, the Balder and the Greta, went unvisited, and still, except for the occasional enthusiast for long-distance tramping and endurance tests, they are lonely places. In the Teesdale fell country alike in spring and autumn I find leagues of rough moorland wind-swept and empty, and there as in Swaledale and Wensleydale the relics of abandoned industry are vanishing into the landscape. There, too, similar economic conditions prevail. Men measure their wealth in acres of scanty but sweet pasture and moorland, in sheep and cattle, in gallons of milk and in the wool-clip, with some quarrying and some forestry. But there is this difference between Wensleydale and Swaledale on the one hand, and Upper Teesdale on the other, that in the former the grouse-moors are of less economic importance and there is less woodland for the protection and encouragement of black game. A good deal of Upper Teesdale is well wooded, and there are more birds. The climate is apt also to be less bleak than that of Wensleydale and Swaledale, and living conditions in Upper Teesdale struck me as being a little easier than in the more southerly dales. There is, however, still another difference, that in Wensleydale and Swaledale the landscapes are moulded of limestone only, and in Teesdale of volcanic dolerite and rhyolite as well as of limestone.

The Pennine foldings—there is no such thing as a Pennine Chain—are of immense antiquity, and their highest point, Mickle Fell, 2591 feet above sea-level, is a molehill compared to what it was before the processes of denudation had their way with it and with the surrounding hills. These Pennine foldings resulted originally from violent volcanic activity in remote Brittany—the Armorican earthstorm—and they were further complicated by an east-to-west folding from the Cleveland Hills to the Isle of Man. These foldings took place towards the end of the Carboniferous Age, when the lower limestones had already been laid down. Then occurred a terrific upthrust and a massive block-faulting, lifting the whole area another three thousand feet or more. It extended over a long period of time during which the crust of the earth in this region was unstable and the rainfall was torrential. Now, when the traveller penetrates into Upper Teesdale, it is not only the puritan nature of limestone scenery that takes his eye. Alike at High Force, at White Force, Cauldron Snout, Cronkley Fell and High Cup Nick he is taken by the grim shafting of plutonic rock, black crags sixty to eighty feet high above the sharp limestone screes; and this intrusion of columnar basalt, the Whin Sill, is the most striking feature of the Upper Teesdale landscape. The flow of lava originated in the volcanic area of Shap, and the geologists feel moderately sure that the volcanoes were not, at the time of their greatest activity, at the bottom of the sea. The lava converted the limestone above and below it into the rough marble common in the district.

Nor was Teesdale free from the powerful agencies of glaciation. Indeed the Swaledale and Wensleydale glaciers, big as they were, were not comparable in size to the Teesdale ice, which, pushing one snout over the hills into Tynedale, pushed another over into Swaledale, contrived to direct its main flow along the present course of the river, and deposited its terminal moraine in the North Sea along a portion of the sea-floor now known to Teesmouth fishermen as the Rough Ground. Then from the icefields of Northern Europe came the Scandinavian ice-sheet to turn the Teesdale glacier south along the fringe of the North Riding coast, add its abrasive scouring to that of the northern ice and deposit its boulders of Shap granite as far south as Bay. These conjectural movements of the Teesdale ice have importance first because the landscape can thus be interpreted and secondly because the botanist seeks for those relics of pre-glacial vegetation which, on isolated nunataks, survived the onslaught of the ice and the great cold.

In Upper Teesdale as in Upper Swaledale the hay harvest is of prime importance, and here, as in the rest of the fell country, the margin of leisure and security for the farmer is narrow. League upon league of moor and mountain, thick deposits of peat in which the bleached stumps and roots of ancient trees are still visible, black and forbidding pools of water, slack and marish ground, the whistling of the wind in harsh ling and tough grass, with glimpses, from the tops, of rich green river valleys to westward and eastward; on occasion the roar of falling water; the clouds rising over the level tops, the rush of shadow on the grey-green slopes, the whitewashed steadings of shepherds and farmers; these things characterize Upper Teesdale—these things, and the plantations of spruce fir mostly on the Durham side of the river.

Making for the kelds of Tees on the slopes of Cross Fell, I crossed the bleakest of moorlands two thousand feet above sea-level. The wind was bitterly cold out of the north-east. There were whinchats, curlew and grouse. In this locality the dotterel once bred, but I have never seen the bird either here or in the East Riding, where it was also once common. Both red grouse and black grouse were rare too, and if ravens once bred regularly on Falcon Clints on the Durham side, I saw no ravens. Indeed this high moor showed few signs of wild life. As I walked, I wondered if, not well conditioned to this country, I should love it or hate it. It is hostile to human life. Not born to this land, I was an intruder.

Tees was a mere beck in its stony bed. I looked north, and saw the marshy depression a mile away, where the South Tyne took its rise. I had no great heart to go farther, and, turning, made back along the right bank of the stream. Four miles I pursued its windings across a moderately level moor, though I had strayed beyond the border of the North Riding. I noted the broadening of the stream at the Wheal, from which the water begins to carve for itself a gorge through the hills, and in a mere half-mile descends a couple of hundred feet. This was Cauldron Snout, and here, below the foot-

bridge, I stood in the North Riding to watch the white fan
of water rushing down between the dark columns of basaltic
rock. The fall is not sufficiently accessible to have become a
show-place like High Force, and my own opinion is that
Cauldron Snout is finer than High Force. The land is more
naked, the forces at work are more elemental, and nowhere
else in the country does there exist so deep a fall upon so
large a stream. The effect of the basalt is that of a ruined
staircase in grim rock, and the water comes down not in a
single mass but with lace-like patternings very attractive to
the eye. I crossed the footbridge and went up Widdy Bank
Fell to see how the lava-flow turned the limestone above it
into coarse, granular marble, which, weathering, breaks up
into calcite sand-crystals. Here, too, I looked for *Gentiana
verna*, but looked in vain. Perhaps it is still there, but perhaps
also the collectors have denuded the locality of its blue stars.
They have, I know, been actively in pursuit of rare alpines in
this locality, and their depredations have almost certainly
deprived the botanist of studying certain pre-glacial flora *in
situ*, so that there will always remain a gap in their knowledge. There certainly remained a gap in mine. I came down
from Widdy Bank Fell to the river, stood on the footbridge
and watched the water rushing down below me. Had there
been, that day, a more copious flow of water, it would have
been a great spectacle. As it was, there was insufficient flow to
satisfy me, and no great volume of sound. I took the track
from the bridge, following the course of Maize Beck towards
the two or three farmsteads called Birkdale. These I left for
the open moor between Meldon Fell and the beck, and,
aiming west, came to the beck at a sheep-wash. Here I crossed
from Westmorland back into the North Riding and followed
the stony stream across the moor for another two miles or so,
then turned my back upon the water and, making over a
plateau of limestone, went forward swiftly towards a gap
between the hills. It was thus I came to High Cup Nick, in
Westmorland, where a small stream traversing the high
plateau comes to an eighty-foot precipice of basalt and
cascades into the gulf below. The Whin Sill is sheer, and
below it lies a steep scree of detritus. It is an impressive
spectacle. Here, I am told, you may meet the Helm Wind,

though I escaped it. It blows often for nine successive days and makes a noise like that of a stormy sea. Carts may be overturned by it, and trees uprooted, and a few miles away no wind is stirring. Here I was not far from the height of Mickle Fell, but found it hard to pick out from the other hills, and I did not climb to its summit. Indeed, except for the fell-walker, Mickle Fell has little attraction, and to climb it that day I should have needed a double allowance of double summer time. Back I went round the spurs of Cronkley Fell, which are, in truth, only shoulders of Mickle Fell. They are high, steep and forbidding, but though they seemed to me to be pretty bare of vegetation, they, and the shallow tarns at their feet, are quartered by the botanist in search of rarities. I made for Cronkley Bridge, but instead of crossing it, I kept to the Yorkshire side of the river, found the Pencil Mill, where shale-beds were worked for slate-pencils in the days when I was a small boy, and the next reach of the river brought me to the most northerly point in the Riding— latitude 54° 39′ 50″. There I swung back to the east with no intention of turning out of my way again, and yet I was led into the hills once more to look at White Force. Sometimes White Force is dry or all but dry. I found it half-dry. There was more basalt, here sixty feet thick and resting upon marbled limestone, and I enjoyed the grim primitiveness of the gorge. Then I came down by the bridle track to Skyer Beck and Blea Beck. Here in the hillside above me I found slight traces of old ironstone workings, which, I should think, were never very profitable but which reminded me of the red gashes in the Bilsdale scars a long way to the east. Thus I came down to the Castles at Holwick and to Holwick Crag, noted on his map by Saxton in 1577. Here, as Derryhouses pointed out, the melt-waters of the glacier carved out a channel of their own alongside the glacier channel. I found myself on level ground after that, and came to the region of quarries where the Whin Sill provides first-class road-metal.

I went to High Force, but not that same day, and I went there by the Durham road, not the Yorkshire. It brought into my mind three recollections : one, of a gaudy picture of High Force seen in a railway compartment and never quite for- gotten; second, of Turner's drawing of the Force; third, of

High Force as I saw it once, with the central boss of rock almost, but not quite, hidden by the rush of water. The first and the third I think repellent for different reasons. The railway-train picture had neither art nor accuracy, and my own recollection was always nightmarish. I could not endure a fall that blew its trumpet without stopping to take breath, and I found menace in the voices within the main voice of the fall. Turner's fisherman with his huge angling-rod and the lad with the landing-net seem quite unimpressed by the clamour of the waters, by the arch of rainbow rising from the foot of the main fall to the lip of the lesser, and by the fact that the slenderer cascade seems not quite of this world. They remain for ever free from hypnosis. To them the gloom is less than Stygian and the light less than elysian.

High Force has been made very comfortable for the sightseer. The sixty-foot cascade falls into a pool in which there is no risk of being drowned. He need not, as a matter of fact, go nearer to the fall than the windows of High Force Hotel, from which he may see it with the slope of Noon Fell backing it and a fringe of spruce fir to frame it.

High Force has produced no poetry of great merit. And inevitably the poets fall into octosyllabic couplets through the sad influence of Scott :

> Fill'd was the air with music true
> (Though loved, alas ! by far too few).
> For Nature's sounds are sweet to hear
> If listened for by trained ear.
> The Tees itself, though far away
> Threading its course through distance grey,
> Proclaims aloud with mighty roll
> Its progress to a far-off goal;
> And rushing madly headlong o'er,
> At High Force leaps with ceaseless roar.
> Thence bubbling, hissing, onward goes,
> Till lost to view in deep repose.

That is about the measure of it.

In 1773, romanticism was not yet quite sure of itself, and Nathaniel Spenser, coming this way, expressed himself in more pious terms : "The water of the river, having collected itself together at the top of a frightful precipice, falls down with such a prodigious roar that it is heard at a great distance; for the perpendicular is twenty-three yards. The force of the water dashing against the rocks fills the mind with horror, but the scattered rays of the sun shining through the misty particles gives the whole the appearance of a most beautiful rainbow. The whole scene is so amazingly delightful that the spectator is lost in admiration at the infinite wisdom of the Creator of the Universe, and filled with the most elevated notions of His power and majesty."

When the American bragged to the Yorkshireman of the thousands of millions of gallons pouring hourly over the lip of Niagara, the Yorkshireman answered that he, for his part, didn't see owt to stop it. I feel that way, rather, about High Force.

The river just above the fall is very imposing. The view below the fall is also very fine. Spruce fir is still dense on the Durham side. The Yorkshire side is craggy, and above the crags the steep shoulder of Green Fell.

Much of the water that flows into Tees on the Yorkshire side takes its rise beyond the border. Lune Forest and Lunedale, with Lune Moor and Mickleton Moor, lie within it. These areas are not easy to explore and give much hard travel. Anyone interested in the old lead-mining would have to explore them, for here the London Lead Company worked assiduously and profitably for a long time. Some Derbyshire miners came north, but I think they lived in County Durham, not in the North Riding. The main stock here is Scandinavian, and it got here not from the east but from the west. It remains sparse and scanty. I should say that the average density per square mile is less than that for the whole Riding, which has a quarter of a person to every square mile. The most important people hereabouts are the quarrymen.

When I came down to Middle Teesdale, I reflected how there were places in England about which it was impossible in plain prose to say anything original or new. So many people have exercised capability and originality upon them that it is now impertinent to try to add to their number. Mind you, the thing could be done by the artist: a Van Gogh landscape is not a Rembrandt or a Titian; a Cézanne is not a Ruysdael. It

269

could be done, I suppose, in poetry. I do not, however, see that it could be done in essay or topographical prose. Travelling eastward along the course of Tees, to such places I now came. Could I add anything to the extant descriptions of Rokeby Hall and Rokeby Park, Mortham Peel and Brignall Banks? Could I add new beauty to the wooded glens of Greta, or add a new significance to the loveliness of Thorgill? No great admirer of Scott's octosyllabics, I think Scott made a good job of this area in *Rokeby*. Lacking something of Ruskin's fervour for Turner, I think Turner made an excellent job of Brignall, Egglestone Abbey and the meeting of Tees and Greta. I do not know if Macaulay ever came this way, but he put Scargill into "A Jacobite's Epitaph" with greater effect than he put Janiculum into the lay of "Horatius." And what these forgot the topographers have remembered. From Whitaker and White to Pennell and J. S. Fletcher, they have quartered this ground. It is the topographer's Beulah.

That was exactly as I found it. In describing the North Riding, though economical of superlatives, I had often praised. In Middle Teesdale, others, having exhausted the gamut of adjectival splendour, made my mind slow to react and my pen loath to describe. This was river scenery at its North Riding best; half wild, half tame, the streams not yet forgetful of their mountain springs, the scars and gorges not yet levelled to the alluvium of the Vale of Mowbray. I found fine woodland, many noble trees. I found rich pasture and fertile arable. Then I let my mind sink back upon itself. I made no notes. I did not consciously observe. On reflection, I believe I felt rather than thought that woodland must be luminous to be attractive but that falling water is more impressive in darkness. In Middle Teesdale I had the best of both woodland and water.

I made up my mind that it was hopeless to repeat what others have said. The history of Middle Teesdale centred upon Barnard Castle and the Balliols, which lay over the border in County Durham. Men seeking the past in Teesdale were fain to fall back upon the four or five acres of Roman camp at Greta and the Hand of Glory at the inn on Stainmore, upon Dickens and Phiz investigating the boy-farms of

Bowes and seizing, with some lack of justice, upon one Shaw as the original of Wackford Squeers. They relied upon the "Felon Sow"—I have never found this ballad amusing—and upon the famous Rokeby advice to growing lads. These things are in all the books, together with much Scott. There are also pictures of the tombstones in Bowes churchyard erected to the memory of certain Smikes.

Most of the topographers came here before this corner of the Riding was cleaned up. The bridges were narrow, the inns quiet, the roads rough. Bowes was a one-street village of half-ruined houses. Bowes Castle and Egglestone Abbey were nettle-grown and neglected, and nobody cared that Bowes was the Lavatræ of the Romans. Nobody went to Barningham, Lartington and Romaldkirk. Save for the scenery, this was a lost land, an outpost, a Lyonesse of the Riding. Even now, the area needs reinterpretation. The riverscapes ought to be painted by men familiar with modern techniques, and the local history needs much overhauling by men who know the value of family letters, business ledgers and human ecology.

How might this be done?

In the early eighteenth century, throughout that century and almost to the end of the nineteenth, the nobility and squirearchy entertained genius in their country houses. When nowadays a country estate comes into the market it is bought by a government department, by a schoolmaster, the Y.H.A., the county authority or the nearest industrial combine, and genius is not admitted. In Middle Teesdale, I suggest, the North Riding County Council ought to buy a biggish country house standing in its own grounds, furnish it handsomely and dedicate it to the use of scholarship and genius. Ultimately this would pay a better dividend than travelling scholarships and research fellowships, and it would be a gracious gesture.

As for the ordinary traveller, I suggest that the best way to make the most of Middle Teesdale is to read Ruskin, in "Modern Painters," on surface and depth in still water, on the difference between the fall and the plunge in moving water, on the effects of light on foliage. Even his errors will assist the untrained eye.

In Upper and Middle Teesdale there will be no more

scarring of the fellsides for galena, no more "hushing." There may be big-scale afforestation in Middle Teesdale, particularly on the Yorkshire side. The quarrying of the Whin Sill will continue. Dairy-farming will prosper more than mixed farming. The economist on survey will mark down Teesdale for holiday, rest and recreation. The existing road system is adequate. Hotel accommodation is not.

In this chapter I shall not deal with the windings of the Tees. I shall take a giant's leap to Tees-side. And if industrial significance is to be the measure of importance then Tees-side is the most important area in the North Riding. This was not always so. At the beginning of the nineteenth century, for instance, the one-street town of Yarm was more important than either Stockton-on-Tees or Middlesbrough, but since that time industry has steadily shifted towards the east, Yarm has now little importance, Stockton has lost what Middlesbrough has gained, and still the eastward shift goes on, so that Eston, Grangetown, South Bank and Redcar are rapidly gaining what Middlesbrough is losing. The best parallel to Teesmouth is London River. Yarm stands at the first practicable spot where the Tees could formerly be bridged, and in the Middle Ages, with its wharves and cobbled market, its shipping and customs, it was a famous port. Its bridge had high strategic value, its shipping was notable as early as 1182, it traded with Scotland, France and Flanders in wool, hides, corn, salt and wine; it was a centre of linen-weaving and cloth-making, and even as late as 1841 it had some value as a port. Now it is a quiet market town, a pleasant place to visit, and such a convenient centre that all roads seem to lead to Yarm, which, in the present, preserves the past yet holds small promise of future growth.

Middlesbrough is a mushroom town. There in ancient days existed a cell of Whitby Abbey in the midst of a grey solitude visited only by grey seals and the grey waters of the estuary. It held, at the beginning of the nineteenth century, four farmhouses with a population of twenty-four persons. The church was in ruins, and the churchyard, now and then used for burials, had no containing wall, hedge or fence. Twenty years later the population stood at forty, and then came the beginnings of change.

The story of rail-routes in the North Riding takes us first into County Durham, where, on 19th October 1827, the proprietors of the Stockton and Darlington Railway resolved to extend their line to Middlesbrough. According to Joseph Pease in 1863, "the silence and solitude of this part of the Tees were only broken by the presence of a few grey-headed seals and a few shrimping-women." He, and Edward Pease, with other Quakers, bought five hundred acres of this silence and solitude for building coal-staiths and a town. They were the Middlesbrough Owners.

Viewing the projected railway as a golden chance, the Bishop of Durham demanded a large rake-off, but, in spite of that, on 27 December 1830 the opening of the new branch line to Middlesbrough occasioned the striking of medals showing the start from Darlington, with a perspective view of the coal-staiths at Middlesbrough, and, on the obverse, a representation of the suspension bridge near Stockton-on-Tees. A new locomotive, the *Globe*, on four coupled wooden wheels, left Darlington after ten o'clock in the morning. The bridge was inspected. Then the train passed through "the romantic vale of Cleveland" with a number of loaded wagons, one of which held a solid block of coal weighing three and a half tons. At Middlesbrough the passengers watched the shipment of the first cargo of coal on the *Sunniside*, and then sat down to one of those huge Victorian banquets, though Victoria was not yet queen. The great block of coal was shipped next day in the brig *Maria* for London.

That was the beginning of the greatness of Middlesbrough. It started life as Port Darlington. The local clay was good for brickmaking, house-building went forward according to the plans of the Middlesbrough Owners, and the population grew. In 1831, 383 people dwelt in the parish, 154 in the township.

Ten years later, parliament passed the Middlesbrough Improvement Act to make provision for lighting, policing and cleansing the town, and establishing a market which meant prosperity for the farming folk of Cleveland.

The year before that, in 1840, two men of importance, Henry Bolckow and John Vaughan, established in Middlesbrough the iron and steel works which became famous as

T

Buttertubs Pass

Bolckow Vaughan's. In 1841, 73lb. rails were being rolled at Middlesbrough for the Stockton and Darlington Railway.

The lias ironstone of Cleveland, averaging thirty per cent of iron, had since 1836 been worked in Eskdale and shipped to the Tyne. Tees then took the place of Tyne, for in 1850 John Vaughan found out that the main seam of this lias ironstone came through the Cleveland Hills to the tidewater and the South Durham coke at Middlesbrough. Already Bolckow Vaughan's had furnaces at Witton Park, and in 1851 the Cleveland ironstone began to go there, and later to Middlesbrough itself. From the beginning the waste gases of combustion were used by Vaughan to raise steam and heat the blast. Thus he saved about a million and a half tons of coal a year, and his furnaces turned out nearly twice as much as hot-blast furnaces elsewhere. They were small furnaces, from forty-five to fifty feet high and of capacity about five thousand cubic feet. In 1864 Vaughan tried a seventy-five-foot furnace, soon the eighty-foot furnace with twenty thousand cubic feet capacity became standard size, and the small furnaces were done away with. By 1870 the eighty-foot furnaces were producing between 450 and 550 tons a day.

The next development came in 1879 when E. W. Richards, manager of Bolckow Vaughan's, put the resources of his firm at the disposal of Sydney Gilchrist Thomas and his cousin Percy Gilchrist. Gilchrist Thomas, a clerk in the Thames Police Court, had been educated in the classics but had a passion for metallurgy. He and his cousin wanted to make phosphoric ores available for the new steel-making. The world was full of phosphoric ores and there was a fortune in the new process if the cousins could succeed. They succeeded. "Middlesbrough was soon besieged by the combined forces of Belgium, France, Austria, Prussia and America." The new process meant everything to Germany and Lorraine, a great deal to Middlesbrough.

In 1851 Middlesbrough might easily have been called a town. By the end of the 1880's more than a quarter of the total number of British ironstone miners worked in the Cleveland Hills, and a third of the British pig-iron was made in and about Middlesbrough. Subsidiary communities like South Bank and Grangetown were springing up around the chief focus, and the whole area was peopled by a highly specialized industrial community. In 1900, over 100,000 tons of iron were shipped from Middlesbrough, but this was not the town's sole industry, for, in 1859, a boring down to 1200 feet had revealed salt. Engineering difficulties had to be overcome, but by 1882 salt was being made. In 1892, over 200,000 tons were produced.

A third industry, the Linthorpe Pottery, lasted only a matter of ten years, from 1879 to 1889.

From all this solid information it may be deduced that Middlesbrough continued to grow. A royal charter of 1853 made the town a borough with the motto *Erimus*. Henry William Ferdinand Bolckow was, naturally, the first mayor. In 1866 he presented seventy-two acres of ground for the Albert Park. In 1867 he became the first member of parliament for the town. In 1868 the Royal Exchange was opened. In 1887 Middlesbrough got its town hall and Carnegie Library, and in 1888 earned the dignity of county borough. In 1901 the population was 91,302. By 1911 it had risen to 104,767.

Prosperity to Middlesbrough brought disaster to Whitby. In 1863 Whitby harbour accommodated 1,300 tons of shipping a week exclusive of fishing boats. By 1882, barely 500 tons a week entered the port, and if in 1881 Petermann had constructed another economic map of Britain he would have omitted the sailing-vessel symbol from Whitby and made the fish symbol less like a whale and more like a herring.

When in 1866 Bolckow presented the Albert Park to the town he spoke of Middlesbrough as "somewhat gloomy," which is what comes of building towns in the nineteenth century. It is indeed a Victorian town, and if, after calling it that, it needs further description, I hesitate to choose the adjectives. Nevertheless, Middlesbrough has given me a good deal of pleasure. I have seen it in November gloom, when its garish lighting, busy streets, muddy pavements and hurrying crowds have pleased me. On grey, rainy afternoons in summer I have not been repelled.

The town is not now so prosperous as in late Victorian days. Nowadays we speak less of Middlesbrough than of Tees-side, and thus I encounter the difficulty that the Durham and the Yorkshire sides of Tees form one economic unit. Calling to mind the majestic industrial activity of Britain during the war of 1939 to 1945, I consider how much of it centred upon Tees-side. The story, beyond detailed telling, lies in the history of individual firms, their subsidiary companies, agencies, offices and representatives in various parts of Britain and the world. The mere collection of information would take years. I have had hints, and often no more than hints. On a railway journey from Leeds to Wetherby this very afternoon, I noted at Osmondthorpe that the railway lines bore the stamp of Cargo Fleet, 1944. A paragraph in the *Times* tells me that Smith's Dock Company of South Bank designed and built sloops. Head Wrightson and Company of Thornaby-on-Tees have issued a brochure dated from Teesdale Ironworks, May 1946, summarizing their war activities. In years of peace this company supplies machinery and equipment for the winning and processing of coal, oil, iron and steel and non-ferrous metals, together with equipment and components for railways, ships, aircraft and motorcars. In war-time it turned to the production, with other companies, of large landing-craft, gunboats, rocket-ships and prefabricated parts of frigates, tugs and tankers. It designed and built the Pluto drum. It constructed a floating caisson for Singapore after the departure of the Japanese, produced 22,000 submarine mines, components for mine-sweeping and boom defence-work, submarine detection equipment and underground storage in cast iron and steel. It developed the simple but elastic Bellman hangar, made armoured cars, radar towers, Mulberry centre-spans, built steel railway wagons and Bailey bridges, completed mining plant for other countries, designed plant for making rubber from a Zululand wild vine, manufactured drop-forgings and castings in steel and special alloys for aeroplanes, tanks and armoured cars, produced a quarter of a million bombs, made ball races for Merlin engines and machinery for manipulating steel and non-ferrous metals. Head Wrightson and Company, moreover, manufacture oil refinery plant, build blast furnaces and go ahead with classes for apprentices, provision of sports facilities and welfare schemes for their employees. This review of the work of a single firm does not exhaust the catalogue of Thornaby's industries, which, in war and peace, include sugar-milling and flour-milling.

The Tees Estuary is no natural harbour. Originally it was shallow and obstructed by sandbanks. The course of the river from Stockton to the sea made a huge S. In 1810 the Tees Navigation Company constructed a cut two hundred and ten yards long, which shortened the course of the Tees by two and a half miles, though navigation was confined to ships of 150 tons burden. Middlesbrough began to prosper as a coal port. Between 1841 and 1850 over eleven million tons were shipped. In 1852 the Tees Conservancy Commissioners took control of the river, Yarm lost its shipbuilding industry to Stockton, and *Advance*, built by the Stockton Iron Shipbuilding Company on the south side of the Tees, was launched in 1854. Other firms began to build ships—Pearson Lockwood; Craig Taylor; Richardson and Ducks; Backhouse Dixon and Company; Harkess and Company; Craggs and Sons. Cleopatra's Needle was fetched to England in a Stockton-built boat. All these yards were closed down in the grim years of depression beginning, for this area, in 1921. Revival began with Smith's Docks and the Furness Shipbuilding Company and with the establishment of a body of pilots for the estuary. Joseph Pease raised £6,000 for the lighting of the river, and Joseph Taylor and William Fallows, with the aid of a pilot, placed the lights. Nowadays, so well lighted is the Tees that no pilots are necessary. The Commissioners built breakwaters and deepened the channel, and foreign ships came in for iron and steel, and particularly for rails. In 1906 Smith's Docks secured an option on land at South Bank, and in 1907 laid out two dry docks, a shipyard with four berths and an engine shop for building marine engines. These works were speedily extended, the site was doubled in area and further extensions are now being planned. During the first world war Smith's Docks produced Z-class whalers for submarine hunting; during the second world war, frigates and corvettes. Tankers of 6,000 tons and over are built here, and repair work never stops.

The Furness yards had their origin during the first world war. This was at the direst moment of the U-boat peril. The site at Haverton Hill consisted partly of reclaimed land, partly of land below high-water level. A million tons of ballast, handled during a period of acute labour shortage, raised the ground-level, and within five months the first keel was laid for a vessel of 10,300 tons deadweight. Since that day the Furness yard has turned out giant whale-factory ships of over 23,000 tons gross—*Southern Venturer* and *Norvhal* in 1945, *Southern Harvester* in 1946.

Since 1854, the Tees Conservancy Commissioners have reclaimed four thousand acres of marsh. Building walls to establish a regular channel for shipping, they dredged this channel and dumped the dredgings over the wall together with millions of tons of slag and ballast. The reclaimed land, useless for agricultural purposes, made sites for ironworks, shipyards, chemical factories and graving docks, most of them on the northern bank of the river.

Between 1908 and 1938 Teesmouth declined in importance because there were too few wharves for general use and ships had to be moved for bunkering, but in 1942 plans were put forward to build a huge system of open docks down-river from Middlesbrough. These plans coincided with the schemes of Dorman Long and Company and Imperial Chemical Industries to establish huge new undertakings in the same area. These plans are going ahead. Messrs Dorman Long and Company are erecting, on a 650-acre site, at a cost estimated at eight million pounds, a universal beam mill, the only one of its kind in the country, which will mass-produce steel sections. The mill will have a capacity of 350,000 tons a year, and will be supplied with high-quality construction steels by means of new, large, open-hearth plant. Close by, on the Tees foreshore, the same firm proposes to set up a central ore unloading, ore preparation and sintering plant. It will cost a million pounds.

South-east of Dorman's site, on the Wilton Castle Estate, Imperial Chemical Industries proposes to spend ten million pounds on "the greatest single industrial project so far announced by British industry." Five years should see the project completed. Already it is drawing labour from as far away as Staithes. It will keep three thousand people at work on the building, and eventually ten thousand people will be employed in the works. The 3,500-acre Wilton Castle Estate will be divided almost equally into a northern and a southern half, with the administration centrally situated in Wilton Castle. To the north will lie the industrial plant for producing heavy organic chemicals from coal and oil; installations for the making of sulphuric acid, an electrolyte chlorine-caustic soda plant and a vacuum salt plant : to the south, playing fields and a carefully planned housing estate. Mr G. A. Jellicoe, President of the Institute of Landscape Architects, will superintend the whole layout. Labour for the project and for the works will be drawn from the towns and villages of Tees-side and Cleveland, coal will come from Durham, oil from the docks, salt from the Teesmouth industry, water from the estuary. Road, rail and dock facilities will be improved. Meanwhile the Tees Conservancy Commissioners propose to instal new coaling plant, deepen the navigable channel and provide an oil-fuelling station down-river.

The policy of the Commissioners is to anticipate require-ments, not to wait upon them; to provide first-class facilities for shipping before the urgent necessity for them arises. Dorman Long's enterprise will cheapen the production of steel and thereby decrease the chances of a Tees-side slump. Both Dorman Long and Imperial Chemical Industries will import much raw material, and their finished products will go down-river from the new dock near Grangetown. This dock will have elaborate loading and unloading equipment, trans-port facilities by road and rail, transit sheds for general cargo, and deep-water berths at all states of the tide. Oil bunkering will be completed while vessels are discharging or loading. Coaling facilities will be provided at the ends of the main wharves. South Bank, Grangetown and Redcar will grow greatly in importance as industrial and residential towns. Trading Estates are being constructed at Stockton, Middlesbrough and Skelton to induce women in those areas to enter industry on either a full-time or a part-time basis, and this means that Tees-side in times of depression will no longer be a mere reservoir, as it has been in the past, to pro-vide domestic helps for other parts of the country.

Accompanying these important industrial developments goes a resolution that Tees-side shall never again lapse into long periods of depression. Here the keynote of change is expansion, but such expansion is partly dependent upon a rising prosperity curve of the world as a whole, upon the co-operation of local and national government, and the will of the people to work. As the schemes now stand, they form the most ambitious plan of industrial expansion in Britain.

Who did the planning?

In 1945 the Tees-side Industrial Development Board defined its policy and prepared a solid basis on which it could build. In 1946 it further consolidated that basis. The Board recruited its membership from the municipalities of Tees-side; from Redcar, Guisborough, Saltburn, Marske, Skelton, Brotton, Stokesley and Whitby; from the Tees-side Chamber of Commerce and from the local trade unions, with co-opted experts on water-supply and transport. It took in hand the education of local members of parliament and local public opinion; surveyed the facilities for provision of gas, water, electricity and transport, and made suitable recommendations; compiled estimates for the supply of male and female labour; pressed for attention to the industrial future of Cleveland; catalogued expanding industries and new industries; suggested solutions to the problems of individual firms; kept a register of unoccupied and vacant industrial sites; agitated for improved residential hotel facilities in the whole region, and enlisted the co-operation of the Board of Trade, the Ministry of Labour, the Ministry of Town and Country Planning and the Ministry of Supply. Such achievements represent foresight and energy. They do not prelude a proliferation of industrial ugliness along Tees-side or its penetration far into the Cleveland Hills. Prosperity and mean streets will devastate neither the new Tees-side nor the new Cleveland. The plans hold the hope of a clean, well-ordered industrial region, housing a population far removed indeed in spirit from that which, in the Middle Ages, knew and chanted the *Lyke-Wake Dirge* printed in all the anthologies :

This ae neet, this ae neet, ilka neet and all,
Fire and fleet and candle-leet, and Christ receive thy saule—

a population conscious of the work it does, well-informed, politically alert and modern-minded. The plans are there, the traditional skill is there, and the work has begun.

Not more than a week ago as I write this, I took the journey from Thirsk north along the Stockton road, stopped to run my fingers over the magnificent bench-ends and the Hardy Standard in Leake Church, turned into Osmotherley and found it enjoying a clean, leisured prosperity, and then swung northward into the National Trust property at Scarth Nick, where I found not merely warnings that the moors might still prove dangerous with unexploded missiles but also a number of motor-parties by the running stream and the high slopes brown with last year's bracken. This is a fine property. Industrialism will not penetrate here. And, as I went along the valley-road from Broughton to Kildale, I was glad that the great fold of hill to my left, the fold cutting me off from Tees-side and Teesmouth, marked the southernmost limit the new industrial expansion will reach. Over that fold of hill lay the wide waters of the estuary and the grey drift of smoke from the drab towns along its shores. Those towns and their inhabitants are part of the hope we have that the new world will better the old.

I mounted the ridge and looked northward to Tees-side, remembering Tees at Cauldron Snout, at High Force and at the junction of Tees and Greta, and as I stood with the drift of snow at my right hand (the month was April, late April), I was inclined to hail Tees as the noblest of the North Riding rivers.

Chapter XII

SELVEDGE AND PENEPLANE

When in revolt against first-class roads and the constant flow of motor traffic, and when, at the same time, you have no urge to blaze your own trail into the waste places, you might do much worse than hurry from Thirsk across Cod Beck and take the road through Sutton-under-Whitestonecliff to the crest of Sutton Bank, and, with salutation to the bold crag of Roulston Scar, the great plain stretching away to the western fells and the shadowy green encircling Lake Gormire, pursue the metalled road as far as the Hambledon Hotel, once called the Blücher. There you will find a road that was once a Road—the disused coaching-road to Yarm and the North. This road you may follow. Now it skirts the steep and shaggy scar, now its stretches away in front of you across the ling, with level ground on either side. You will walk without anxiety, for you cannot miss your way; you will walk in solitude, for there is no traffic and there are no people. For sufficient company you will have the occasional sentinel pines, the clumps of birch-trees and the moorland birds. Keep your eyes open, particularly where the track approaches the scar, for buzzards, and, for the rest, take it as it comes. A thousand feet above datum-line the air is clean and fresh, and the intakes and steadings, the dry walls, the sheep and cattle, the thin, snell winds, all speak to you of upland country. Below there, in Sutton-under-Whitestonecliff, is the relic of an old crab-mill where they used to make verjuice as a substitute for vinegar. Below there, north of Thirsk, is Nevison House, dubiously the birthplace of Swift Nick, hanged at York in 1685. Down there, too, is Kilvington, where human bones used to protrude now and then from the earthen floor of the church. A mile away from Kilvington, at Thornton-le-Street, you might still find a furlong of the old Roman road, and at Borrowby you might recollect, from George Fox's Journal,

282

that here "was a preist and severall freindely people yt mett togeather, and the people were convinced and have stoode ever since and there is a greate meetinge in yt tounde." And this may cause you to wonder at the energy and fervour of men like Fox and Wesley, who rode the length and breadth of the land from hamlet to hamlet preaching in the simplest of language to the simplest of men. Nowadays, unless we are communists, we aim to convert England from the top downwards instead of from the bottom upwards. Down there, too, is the curious township of Leake, with rich bench-ends in its church, a beck called a *stell*, and a stone-built seventeenth-century hall with a massive black oak stairway. Down there is Jeater-houses, where a small colony of jet-workers plied their trade, and Brompton, where handloom weaving went on until the nineteenth century had almost seen its final day. Over Silton lies below you, and not far away from there is Hob Thrush Hall, a cavern in the hill haunted by a large-scale supernatural being. Old brick granges of the seventeenth century, old churches, old villages and steadings where a strain of Danish invaders settled, where linen-weaving was a principal industry; old quarries in the scar, and ancient hanging woods characterize the plainland below, and through the level land the slender threads of traffic communication run without knots and loops. As you move northwards over Arden Moor towards Black Hambledon, you climb steadily to well over a thousand feet, and then you slip down towards the famous Chequers Inn at Slapestanes, and the dignified village of Osmotherley, once a linen-weaving centre, much more important then than now. If from Osmotherley you venture into the Cleveland Hills, you may well find your heart's desire on the height of Burton Head, highest point of these north-eastern uplands, and you will walk in places where illicit stills used to produce raw liquor for the Cleveland ironstone miners. Here in this country, at Urra, in Scugdale and Raisdale, the wilderness so took hold of my youthful memory and gripped it so tightly that it has haunted me ever since. But you, maybe, in a less impressionistic age, will remain untouched, and you will go down from Black Hambledon by way of Crathorne and Kirk Leavington to the railway, the windings of the Tees and the ancient port and shipbuilding town of Yarm, now left with its little market and its memories.

I don't want to sentimentalize over this selvedge of the plainland, but I assert that this western edge of the Hambledon Hills is a pleasant place to live in, belonging to the uplands and the lowlands, possessing a spaciousness, and a rural grace denied to the middle region of the peneplane. For, make no mistake about it, when you walk in the Vale of Mowbray and the Plain of York you are walking in a factory —a factory that produces sheep, cattle, poultry, corn, field peas, beans, potatoes, sugar-beet, flax and such. The modern farmer more than ever in the past thinks of his farm as a factory, works to a schedule, calculates in man-hours of productivity, and is impatient of mere beauty.

For a time now you have done with the uplands. You are in a land where only the roads and the towns have a history, where there is almost nothing to take the eye of the antiquarian, the social surveyor, the artist, the botanist, and everything to interest the agricultural economist. He will tell you that the acreage of flax, for instance, is bound to increase during the next few years.

This is the flat land between the moors of the east and the fells of the west. It is a wide, fertile peneplane through which Swale, Wiske, Leven and Tees wind between banks of red boulder clay. It is the Vale of Mowbray, sheered level by long-vanished ice, overlaid with the detritus of a final glaciation, distinguished for its value as farming land and fattening ground for upland sheep and cattle. First-class roads and main-line railways reel through it, but everywhere it is shot with secondary roads, farm-tracks, footpaths and ancient green lanes. Along the windings of the Tees, which are not far distant in time from the ox-bow stage of river-evolution, there is more woodland and much more pleasing country than you would expect. South of the Tees lies the land of the yeoman farmer, adequately watered, not too densely populated, with sparse woodland and scattered parks, red brick granges with old, rich tiling, and few signs of baronial occupation in the Middle Ages. Here and there the soil is light, and along the course of the Wiske there is sometimes danger of flooding. The soil is reddish brown, or a burnt red, for this was a strip of the Permian desert. There are few vestiges of any manorial system here, and still fewer of monastic establishments. Once densely wooded, when it became open agricultural land it showed a community of windmills, and they, with the spired churches, were formerly the conspicuous landmarks. It is not, when you think of it, strange that the flat lands should be lands of spires rather than of towers, and that village names should go in pairs, like East Rounton and West Rounton, High Worsall and Low Worsall, Great Smeaton and Little Smeaton, North Cowton and South Cowton (though there is also East Cowton, and Cowton Moor where the Battle of the Standard was fought). It is also natural, I think, that the place-names should be mainly Anglian and not Danish, and that *leys* and *tons* should preponderate over *wicks* and *bys*. There are plenty of moors, but these are not moors in the common usage of the word; they are second-quality agricultural land that remained unenclosed until recent times, and I should say that, with the exception of a few Tees-side hamlets and their surrounding fields, this land in the Middle Ages was not intensively cultivated, but given up to marsh, moor and forest. The only industry, apart from farming and weaving, that has ever distinguished this strip of Permian landscape is the manufacture of tiles. This industry has fallen upon evil days, and is now in the final stage of decay.

The great roads that cross the Vale of Mowbray do not commonly touch the villages. From Catterick to Cliffe and Piercebridge the villages stand away from the road, and from Scotch Corner to Bowes only Rokeby stands upon it. Both roads are Roman, and this may be the explanation, for the Romans engineered their highways for military rather than for trading or residential purposes. The consequence is that the great roads are used to-day as they were used in Roman times—as speedways—and they are dull now as they were dull then.

The villages are not without dignity, the minor roads not without grace. I like the road, for instance, from Richmond by way of Aske Hall to Gilling and Melsonby, the road from Scotch Corner through Middleton Tyas to Croft. I like the villages of Cleasby and Croft, Hutton Magna and Ravensworth, Ovington and Brignall. More important, to my mind, is Morris Grange, some four miles north of Catterick and east of the Great North Road, for here stands one of the finest sanatoria for children in the whole country, and upon Morris Grange the North Riding County Council bestows a great deal of care and thought. As I move westward to the fells I note a greater proportion of woodland and a larger number of country mansions. Castles, moreover, begin to show themselves again, but not till I find myself west of the Great North Road do I look for battlemented towers and ruined peels. Amongst the ancient relics of this land, I think that which interests me most stands in a couple of private parks, Forcett Park and Stanwick Park, between the Bowes Road and the Tees at Cliffe. Close by this relic stands Aldbrough, and wherever you find an Aldbrough there is pretty sure to be something that goes back beyond Anglo-Saxon times. Sure enough, this relic is pre-Anglian, I think it is almost certainly pre-Roman, and it is unmistakably big. The earthworks are so extensive that they preclude any possibility of their being merely the boundary-lines of a military camp, their shape and layout imply their being of Brigantian origin, and I believe they mark the site of a populous British settlement. Perhaps this was the capital town of the Brigantes. More than that I will not say.

I delve into the records of this quiet land to find that it has produced remarkable men. At Smeaton was born the planter of Maryland, Lord Baltimore; Kirby Wiske produced two giant scholars, Roger Ascham and George Hickes. Ascham, tutor to Queen Elizabeth, had ideas on education and archery, knew Greek and wrote sturdy English and Ciceronian Latin. Georges Hickes, of plain farming stock, was a great student of the ancient northern languages : his labours were published at Oxford in 1705 in three volumes folio as *Linguarum Veterum Septentrionalium Thesaurus Grammatico-Criticus et Archæologicus, Auctore Georgio Hickesio.* The critical text is in Latin, but, in their original character, "the wild and mysterious semblance of the Runic, the ancient solemnity of the Mæso-Gothic, the neat and legible Anglo-Saxon, and the black Icelandic." Burnet reports of Hickes that he was a bad-tempered, sour old fellow, but he laid massive foundations for the fabric of romanticism. According to Leland, John Wyclif was born at Hipswell. From Wickliffe came Archbishop Thoresby, and, without emphasizing the distinguished history of Neville, Scrope, Aske, Askwith, Boynton, Conyers and Gascoigne, I must include the wife of John Jackson of Marsk, for, says her monument, "for conjugall love and bowells of mercy shee was much more then vulgar." And I must mention Henry Jenkins of Bolton-upon-Swale (he was born at Ellerton-on-Swale), who, though he made no noise in the world, died in 1670, being then 169 years old. By his own account he remembered the Battle of Flodden and the carousals of his master Lord Conyers with the Abbot of Fountains before the Dissolution. The testimony of this simple old man appears to be authentic, for he was not reckoned clever enough to produce convincing lies. Then there was a certain J. Phillips, who must have been a considerable wizard in his time. In a stone-heap on Gatherley Moor near Brignall were discovered a couple of leaden plates rudely scratched with planetary figures and vindictive writing : "I doe make this, that James Phillip, John Phillip his son, Christopher Phillip and Thomas Phillip his sons shall flee Richmondshire and nothing prosper with any of them in Richmondshire." And, on the second plate, "I do make this that the father James Phillip, John Phillip, Arther Phillip and all the issue of them shall come presently to utter beggery and nothing joy or prosper with them in Richmondshire." As he cursed them, so it fell out, and how this should all happen in "a low, warm, fertile tract without one market town or one considerable object of antiquity within its limits," I do not pretend to know. Jenkins and Phillips belonged to important sub-species of humanity.

Of this area, Whitaker reported that the population was slender, and dispersed in clean and pleasant villages. "Many of them surround spacious greens, and a vast elm frequently marks the place where the sports of the young and the conferences of the aged have taken place for centuries." Elms are not deep-rooting trees, and neither young nor old now congregate upon village greens. Things in these villages have changed, though whether for better or worse I do not know. From Melsonby you may still view the ramparts of Cleveland across the Vale of Mowbray, and from a long way off you may still see the tall spires of Ainderby Steeple and Patrick Brompton. At Middleton Tyas I still found a vague memory of long-abandoned copper works, and at Croft I saw the giant tomb of Richard Clervaux, eleven feet long, five feet broad and four feet high, dating from 1490. Cedars of Lebanon grow at Scruton, though I believe their number has diminished. Cedars of Lebanon, incidentally, thrive better in England than in their native land. Croft Bridge across the Tees is still as fine a piece of work as when it was "the grete Bridge at Crofte . . . beinge of six myghty large pillars, and of seven arches of stone worke; the most directe and sure way and passage for the Kinge or Sovraigne Lordes armye and ordynance to resort and passe over into the Northe parties and marches of this his realme."

I take it that the less ignorant and more wealthy inhabitants of this fertile Vale of Mowbray must, during the early seventeenth and the eighteenth century, have tried to make life tolerable for themselves by concentrating upon massive domesticity in the seclusion of deciduous parklands. Doing this, they shut out the levels and made their life less naked. They brought this way either Inigo Jones himself or his designs, they fetched in Roger Gale, they planned their houses round border peels or ancient tithe-barns, they built terraces and classical temples, they concentrated upon interior decoration, they bought old masters and provided showplaces for the people of less fortunate centuries. Sometimes, as at Hutton Magna, they left well alone; sometimes, as at Brough Hall and Hornby Castle, they built from the ground upward in the massive style of their own day; sometimes they used old masoned stones, sometimes they quarried new stone, and sometimes they built with Jacobean brick.

Their churches impress me as belonging to a different school of ecclesiastical architecture from the churches of the remainder of the North Riding. In this I may be right or wrong. It is not of the details I speak; it is the general impression they give me. The change-over begins, I think, with Grinton Church in Swaledale, and it becomes more marked as I travel towards the Tees. Some of these northern churches are of great antiquity, and some, until recent years, were neglected. Cundall's Anglian cross is the lintel of the church door; Danby Wiske has a twelfth-century tympanum—"plain and homely work," says Whitaker, "with its singularly rude sculptures." Romaldkirk has a fine, large church, but Whitaker reported of it that the walls, floor and pews were damp and neglected, and the churchyard was grossly over-crowded; Startforth is another old church, and in Whitaker's time Hutton Longvilliers had a big hole in the roof; Hornby Church seems to be late eleventh-century; Middleton Tyas gave me a curious quadrant window, and I liked the north arcade of Fingall Church. The general impression remains, however, of churches with tie-beam roofs and of considerable age, built on a bigger scale than that to which I am accus-tomed, then left for long periods to decay and neglect, and finally set in reasonable shape.

As you make your way southward you may leave the Great North Road and find the little towns and villages that stand east and west of the highway, or from time to time mark how the road rises here and there where the retreating glaciers left terminal moraines of boulder clay and detritus behind them. You will come into Northallerton and amuse yourself by wondering how many kings of England have passed through it, speculating how many armies have gathered here to make inroad upon the Scots, and wondering what is going on behind the windows of the County Hall. Instead of giving you the history of Northallerton, I propose to deal with Northallerton as an administrative centre.

It is not within the capacity of all people to see a village, town, city or county area as a going concern. If it were, we should not need to teach or learn history in our schools. Human vision sees a landscape as a slow-motion picture. If things move, they move with comfortable lassitude, the lines remain relatively static. Often, indeed, when the lines happen to satisfy our sense of beauty, we are inclined to wish they would remain so. But forests melt away like clouds in a summer sky, waterfalls recede towards the mountains, the sea takes its eternal toll of the coastline, rivers in flatland develop increasing sinuosities; where there existed a wilderness an abbey rises like an exhalation from the ground, a bold crag

High Force, Teesdale

is crowned by a fortress of stone, and castle and abbey in their time decay, their human population vanishes, they are given over to the weasel and the bat, the owl and the rabbit. They were once going concerns. And finally, of course, they went. They went, I suppose, either because they ceased to function or because they went in the wrong direction, they went too slowly or too quickly, or, again, because they went rotten.

They represented administrative systems that proved insufficiently flexible, insufficiently adaptable to conditions that themselves were in a state of flux or change. No medieval castle could survive the use of gunpowder, no manorial system the challenge of new methods of agriculture.

The North Riding of Yorkshire is an administrative area controlled from the County Hall at Northallerton. Obviously the County Council, in existence only since 1889, has not yet gained the immense administrative experience of the Roman Catholic Church or the late Babylonian Empire. Like Macbeth, it is but young in deed. But administrative bodies are not composed of fools and ill men who, said Erasmus, must learn all their lessons from bitter experience; they can learn from the bitter experiences of others. Some historians declare that the empires of the ancient world fell to pieces because their governments were too centralized; some argue that they fell because their governments were too decentralized. The wise administrator will seek the *via media*. Local government will resent the over-interference of central government in matters of local concern, but will not be too proud to ask for advice and help from the more experienced central administration. The balance between local and national government is subjected to disturbances, and both forms of government must ensure that it is not altogether upset. In the records of the North Riding County Council I have found no evidence of any violent disturbance of that balance. It is equally clear that local administration should preserve the good will of the people whose affairs it administers, and I have always heard the County Council spoken of with respect and often with admiration. This is remarkable because the population of the Riding is here widely scattered, there densely congregated, is here engaged in hill-farming, there in heavy industry, in mixed agriculture, stock-breeding and catering for holiday-makers. It is remarkable because the county councillors themselves are drawn from widely distant areas with widely diverging interests; they represent different views in politics and different social strata, sharing only a common interest in and a common enthusiasm for the North Riding.

Even county councillors are amateurs in the art and science of government, and government nowadays is so complex and so expensive that professional help has become essential. For the experts as well as for the amateurs, county halls have sprung up all over the country, to house files, typewriters, adding-machines, clerks and typists. People deplore the complexity of the modern administrative machine, but I think that the more complex it grows the less likely it is to break down. In some way it is analagous to the National Debt, which, the more it increases, the more it ensures freedom from revolution.

Before 1889, local government in the North Riding was in the hands of the Members of the Court of Quarter Sessions, who authorized no expenditure unless it was vitally necessary. During the year ending Michaelmas 1888 they spent only £45,284. When in 1889 the County Council took over, the chairman of the Works Committee, Mr Rowlandson, pursued a policy of strengthening and widening bridges, and turning district roads into main roads. This was sound social practice. Then the new council put electric light into the county asylum and improved the sewerage there. They put vigour into the analysis of food and drink. They spent money on new police stations at North Ormesby, Hovingham, Bedale and Great Ayton, and brought up to date those at Thornaby, Eston, Grangetown and South Bank. They built a new Court House at Malton. These works took time, energy and money. In 1903–4 the new County Hall was planned to house the administrative staff under one roof. In 1903 the total expenditure was £101,951. By 1909 it had risen to £300,402. New bridges had been taken over, more roads improved. By 1910 there were 48,000 children in the elementary schools, blind, deaf and defective children were being cared for, and new schools had been built. The councillors were of the opinion that the national exchequer should find more money for education. The Council had also provided smallholdings, built a new police station at Northallerton and taken over the old age pension scheme of 1908. In 1906 the new County Hall was ready for occupation, but, remarked the chairman of the County Council, "the time is I fear not distant when further office-room may be necessary." A Yorkshire Reference Library was housed in the new County Hall.

By 1911–12 the cost of maintaining the 532 miles of main roads had risen to £41,849, and the elimination of sharp turns had begun. The road near Middleham Bridge was raised to prevent flooding by the Ure. Footpaths were made and reconstructed. New blocks were added to the County Asylum, new secondary schools were built in Easingwold, Malton, Saltburn and Whitby, schools were enlarged at Guisborough, Northallerton and Pickering, and Yarm secondary school was begun. Evening schools were started particularly for the benefit of miners. New council schools were built at South Bank, Kirby Sigston, Loftus and Lingdale, the council took over four voluntary schools and made more provision for school gardens, manual instruction, cookery and needlework. Travelling vans for cookery instruction were proving their worth. Swine fever and anthrax were giving anxiety. The administrative staff had overflowed from the County Hall into other buildings. Expenditure had risen to £294,881 13s 1d. The total population of the Riding in 1911 was 314,814, and in 1912 the assessable value of property for the county rate was £2,008,940. John Hutton was still chairman of the council, as he had been from its inception.

The next report is dated February 1919, and by that time the first Great War had come and gone, leaving a legacy of foundered, damaged and neglected roads, impaired bridges and choked drainage systems. Part of the County Hall had been a Red Cross hospital from August 1914 to January 1919, the grounds had been given up to allotments, the basement had been used as a miniature rifle-range, and accommodation had been found for the War Agricultural Committee, the War Pension Committee, the Women Land Workers and the Appeal Tribunal. Northallerton Grammar School was for some time taken over by the military, and the school was housed in the new wing of the County Hall. The

County Council faced new responsibilities. It established clinics for tubercular patients, appointed five full-time nurses for infant welfare and school medical services, increased the number of school gardens, provided more vans for cookery demonstrations, and established a permanent centre for the teaching of handicrafts at Thornaby-on-Tees. It opened new schools at South Bank, Cargo Fleet and Pickering Marishes, improved the accommodation of many others, projected a technical college at Middlesbrough, and housed children of school age in army huts at the new village called Dormanstown.

By 1922 the North Riding County Council owned 3,200 acres of land let out to smallholders, and had begun to concern itself seriously with the control of sheep-scab in the Pennine area, with the scouring and cleaning of drains and streams, with the reduction in numbers of rats and mice, and with the breeding of light and heavy horses, of pigs and cattle. In education it began to adopt measures to minimize the effects upon children of growing unemployment along Tees-side by providing school meals, and establishing clinics at Thornaby, Grangetown, Carlin How and Whitby. Its scholarships scheme was overhauled and brought up to date, it established child welfare and maternity centres, and pursued an enlightened policy of opening new schools for secondary education.

The growing amount of unemployment began to throw an additional burden of responsibility upon the County Council, and certain public works were undertaken. Watercourses in the Plain of York and the Vale of Mowbray were cleansed, and work was undertaken along the Wiske and in the Derwent and Rye drainage area. The Rural Development Sub-Committee, refused financial aid from the National Exchequer, did what it could within the limits of its own means, and provided lectures, concerts and demonstrations. It tried to resuscitate the Whitby jet industry, revived the making of wattle hurdles, showed village blacksmiths and wheelwrights how to modernize their methods, and organized rural industries exhibitions at Northallerton, Scarborough and Richmond. It pressed the education committee to provide library facilities for the whole population of the Riding.

By 1925 the population of children of school age had begun to decline in number, and half a dozen small schools had been shut down, the number of teachers was reduced and classes were reduced in size. Building of new schools went on in Eston, Thornaby, Redcar, Dormanstown and South Bank, though trade depression had resulted in the reduction of the number of secondary school pupils from 2,966 in 1922 to 2,649 in 1924. The Yorkshire Council for Agricultural Education organized lectures on veterinary hygiene, agricultural economics, horticulture, poultry-keeping, production of clean milk and butter-making. On public works the County Council spent, in 1925, £150,000, and built a new road from Middlesbrough to Marske. Stock-breeding was subsidized and a register of ratcatchers was compiled.

Unemployment figures were still heavy, and in the winter of 1925–6 men were paid to clear twenty-eight miles of ditches and drains, but "the unemployment schemes, which were in operation for four winters, only touched the fringe of the drainage problem in the North Riding, and there are many miles of watercourses in the Riding still so obstructed that considerable areas of agricultural land are inadequately drained." In the summer of 1925 and again in 1926 a motor-van equipped with oxy-acetylene welding plant, emery grinding wheels, power drills, a portable forge and a small oil engine, toured the Riding for the instruction of village blacksmiths, and a register was compiled of smiths able and willing to make ornamental wrought-iron goods. Two more rural industries exhibitions were held in 1925, one at Pickering and one at Stokesley. In 1926, one was held at Northallerton, and in 1927 one at Whitby. The County Library Scheme was developing rapidly. By 1928 thirty-four schemes of public utility had been carried through for the relief of unemployment. The majority of these were in the Cleveland area, and included improvement to Staithes harbour. Stricter supervision of milk supply had become necessary under the Milk and Dairies (Consolidation) Act of 1915, which, however, made no provision for the inspection of cowsheds and dairies.

From the 1931 report it is possible to gather a notion of the sheep population in the North Riding. Dipping against sheep scab had become compulsory, and the figures for 1928,

1929 and 1930 were : 1,232,480, 1,236,021, and 1,241,837. All sheep exhibited at all the autumn store sheep sales were inspected for scab. Over 120,000 cattle were inspected in those three years, and a total of 238 tubercular beasts were discovered and destroyed. "Cows are now kept very much cleaner than formerly; especially is this noticeable where milk is produced and sold off the premises as raw milk for human consumption." The work of the veterinary inspectors was largely to give advice on the importance of cleanliness, fresh air and sunlight for cattle. After exhibitions at Leyburn and Whitby, the Rural Development Sub-Committee regretfully closed down its useful work. Further extension of office accommodation at the County Hall had become necessary. The Reference Library had continued to grow in size and value, but was badly housed. In education, a progressive policy was adopted in medical and dental services, technical education and the provision of new schools, playing-fields and library services. Small schools were still being shut. Agricultural education was consistently pursued, with more lectures, sampling of fertilizers and feeding-stuffs, control of weeds, inspection of livestock and pedigree stock-breeding. The Reference Library at the County Hall continued to grow, and the number of secondary school children increased to 3,532 in 1933, and the number of students in evening institutes rose to 3,946.

By-laws now regulated the putting up of petrol pumps and filling-stations. The Riding was divided, for this purpose, into a prohibited area, lying west of the Great North Road and comprising also the North York Moors, and a controlled area. In the prohibited area no person would in future be allowed to put up a visible filling-station. The controlled area consisted of the Vale of Derwent, the Vale of York and the low land between Piercebridge and the coast. New filling-stations would there be permitted only in accordance with the by-laws.

Another by-law was passed to check unnecessary noise in the Eston urban area, and caravan dwellings and gipsy camps were brought under control by still another by-law. Regulations for cinemas were recommended by the licensing justices in petty sessions. Sixty-seven miles of new footpaths were made between 1931 and 1934, twenty of the 619 bridges were overhauled or rebuilt, traffic lights were installed at Redcar and Eston, sixteen road-schemes were completed under unemployment assistance work, petrol lorries began to replace the Council's steam wagons. The most important event during these years was that the local boards of guardians ceased to exist and the County Council took over their work.

The year 1937 saw ten internal drainage boards take over much of the County Council's drainage work. The Council agreed to contribute financially to the establishment of the Yorkshire Institute of Agriculture at Askham Bryan, and the whole serious problem of water supply came up for consideration. The Council promised £34,307 towards the cost. Schemes were drawn up for the urban district of Malton and eleven rural districts. Road-mileage maintained by the North Riding amounted to 3,095.7 miles, but of these 2,424.99 were unclassified roads; twenty-two bridges were overhauled, the abolition of level crossings was undertaken at Barton Hill, Malton Road, Baldersby Gate and Sleights. The York-Scarborough road began to take on its present appearance, with twin carriage-way and cycle-track layout. Traffic circuses were constructed or contemplated at Catterick Camp, Richmond, Scotch Corner, Haxby, Busby Stoop, Baldersby Gate, Upsall Corner, Marske, Eston, Redcar, Whitby (at Station Corner, Four Lane Ends and Chubb Hill), Seamer and Yarm. Roads were given roughened surfaces.

A South Tees-side Joint Town Planning Scheme included a road with twin carriage-ways, cycle-tracks and footpaths, free of all building developments, to run from a crossing of the Tees south of Victoria Bridge, by-passing Middlesbrough and reaching Saltburn by way of Eston and Kirkleatham. Richmond had prepared a scheme of town and country planning, and the North Riding committee consulted with York Corporation on proposals of co-operation.

Clean milk still claimed attention. In 1937 there were twenty tuberculin-tested herds in the Riding. Each herd was examined twice a year, one examination being conducted free of charge, to encourage producers of T.T. milk. The Council formulated a standard of structural requirements for byres and cowsheds. A new courthouse was sanctioned for North-

allerton, the old, dating from 1785, being "in a deplorable
state of repair."

Planning schemes were being prepared for the urban districts of Loftus, Malton, Pickering, Skelton and Brotton,
Scalby and Whitby; for the rural areas of Aysgarth, Bedale,
Croft, Flaxton, Easingwold, Helmsley, Kirbymoorside,
Malton, Masham, Northallerton, Pickering, Reeth, Richmond, Scarborough, Startforth, Stokesley, Wath and Whitby.
Professor Patrick Abercrombie was consultant, and a
planning officer and staff were appointed. The Riding was
zoned. There were six zones : moorland, special landscape
rural, normal rural, coastal, temporary restricted development, immediate development. "The general provisions of
the schemes will operate in all zones," says the 1937 report,
"to secure seemly and attractive development having regard
to appearance, convenience, amenity and hygiene."

The 1940 report covers a great amount of organized
activity resulting from the outbreak of the second world war.
The Council had to take interest in swine fever and warble fly
as well as in sheep-scab and foot-and-mouth disease, tuber-
culosis and anthrax. Lake Semmerwater went through drastic
treatment. The Ouse Catchment Board's mechanical
excavator was hired by the county council, the level of the
lake was lowered by approximately two feet, and 420 acres
of waterlogged land above the lake were improved for agriculture. (A good deal more land awaits reclamation in the
same area. Much is still waterlogged.) The local landowners
shared the cost.

The Council began to take interest in the rabbit as an
agricultural pest.

At the outbreak of war the County Council had a programme on the way costing £1,200,000 for education, and
had had a congratulatory message from the Board of Education to encourage its fulfilment. The war "applied the brake
to school-building machinery at its maximum momentum,"
and since the North Riding was scheduled as a reception area
for evacuated school children, the problems of reception came
first on the list of educational priorities. A great reorganiza-
tion of services became necessary. Shelters had to be provided
in the neutral areas of Eston, Redcar and Thornaby. Black-

out for the schools cost £6,700. Some of the small schools that had been closed were reopened during the war. The school camp at Runswick had, of course, to be given up.

In 1940 the County Library owned 105,000 volumes, and the issue of books had grown to 1,069,000 in 1939. Where reading flourished, gun and game licences languished, and the revenue from armorial bearings showed a decrease. Primroses were included in the preservation of ferns and plants by-law. Cycling in the subway under Saltburn railway station was prohibited. There was no money available for water-supply schemes. Twenty-one bridges were being doctored, and the County Council made itself responsible for the approaches to and the carriage-way over ninety-one railway bridges, in consideration of an annual payment by the railway company. The banking of 373 roads at bends proved the liveliness of the road engineers, and parking-places or "lay-bys" were provided for lorries and cars, notably at Robin Hood's Bay, at the top of Sutton Bank and at the top of Birk Brow. Motor snow-ploughs were brought into the Riding. Precautions were taken for traffic safety during the war, A.R.P. organization was quickly and thoroughly carried through. Though much expenditure was cut down, the war brought tremendous increases, most of which, fortunately, was payable by the National Exchequer.

The 1945 report is the latest in the series. There was a further demand for smallholdings in the Riding; foot-and-mouth disease was troublesome, sheep-scab seemed to be invading the Riding from adjacent territories, rats and mice were again scheduled as important public enemies, and the Council's interest in stock-breeding was suspended. The laboratory in the County Hall became the centre for the distribution of penicillin to hospitals in the Riding. In May 1941 the County Hall was set on fire by incendiary bombs, but, though the water-mains were empty, a static water-tank filled the previous evening gave enough water to confine the damage to a couple of rooms.

During the war bombs were dropped on 418 separate occasions. About 3,000 high explosive bombs or parachute mines fell, in addition to thousands of incendiaries. Damage was done at Thornaby, South Bank, Grangetown, Redcar,

SELVEDGE AND PENEPLANE

Whitby, Scarborough, Flaxton, Loftus, Saltburn and
Masham; 15,317 buildings were damaged; civilians were
killed in Skelton and Thirsk as well as in the towns already
named; in all, 149 people were killed and 746 injured. The
first enemy aircraft to be shot down in England fell outside
Whitby on 3 February 1940, and the first civilian casualties in
England occurred at South Bank on 25 May 1940. The alert
was sounded 177 times in Wensleydale, 317 times in Scarborough, 480 times in Cleveland. Volunteer wardens from
the North Riding were loaned to the Sutton and Cheam
borough council during the flying bomb attacks.

There was, during the war, an increase in juvenile delin-
quency. The education services went on. At one time, 30,000
evacuees were at school, the education committee became the
largest caterer in the Riding, providing 20,000 children with
dinner every day, and the service was still expanding. Three
new schools providing a special type of rural education were
opened during the war. The number of secondary school
children rose to 4,687 in 1945, over 91 per cent of them from
the elementary schools of the Riding. Children provided
10,000 garments a year for the Red Cross and H.M. Forces,
worked on the farms, and gathered urgently needed plants
and herbs. The number of issues from the County Library
rose to 1,500,000, with 68,000 borrowers in 1945. All
children living more than two miles from school were now
carried by bus at a cost of £12,000 a year. Scarborough sur-
rendered its schools to the Riding on 1 April 1945.

The Planning Committee approves the siting of electricity
and telephone lines, substations and telephone kiosks, and
outdoor advertisements are also subjected to control.

Generally, in spite of the war, the County Council
expanded the range of its services to the community, and
within its present duties may be included the care of the aged
and infirm, of the blind, of mentally defectives, of tubercular
children under five, and there are homes at Pickering and
ward in the Riding has been closed. Of children deprived of
normal home life, 45 are boarded out, nurseries at Guisborough, Kirbymoorside and Northallerton provide for 53
children under five, and there are homes at Pickering and
Scarborough for 79 children over the age of five.

The roads of the Riding had had hard wear during the war years because a number of armoured units carried through intensive training within its borders, but they stood up to their work without breaking.

The County Planning Committee gave consent, advice or direct refusal to proposals submitted. Here is a sample :

Dwelling-house at Row Brow Farm, near Lady Edith's Drive, in the Scarborough Rural District.	The site is in a locality of special landscape value and immediately adjacent to a large area set apart as a Private Open Space; and any building erected there would be detrimental to the amenity of the countryside. In addition, the site is not served by sewers, water supply or adequate road access. Consent was refused.

Now, I trust, you have some notion of what goes on behind the windows of County Hall.

You resume your journey southwards. You come to Catterick and note the ordered ramifications of Catterick Camp, and how the old bridge of Catterick is now enclosed within the new—that old bridge for the upkeep of which so many medieval Yorkshiremen left xijs ivd or some similar amount, *for the wark at Katryk brigge*. You will note the sign of the Mouse at the inn, the ponderous traffic-flow and the sluggish waters of the Swale. You will come south to Bedale with its good old church and its general air of content and prosperity, its spaciousness and cleanliness in the midst of fat farming country. Bedale was there before the Normans came to England. Leeming and Leeming Bar are equally old, and there you will come to nursery gardens famous all over the country. I have heard it said that "there is something in the soil" here which gives a richness of colouring to the roses and Harkness's famous lupins, and to pass along this road when the lupins are in bloom is to gather a memory not easily forgotten. Then there is Topcliffe upon Swale, a former stronghold of the Percies, and a little town that has given something to English history. Was it here, in the upper chamber of the moot hall, that the Scots handed over Charles I to the Parliament men? Paulinus is said to have baptized converts in the Swale close by. There is a supposed Roman camp at Cock Lodge, and in the angle of the Swale a mile down-river you will find one of the three *mai-duns* of the Swale valley. This is Maiden Bower with its seven terracings, and, so far as I know, no archæologist has troubled much about the place. Over the ford, south and east of Maiden Bower, you will find Leckby Carr, once a botanist's paradise because it held so many rarities now vanished. Aisenby, not far away, boasted one of the last Yorkshire witches, Peg Lumley, who lived and wrought her spells during the first half of last century. Not far away also is Baldersby Park, once the residence of George Hudson the Railway King, about whose life the books are reticent even after a whole century.

You will come to Dishforth with its great hangars, its seventeenth- and eighteenth-century atmosphere and its good Jacobean architecture, and so finally to Boroughbridge and the southern boundary of the Riding. Of all the towns and villages between Tees and Swale, from Croft to Boroughbridge, there is not, perhaps, a single one where you would deliberately choose to live. You would feel isolated, motionless in a backwater of the stream of progress. What, in reality, would you be missing? From Topcliffe you could write to the *Times*; at Bedale you could read *Hansard*; at Northallerton, Thirsk and Easingwold you could discuss the articles in the *New Statesman*, and everywhere you would find a rich, satisfying life grounded in reality. Here the roots of humanity still strike down into the soil. Existence is anchored. Men don't drift between Matthew Arnold's two worlds here—one dead, the other powerless to be born. Candidly, I know many folk who delight to amble through this country in their cars, and I find that, without definite aims though they may be, they find their experiences as satisfying as when they went through the Cotswolds, or explored the Dauphiné, or came down through Aberglaslyn or the Cheddar Gorge. And they talk about the little villages they have discovered, the charming views that have held them, the pleasant people with whom they have talked. I myself have told you something of walking in this great plain, and the sort of thing you may expect to find, but I have not, within the compass of this volume, been able to describe the half of what there is to see. The perpetual illusion of discovery remains yours to enjoy. If in the last few pages I have condensed experience, the condensation has been deliberate. There are times when allusion is of greater merit than detailed description, and this is one such time.

Any day, wet or fine, hot or cold, is a good day for walking, but May, with plenty of sun, the wind fresh, the air so clear that the distances are not veiled, gives the perfect weather. It was in such weather that on 19 May 1945, I crossed the border from Ripon into the North Riding at about a quarter to eleven in the morning. One likes to be precise about these things. Across the broad Ure the road climbed steeply. Behind my right shoulder a cuckoo was shouting, and a charm of finches occupied the grey willows to the left of the road. The willows, I fancy, had been planted there below road-level to drain the marshy ground, but the vegetation was rank and lush, with its roots in mud. Presently there was a beck and there were ducks on it. And so through Nunwick, where there are now no nuns, to Norton Conyers.

The exterior of the famous house has been much altered since James I slept there on his way from Scotland to take the English crown. The bow-window and the Flemish gablings are additional, and the frontage of the house, beneath its grey surfacing, is really of brick. Lady Graham explained to me the intricate story of how Norton Conyers came into the family, and took me into the house. The oak-panelled hall is magnificent with paintings of the eighteenth-century Grahams, and over the fireplace hangs Ferneley's picture of the Quorn in 1822. I have forgotten how many gentlemen paid twenty guineas apiece to have their portraits painted into the big canvas, but, the painting finished, they diced for its ownership and Sir Bellingham Graham threw a double-six. Almost the length of the hall extends a fine oak table, and to the right an altar-table whose top is of English craftsmanship but whose lower work is Dutch or Flemish. The hall has a double door of mahogany with brass lock, and

the morning-room beyond contains a couple of good Romneys
and a fine Zoffany. The Romneys are individual portraits. In
the Zoffany, an eighteenth-century formalism blends with
what I should call a feeling for Versailles landscape. The
master of the house, dignified by an eighteenth-century cor-
pulence, rests in an easy chair beneath a spreading tree. His
family poses respectfully round him, with a blue-green
pastoral background. A good Zoffany.

"Now," said I, "for the hoofmark on the staircase."

"You know the story?"

"Everyone knows the story! Sir Richard Graham was
badly wounded at Marston Moor. Endowed with more than
its share of equine common sense, or plain horse sense, his
horse turned out of the battle with its master, and, hotly
pursued by a band of Ironsides, made for home. Knowing
the right place for its wounded master and without waiting
for him to dismount, it galloped into the hall and up the
staircase, leaving the clear imprint of one of its hoofs in the
solid oak of the bottom step."

"Yes, the hoof-print proved a trifle awkward there. People
used to trip on it, so it was transferred to the landing. I'll
show you."

Three hundred years of beeswax and turpentine crave
wary walking. When we came to the panelled staircase there
in truth was the hoof-print, and, looking down on its clear
outline, who would dare to judge it merely a curious mal-
formation in the grain of the oak? Should one not rather
profess a willing suspension of disbelief?

James I had occupied a massive four-poster in a rather
small bedroom. Over the fireplace hung the portrait of James
with his wife and little Prince Henry. So pleased with his
entertainment at Norton Conyers was the royal Scot that, the
story goes, he gave this picture to the family. It seems
authentic in that James is made to look more the philosopher
than the fool.

In most country houses, Jacobean has been supplemented
by eighteenth-century. Norton Conyers is no exception.
Seated at the ancestral oak, the squire and his friends smoke
their pipes, tell their stories, talk politics and sport, drink
their wine, and, finally, are carried off to bed. In the drawing-

room beyond, classic in style rather than Gothic, the ladies of the household sit at their embroidery frames, their music or their sketching. So, at Norton Conyers, the Adam-style drawing-room presents contrast with the hall.

For a time Charlotte Brontë was governess in a family named Greenwood, and, while in Harrogate, the Greenwoods paid a friendly visit to Norton Conyers. This visit has led to much debate. Did Charlotte Brontë use Norton Conyers as a setting in *Jane Eyre*?

"I'm not going to express any dogmatic opinion about that," said Lady Graham. "There are other houses with good claims, as you know, and the artist, the novelist, hardly ever uses a precise, photographic memory. The imagination makes composites, choosing a fragment of this, a trifle of that, a suggestion of the other, and these become fused into one picture."

The frontage of Norton Conyers faces west and has a wide terrace with a sunk fence. From the windows and the terrace the view leads the eye over a wide park, but with no noble trees. South of the house is a chapel with a clock tower. It looks rather like the stables. The north side has a bowling-green where Charles I played, and where, no doubt, he stammered words of encouragement to his woods as they trundled over the green. There is a large walled garden with an orangery.

Two or three hundred yards north of Norton Conyers lies the village of Wath. A *wath* is a ford, and here the ford is over Upsland Beck, which is now bridged. Wath is clean and prosperous. Its church holds the memorials of the Graham family, and, inspecting them, I thought how churches must necessarily be visited as arks not only of religion but also of local history, and, often, of local custom. Here are six bells, and the tunes chalked on the wall as well as upon a large chart of the change-ringing.

I paused for a moment before a tablet to the memory of a small daughter of Sir Digby Cayley : the poor child seemed a long way from its home at Brompton.

From Wath I might have followed the course of Upsland Beck, but I pursued the road. To my right lay a five-acre field of young flax, a far brighter green than that of the corn. On

The junction of the Greta and the Tees

the other side of the road stood the farm, where I made inquiry about the flax.

"Last year, seven acres of flax. This year, five acres. Next year, probably none. You see that stack a hundred yards south of this? Last year's crop, and the rats are in it! The straw's light, and there'll be precious little return on the crop and the labour. The flax-mill, near Selby, hasn't yet sent for the stuff. There's a farmer near Thirsk who grows a lot of flax, and he's in pretty well the same predicament. If the manufacturers don't mend their ways there'll be no more flax there, or here either!"

So that was that! I was, however, under no delusion that flax was a new crop hereabouts, or a war-time emergency crop. The old maps of the Riding show flax-mills and paper-mills well scattered over the arable lands, and all that has happened is the usual and lamentable, though no doubt economical, centralization of the flax-growing and linen-weaving industries of the country. Flax, besides being useful, lends an added richness to the rural spring.

I pushed northwards to Sutton Howgrave. Here there is Sutton, there is Howgrave and there is Sutton Howgrave, and the three in combination hardly amount to a village. Of Howgrave Hall there is left only an outer shell of dilapidated wall in the middle of a field, and the inn makes no claim to be more than a cottage promoted to innship by the addition of a dart-board, a couple of ingle-benches and some beer. It was excellent beer. The innkeeper was reading the *Northern Echo*. Each provincial newspaper has its own territory, and the *Northern Echo* goes not much farther south than this. Part farm-man, part innkeeper, the landlord had little good to say of farmers. They were, he said, a damned sight too prosperous. Handsomely subsidized for their crops of corn and potatoes, they were an idle lot.

"But," I said, "surely the North Riding War Agricultural Executive Committee keeps on stirring them up?"

"If," he said, "any farmer thinks himself badly done to, off he goes to the N.F.U. and kicks up a hubbleshew."

"A what?" I asked.

"A hubbleshew!" he repeated.

"D'you know the last time I came across that word?"

x   305

"No."

"Two years ago," I said, "in Beaumont and Fletcher."

"Never heard of 'em!" he said.

I explained that here was a word which in the early seventeenth century had evidently had national currency, which had gone to ground and which had, in the twentieth century, again poked its nose out into the light of day. He did not, however, profess interest. The word was part of his limited vocabulary, and that was all he knew or cared.

"What about tractors?" I asked.

"Oh, ay, they've all gett'n tractors, but nobody knows owt about t'war i' these parts," he insisted.

As I finished my beer I asked him about the *Howe* and the *Grave*.

"Where there's a howe there's a grave," said I. "You're a trifle tautological hereabouts. Is there a howe?"

"Ah deeant knaw!" he said.

Sutton Howgrave, it seems, offers a promising field to the archæologist, but, for all that, I hope he will keep away. He is unlikely to discover anything new about bell-barrows, disk-barrows, round barrows, long barrows or plain howes at Sutton Howgrave, and the place looks as though any sort of hubbleshew would get on its nerves. Leaving the inn, I considered the farming. It was first-rate, and the land was in good heart. Perhaps the hedges were not so trim as in pre-war days, but what they had lost in tidiness they had gained in loveliness, and I have never been convinced that a three-foot lopped thorn fence gives adequate shelter from sun and storm to any sort of stock.

Lambs have queer ways. I have grown used to the sight of lambs standing on their mothers' backs, but here was a pasture to the left of the road with seven or eight heaps of artificial fertilizer in it. Upon every heap a group of lambs was concentrated.

From Wath onwards the mild air was heavy with the droning of Halifax and Lancaster bombers from the aerodromes of the Vale of Mowbray. They seemed to be flying in all directions, as whim dictated, but finally I found a scheme to cover their activities.

Turning left along the main road into Wensleydale, I

noted Upsland, a single farm, in low-lying carr country, and between the farm-buildings and the road a great pond of stagnant water. On the Survey map this pond is a moat, and I have no doubt that it is a moat and that Upsland was a moated grange. Thornbrough Moor is low-lying agricultural land; the water-table lies near the surface. Good trees are rare, but there is neither moor nor marish. Beyond Thornbrough and approaching Nosterfield, I grew certain that this locality had witnessed, in Anglian and Danish times, the making of history, that it was an important focus of event. The great earthwork, covered with trees, to my left confirmed this, for the ridge or rampart, visible through the trees, invites the archæologist to thorough exploration.

I refuse to believe that *Nosterfield* is a Latin-English portmanteau word. I prefer to think that originally the name was *Paternoster Field*, for when these words trip from the tongue it will be found that *noster* goes less easily with *pater* than *noster* with *field*. Etymology betrayed me into taking what the map showed as a field-path from Nosterfield to Well. There was, indeed, no footpath, but a large amount of barbed wire. I came into Well at the top end of the village and looked with some sinking of enthusiasm down the village street. Forty years ago Well was as picturesque a spot as any in the Riding. I found it an occupied, almost a distressed, area. There used to be thatch, but there is no thatch now. The Royal Army Ordnance Corps had a local headquarters here. Not far away, visible from the hill above the village, was a hundred-acre bombing-field. The whole place reminded me of Rex Warner's *The Aerodrome*. Still, I explored. The little stream, the Well, which runs down the main street, is neither so imposing as the beck at Thornton Dale nor so noticeable as the beck at Low Kilburn. It made no music. The little almshouses are still there, but their exterior seems preferable to the glimpse of interior I caught as I went by. In the churchyard, close by the chancel door, was a stone shaft, the remnant of a cross, and obviously it had formerly been used chiefly for sharpening knives, scythes, bill-hooks and sickles. The old font was in the churchyard, as it was at Wath. The doorway was not particularly good Norman work. Within the church, the wooden font-cover is reputed to be the second oldest in England. Its date is 1352, and though I am no authority upon medieval woodwork I think it is of French workmanship. There is a recumbent effigy of Sir John Neville, fourth Lord Latymer, who died in 1577 and had his figure carved in a good freestone which, being rather soft, lends itself to treatment with a pen-knife sharpened, I dare say, on the cross-shaft in the churchyard. So, at least, thought one Marmaduke Danby in 1618, and though I shall probably never learn who Marmaduke Danby was, or any circumstance more of the thoughtless hour in which he immortalized his name, I shall remember him when I have forgotten Sir John Neville, fourth Lord Latymer.

Yet, Latymer? Latymer? Of course it was a famous Lord Latymer, ancestor of Sir John, who slew the great dragon of Well, and upon this legend I have time and patience enough to dwell. Here in this village has been excavated the biggest Roman bath, outside Bath itself, in this country. This was an important focus of Roman civilization in the north, and where there were Romans there were, later, the Romano-British. Now the emblem of the British kings was the dragon, and what more likely than that, here at Well, in his stronghold, a British king was defeated by invading Angles, and killed on the spot? Somehow, quite naturally, the leader of the Anglian horde became identified with the ruling family hereabouts, and Latymer got the credit for slaying the dragon. And Nosterfield might easily be associated with the whole affair. Plausible, but, unfortunately, there is no evidence.

From the hill above the village I stood to watch the big bombers converging from all quarters upon the bombing-field, the puffs of white smoke as the Halifaxes and Lancasters passed over the ground, and I heard, after intervals, the faint noises of explosions.

In Well, for anything I know, the ancient hospital with its Gothic arches may still survive. The man at the post office knew nothing of it. It was a hospital of St Michael, founded in 1342 by Sir Ralph de Neville, Lord of Middleham, for a master, two priests and twenty-four poor brothers and sisters. Apparently the endowment survives, for the alms-houses just above the church bear the Neville arms. The Nevilles were the great family at Well.

"Here lyeth buried Sr Jhon Nevell, Knight, last Lord Lattimer, who died the 23 of Aprill, 1577, who mared the Lady Lucy theldest daughter of Therle of Worseter, and she lyeth buried in Hackne Church, by London, and by her left 4 daughters and heires, whoes matches are here under expressed."

There is something pathetic about this. The inscription insists that though the Neville line comes to an end the Neville blood still flows in human veins. Something pathetic, too, in the tiny chairs within the church, grouped for the infants' Sunday-school.

On the left of the road at the crest of the hill the Well Scar limestone quarries and kilns showed smoke without human labour. It was Whitsuntide. From the brow I looked eastward over the wide Vale of Mowbray, and because the sun was westering I saw plainly the White Horse of Kilburn, the clear outline of Black Hambledon, and, at the northern extremity of the moorland plateau, the cone-shaped outline of Rosebery Topping. All day, from noon until five o'clock, I had been following a low ridge that gave me visions of the western hills and of the eastern uplands. The Vale of Mowbray looked fat and prosperous. Everywhere little villages, sometimes not more than a few clustered houses. Everywhere plenty of green woodland, and everywhere Dutch barns with red roofs not at all out of harmony with the landscape.

Over the crest I went down into West Tanfield, and there, sitting on the wall that cinctured the churchyard, I set my memory to work upon what I had so far seen that day. The name of Norton Conyers brought into my mind that Sir Richard Norton, Lord Chief Justice of England, who died in 1421. He was the gentleman who told Falstaff that his means were very slender and his waste was great, and who, having committed Prince Hal to prison for striking him in his very seat of judgment, was by King Henry V confirmed with honour in his office. Shakespeare used him as a whetstone for Falstaff's wit and as a pillar of the English state, and this same Richard Norton was buried in the transept of Well Church. Of his blood came that Richard Norton who with his eight sons took part in the Rising of the North; and when, in early Stuart times, Norton Conyers passed into the hands of

309

the Grahams, it was to a branch of that great stock of the Grahams that the flower of Montrose was given. Thus, and here at West Tanfield with the Marmion Tower within range of my eyes, I was reminded that the story of England is a rich fabric centrally wrought of rural threads, that Wath and Well and West Tanfield have played a part, have contributed a thread, to the rich brocade of history.

From Wath, moreover, I take this epitaph :

> Enobled virtue lyes within this tombe,
> Whose life and death inferiour was to none;
> Her soules in Heaven this tombe is but a tent,
> Her endlesse worth is her owne monument.

I like this for the sentiment expressed, but chiefly for the subtle rhythm of the last line. Repeating that line, I rose from the churchyard wall to look at West Tanfield. There are times when one is more intent upon trout than upon tombstones, and Tanfield is the place where, for me, trout and tombstone meet. The tombstone was put up by voluntary subscription to the memory of Francis Maximilian Walbran, who was accidentally drowned whilst angling at Tanfield, 15 February 1909, aged 57 years. Below the inscription on the Celtic cross is a pediment upon which fishing-gear stands out in relief : basket, landing-net and rod, and three plump trout disport themselves in a series of impressionist waves. That there are fine trout in the Ure at Tanfield I know from my own observation, from careful and patient experiments in dry-fly fishing. That I, too, was not accidentally drowned was probably more by luck than management, for I didn't know the river then so well as I do now. Let nobody play the fool with Ure or Swale or Wharfe. Shallow and deep water, slack and fierce current, can be very treacherous, and as for the trout-fishing in the Ure, the Yorkshire Anglers are jealous of their rights and the water-bailiff knows his job, even to the picking-out in fresh mud of the tracks of an otter followed by her young. The fine trout hereaway are not, moreover, native to the brown water, but are bred in a hatchery not far away. I remember once looking over this hatchery, but, truth to tell, it was a long time ago and I have forgotten precisely where it lies.

Usually I have been happy, at Tanfield, to look from the bridge up the first reach of the river and rejoice in the Englishness of the scene. It presents the sort of picture that is given a half-page of the *Times*. It makes no demands of the sun, for it is as fine in stormy autumn and black winter as in May. It has no sublimity, and therefore is satisfying. It is never querulous, never moody. Along this river reach I have watched kingfishers in undulating flight. Best of all, perhaps, I have watched trout ring the calm water, after sunset and the dropping of the wind; and often, curious in these things, I have tried, yet always failed, to analyse the content of that serene mood which anglers know, and the villagers that lounge on the bridge on summer evenings. It is a mood always associated in my mind with river scenery, and I have experienced it even on the banks of the Nile.

Here, however, I have a duty to history. Tanfield Church and the Marmion Tower may fulfil that duty. Walking down the churchway path was a young woman, a sightseer. I caught her up.

"You've read Scott's *Marmion*, of course?" I asked.

"No," she said, "I have not!"

"But bless your life, you must have!"

"No!" she said.

How she contrived at school to remain ignorant of the last words of Marmion remains a major miracle, but let that be. She is, perhaps, all the better for never having been told that *Marmion* is poetry. Here in Tanfield Church lie the alabaster effigies of a Marmion couple, wrought shortly after 1400. Here, too, are other stone figures that have obviously lain out in the rain for a century or two. Contemplating the weathered relics, I was minded to remark that originally such effigies were carved in wood and that stone became popular because wood gave no firm assurance of perpetuity. In York Minster, the images of the kings show how the carver in stone followed the technique of the wood-carver. With the institution of Guy Fawkes' Day, there developed an irresistible urge to use wooden effigies as guys, and those left over from the annual burnings came to be used as gateposts and hovel-props, as Mizraim became merchandize and Pharaoh was sold for balsam.

I proved less interested in the Marmion tombs than in the Marmion Window, the most easterly of the windows in the north aisle. This window was good, far superior to the modern windows. At the top on the right was a weird moon-face with a shadow darkening it, but what medieval magic lay in its symbolism I did not know. The woodwork is modern, and good. I know a man who collects information regarding musical instruments carved in ecclesiastical wood or stone; he would be interested in the carved musicians on the vicar's chair, and on the curate's. One plays the fiddle, another the harp; the third has a bassoon, the fourth a long horn. The bench-ends have heraldic birds and beasts.

The Marmion Tower stands just above the church, and I found it hard to express my opinion upon it. The fifteenth-century window, the oriel, is of later date than the featureless walling of the Tower. The ground-floor rooms on each side of the gateway were in occupation : they were full, so far as the obscurity allowed me to see, of old chairs and lengths of rope.

The inn at West Tanfield is an angler's pub, and what that means is too well known for detailed specification.

CHAPTER XIII

THE PEOPLE AND THEIR DIALECT

FIRST I shall describe to you a certain Mary Allatson, a daleswoman, now dead, but whom I well remember. She stood not quite five feet in height and was a thin, wiry woman with small bones, a great talker and a prodigious worker, a complete extrovert, not at all given to introspection or generalizations of any kind. She accepted daylight and darkness, rain, wind, sleet and sunshine, without question. She took poverty and toil as completely natural, and showed never a sign of wanting to escape from either of them. Often she got out of bed at three o'clock in the morning and did a day's work before lazier folk were stirring. She was sharp-tongued yet not malicious, and she never gossiped about her neighbours; she attended rigidly to her affairs, she was businesslike, hard in bargaining yet not, I think, greedy. She bustled, she never lounged or lazed, and favoured hard chairs. Conservative to the backbone, she had no patience with new-fangled ways, and detested innovations of any sort. She had no wit and little humour, yet could hold her own in argument so long as argument had either practical or personal bearing. Town life and town folk she mistrusted. Both were completely alien to her. Without much book-learning, she knew her Bible and her *Pilgrim's Progress*. They were her books; she hadn't any other. I would not say she was religious. Apart from orthodox acknowledgment of the existence of God, which she took for granted as she took sunrise and sunset, she was a pagan. The strange play of chance in life she recognized well enough, but not the finger of God. In a way she was callous. When, old and wrinkled and tough, she heard that So-and-so had died, she would chuckle and say, "Mak' room for mair! Mak' room for mair!" The business of living had to be carried on. She liked elbow-room. Even the village street was too thrang for her, and three people made a crowd. She was a stoic by nature, not by training.

313

She preferred her own company to that of others. Monotony and solitude did not frighten her, and amusements never appealed to her. I doubt if she knew there was a village cricket team, she despised card-players, she never set her foot inside a cinema, and the Women's Institute meant nothing to her. I heard her say never a word in praise of beauty, many words in praise of utility. Perhaps she had no eye for the beautiful, and certainly she cared nothing for music and poetry. Music was hymn-singing and poetry was anything in rhyme or jingle. Was she a good woman? Really I don't know. People talked about her actions, never about her morals. If to be good is to be a regular chapel-goer and a total abstainer from alcoholic liquor, then Mary Allatson was good.

You see her, then, as a thin little woman, active and industrious all her life. Now for features that have more to do with heredity and less with environment. She was dark in complexion, with sallow skin like wrinkled parchment; brown-eyed; she had dark, straight hair without trace of kink or curl, never luxuriant, fine rather than coarse, parted neatly down the middle and drawn tightly back over the ears and knotted up into a little bun. Her eyes were neither lustrous nor contemplative nor twinkling, but screwed up, sharp and restlessly inquisitive. They darted. Her brain-case was long and narrow; she was strikingly dolichocephalic, thin-faced, with sunken orbits and high cheek-bones; rather small, regular teeth, and a jawbone that narrowed to a sharp chin.

Mary Allatson represented an important North Riding stratum of population. If you look for it to-day, you will find it in the fields and cottages. It won't be wearing anything like the cotton sunbonnet Mary used to wear, but it may be in shapeless skirt, faded blouse and clogs, and you will recognize the features, the harsh, sharp voice, and, on closer acquaintance, the character. You will find it in the western dales and the fell country, you will encounter it in the north-eastern moorlands, and sporadically in other places. It is characteristic of the barren lands.

The tough physical fibre and the rigidity of character of Mary Allatson's type indicate a struggle for survival carried on for many centuries. The habitat of the type to-day is that of yesterday, and it was dictated not by choice but by necessity. The slender bones, the narrow skull, the small stature, are all those of the long-barrow people, the Neolithic type you may study in textbooks and anthropological museums. Reporting on their presence in Hampshire, W. H. Hudson thought the little dark people were increasing in number at the expense of their big, clumsy, blue-eyed, slow-witted Saxon neighbours. In the North Riding to-day they are holding their own but not ousting other types. They may be trusted never to vanish, but they have to maintain themselves in competition with other tough elements in the population. You will not often find them in towns. They form the oldest breed in the North Riding and have contributed much to that strange composite called the Yorkshire character. The menfolk of the breed make excellent poachers and gamekeepers.

The second figure in this portrait gallery intrudes upon my notice before his proper turn. That is his way. He is something of a mystery. I can tell you neither his name nor his occupation, and beyond the fact that he was a North Riding man in his thirties and that his work lay with farm-stock I know nothing of his history and character. I saw him sitting in the sun on the steps of Masham market cross in August 1924. He was alone and at his ease. A little below average height, with thick limbs, big hands and an immensely solid trunk, he was broad-shouldered and deep-chested. He was naturally swarthy, but the smooth, clear skin of his face and neck were burned a transparent golden-brown. If his hair had not been closely cropped, I think it would have curled, or, at any rate, would have developed a wave. He was bullet-headed, a pronounced brachycephalic type, and handsome in a southern style, with firm chin, well-shaped nose, straight forehead, thick eyebrows and determined mouth. When I first saw him, I said, "A Roman!" Then, at once, I corrected myself. "No," I said, "he's straight out of the Bayeux tapestry!"

I have had no reason to modify that judgment. Straight out of the Bayeux tapestry he was—one of William's Normans or Frenchmen, a Mowbray, a Roos, a Bulmer, a throwback to one of the great Anglo-Norman families that, dominating the North Riding in the Middle Ages, have quitted the pageant of history. By some fortuitous combination of genes the type had come to life again in Masham market-place, and there he was, exactly as in the tapestry. You ask, "Is this a rare type?" and I answer, "Not particularly rare, but seldom found so perfect as in this specimen. Look for these men on the big farms in the Plain of York or the Vale of Mowbray. Look for them especially amongst horses, for they seem naturally attracted to the life of a wagoner and are happiest in stables. You can find them carved in stone on the Wagoners' Memorial at Sledmere in the East Riding, and they exist, in effigy, upon many a medieval knight's tomb. Look for them and you will find them without much trouble."

Next I come to a giant of a man, Solomon Hardwick by name, yet anything but a Solomon by nature. He was a great golden-bearded fellow in his prime, with the strength of an ox, the generosity of a fool and the good nature of a spaniel. Reckless, arrogant and boastful, he never lost his self-esteem, and prided himself always more upon physical strength than upon brains or cunning. He was by trade a village butcher, and it was right that this should be so, for he genuinely delighted in handling the weapons of his craft and there was a powerful strain of barbarity in his nature. I have watched him, bloody-handed, roaring with laughter, take up huge lumps of raw liver, fresh from the carcass, and cram them into his mouth, blood staining the golden wires of his beard. He roared still more loudly and much more menacingly when I refused the oozing fragment he offered me.

"Good for ye, lad!" he growled. "Put blood into your heart!"

The Solomon Hardwicks, the Vikings of the North Riding, are not very common nowadays. They have no *métier*, there is not enough hand-to-hand blood-spilling to persuade them to persist in the modern world. I found one putting up a signpost on the Roman road beyond Stape, and I have encountered a few amongst the fisherfolk from Saltburn to Filey, but the blue-eyed, red-headed giants have dwindled in number and are, I fear, doomed to be merged in the majority. They were a type, but it has largely drifted into a more common and more dominant stock, represented pretty well, I think, by my own great-grandfather, Robert Merry Cross of Scalby, and his wife. They exemplify, I think, a combination of Anglian and Danish stock—tough, cautious, straight-spoken and even blunt in expression, rigidly honest, puritanical, and with a streak of hardness running through soft places in the heart. Those soft places are for livestock, dogs and children, for the implements of their craft and for the fields they farm. They are not particularly gentle to women. The women are their partners, not their inferiors in any way. These men and women are not smooth-tongued. When they suspect anyone of an untruth they do not say, "That doesn't sound quite like the truth," but "Thoo knaws varry weel thoo's leein'!" This absence of the diplomatic touch in common talk is one of the first characteristics noted by strangers in Yorkshire. It takes, I believe, a lot of getting used to, and some southerners never do get used to it. It is one of the reasons why Yorkshire writers remain as a rule outside the main stream of English literature. It is one of the reasons why Yorkshire poetry is either imitative and worth-less or genuine and unintelligible.

These North Riding farmers are shrewd bargainers. Some-how they have never accepted fixed prices even in the shops where they buy clothes and articles for household use. This, I suppose, is due to the fact that the goods they have to sell are subject to bargaining and fluctuations of market price. Chaffering, however, is in the blood. The North Riding farmer trades on it. It forms part of his humour and self-esteem. He is proud of it, and yet he has a notion of fair prices. I knew one old farmer, William Hardcastle, who used to plough up Cromwellian bullets in his fields. His price for a bullet was a shilling, and when an American globe-trotter offered him ten shillings and insisted upon his taking it, he was offended and indignant. One shilling, one bullet. That was fair dealing. Ten shillings was crazy.

The Anglo-Danish stock has plenty of brains, but they don't get—or used not to get—very much chance of proving their worth. When they do, you get an Adam Sedgwick or a John Wyclif. My own opinion, for what it is worth, is this: when a young man leaves the land for town life, he is often bewildered and spends years finding his feet. By that time it is hopeless for him to try to make a great figure in the world, but his children—that is another matter. They go to school, they win scholarships, they become lawyers, doctors, politicians, professional men of all sorts. They even learn to make friendly noises.

Finally, there is another type of North Riding character. I shall, for purposes of analysis, take a woman as my illustrative material. She may resent this, but I can't help it. She best serves my purpose. Well, then. She is stocky in build, or rather gives that appearance. Sturdy is a better word. She strides rather than walks, and strides with purpose, as though there went something or someone in front of her with which or with whom she was eager to catch up. It is the same with her greyish-blue eyes, which are always looking for something ahead. It is the same with her speaking, which is always trying to catch up with her ideas. She has a careful, shrewd, analytical mind, resourceful and inventive, with a strain of melancholy threading it, and a powerful imagination.

This is the seafolk type. You can trace the salt of the sea in its mentality. It is not, be sure, the longshoreman, the beachcomber, the gatherer of flithers from the rocks, but the born shipmaster, dominating and adventurous, never satisfied with familiar horizons, always exploratory and always restless. It is Captain James Cook, it is William Scoresby father and son, it is the Whitby master mariner, with palish features, pale hair and pale eyes; Scandinavian or Danish, yet the Norse or northern blood infused with English, giving it something that, though it comes out in an Ibsen and a Nansen and a Stefansson, the Scandinavian blood too rarely possesses—drive, imagination, power of leadership.

This completes my portrait gallery, for I shall not ask you to study the intermediates, the infinite gradations between type and type; the nondescripts, the North Riding folk by adoption, the townbred folk. The specimens I have chosen to exhibit are indigenous to the land, but the centuries have witnessed some dilution of the native breeds. From medieval times down to the end of the eighteenth century, for instance, criminals fleeing from the headsman's axe or the hangman's rope often sought refuge in the remoter gills and dales, where they were fairly safe. Irish haymakers and labourers have settled within the borders of the Riding. There are gipsies, of whom I know nothing and can report nothing. The Cleveland iron-mines were not worked exclusively by North Riding men, nor were the lead-mines of Swaledale and Wensleydale. Moreover, when in the nineteenth century the Silver Pit began to yield huge quantities of magnificent fish, a few families of fishermen settled along the North Riding coast from as far away as Devonshire. Boarding-house keepers and publicans are not invariably native to the districts where they follow their trades, and many people who have made their money in Leeds, Bradford or elsewhere have settled in the North Riding dales. There is also a sifting of artists and writers, and the war, no doubt, has had some influence upon the population.

In general, however, because the North Riding is very largely agricultural in its economy and because agriculture demands a static population, the dilution of the native blood has not been serious. In the remote villages there is still inbreeding—the gravestones show it—but there is no evidence to prove that this has resulted in a high percentage of idiocy. I hear of few idiots and see still fewer.

Now, I suppose, I must describe how life is carried on in the North Riding, and I shall begin with the small farmer in the north-western dales. When I was last in Upper Wensleydale it was the fag-end of July, and I stopped by the roadside for a few minutes to watch three men scything a meadow, a small and uneven intake. There was something very beautiful in the swing of their bodies, the rhythm of their movements, the clean swish of the scythe-blades and the regularity of the swath they were cutting. I can handle a scythe myself, but not so technically as this. This was a fine sight and worth watching. But there was more to the picture than the beauty of the scything. This was the hay harvest, the first and last of the year, and thin, poor stuff was the grass they were cutting. Every scrap of it had to be saved for winter fodder, or it would be a sorry time for the cattle and for their owners when the snows came. The lovely superficial overlay a grim reality, and the grim reality was this : the small farmers, owning or renting thirty or forty acres of grazing land and meadow, live desperately close to the poverty-line. They survive only because they have made up their minds to survive. For them, life and the struggle for survival are the same thing. Sometimes there is insufficient food on the table, and only a few coppers either in the china pig on the mantelshelf or in the housewife's purse. Menfolk and womenfolk alike have little time for rest or relaxation. They avoid the alehouse. They visit the cinema maybe once in six months. The ordinary wireless programme is too remote from their daily lives to interest them, and a trip to Ripon or Harrogate is a rare treat. Yet they find their moments of leisure profitable. The W.E.A. has a resident organizing tutor in the area. The Women's Institute also flourishes, and for the boys and girls there are scouting and guiding. The brass band is a regular feature of village life, and sports meetings are highly popular. Cricket seems not to flourish greatly in the dale country, and the winter traveller sees few football pitches. Farther down Wensleydale and Swaledale both games prosper because those areas offer easier living and greater leisure for the young men. Richmond, for instance, has had a cycling club, a working men's club, a mechanics' institute, clubs for hockey, cricket, golf and rifle-shooting, a branch of the Girls' Friendly Society, a horticultural society and the Richmondshire Choral Society. Some of these may now be dead or moribund, but other clubs and societies must have taken their places. Do not think that the dalesman is a brainless illiterate. He may not read much or rapidly, but he reads carefully and co-operates with the writer, which is more than can be said of many professional critics. I have known dalesmen who read Leibnitz and Spinoza. One of them, when I last met him, was wrestling with Whitehead's *Adventures of Ideas*. All seem to take much interest in the contributions of science and technology to agriculture, even though they can't afford to experiment with new methods and machines. I should say that the men of Wensleydale and Swaledale are more intellectually active than those of the north-eastern moors, Cleveland and the Vale of Pickering. They have inquiring, speculative minds, and I am afraid some of them are beginning to think they should be getting a squarer deal than local or national administration allows them. For example—

320

Bedale

though it is a West Riding, not a North Riding, example—as I went down from Buckden towards Kettlewell, there on the fellside to my right, in huge letters twenty or thirty feet high, sprawled across the dull green of the upper slope, I read these words : WE WANT THE GRID. For my part, I think I believe in the sort of discontent that arises from the constant presence of an irritant because ultimately this leads to a growth of better living-conditions. Hence I doubt not that the hardness of life for the small farmer in the upper dales will steadily be mitigated.

Farther down Wensleydale, between Leyburn and West Tanfield, farms are bigger and farmers more prosperous. The population keeps abreast of the times in those things which concern it. A group of farmers, for instance, from the Masham area, takes a day off to visit the agricultural research station at Askham Bryan, to see for itself the latest machines in operation. Men are eager to do their best for the land. They are ready for experiment, they respond to suggestion, but as yet they don't get enough guidance, and I suspect a lack of vision amongst the men at headquarters. Technical advances are not enough. Machines can play their part, but Northallerton by this time should have become a big centre for agricultural research especially in the field of genetics. The future of the land lies more in the hands of the geneticist than in those of the veterinary surgeon or the firm of Massey Harris, and Northallerton, as the administrative centre of the Riding, ought to realize this truth.

The pick of North Riding farming lies in the Vale of Mowbray, and there is a lot of it. The Vale of Pickering is not so well farmed as it ought to be. In Bilsdale, Bransdale, Rosedale and Upper Farndale, the conditions of Upper Swaledale and Upper Wensleydale are repeated. There are excellent farms between York and Malton. Eskdale is good pastoral country. The coastal strip from Whitby to Filey shows some good farming, some only moderate. From Stokesley to Guisborough I found little to complain of. The stock-breeding in Kildale and Westerdale is largely a hit-or-miss affair. It is, however, no business of mine to make an accurate agricultural survey of the North Riding, and I am glad of that, because I should make a poor job of it. What I record here is a series

Norton Conyers

of personal impressions, and they may be right or wrong, just or unjust, adequate or inadequate. How should I know? All I can do is to compare North Riding farms with, for example, the thousand-acre farms of the East Riding, and set down what I think. If my impressions are distorted, I regret it.

All over the North Riding to-day, on main roads and by-roads, you will meet the baker's van. I don't know why I should regret this, but I do. Other travellers may look upon the baker's van as a commonplace economic necessity, but for me it means that North Riding housewives are ceasing to bake their own bread, cakes and pastry. The big ovens set into the wall by the fireplace, ovens that would hold batches of a dozen or fifteen loaves, are going out of use. Going, too, is the huge flour-bin. Gone are the earthenware cream-bowls, the barrel-churns, the cumbersome cheese-presses. If the farmer's wife still makes butter she doesn't roll it and stamp it with a butter-mould, put it into a big, square butter-basket and carry it to market as she used to do, sitting by her husband on the driving-seat of an old covered wagon, light buggy or smart gig, returning home at dusk with raisins, currants, treacle, tea and what-not. I don't say that marketing has fallen into decay, but it isn't what it used to be. Hucksters from the big towns have taken a lot of it over. They are the modern representatives of the old packmen who used to journey on foot from farm to cottage, from cottage to farm, with needles, thread, tapes and buttons, ribbons and stuffs, in the very manner of Autolycus. They ceased to operate about half a century ago, or perhaps even longer than that. Even then they were a dying race, because in the villages you would find a Manchester House—my own grandfather owned one —to which the country housewife could go for her necessities. One thing, however, my grandfather neither bought nor sold, and that was the crudely printed, double-column broadsheet in which the packman commonly dealt. This sort of broadsheet you will not find on exhibition in the museums, for its contents were often lewd to a degree, and the packman carefully picked his customer, usually the cowhand or wagoner, not the farmer himself. I dimly remember the last of the packmen : he was a nasty, leering old fellow with what he thought was a persuasive tongue.

Speaking at the moment only of the Vale of Pickering and its dales and gills, I should say that that area was sadly deficient in folk-song. I do not recollect hearing a genuine folk-song there. Over in the East Riding, at North Grimston, I remember an old fellow singing a bastard folk-song called "Salvation," and there was a clumsy dance to it. I have heard genuine folk-song at Veryan in South Cornwall, but North Riding people are not, I will say, great singers. Their chapel-singing is almost invariably atrocious, and the ploughman would rather bellow "Nelly Dean" or "Lily of Laguna" than anything straight from the soil. If in North Wales, at Mold or Bala, you are likely to meet half a dozen young men at dusk standing at a road junction and singing to the sunset, you are not likely to encounter the same thing in the North Riding. I have heard market-women in Italy singing color-atura stuff in a lakeside tunnel, but nothing like that has ever greeted me on my entering Thirsk or Malton. Christmas carolling, even, isn't first-rate. There remains a Thomas Hardy touch about it, but the merest touch. The business doesn't flourish by reason of sheer delight in singing.

In the same way bell-ringing doesn't flourish either. In Elizabethan London, citizens inflamed with sack and enthusiasm would set the bells to change-ringing. There is nothing like that in the North Riding. Such conduct is contrary to North Riding character.

But stories of ghosts, bargasts, hobgoblins and fairies, indeed yes ! Wise men, wise women, wizards and witches by land and water. In the North Riding character exists a strong sense of the uncanny. There are unlucky birds and beasts, lucky and unlucky things to do. My grandmother on my mother's side could charm away warts and did so to my know-ledge (the wart was on my wrist, and I was eight years old), but she is dead (she died walking through the fields), and so far as I know nobody has succeeded to her gift in that particular village. She also had second sight, which the philo-sophers no longer sneer at. Many North Riding women have second sight. They have the knack of breaking through the spatio-temporal web that envelops the rest of us, and they enjoy premonitions of death and disaster as you and I enjoy a promenade concert or the ghost stories of M. R. James.

In his younger days, my father was the crack sprinter of his village, and at weddings commonly won the ribbon that, before his time, was the bride's garter, the winner of the race having the right to remove it from the bride's leg. He was also, I am told, the treasurer of the annual club-feast, but of the actual feast I remember very little except that the two taverns were open all day, the village street was full of drunks, there were swings and roundabouts, cocoanut shies, athletic sports, sweet-stalls, and a brass band in scarlet and blue, paraffin flares at nightfall and a great deal of good-tempered fighting, and that the whole glorious set-up took place along the village street. The running for the ribbon and the annual club-feast have long been abandoned.

The age-old custom of riding the stang, of which Hardy makes a feature in *The Mayor of Casterbridge,* was dead before my time, though I have heard my grandfather speak of having witnessed the whole complicated ritual, and he repeated the nominy which accompanied it. But if riding the stang had fallen into desuetude, the old Christmas mumming-play of *Saint George and the Dragon* had not, and I myself have played in it, though I forget what part I took. The words as I recollect them were almost identical with those of the Cornish version. It was, in the North Riding, more of a pagan rite than a Christmas play, and as a boy I was mightily impressed and awed by its ferocious fertility-rite.

If you look into Anglo-Saxon literature you will soon discover that one of the favourite forms of poetry was the riddle. Doggerel has taken the place of poetry, but the riddle is still popular.

> As Ah went ower Moory Moss
> Ah met a man on a grey 'oss;
> He wept an' he wailed
> An' Ah axed him what he ailed,
> An' he said he was gaain' to his feyther's funeral
> 'At dyed seven year afoor he was born.

When an old custom dies, is it any use trying to rejuvenate it? If the mell-doll and the mell-supper have vanished into limbo and the harvest festival has taken their place, if the plough-stots no longer dance their way through the village, it

means, I think, that these things have had their day. I am not
sure that the old sword-dances shouldn't be let quietly perish.
When I hear of the Sleights Sword-dance being taught in
schools, I suspect the thing is already moribund or likely soon
to be so, and I am no admirer of earnest young men and
women dancing country dances which, alive in Shakespeare's
time, have lost their ancient liveliness. I don't think I regret
the passing of the mell-supper, or witch-crosses, or the
horrible superstitions people used to hold. I wouldn't care to
believe in bargasts and gabble ratchets. In my young days
there were plenty of young men and women not sure whether
they believed in fairies or not. They were careful how they
talked of fairies. The older folk didn't believe in them.

Farm servants were hired from Martinmas to Martinmas,
presumably after the farmer had been paid for his harvest
and had cleared his debts, and as a rule the ploughlad or
wagoner took no instalment upon his wage during the course
of the year. When Martinmas came round again, off he went
to the nearest village to be measured for a new suit of clothes
or to buy a bicycle with Bowden brakes, three-speed gear and
plated rims. Careful with his few pounds, he spent them
wisely and then took himself to the hirings. The usual
question from his friends was : "Estha gettn hired or istha
stoppin on?" This question became a catchword in the towns.
I believe the man seeking work should have carried with him
some mark of his craft—a wagoner's whip or a shepherd's
crook—but as far as I recollect all he did carry was a bunch
of ribbons in his hat. What he most looked for was a good
meat-house, where he would be handsomely fed. It is reported
of one old farmer that, repeating the Lord's Prayer in chapel,
he came to "Give us this day . . ." when from the back came
the indignant roar of his wagoner : "Ay! Cheesecakes wi'
lids on!"

Gipsies were regarded with mingled awe and suspicion—
awe because they told fortunes, suspicion because they were
held to be thieves. They were never welcome. On the other
hand, tramps, roadsters or rangers—they were known by all
three names—were never turned away from the farms. They
could rely upon a bite of supper and a bed in the barn, and
no work was expected of them in return. Many of them had

forgotten their real names—they were simply Lincoln Bill or Poor Patsy; most had been in jail, they slept out in deserted quarries during the summer months and in winter crossed the Vale of Pickering to take up quarters, three or four of them together, in the high barns of the wold country. One North Riding vagrant, Edward Simpson of Whitby, achieved nation-wide notoriety and a measure of grudging admiration from collectors of flint weapons. He carried on his trade between 1840 and 1860, and came to be known as Flint Jack. I have a few of Flint Jack's forged Stone Age implements, but some time ago they got mixed in with a number of genuine speci-mens and now I cannot for the life of me sort out the fakes from the genuine specimens. The fakes have the true patina of antiquity. Flint arrow-heads and spear-heads are known in the North Riding as elf-bolts; in Shetland, I believe, they are called elf-shot.

The Yorkshire dialect is one of the very few English dialects of world-wide importance. Wherever the traveller in this modern world may find himself, whether in the steaming jungles of Yucatan, the icy wastes of Spitzbergen, the tropic desert of Atacama or the bazaars of Bushire, he is apt at any moment to hear the broad accents of the broadest of our English shires. Wherever two Yorkshiremen meet, there is already forged between them the bond of their dialect-speech. With a large and energetic membership in Yorkshire, the Yorkshire Dialect Society has even more subscribers in the United States of America than in the East Riding, and there exists a greater number of publications in and about the Yorkshire dialect than in or about any other English dialect. No village entertainment within the borders of the county would completely satisfy its audience unless some part of it consisted of a play, sketch, dialogue or monologue in broad Yorkshire, and a synthetic Yorkshire accent is welcomed by radio, music-hall and theatre. I need not here explain the devastating effect produced by a highly educated Yorkshire-man (and there are a few) suddenly and feloniously switching over from Standard English to the broadest of dialect-speech —a procedure apt to strike respect, terror and dismay.

Yorkshiremen discussing their dialect either in the dialect itself or in the English of current speech will sooner or later speak with pride of its vast antiquity, and with equal or greater pride of its purity. They will tell each other and the credulous listener that theirs is the tongue of Cædmon, will boast with ferocious dogmatism of their Viking vocabulary, and with arrogant confidence assert that their peculiar idiom has descended in the purest state from darkest antiquity. If they have philological grounds for this belief they conceal the fact effectively under a mass of iteration. It is something they accept on trust as their ancestors accepted the literal truth of Scripture. I hate to disturb this confidence or controvert their dogmatism with a dogmatism equally massive.

The members of the Yorkshire Dialect Society would be the first to admit that there exists not one single, coherent dialect spoken within the boundaries of the whole shire. The speech of Hallamshire is far removed from the speech of Richmondshire, and the dialect spoken in Joseph Wright's Windhill is by no means the dialect of Herbert Read's Kirby-moorside. If students of the Yorkshire dialect assert that, broadly speaking, there are two distinct dialects now widely spoken in Yorkshire, this again is to make the roughest of classifications, for I have heard people with phonetic training and attentive ears claim that they could with ease distinguish between the speech of Leeds and that of Bradford, and that the dialect of Huddersfield was as far removed from that of Morley as the dialect of Middlesbrough is removed from that of Reeth. The rough classification, however, serves its purpose well enough, and it is that there is one dialect of the West Riding of Yorkshire and another common to the East Riding and the North. The dialect of Wetwang or Friday-thorpe in the East Riding is substantially the same as that of Danby or Stanwick or Bedale or Hackness, and this is confirmed by the fact that Turner's dialect stories in the speech of the Wolds are in identically the same idiom and are recited by dialect-speakers with the same intonation, as the traveller will find existing many miles to the north across the Vale of Pickering. Moreover, Atkinson's *Glossary of the Cleveland Dialect* contains few words or phrases which would not, to a native of Driffield or Market Weighton, convey the same meaning as would be put upon them by a native of Rosedale or Eskdale.

Yet this again is to speak generally and broadly, for when I think of the dialect spoken in Swaledale and Teesdale I am at once aware that there exist slight differences in vocabulary and subtle differences in intonation between that dialect and the dialect of the rest of the Riding. Further, the dialect spoken by those whose business is with the sea is not exactly the landsman's dialect. I say nothing of the speech of the North Riding towns, for that is but a bastard affair compounded of dialect intonation and Standard English pronunciation or mispronunciation, with aspirates cropping up where they have no business to be, and vowels varying from the broad to the standard. It is the basic dialect with which I am concerned. Up to this point my remarks should have carried conviction. The North Riding will agree that the East Riding speaks substantially the dialect native to the North Riding, and that, as my namesake John Harland of Swaledale wrote, the dialect of the West Riding is a barbarous jargon, the result of an influx of industrial workers into the manufacturing towns from the beginning of the machine age down to the present day. The North Riding will agree, too, that its coastal dialect is subtly different from the inland dialect, and that there are words and idioms peculiar to the recesses of the north-western dales. Now let me turn for a moment to this question of the antiquity of the North Riding dialect. Has it in truth existed unchanged from Anglian and Danish times, or are those who make this assertion in some error?

The question is hard to answer, for the only reliable evidence is contained in written documents which only a trained philologist can interpret. It is true that we have the evidence of glossaries and comments upon the dialect, but these for the most part date only from the late seventeenth century. There is not much of earlier date. But obviously unless a dialect, like a whole language, is subject to change, that dialect is as dead as Sanskrit or ancient Greek. In any living dialect there is continuous change, and unfortunately the change may furnish evidence of decay and dissolution. Examining the brief glossary of dialect-words given in Marshall's *Rural Economy of Yorkshire* in 1788 I find words which are no longer "slipper upon the tongue" as they were in Marshall's day.

328

Writing in the second half of the nineteenth century, John Harland lamented that during a brief ten years' absence from Swaledale, he found on his return that words with which he was formerly edified had vanished from the local speech, and this was his justification for putting together his wholly inadequate glossary of Swaledale words. I pick up Atkinson's work, again of the later nineteenth century, and there I see words and phrases which, lively to my youthful ear, are now dead. When, to verify my findings, I go back to the *Yorkshire Dialogues* of the late seventeenth century, I discover that between their date and that of Marshall the vocabulary of North Riding speech was impoverished by the disappearance of word and idiom alike. Lastly, the Yorkshire Dialect Society has for some years realized the importance of making gramophone records of dialect speech before that speech becomes hopelessly corrupted or altogether extinct. Only thus, and neither by the symbols of the phonetician nor by the desperate orthography of the dialect-writer, can the dialect at present spoken be accurately preserved for posterity.

In the days of Cædmon the sole recording instrument was the quill of the scribe, and the scribe stands as an obstacle between the spoken dialect of past centuries and the modern student of that dialect. We underestimate the bulk of that obstacle. The scribe was engaged in an essential occupation. Into his hands came the monastic records, legal documents, wills, records of national and local events, myths, legends, traditions, meditations and exhortations. Even in the fourteenth century the written English of the North Riding was not vastly different from the written English of the rest of the country, including London.

"In the name of Godd, I Henry Wartre, preste, xxv day of Aprell, the yere of oure Lord Criste MCCCC mo. XXXij, makes my testament in this maner. First I wyte my saule to Ihesu and to oure Lady Sancte Mary, and all blissed company of heven; and my body to be beryedd whare Godd will dispose for me, if I do noght. Also in wax to be brent about me ij sereges. Also I wite to ilka preste at my messe and at my dirige beyng iiijd. Item I wite to Sancte Petre werk of York vjs.viijd. Also I wite to Annes Drynge a rede docer wt. a banquere and all the whysshyns. Item to the forsaynde

Annas I wyte a rede coverlett, with the tapett of the same. Item to Annas Westen j matres that I lige on. Item to Alice Page j litell kyste. Item to Richard Drynge j lange kyste that stands in Sir John Pratt chaumbre."

That is an extract from the will of Henry Wartre of Scarborough, and its date is 1432. The surprising thing about this document—and it is a thing that can be paralleled from the many hundred wills of the same and subsequent centuries—is the rarity of purely Yorkshire words and inflexions, and even of Yorkshire pronunciations. *I makes*, *Sancte Petre werk*, *lige*, *kyste*, *lange*, *that stands*, are all Northern forms, except for *werk*, which ought to be *wark*. Otherwise the document is in the usual scribal English of the period. The whole mass of written evidence, indeed, goes to show that, from the time of Cædmon onwards, in the northern counties as elsewhere, there existed a powerful scribal tradition of spelling and grammatical structure, and that departures from this tradition are exceptional. They exist but they are not common, and hence the task of discovering how the North Riding dialect was actually spoken in the Middle Ages is wellnigh impossible.

Many philologists, indeed, believe that our modern dialects did not properly emerge until the seventeenth century, that the seventeenth and eighteenth centuries were the heroic age of dialect speaking, and that from the end of the eighteenth century began the period of degeneration and decline. With this view I do not entirely agree. Chaucer's parson, for instance, was conscious of wide differences in speech between himself and the northern men; Caxton is aware of dialectal variations; Shakespeare, writing dialect, produces a speech utterly different from the rest of his English; Raleigh spoke with a strong Devonshire accent, and Milton draws a distinction between the upland hamlets and the educated town. Yet I believe that during the Middle Ages there existed a northern dialect spoken with considerable uniformity from the Firth of Forth to the estuary of the Humber, and that only at the beginning of modern times did this great northern dialect develop a number of sub-dialects which grew in strength until they reached the dignity of independence. The emergence of two separate Yorkshire dialects in modern times would explain the sudden interest taken by seventeenth-century writers who saw dialect as something new, rich and strange. Forthwith they must needs employ it for purposes of poetic composition, producing barbarous eclogues in octosyllabic couplets far removed indeed from the tradition of Theocritus and Spenser, and often mutilating pronunciation to secure adequate rhyme. True, their subject-matter is elemental, for one of these dialogues deals with the birth of a calf, the other with the slaughter of an ox, and without being exciting they are at least interesting, for they contain words which since the seventeenth century have either changed their shape or become extinct. The ordinary reader must needs go through them with the aid of a glossary and a series of footnotes, and, doing so, will realize that if he could by some trick of time be set down amongst the peasantry of seventeenth-century Swaledale he would find himself hard put to it to understand their speech.

Now I would raise another point of importance. If a Yorkshireman should assert the preponderance of the Scandinavian element in his vocabulary, I should challenge the truth of the assertion. The North-West Midland poet of the Middle Ages, author of *Pearl*, *Patience* and *Gawayne and the Grene Knight*, used many more words of Viking origin than, for example, Richard Rolle of Hampole, and the place-names of the North Riding show a preponderance of Anglian over Danish forms. The Danish element is indeed strong, but not as strong as is made out by amateur dialect-students who, given Danish and Anglian analogues for a word, ascribe its origin unhesitatingly to the Danish when the probability is that the Anglian derivation is the right one.

Discussing origins and history, I would here put in a word for the study of the ancient and modern dialect of the Friesian Islands; I think this would throw a good deal of light upon the North Riding dialect. As for Celtic origins, they are hardly worth pursuing. Celtic words and phrases survive, but nobody knows why. *Brock* the badger is one of them. Celtic numerals, until recent years, were used by shepherds only. Again nobody knows why.

Dialect speech is a matter of word, idiom, rate of utterance and intonation, and though word and idiom may perish, rate of utterance and intonation show few signs of decay. Old customs and old gear are subject to processes of educational and economic change, and with their disappearance part of the dialect dies. A modern kitchen-range replaces the old plate hearth, and *reckin-crewk* and *rannel-bawk* are forgotten. Mechanized agriculture kills a word like *swingletrees*, and radio weather forecasts lead to the vanishing of *snell*, *snarry* and *sowmy*, a *rooak* becomes "hazy conditions" and "overcast" takes the place of *owerkessn*. Moreover, the rural population, now in closer contact with the world, tends naturally to adopt the speech-habits of townsfolk, and though amongst themselves they use the racy and vigorous dialect they slide into the speech of the village school whenever they talk to bettermy folk. Thus *shoggles* become "icicles," a *smout* becomes a "tunnel," and a *laith* becomes a "barn." More and more it grows difficult for a stranger to penetrate the outer layer of school-taught English to reach the core of dialect speech, and ever more and more intent of ear must the student of dialect become to catch the vanishing nuances of pronunciation. How few years must elapse before the almost Irish pronunciation of the doubled consonant in such a word as *butter* becomes extinct, and how long before the inflected genitive creeps into *yon lass beeats*, or the whole phrase becomes "that girl's boots"?

In isolated areas the dialect seems not to be losing ground, but this state of affairs will not outlast the closing of isolated schools. When I went to Rievaulx, the lads playing by the roadside—*on t' cam-sahde*—were using the dialect with vigour and accuracy, and Rievaulx is not the only isolated hamlet in the North Riding. North Riding members of the Yorkshire Dialect Society have on occasion complained that their dialect is not receiving the attention it deserves and the scientific study it merits, but for my part I am glad of that, for many a flourishing wild plant transferred to a cultivated garden droops and dies, and dialect-speakers confronted by a recording apparatus are apt to develop an awkward shyness that militates against the authenticity of the recording. To teach the dialect is useless. Minute shades of pronunciation cannot be taught. As for literary composition in the dialect, it is usually a failure. This is one example of such a failure.

It is an adaptation of the first speech in the *Agamemnon* of
Æschylus :

The watchman talks to himself.

Noo distha knaw, thoo greeat fond lubber, thoo,
It's ten year, ay, ti t'varry neet, sen fost
Thoo set thisen to leeak oot ower t'dikes,
Gloorin' like a gaumless feeal—fer nowt !
Ah tell misen at yah neet, alawand,
A leet'll fire yon eldin up on t'rigg,
T'low on Blakey Toppin'll leet up
An Ah s'll stevn oot an wakken t'oose.
It's despert wark. Me ees is gannin' blinnd,
Bud yit, i' sowmy neets, wi' rooak an' raan,
I' snarry winds, wi' rind on ivvry steean,
Me awd beeans shakkin', shoggles o' me lugs,
Neea matter what, Ah dozznt gan to sleeap.
Yah neet as black as pick yon low'll leet
An' Ah mun set misen ti beeal oot.
Ah's flaid ti sing, Ah e neea mind fer laykin,
An jalous, noo, at if Ah shut me ees,
Ah'd sleeap an nivver wakken onny mair.
Thrang ? Ay, Ah'd need ! An yit Ah tell misen
Ther's nut a steean at went ti build this spot
Bud ez a coss on't.

And *The Solitude of Alexander Selkirk* is no more successful :

Ah's t'gaffer of ivvrything 'ere,
An neeabody threeaps wi' me ;
Neeather beeast ner bod, ti be seear—
As far as Ah'm yabble ti see :
Ti them fooaks at thinks looanliness grand
Ah wad mak a noraation and rant
Whaal Ah'd lettn the feeals understand
At Ah've a seet mair an Ah want !

The weaknesses are obvious. The only first-rate verse and
prose that might be composed in this dialect would be the
work of one who habitually thought in the dialect as Burns
thought in the Ayrshire dialect. But in any event this dialect

is no mine of jewels. It is too rude, utilitarian and rough. It is nesh only to those familiar with its sounds.

Those who compile dialect glossaries are usually folk of mature years and education who, very naturally, include words and phrases familiar to them in their childhood. Some of the words in John Harland's *Glossary of the Swaledale Dialect* (1873) were already obsolete when Harland recorded them, and I have reason to think that this applies also to other glossaries. I submitted a list of a hundred dialect words to a class of North Riding school-children and found that about half the words were totally unknown to them. Others they completely misinterpreted. A truthful modern survey of the dialect would clearly have great value, but so far as I know no such survey is in process of compilation.

Next, many dialect words have more than a single pronunciation : *greeav* or *graav*, to dig; *heeam* or *yam*, home; *leean* or *looan*, lane; *sweeal* or *swaal*, to throw. Compilers of dialect glossaries are not always careful to indicate the variations and the reasons why they exist. I believe I am right also in supposing that no comparative survey of the sub-dialects in the North Riding has yet been undertaken to indicate the existence of special, mainly occupational, words, and sub-dialectal differences in pronunciation of the same words. The following Swaledale words from Harland's glossary are not familiar to me as North Riding words : *addle*, to earn—I know this only as a West Riding word— *ajye*, awry or crooked; *aswin*, oblique; *barf*, a mound; *barn*, a child; *belive*, presently; *blirr*, a blaze; *dormon*, a main cross-beam; *gruve*, a lead-mine. Where I have quoted nine examples there exist probably ninety or more. The special task is not mine to undertake here, but it should be done without much delay. Similarly the special sub-dialect of the fishing community demands investigation; the speaking-rate differs from that of the inland folk, the pronunciation is different, and no doubt there are technical and occupational words which demand recording. It may turn out that this sub-dialect may extend northward and southward along the east coast and prove after all to be almost an independent dialect. The more closely the North Riding dialect is scrutinized, the greater the number of problems that emerge.

"Leeakstha, lad! Mebbe thoo's takkn up wi t'lawcal talk an anters thoo's gaain ti deea some wark on it. Noo i'steead a gannin aboot wi a nawtbeeak i thi 'and an axin questions fer all t'wolld like a skeealgaffer thoo mun get thisen a gave-lock er a shackfork an set ti wark amang t'fooaks thersens; Thoo'll e to be yan on em, neeather better ni warse. Thoo'll seean finnd oot all thoo wants ti knaw, an a bonny seet seeaner 'n onny other rooad. Get od o t'lahtle bairns, ax em t'wods bud deean't aggle. T'young taistrills'll knaw mair aboot pawtin bods an aboot sooart o thing thoo's set on, an if thoo skelps em thoo'll larn nowt. Awder folks is ower thrang wi skep an ken, wi strickle an stang an mell, an t'mair thoo canges t'mair they'll glower. Bud mebbe them at's past wark'll e summat ti tell ya. Thoo'll finnd em threeapin at t'toon end an doon o't'brigg, and thoo'll e ti deea a despert lot o beealin i ther lugooals afoor thoo ez em wick eneeaf ti gan wi tha ti t'yalhoose. Yal's nobbut walsh nooadaays, bud it's strang eneeaf ti raffle up t'brains o' sike-like an set em on ti a noraation."

And if the reader can make anything of that, he may congratulate himself on knowing a little about the North Riding dialect-speech.

CHAPTER XIV

THE CITY OF YORK

MRS ROBINSON is a West Riding woman by birth. She was schooled and took her degree in Leeds and now lives in York. I sat with her in Terry's Café and we talked about York.

"York," said I, "offers a challenge. As a big railway centre it is nothing like Crewe, as a cathedral city and county town it is nothing like Salisbury and Lincoln, as an industrial city it is neither a second Leeds nor a minor Bradford, and as a market town it is not a magnified Thirsk, a greater Easingwold, a vaster Beverley. It is Roman, Saxon, Norman, Tudor, Georgian and modern. It is the capital of the North yet it is not megalopolitan. Tell me about York!"

"I love York," she said.

"A mere emotional reaction! People also love Pudsey, Sheffield Brightside and Hunslet. You must do better than that."

"When you travel from Leeds to York," she said slowly, "you cross a frontier."

"From the industrial to the agricultural?"

"From the utilitarian to the decorative, from the modern to the historic, from the grim to the gay."

"From Faust to the Russian ballet?" I suggested.

"From the serious to the fantastic."

"Listen!" I said. "Listen carefully, because I'm going to be rather difficult."

"In York," she said, "we take difficulties easily."

"All right! Do you know anything about the theory of the second adolescence?"

"I do not. It sounds like something out of the psychoanalyst's secret drawer. Go on!"

"When people arrive at middle age," I said, "they often go through a difficult phase reminiscent of the troublesome period of adolescence; they develop an acquisitive restlessness, a sharpness of temper, an irritability; they become ultra-

336

sensitive; they become ambitious; they dash after material prizes and ache for medals and distinctions; they pass through a dark turbulence of spirit. Those, roughly, are the signs of this second adolescence. Now I have the idea that this second adolescence may apply not only to individual human beings. Communities and whole civilizations may pass through it, and I fancy that the industrial communities of Britain are now going through that stormy phase of their existence. You wouldn't deny, for instance, that the cities and big towns of the North and Midlands are grim, restless and irritable, ambitious, jealous, grasping, psychically disorganized?"

"I would except York."

"So would I."

"The industrial cities, you suggest, are in their early forties? And York, I take it, has passed through her second adolescence, found her way out of the spiritual wilderness, and is now psychologically adjusted to a sparkling fifth decade? Still full of life, anything but senile, and conscious that there are values higher than those of mercury-vapour lighting, muck and money?"

"Exactly."

"You know," she said, "I belong to York in this, that I swallow theories very easily. Still, I prefer tangible evidence."

"Evidence forthcoming?" I asked.

"Plenty. For one thing, I've found York full of individuals. The mass mind does not triumph here. York has offered me more queer people to the square mile than any other place I know."

"Queer people," I warned her, "gravitate together."

"Maybe. Or maybe York brings out the queerness in folk. Anyhow, here they are. Cranks and cults, côteries and cliques. Monastically minded young men, fierce poets of both sexes, mild-mannered anarchists, absent-minded but brilliant women. York cherishes the individualist. York is a circus in which the eccentric can demonstrate and sober conventionalists don't jeer. And people dress as they like. Fashion worries nobody."

"Cathedral city atmosphere," I commented.

"I agree. And nobody bothers about the money you have or haven't got. People sing in York. The milkman sings, the errand-boy whistles, the window-cleaner hums a tune. You could break into a double-shuffle in the middle of the square yonder and nobody would be surprised. York's shabby, perhaps, and rather poor, but careless and gay. She's lived through her second adolescence."

When she paused for breath I intervened.

"That," I said, "will serve admirably as an introduction to the City of York."

"But," she objected, "I've said nothing about the City."

"The people," I said, "are the city."

"The people living," she added, "and the people dead. There's something of Vespasian and Severus, of Paulinus and Wilfred and Cuthbert, of Anlaf Cuaran and Harold Godwinsson, alive in York to-day. I was standing in a bus-queue in Rougier Street a couple of days ago, along with half a dozen young naval men. They were talking—about what, about whom? About Jonathan Martin, the Minster firebug. They'd somehow mislaid the date when Jonathan set fire to the Minster."

"Ay," I agreed. "If York owes much to the living it owes still more to the dead. A man must reckon with history—with Anlaf Cuaran and Nicholas Blackburn, for instance, and most certainly with Jonathan Martin—the very moment he walks through Micklegate Bar."

"You know the history of York?" she asked.

"All the histories of York that I've read," I answered, "seem to bear as a burden the grim psychology of the West Riding. I have not found them gay. Instructive, certainly. Desperately instructive."

"Let us," she suggested, "begin at the beginning."

To seek beginnings is often to answer questions; the great trouble is to frame the questions. The first question about York frames itself, but only, I think, when you enter the city by the road from Poppleton or Wetherby, or if you notice the curious dip from Blossom Street to the railway station, or if you see The Mount marked on Bartholomew's shilling map of the modern city. All round York the levels stretch to the horizon, yet the Wetherby Road shows them giving place to little hills. Here is one to the left of the road with the wreck of a windmill on its summit, and there are dips and climbs in

338

the road itself. What are these hills, and why do they occur in the midst of the plain?

The answer comes, as it comes so often, from the geologist. "These hills," he explains, "are glacial rubbish. York is built upon the east-to-west ridge of rubbish left behind at the extremity of the ice-sheet that flowed down from the northern mountains, filled the Vale of Mowbray and the Plain of York as far south as this point and then shrank back at the close of the last Ice Age. York stands on the moraine," says he, "and what the North Riding looked like in those far-off times you'll be able to picture : to the north, a flat sterility of marsh and moss as inhospitable as the barrens of arctic Siberia; to the south, vast floods surging through and submerging the midland forest-lands, swirling away in a south-easterly direction and leaving huge deposits of alluvium; then this long, irregular moraine, a frail bridge between the eastern and western highlands of Yorkshire, here broken by the floods and there holding firm, providing the first practicable track across a wilderness of ice, frozen mud and reedy morass, vast rivers and shoreless lakes. The moraine explains not only the existence of a settlement here at York but also the direction of the first roads."

The pictorial quality of the geologist's imagination is surprising, and the more vivid it is the more I believe in its accuracy. The Ice Age and the Great Thaw, however, is not Mrs Robinson's beginning. Hers is the historical beginning. Guiding me through the narrow streets from St Helen's Square into Petergate, she suddenly switches me up an alley to the right and, climbing the city wall behind Lund's shop, we look from above and concentrate attention upon a fragment of history pretty well the size and shape of a man's grass-grown grave.

"Here," she says, "is the beginning."

It is, I believe, the sole extant fragment of the original vallum cast up by the Romans when they resolved to extend the Pax Romana to the turbulent Brigantes. This is a corner of the earthwork, rounded off in Roman fashion, and from its position antiquarians have plotted the lines of the first Roman camp on the tongue of land between the Foss and the Ouse. Its tangible, visible presence demonstrates the learning and

339

skill of the antiquarian who, twelve feet below modern ground-level, established its width, height, compass-bearing and date. Mrs Robinson tries to show me the original lines of the whole rectangular fortification, but, because monographs will give me all I want to know on that subject, I am inattentive.

"This," I say, "might be the grave of man or wolf-hound. Why don't the Friends of the City of York, or whatever they call themselves, set up here some indication of what this grass-grown mound is, commemorating in fine gilt lettering the foundation of the City and the name of the founder?"

"I don't know."

"Nor do I. What next?"

"The Museum of Roman Antiquities?"

"I am in no mood for museums."

We went, therefore, to the Minster, and there I ran into a trouble sure to afflict even the most logical. Philosophers discuss spatio-temporal relations as though space and time were on the most friendly terms. Let the philosophers visit York! In York, if you get your spatial relations right—in other words if you survey topographically—then the temporal relations prove obstinate; on the other hand, if you resolve to cover the city's monuments chronologically, time leads you a bewildering dance from street to street. The hot-footed sightseer succumbs to partial aphasia or complete black-out, and even the most leisurely will need time to adjust his vision. I would challenge Tom Macaulay himself, or John Ruskin, to remember York Minster from a verger's *recitativo* or his own *O, altitudo!* The trouble originates in trying to see everything. Seeing everything, one remembers nothing. On this occasion I fell into temptation but evaded it by expunging from my mind every impression but one.

We were admitted to the crypt, the verger clicked down a switch, pulled up a wooden trapdoor and revealed, seven or eight feet down, the base of a pillar. Calling the fragment of Roman vallum Exhibit A, I could match this Exhibit B with all the diagrams and sketches of Roman architecture in the books and with such wreckage of Rome as I have seen between Rome itself and Hadrian's Wall. Indeed, had I stumbled over this fragment in Asia Minor or Central Park,

I should still have said, "This is characteristically Roman!"

To rewrite the history of York from the Ice Age to our own day is a task for which I am fortunately ill qualified, yet I may, perhaps, be allowed to pose questions. One of these questions perturbed me as I considered this relic of Rome. Granted that Roman poets and historians make a mere half-dozen references to York, in the great days of the Roman peace York was certainly a thriving city, and when Britain was a major granary of Rome the neighbourhood must have been well studded with villas. From Old English poetry it is clear that the Anglian invaders considered Roman sites the work of superhuman hands, copiously haunted by bad spirits, and they left these sites alone. They preferred to settle away from them. York, however, shows few traces of Roman occupation *in situ*. Why is this?

The historian shrugs his shoulders and I have no theory to offer. Then, again, how comes it about that a Christian church, the Minster, stands upon a Roman site? Here, perhaps, we may follow Angelo Raine. The emperor Septimius Severus, a little, swarthy, bright-eyed African whose Latin carried a strong Phœnician accent, died at York. Here, too, died Constantius, and here Constantine, son of Constantius and Helena, was proclaimed emperor by the army of Britain. Constantine had been brought up by Diocletian in the creed of Mithras, the old Roman gods were all as dead as mutton, and between the cult of Sol Invictus and Christianity the gulf, in those days, seemed narrow. Constantine became a Christian, Christianity became the official religion of the Roman Empire, Mithraic temples became Christian churches, and when the last Roman garrisons ebbed back on Rome the local inhabitants continued Christian worship. Through the grim days of the Anglian Conquest they lurked in the abandoned Roman sites, and where Christians lurked the barbarians ceased to fear. York suffered eclipse but not annihilation, and when the barbarians embraced the new religion they built their first church on the old sacred site. Thus, or approximately thus, Angelo Raine. His theory is possible but not convincing.

Another question. When a stranger enters Leeds he does not ask to see the Red House or the Coloured Cloth Hall as, in York, he asks for the Merchant Adventurers' Hall or Margaret Clitheroe's House. He knows well enough that long ago Leeds demolished the old to make way for the new. Why hasn't the same thing happened on an equal scale in York? Why is so much of Old York spared? Why haven't the old streets been widened and why haven't the alleys and courts been abolished?

The answer this time comes from London. Though much of Old London has vanished, much remains, and it remains because, during the late seventeenth century and the whole of the eighteenth century, the wealthy London merchant, whose business had been carried on in his house in the city, built himself a fine new house in the country with a garden and an orangery, yet still maintained his old premises as warehouse and office. The city streets were too narrow and the business premises were dingy and sunless, but the city remained the hub of trade. Exactly the same phase of social evolution took place in York, and the York of the tourist and antiquarian was spared.

Even so there arises another question. The most casual investigator soon discovers that the Romans and after them the Minster-builders quarried and used the beautiful magnesian limestone of Tadcaster. The stone was there in vast quantity and could easily and cheaply be brought to the city by water. Why, then, did not the medieval and seventeenth-century house-builders of York use this stone? Why did they prefer, as they evidently did, to put up half-timbered houses?

I think I can answer that. Within the city walls building-land was expensive, and consequently sites were limited in area. But you could build a big house on a small site if, using the ground floor for business, you bracketed out the first floor and made it overhang the pavement. You could do this with half-timbered houses but not with stone, and thus the half-timbered house was popular because it gave something for nothing. Hence the Shambles in York.

Do not imagine that the problems presented by the city are all set down here or that they are all explainable. York is an English city, and all England is littered with problems. Nobody, for example, knows why the great Wansdyke was built on top of an excellent Roman road, and no York archæologist can explain the quatrefoil shape of Clifford's Tower on its grass-grown motte. He can tell you that the closest resemblance exists between Clifford's Tower and a tower at Etampes in France, but that is a parallel and not an explanation.

All this as I stared down at the base of the Roman pillar below the crypt of York Minster.

"This magnesian limestone!" I said suddenly.

We left the crypt, the verger locked the iron gate, we came out of the Minster into the strong sunlight. A little quest began.

Walking across Lendal Bridge towards the Minster, you naturally look down-river and the river frontage inevitably reminds you of Bruges, Antwerp, Rotterdam. You stop to admire the noble width of the Ouse, the swans, the irregular skyline of warehouse roofs and the plunge of the sunlit walls into the river. Twenty yards downstream you note a little landing-stage, with perhaps a small craft tied up to it, and you say to yourself, "I should like to walk down there!"

Easy to say, but not so easy to accomplish. The way lies through the blitzed Guildhall down into the cellars, the former A.R.P. headquarters of the city, and there you need the little Scots caretaker and his jingling keys. He took us down to the landing-stage and explained.

"Nowadays," he said, "you see the Ouse always full of water and the level doesn't seem to vary much. It wasn't always like this. I remember it before they tinkered with it. The Ouse was a tidal river then. At ebb you could often walk across the bed of the stream from one bank to the other, but at flood the water rose twelve feet or thereabouts. This landing-stage isn't the medieval staith, of course, but the old staith stood on roughly the same site." Turning to unlock an iron gate, "Now this," he went on, "is Common Hall Lane. It runs under the Guildhall up to daylight."

Facing the dark, overarched, steep incline of Common Hall Lane, I knew we were looking directly towards St Helen's Square, named after the mother of Constantine, and towards Stonegate; and how, I thought, should Stonegate be so called unless it were the road by which stone was carted from the river-front for the building of the Minster? Overhead were great beams of oak, underfoot the lane was cobbled, on the right was cellarage and on the left ranged a series of chambers once used for storing goods brought up-river and landed at the staith. Now they were bricked up with Jacobean bricks and their interiors filled with concrete which here had caused the walling to bulge outwards and there had oozed out at ground level. The lane was roughly as wide as the Shambles. The stone flags higher up came from the floor of the blitzed Guildhall. A modern door of old design took us out into daylight.

Down there under the gutted Guildhall I had been cut off entirely from the York of banks, insurance offices, building societies, railway offices, cafés and shops; Common Hall Lane was out of modernity altogether. But does that explain why, under those big oak beams, the only figure I thought of was that of Joseph Addison, the parson in a tiewig? Why Addison?

Again in the open air, the temptation to quote came upon my companion : "Time, which antiquates antiquity, and hath an art to make dust of all things, hath yet spared these minor monuments."

"True," said I, "but the major monument above Common Hall Lane is now a worthless ruin, war is more ruthless than time, and nobody now will ever see York's Guildhall as it was before the bombs blasted it."

What, therefore, would profit my describing it? And, furthermore, why should I let a too vivid imagination play upon the past? I lack the confidence essential to the romantic chronicler who so carefully describes the first appearance of Roman legionaries at Eboracum, the course of the fighting with the indigenes, the slow extension of Roman power and the settlement of the country, the slaughter of the Ninth Legion Hispana, the funeral rites of Severus, the proclamation of Constantine, the withdrawal of the Roman garrison; I may not describe the life of the Roman streets, the shops, the slave-market, the circus, the marchings-out and marchings-in of the legions, the changing of the guard at the prætorium, the saluting of the eagles, the rites of Mithras. Nor may I like a patient bookworm thread the long and bloody chapter of daylight stabbings, drunken carousals,

344

burnings, lootings and midnight murders which makes up the
tale of Anglian and Danish York, nor pause for the four
plates in colour illustrating Paulinus's christening of King
Edwin of Northumbria on Easter Day in the year 627 A.D.,
the building of the first church in stone that followed the
baptism, the fire of 741 A.D. and "the most magnificent
basilica" subsequently built by Archbishop Albert. Alcuin may
not display the treasures of the Minster Library, nor may I
clarify the shadowy lineaments of the great builders. The roll-
call of their names must be enough : Thomas of Bayeux,
Archbishop Roger, Walter de Gray, John Romanus, Archbishop Melton. This story is told by the chronicler.

I leave the authority on ecclesiastical architecture to describe the west front of the Minster as "more architecturally
perfect as a composition and in its details than that of any
other English cathedral," the great window above the west
door as "an unrivalled specimen of the leafy tracery that
marks the style of the fourteenth century," and the late Perpendicular east window as "one of the finest in the world." I
leave him to detail the beauties of All Saints in North Street,
the Norman work in the churches of St Denis, St Margaret
and St Lawrence, and to reveal the Roman masonry in the
foundation walls of Holy Trinity in Micklegate. Let the
ecclesiastical historian patiently trace the story of the Benedictine Abbey of St Mary, the wide temporal and spiritual
powers wielded by its mitred abbots, the fluctuation of its
fortunes, its quarrellings and reconciliations, and how after
the Dissolution much of its Early English and Decorated
stonework went to build the King's Manor as a palace for the
Lord President of the North, and how that palace afterwards
became a school for the blind. Let the classical antiquarian
display the ten remaining sides of the thirteen-sided Multangular Tower and trace the Roman masonry in the city wall
between the Tower and Bootham Bar. Let him demonstrate
the existence of Roman baths beneath the inn called the Mail
Coach.

York is inexhaustible. You may prefer to look at the
daffodils in bloom along the slope of Tanner's Moat, sit in
the public garden, row a skiff on the Ouse, or stroll along the
city walls remembering how traitors' heads were displayed

at Micklegate Bar, recalling that the name of Monk Bar now pays compliment to General Monk as once it did to Danish Guthrum. You may have such an eye for eighteenth-century dignity as will take you to the designs of the Earl of Burlington for the Mansion House and the Assembly Rooms. You may note that York's civic theatre was founded in 1765 by Tate Wilkinson, and bear in mind that York, though without its Jane Austen, was then a place of fashionable resort; that here were horse-racing, balls, routs, midnight masquerades. You are interested in social and economic history? Here flourished medieval guilds and merchant adventurers, and here operated George Hudson, the Railway King. In drama? Here from street to street on the Feast of Corpus Christi lumbered the tiered pageants of the York Cycle of mystery plays. You are taken up with medieval wood-carving? Here in York were two distinct schools of the craft, both as famous in their day as the great school of the Ripon Carvers. I doubt if any other city in England has so much to offer in so small an area, and I am very pleased that the schoolchildren of York are systematically taught the details of their city's history.

But I am for the Minster, and I go alone.

In some old library or bookshop you have perhaps drawn out from its place on the shelves a great folio bound in leather —such a volume as Charles Lamb loved to handle—of one of the Jesuit theologians or the medieval philosophers, and, opening it at the title-page, have been halted by the bold red and black, the tall Roman print, the convolutory wording that says to you, "Think well before you go further!" The west front of York Minster is the title-page of a great volume. It bids the visitor pause, saying, "Once penetrate this towering sublimity and for the good of your soul you enter the purlieus of the world invisible." I open most books with neutral feelings, yet some books demand a chastened and humble mind: Thucydides, Shakespeare, George Berkeley, Charles Doughty, Augustine of Hippo. Some music makes a similar demand. Who dare swagger against Mozart or bite his thumb at Beethoven? Similarly it is well to stand up in presence of William Blake and Michelangelo. Still the philosophers impress me most. York Minster is a vast philosophical treatise, a logical expounding of the transcendental. The architects and builders knew the symbols, they set a meaning into the stones, every measurement was significant and every carving declaratory, they rejoiced in the mathematics, delighted in secret harmonies of length and breadth and height, and exulted in the allusive balancing of light and shadow. Some of them walked familiarly in the dazzling darkness and lightless brilliance of transcendental revelation. Every chip of oak, every dab of mortar, had significance, and the whole building was an allegory of the greater allegory of the whole earth.

Rhetoric? All cathedrals are rhetorical, and why not? Some have the fantastical quality, some are overheavy with ornament, some are repetitive, and some plainly vulgar. York has a massive rhetoric of its own. Do I value it at its proper worth?

No. Before I accept the rhetoric wholly, I must know the meaning of the matter that justifies it, and because I am a modern I can never fully understand the matter, nor am I helped to understand it by guide-books and histories.

Commonly it is by small doorways that we enter into great mysteries, and the doorway of a cathedral is rightly small in proportion to the size of the interior. Religion is a mystery, and mysteries are dark, making play with gloom and indirect lighting. The walls of this world are solidly opaque, yet they open on another world full of light and intelligence. The Church of God rests upon the rock and yet is on the march. It is remote and near, universal and parochial, simple and learned, silent and full of voices, and though as a rule I find paradox disturbing I accept the paradox of York Minster because it holds so many of the paradoxes experience has revealed to me.

Self-scrutiny is notoriously a treacherous business, but when I try to analyse the emotional tone of my mind as I stand within the great building I find that the builders have had much to do with it. In all great churches and in most small ones, there are two physical and spiritual urges : one is towards the east, the source of light and life; the other is upwards; and couples itself with the desire of the lowly for the exalted, of the little for the great, of the incomplete for the complete. These two powerful urges are accompanied by a diffused sentiment of pity and reverence—pity for the dead and reverence for the past. There is also a keen sense of being alive. Here below the grave-slabs lie the dead, and here stand I. Whose hands fashioned that moulding or carved that winged angel, and where is the dust of them now? Here in my turn am I, and for the moment my feet echo upon the Minster floor, my breath is lively in the still air. The secret and selfish joy that this is so is tempered by a regret that soon it will not be so, and that nothing can be done about it. To the gift of life there is attached a penalty.

Now since rhetoric is out of fashion let us go back to plain prose and raise a troublesome question. Medieval cathedrals were full of colour. Woodwork and stonework were rich with blues, reds, greens, gold and silver, and the windows slanted their crimsons and amethysts to the floor. Symphony of colour blended with the colouring of sound, with incense-burning, regulated movement, pillared candles; and the combined effect produced what the psychologist calls mass induction of emotion. But the seventeenth-century puritan spirit believed that religion could not be induced from without; it arose within a man's self. The nineteenth century preferred whitewash to colour. To-day the majority of people are neither individualist puritans nor are they convinced of the validity of the association between religion and sensuous appeal, so that the question as to whether York's medieval wealth of colour shall or shall not be restored is giving rise to debate. For many people, to paint natural oak and stone is to gild the lily, but still this is a question of æsthetics, not of faith and not of morals. If the whole interior is to blaze with colour, what will happen to the natural play of light and shadow within the building? Should cherubim, those beings whose element is flame, be painted up like chorus-girls? Is not to paint upon stone to create a waxwork effect without the flash of life, and is not to do things by halves to produce an impression of "neither nowt nor summat"?

The full effect of reintroducing medieval colour into the church can only be achieved by coupling colour and gloom, by darkening the interior until the glint of gold, the gleam of silver, the dense blues and smoky crimsons blend into incantatory spell. A pity that since Merlin's day nobody knows the cantrip by which the experiment may be made.

The longest of lifetimes is not long enough to learn all there is to learn about the Minster, and, for my part, at every turn and in every corner I find questions I cannot answer and problems I cannot solve. When and where originated the making of stained glass? Did the stained glass workers of medieval York match their colours to the colours of turquoise, amethyst, emerald, ruby? How happened the miracle of the Five Sisters Window? Was the great east window designed as a whole before the execution of the parts? Was it in fact as well as in legend that Fairfax saved the windows of York Minster from iconoclastic puritan soldiers?

At the table in the Chapter House, the Chancellor and I sit together talking about the Minster. The flies buzz. One of the vergers shows a party of sightseers round the building. Occasionally a furniture beetle or a death-watch drops on the polished oak. It is the time of year when the destructive little pests are on the wing. The Chancellor tells me first that my theory about the route by which stone came up from the riverside to the Minster may not be altogether correct. "The problem," he says, "may not be so easy of solution. Though the route seems practicable, the modern street-lines are not necessarily those of medieval York. There were differences, and sometimes big differences. That is all I can say."

Everyone supposed that the Tadcaster stone was long ago worked out, and the Minster had to seek another source of supply, being careful to match the new stone to the old. When new stone is wanted nowadays it comes from Clipsham Quarries in Rutlandshire, to the east of the Great North Road. It seems, however, that there is still a plentiful supply of stone at Tadcaster; the old quarries, in use from Roman times, are not yet worked out, and the Minster may begin using Tadcaster stone once more.

The ancient prætorium within whose bounds York Minster stands was certainly paved. Roman villas had mosaic pavements, usually of stereotyped pattern (Rome had no artistic originality in these things) and executed by British or Continental craftsmen who followed the designs furnished them. But was the first wooden church on the site of the Minster paved? Was Archbishop Roger's crypt? And how was the medieval Minster paved? I bear in mind a West Riding tavern that to this day has no flooring but dry, naked, irregular, beaten earth. I recollect a seventeenth-century complaint about the condition of the floor of Leake Church; within the church the bones of the dead were sticking up out of the ground. On the other hand, the floor of Byland Abbey was paved with tiles each bearing an Ave Maria, and all of uniform pattern. I asked the Chancellor about the flooring of the Minster. In reply he produced a book that any unprincipled bibliophile would set himself to secure. Bound in ancient leather, it is James Torre's description of the Minster in 1699, when yard by yard he reviewed the fabric, illustrating his prose by confidently drawn plans and elevations. Torre was both accurate and thorough, and, despite occasional obscurities, his account may be trusted. His plan of the eastern end of the church shows it to have been thick with grave-slabs, in places so closely set that they almost touched.

"That was the state of the paving in 1699," said the Chancellor. "In 1736 the old grave-slabs were taken up, cut in two and relaid face downwards. This explains the patterned occurrence of those blue-slate rectangular slabs in the eastern portion of the aisles."

He pats James Torre as he closes the volume, and we turn to the subject of the stained glass.

"The medieval clergy," the Chancellor said, "had a duty towards the illiterate. There were certain items of religious knowledge that ought to be known to literate and illiterate alike. Everyone should learn how the events of the New Testament had been foretold by the prophets; everyone ought to know the story of the Nativity, the events preceding it and the events following; everyone should know the sequence of events that took place at Easter. Then they ought to learn something of the saints, the episodes of their lives and the manner of their deaths. These are the chief subjects worked out in the stained glass of the Minster. The windows were the coloured picture-books of the medieval churchgoer. And in those days everyone was a churchgoer."

"And Saint Thomas of Canterbury?" I asked.

"Enormously popular in medieval England. So popular, in fact, that when the reformers went through the missale scratching out the name of the Pope they took good care also to obliterate the name of Saint Thomas of Canterbury."

"That," I commented, "showed Chaucer's good judgment in choosing a Canterbury pilgrimage as the setting for his Tales, and why his pilgrims came from every shire's end of England. Now," I went on, "the Continental cathedrals are proud of their treasures and relics : gold, silver, jewels, rich brocades, chalices, patens, croziers, mitres, and the bones of long-dead saints."

"Of pre-reformation treasures we have only the Horn of Ulfus," came the answer. "Nothing else ancient."

I divagated once more.

"Time after time, when one examines the inscriptions on the bells of North Riding churches, one finds that the bells were made in York between 1660 and 1700. I suppose the old bells had been melted down for ordnance during the Civil War and new bells had to be made and hung in the belfries and bellcotes. But who were the bellfounders of York, and what has become of the industry?"

"No information," said the Chancellor.

Next question. When one enters the great churches of Flanders and Italy it grows clear that ecclesiastical authority made use of great artists. Dim frescoes and gloomy rich canvases cover the walls. In England there are few wall-paintings and fewer canvases. True enough that the art of painting developed late in England, but English ecclesiastics were constantly passing between England and Rome, and they must have seen the Fra Angelicos, the Giottos, the Van Eycks. Having seen, they must have praised. How, then, that in England the walls are mostly bare?

A mystery. I passed on to a further problem. In the twelfth-century churches of the North Riding there is a certain uniformity of design which seems to extend into the East Riding. Village masons operating independently could hardly have arrived at such uniformity, and I am ready to believe that in York existed a flourishing school of twelfth-century church-builders. The Chancellor admitted the possibility, but thought it more likely that the masons looked

351

at one another's work. There may possibly have been an interchange of masons and there may have been itinerant masons.

The most casual eye can see that the great fabric of York Minster is cared for, ample evidence that single-minded devotion rules here. When I looked at it, the north transept had the appearance of a Piranesi wilderness of scaffolding, for the beetle has been hungrily at work here, and the old oak, riddled almost to lace, was being replaced by new timber. Great Yorkshire families have offered oak trees for the essential repair-work. Were there, I asked the Chancellor, any periods of history during which people grew indifferent to the fate of the Minster or when pride in its Gothic grandeur was diminished?

"There were," came the reply, "four periods of great building activity here, and they cover almost all the years between 1220 and 1472. In 1472 the towers were finished, and after that there are no records of extraordinary activity. But if there were periods during which the Minster was neglected, those periods were the years of the Civil War and the earlier eighteenth century when deism was followed by religious indifferentism, when Collins and Toland made way for Gibbon, David Hume and Jack Wilkes, and when the word 'gothick' was a synonym for 'barbarous.' The eighteenth century was much too busy making itself comfortable in its own houses to trouble greatly about the fading splendour of the Minster."

Noting that the late Elizabethan and Jacobean periods saw the enormous development of domestic architecture, I suspect that during those periods also the fabric of the Minster was neglected.

Finally, I asked about the Library of the Minster, for the Chancellor is also the librarian. The question arose because the Church of St Peter in York has never been a monastic institution, and, arguing pedantically, one should hesitate to call it a Minster. I could well understand the need for a library in a monastery, but there would be no such need at York. Yet Alcuin got together, by report, a magnificent library, and though it was completely destroyed in the Norman burning of York, the Minster to-day has a collection of some thirty thousand volumes. Why?

"A big question," said the Chancellor. "First, the library was for the priests and canons, and not all of them were highly educated men. They would need certain books : copies of the Bible in translation as well as the Vulgate; glosses and commentaries upon the various books of Scripture; books for the instruction of the deputy canons, elementary service books in Latin, copies of the psalms, the missal, the offices of the church. It would not be vital that they should understand the Latin; enough for them if they could read the words and repeat them. Then, no doubt, there would be copies of the canon law and the civil law, for no priest would wish to find he had broken, through ignorance, either the one or the other. Further, for their edification would exist copies of the writings of the Fathers of the Church, particularly of St Augustine of Hippo, and, to increase their knowledge of the religious life, copies of the Benedictine Rule with its three great divisions—Opus Dei, Divine Lectu and Opus Manu; the daily services in due order, rules for study and reading, rules for working with the hands in the fields, at the forge or smelt-mill, or in the cloister at copying, illuminating, book-binding and so forth. Then also there would be a little collection of histories and chronicles : certainly a copy of the Anglo-Saxon Chronicle, of William of Malmesbury, Walter Map, Ranulf Higden's *Polychronicon*. Biographies, too— Lives of the Saints, for example—and perhaps a Bestiary. And finally a copy of Cicero's *Rhetoric*, or Priscian and Donatus, possibly of Quintillian and perhaps of Aristotle's *Rhetoric*, in Latin. These books would be useful for those who did the preaching."

"And now?"

"Now, pretty well single-handed, I'm trying to put the library in order again after the war."

"A big task."

"Very big, but made easier, I suppose, because in a way I may claim to know what books there are."

"In a way?"

"Certainly I know what books are in the library, but I am not an authority on, for example, bindings; so that if a recognized expert on bindings asks if he may look over the library I am happy to take him along, lock him in and leave him to his work."

St William's College, York

"And what happens then?"

"This is what did actually happen not long ago. The expert came upon a volume of Lactantius beautifully printed in Greek. What interested him was not the Greek text, however, but the binding. The title-page told him the book was produced in the first half of the sixteenth century. The binding was rather greasy, dirty, worm-eaten and worn, but the tooling could still be made out fairly well. This is the book."

I turned over the pages of lovely Greek type, then fixed my attention upon the binding.

"You note the horizontal panels at the top and bottom," said the Chancellor. "Here, you see, is a fellow playing some sort of musical instrument to the dancers. It's well done. A good design. It proclaims itself of the Revival of Learning. Very well. Now who were the master-spirits of that period in the northern parts of Europe? Here they are in these medallions down each side of the cover. Do you recognize any of them?"

I examined the portraits with the light falling on them slantwise, and they were beautifully clear.

"Erasmus," I said. "Martin Luther."

"And Melanchthon. But here is another medallion on this side, repeated on that : the portrait of a certain H.H. who must have been in England during the reign of Henry VIII. Do you recognize him?"

He was a florid, bearded gentleman, and I was slow to guess.

"The name was Hans Holbein," the Chancellor told me, "and this volume of Lactantius appears to be the sole authentic specimen of Holbein's work as a bookbinder. That," he concluded, "is what I mean when I tell you that I know my books only in a way. Such discoveries as this, they imply the specialist's expert handling."

While the Chancellor was locking away James Torre and Lactantius I examined the showcases in which lay open several of the rare volumes from the Library. The first that took my eye was Higden's *Polychronicon*, its title-page in black and red. The others I looked at casually and they have left no impress on my memory. There, too, was the famous Horn of Ulfus, a unique piece of carved ivory concerning which there is a printed pamphlet and a fascinating theory which I, on the evidence, consider to be more than a theory.

As I left the Minster I worked out a suggestion for the designers in stained glass. Let the artist set himself the task of illustrating the evolution of life on this planet, let the whole vast theme—the primitive fish, the giant saurians, the mammoths, sabre-toothed tigers and all—be brought into the church. Let a window be given to the mastery of nature, showing how under the guidance of God man has won his way from the use of fire, the cooking-pot, the dug-out and the wheel to the mastery of nuclear fission. Dedicate a window to the Newtons, Leeuenhoeks, Cavendishes, Faradays, Rutherfords, that the name of the Lord may be blessed. For if York Minster ceases to change and grow, if its wardens fix their gaze wholly on the past and have no eye for the present and the future, the people will grow careless and think no more of the Minster than of the Castle Museum, where they are entreated not to consume ice-cream on the premises and throw down the sodden paper, and where children swarm whenever the cinema opposite displays the notice "house full."

This, however, is subject to modification. The Castle Museum is rightly popular. In the year 1944 to 1945 over ninety-four thousand people passed through the turnstile, and more than half these people were not resident in York. Visiting the Museum, you at once understand its popularity, for in the layout of the exhibits logic, learning and art take equal shares, and behind all there is the stimulus of harnessed imagination.

Formerly the Castle Museum was the Women's Prison, and here and there occur the names of long-dead debtors scratched into the stonework imported from across the green. The power-house of the Museum is the office, once part of a prison cell, now a pleasant little room with a wagon roof and oak-panelled walls which have not yet been rid of their overcoat of paint or limewash. There the plans are made, the layout of the exhibits new and old is discussed; there Miss Violet Rogers copied the coloured prints of old Yorkshire costumes and there Miss Amy Jordan pondered the talks she delivered to visitors. The floor is stone-flagged but none the worse for that, and the only deficiency I note in this power-house is the meagreness of the collection of reference books.

To anyone wishing to learn what the North Riding was like and how people lived in the eighteenth and nineteenth centuries and what it is still, in some places, like, the Castle Museum is essential, for behind the disciplined energy, art and skill so evident to the visitor he is still aware of the personality of Dr John Lamplugh Kirk of Pickering. In sober truth I can feel that personality dominating the place. Kirk was interested in the machinery of farm and farmhouse. He got together the vast cheese-presses, the enormous forks and rakes, the great ploughs and harrows, the elmwood bread-troughs, ox-yokes, churns, spinning-wheels, grease-horns, flails, straw-band twisters, butter-moulds, turf-cutters, ling besoms and what have you, that cause a middle-aged North Riding man like myself to exclaim in delight, "By Jove, these things were in daily use when I was a youngster!" Here, for example, is the very wooden yoke whose weight I learned when I used to fetch water from the village well, and here is the great plate hearth with its reckans of polished steel and big black-leaded kettle—the hearth before which my grand-father used to fall asleep in the evenings with a couple of dogs at his feet. Here are the very farmhouse chairs, the cream-bowls, the ornaments of plaited straw we used to make in late July or early August before the wheat-straw became brittle-dry. Here's the churn, here's the witchball, and here's the pretty patchwork quilt my grandmother made.

But, of course, many of the exhibits are older than that, and many, to me, are not vastly interesting. In the collection of musical instruments, for example, the serpent reminds me rather of Hardy's Wessex than of York or Yorkshire, and I find the serried rows of batons, glass walking-sticks and the like rather tiring. I go to museums through no diffused or vague impulse but to satisfy a specialized curiosity, and Kirk's nucleus does that for me very well. I discover facts of which I was ignorant : that flint arrowheads with tangs longer than their barbs are characteristic of the Pickering region; that handloom weaving was one of Helmsley's industries between 1800 and 1850; that wooden dolls were solid all through; that Kingthorpe near Pickering was a lace-making centre;

that a witch-cross had to be made of the wood of a rowan tree and cut with a special knife; that the maker of the cross must never have seen the tree before and had to return home by a route other than that by which he came to the tree; that branding-irons were not heated but merely covered with paint, and that flails were in use within living memory near Easingwold and on the Cayley estate, now pretty well broken up, at Brompton in the Vale of Pickering.

Amy Jordan was not merely lecturer to the Castle Museum. She was also a field-worker with a specialist's eye for rural economy in the North Riding, spent her holidays in workshops and rustic forges and talked nineteen to the dozen all the time she was there and twenty to the dozen when she got back to York. Violet Rogers, I suspect, remained *in situ*; her immediate enthusiasm was the Museum itself and Yorkshire costume through the ages. And there, I say, was an admirable team of workers backed by a good committee. For make no mistake, the aldermen, councillors and citizens of York are not lacking in that sort of local patriotism. They do not, I think, boast of their achievements but take the better way of allowing their achievements to speak for them. Well they know that private activities unruled and unchecked could work havoc in Old York. They have their eyes open to all that.

Consider, for example, the hall of the Merchant Adventurers. There is still a corporate body of merchant adventurers in York, though its members are not merchants and not, perhaps, desperately adventurous; they are doctors, lawyers and so forth. The secret of the existence of this and similar corporate bodies is to be found in Chaucer's Prologue to the *Canterbury Tales*, where you will find Chaucer describing his five guildsmen as dressed in the rich livery of one fraternity. This fraternity was a social and religious society to which various guilds belonged—a medieval friendly society. Somewhere about 1300 a number of wealthy York merchants founded a Fraternity of the Blessed Virgin, and a little more than half a century later Sir William Percy presented the fraternity with a site for their chapel and hall. In 1373 Archbishop Thoresby reorganized the fraternity with a hospital for poor folk, a master and two chaplains. Though in 1547 the religious fraternities were suppressed, in 1580 the Merchant Adventurers were formally constituted. Their story has been told, as fully as probably it ever can be told, by the late Dr Maud Sellers, a scholar whose immense learning never became pedantry. She put the Merchant Adventurers of York into history—the history of York, of England, of the world, and, if the hall of the Merchant Adventurers in York is not now as it was towards the end of the sixteenth century, that is because the ravages of time have not yet been repaired. The right stuff has to be looked for in the right places, and the search is no fool's job.

In the hall I found both American and Canadian servicemen. I will not say they were pop-eyed with excitement, but they were seriously impressed. The sole criticism I have to make of their behaviour is that they were shy. Here was a magnificent fragment of Merrie England, and, bless me, I asked more questions in five minutes than they asked in fifty. I showed what in the North Riding they call the cheek of a miller's horse, and though I may visit the Merchant Adventurers' Hall any time I please, they, I suspect, may never see it again. They will show the photographs they took, but photographs are supplementary to the text and not the text itself. Anyhow, I discovered that there is none of the ancient plate left, that the display of guild banners—the banners of glaziers, tanners, clothworkers, merchant tailors, weavers, skinners, dyers, girdlers, masons, goldsmiths, millers, vintners, grocers, ropers, curriers, cordwainers, pewterers, tallow-chandlers, feltworkers and merchant adventurers—is not all indigenous to York. Each banner has a symbolic design, and I should like to see the York tradesmen adopt them, matching the enterprise already displayed in some of the tavern signs of the city. The more colour in York the better.

The present body of Merchant Adventurers holds four courts a year, and its monthly meetings admit new members, deal with problems of restoration and settle the affairs of the ten pensioners still maintained by the fraternity. On the last Sunday in January the members go in procession to the Church of All Saints in High Ousegate—this is the church with the lantern tower from which, after sunset, a lighted lantern guided travellers through the Forest of Galtres—and afterwards return to the hall for wine. The visit I paid was well timed, for I found work in progress following the bombings. Pictures were still to be sorted out and hung; the ambition of the guardians of the hall to restore its sixteenth-century authenticity was far from having been realized. Perhaps it is doomed to remain a platonic idea, yet I was happy to see that the place was not being systematically sterilized by cold-hearted, efficient experts.

As for Margaret Clitheroe's house in the Shambles, workmen were scrambling all over it, rafters were gaping, plaster and dust were flying, the old half-timbered structure was undergoing a major operation : what the nursing profession calls, I believe, general repairs. Of such renovations I am suspicious. My most vivid memory of Rievaulx Abbey is that of the ruin before it was sterilized. The walls were all overgrown with ivy, grass and wallflowers. Young saplings had rooted in the broken masonry, there was a red moon rising, there was an owl hooting, and there were no shaven lawns, no grouted walls. It was a ruin in process of ruination, and I liked it that way, just as I liked finding cattle stalled in Slingsby Castle on the Vicinal Way from Malton to Hovingham. But Margaret Clitheroe's house undoctored would have developed into a threat to life, limb and property. Either it had to go through its operation or it had to be pulled down, and I prefer renovation to demolition.

Not a stone's throw from the Minster, at St William's College, the renovators have carried through a handsome piece of work. The outer oak door is by Thompson of Kilburn, his sign-manual the mouse complete on the right doorpost, mutilated on the left by a soldier who tried to prise it off to take home to Canada. Then comes a cobbled forecourt with carved wooden figures representing the months and their occupations. December sits warming his hands over the fire, his dumb eloquence describing better than words could do it the misery of the medieval winter. Over the doorway to the left stands St Christopher; to the right, the Virgin and Child. The original door leans against the wall within, next to a Jacobean four-poster with a concealed recess for jewels. The oak floors are not original. Nor are the Jacobean chests and the six chairs upholstered in Cordova leather. Most of the doors are Jacobean, and, I think, some of the stairways.

When the renovators walked in, there were many more stairways, for St William's College was then a slum, filthy beyond belief, of tenements, some of which had outside staircases in the fashion of seventeenth- and early eighteenth-century Yorkshire architecture. In Jacobean times the house was a private residence. Before the Dissolution it was a warren of chantry priests, who seem to have imitated the rabbit also in burrowing for themselves an underground passage between their dwelling and the Minster where their sole job was to sing masses for the souls of the dead. There is a niche in the stone stairway where, apparently, they were clocked in and out whenever they used the subway. This seems to be a genuine subterranean passage, not part of the old drainage system. Rumour also reports the existence of another underground way, this time from the Minster to the Bedern, and still another, though where the third one leads to I am not at all clear. I do not think anyone else is, either. Such burrowings puzzle me.

The oldest room is the Painted Chamber, haunted by a mild-mannered clerical ghost earthbound since medieval days. Perhaps he defrauded his patron in the number of masses he sang. He has been seen in daylight, he has been seen at night. Investigation, no doubt, proceeds. His presence does not deter modern ecclesiasts from using the place for many miscellaneous purposes and adorning the walls with portraits of distinguished though defunct archbishops.

I think the furniture of St William's College clumsy, and the beetle—furniture beetle, powder-post beetle or death-watch—is in the oak.

From medieval England to Roman Britain, from St William's College into the private grounds of the Yorkshire Philosophical Society, with the Multangular Tower on my right and the hospitium across the sloping lawn to my left. I have not that sort of learning which can transform a few cracks and chisellings and stains of moss and lichen into a complete Roman inscription, and thus I undoubtedly miss a great deal of intellectual sport. Yet I derive a lot of pleasure from the relics here preserved : Roman pins and needles of ivory, bone and jet; marbles that Romano-British children played with; bracelets, brooches, rings and amulets; coins, drinking-cups, amphoras; Samian ware; lamps, jugs, bowls, jars for various purposes; artists' palettes; tiles with the stamp of the Ninth Legion; lead piping for a Roman bath; proof that Eboracum was a genuine *colonia*; more coins, and coin-moulds; much of the necropolis also; evidence of the flourishing state of Mithraism; death and religion keeping as close company as they do to-day. There are skeletons and skulls, fragments of shoes and sandals. Sometimes the undertakers poured gypsum over the bodies in the stone coffins, sometimes they made a penthouse of tiles to cover the bodies. There are brachycephalics and dolichocephalics amongst the skulls. There is, in the main Museum building, the hair of a Roman woman. Inscriptions bewilder the eye.

As I write this, much remains to be done to set the Roman relics in order. Even when expert hands have done their work, I still fear that these evidences of Roman civilization, Roman life and Roman death will remain cold, grim and forbidding to all but the experts themselves. It is one thing to wander about a Roman camp under the open sky, quite another to survey the ranked and catalogued relics of Rome in a museum. Although I like skulls, it was something of a relief for me, after looking at so many relics, to emerge into the sunlight and to contemplate the lovely remnants of St Mary's Abbey.

Quiet people, and people who want to be quiet, use these gardens; people who knit, people who read, and those who ask no more of life than to be let stand and stare. Several people go there to work. I saw them at it. They were actors and actresses from the York Repertory Company learning their lines. They remind me that I am one of those wretched people who cannot even read out-of-doors. The Repertory Theatre is under the ægis of the City Council and from the boards of their York theatre the actors stand an excellent chance of breaking into West End theatre and into the films. Many have done so, to the loss of York audiences, though it is a good thing for repertory companies to change their personnel fairly often. York hums with dramatic societies dominated by restless, energetic, temperamental producers. It is precisely as you would expect in a city like York. There is more drama to the square yard in York than there is in the whole of the West Riding, and the various amateur societies do well to be ambitious. They can carry it off with aplomb.

For the city is a magnificent setting for drama, for comedy and tragedy alike. Its Danish kings were men of the theatre, ruthless Macbeths and cunning Richard Crookbacks playing out tragedies now forgotten with a copious equipment of fire-brands, knives, mead-horns and ale-cans. In medieval days the pageants of the miracle plays lumbered through the streets. The Council of the North sat here. In the seventeenth century also, "a certain person presented a Petition to the Rebel Parliament desiring a Grant to have the Chapter House of York demolished as being a Useless part of the Church, and the Timber and stone thereof converted to a stable. The petition accordingly was granted, but (and here comes the drama) he died a week before he put his impious design into operation." That is from *The Ancient and Modern History of the famous City of York; and in a particular Manner of its Magnificent Cathedral, commonly called York-Minster . . . the Whole diligently collected by T.G., 1730.* T.G. was Thomas Gent. At the end of the Protectorate General Monk rode into York through Goodramgate and the city willingly broke its puritan bonds. On the night of 1 February 1829 the lunatic Jonathan Martin set fire to the stalls of the Minster, and the Choir was badly damaged, but this incident was of minor importance to the great debate that followed when Smirke, who designed King's College, London, proposed that the choir-screen should be set a bay farther east. A great war of pamphlets began. Gentlemen quarrelled over their wine; footmen bawled at one another in the servants' hall, maids fought in the kitchen. "At a dinner party, given by Mr C——, a gentleman who sat with his back to the fire, feeling rather cold, requested a servant, whose head was full of the argument, to *remove the screen*—meaning that one at the back of his chair—John started from his reverie at once, and quite forgetting where he was called out, he would be damned if it should be stoored for any man." The controversy gave rise to one of the most famous Yorkshire dialect poems, "York Minster Screen," published anonymously by R. Smithson of Yorkersgate, Malton, in 1833.

When the visitor emerges from the Castle Museum he should ask to see Dick Turpin's cell in the prison opposite, and, when he sees the extraordinary figure within, he will know what I mean when I insist that York has a vast sense of the dramatic. If he wants further proof, let him read any history of the city. The drama is not yet complete. Even during Hitler's war, during the Baedeker raids, it had to be the ancient Guildhall that suffered most from the impact of bombs, and before the war York Races and Military Sunday provided plenty of colour and pageantry and something to take the ear as well as the eye.

The narrow streets of the city are busy with motor traffic and people walking and cycling (to see the cyclists in the dusk of a winter evening is a sight rememberable), but there are comparatively few accidents because York demands a highly developed road sense and strangers within the gates drive with extra care. To enjoy the full impact of the city upon the mind it is essential to walk. You cannot see York from the windows of a car.

But this is not to describe York. Hating conducted tours, I see no other way of getting a grip upon the city but to walk about it at my leisure. Often I enter York along Blossom Street, late eighteenth-, early nineteenth- and twentieth-century, exemplifying nowadays an economic segregation, with Micklegate, of doctors and dentists. The modern notion —or is it actually a survival?—parallels the medieval; I have no doubt Chaucer's Doctor of Phisik lived in the fourteenth-century Wimpole Street and his Sergeant of the Law haunted the Parvys at Paul's. Addison's coffee-houses also showed segregations—financiers in one, wits in another, fops in a third. I do not know if the coffee-houses of eighteenth-century Stonegate in York showed a similar segregatory tendency. By Micklegate Bar in two or three dingy streets tanners and barkers followed their trades, and where Nunnery Lane runs outside the city wall Priory Street runs within. Excavations are going on in the neighbourhood of Barker Lane; Roman York is being revealed there, but I have no detail to give. Micklegate Bar was the Traitors' Gate of York. To the

north, railwaymen are still liable to find relics of the Roman
cemetery. Whenever they do so they call in Angelo Raine.
Whenever the Museum of Roman Antiquities grows interested in an excavation it calls in Angelo Raine. He is York's
authority in these matters. This quarter above-ground is not
old; below-ground it holds history by the lorry-load. The
Roman dead were buried across the river towards the setting
sun. So were the dead of ancient Egypt.

Between Tanner Row and the Ouse, in All Saints' Church
the soft-footed ministrants are scarcely visible in the gloom
and the air in and around this little church is heavy, still and
stagnant. All Saints' is not easily found, not easily forgotten.
Hereabouts it is possible to reach the river-front opposite the
Guildhall, but there is little to see and nothing to do. The
York Industrial Co-operative Society's premises are not easy
to overlook and they are important because the co-operators
make much of education and drama. Rougier Street is thick
with buses. Well supplied with public transport, York ought
to do something for its bus-queues. There is little shelter here.

I prefer Ouse Bridge to Lendal Bridge, but usually cross
the river by Lendal Bridge. The Romans, I believe, never
bridged the Ouse. If they did, nothing remains. The medieval
bridges were built of timber. Ouse Bridge, not the present
bridge but an older structure, gave St William a chance to
work a miracle and earn a great reputation when it collapsed
as he crossed it in company with a vast crowd. He saved
everyone from drowning, and York has never forgotten this
charitable action. Lendal is a curious little street. Coney
Street craves wary walking. A Baedeker bomb scored a direct
hit on St Martin's and smashed good stained glass of the best
medieval period. Another demolished an arcade of shops on
the other side of the street. Coney Street leads into Spurriergate, Castlegate and the neglected area in which stands
Clifford's Tower on its motte. I have a print of Clifford's
Tower showing the motte thick with bramble and elder trees,
and, comparing the print with the reality, I prefer the print.
The bare slope of grass is unattractive and the interior of the
Tower has little to offer. There are two sorts of building-
stone : the magnesian limestone and a reddish sandstone
from north of York. The gridded well is associated with a

twelfth-century pogrom and the bodies of the victims were, if the records are to be trusted, flung down the well. It is not obvious why the slaughterers chose to spoil a good well; the killers of little Hugh of Lincoln had more sense. With throte y-corven, he sang his *Alma Redemptoris Mater* not from the bottom of a well. Even in the Middle Ages it was hard to dispose of the body.

In sight from Clifford's Tower stands the Castle Museum and the old jail. The Castle has gone, but there are folk living in York who remember its last fragments. We are now on the narrow tongue of land between the broad Ouse and the narrow Foss, which in places runs like a canal between straight walls. Over Castle Mills Bridge we strike the city wall at Fishergate and follow its curve north-east to Walmgate Bar.

I consider Walmgate Bar wasted where it is. It is a brilliant fragment of medieval fortification with a barbican, and it is still inhabited. The stone weathers clean and silvery. Off Walmgate I had to look for St Margaret's Church, once the Church of St Nicholas-without-Walmgate. It was worth looking for. The south porch, the Norman door, is enormously interesting in its carvings—the orders show the signs of the zodiac and Æsop's fables, and the workmanship is better than that of the Norman carving at Barton-le-Street. It has not yet reached the stage when carving in stone broke away from the technique of wood-carving.

Walmgate, a dull and dingy street, brought me into Fossgate, and, turning right up St Saviourgate, I found Freemasons' Hall merely to remind myself that York freemasons claim the oldest lodge in England, with Edwin of Northumbria as its first Grand Master. Before reaching St Saviourgate I explored the Hall of the Merchant Adventurers. To match my print of Clifford's Tower I have one of this hall showing it in a state of picturesque decrepitude, surrounded by unkempt grass and a broken fence. The roof in those days—not so long ago, either—was thatched. The whole area, and the building, are now tidied up. The hall is a big, half-timbered structure rather like a barn, with plenty of oak, a musicians' gallery and a spacious undercroft. The little office has an excellent photograph of Dr Maud Sellers, whose findings regarding the Merchant Adventurers are to be found in the publications of the Surtees Society. They have value also for the student of dialect, for northern spellings are embedded in the normal scribe's English and these spellings may be interpreted phonetically to throw light upon contemporary pronunciation.

So I came to Pavement, and, over a shop, to the half-timbered residence of Sir Thomas Herbert. I am persuaded that formerly it stood in a walled garden. It has that appearance. Parliament Street and Sampson Square next, with the inns called the Three Cranes and the Mail Coach. Students of Elizabethan London will be reminded of that famous tavern, the Three Cranes in the Vintry. The recently discovered Roman bath was revealed during an extension of the cellarage in the Mail Coach. Here in the grand open-air market the sceptical phlegmatism of gaitered Yorkshire is matched against the sprightly cheapjackery of professional marketeers. Davygate took me to St Helen's Square, called after the mother of Constantine. She, I remember, identified the holy sites at Jerusalem. The mahogany panelling in Terry's Café came from the firm's property in the Caribbean. So I was told when it was first installed.

I never visit York without going into Stonegate, and never find it easy to escape from the short but entertaining street. Stonegate may be called a commercial museum. Its shops form an economic segregation of traders in old glass, china, furniture, prints and books. In Stonegate I am tempted to rage because I never have enough money to buy everything I should like to buy: Georgian silver, Baxter prints, Leblonds, Pollards, J. R. Smiths; Bristol glass, old Spode. Knowing that Petermann's economic map of Britain in 1851 shows glassware made at York, I have yet to trace York glass in Stonegate. But perhaps Petermann meant beer-bottles. Godfrey the bookseller—Godfrey of York—has his shop here, and Knowles the worker in and authority upon stained glass. In peacetime summers American buyers haunt Stonegate, and I never expect to pick up valuable antiques here at bargain prices except when Wall Street totters.

Stonegate leads easily to St Michael le Belfry and the Minster. The base of another pillar of the Roman prætorium was uncovered at St Michael le Belfry, and the verger explains how this church is historically associated with the family of Fawkes. The exterior of the Minster is a study for architects in problems of strains and stresses. Inside the fabric I find religion; outside I find engineering. It is not often that people stand to scrutinize the west front of the Minster. The niches for images are mostly empty; the images that remain are hard to count for a man with a tendency to fibrositis in the muscles of the neck. Here stands St Peter. There are gargoyles and heraldic beasts, and here is a man heaving a great rock. I trace vine-stems and bunches of grapes. Over the north door I find a bat with huge ears, and a wild boar at the other side. Within the Minster, the vergers conduct parties from one point of interest to another, and I have little urge to parrot their information as they go their regular rounds and repeat their regular quips. Yet from them one may still learn something new : that there is a well, King Edwin's Well, in the crypt, and a spring in the Zouche Chapel; that the exploration of the crypt with its herring-bone Saxon masonry was, in fact, a spectacle of learned clerics crawling through little holes and over mounds of ancient rubble and wiping the dust of ages from their spectacles.

I have never climbed the Minster tower.

Bootham Bar, Exhibition Square and the King's Manor lie north-west of the Minster. In 1946 Bootham School published an ecological survey of Askham Bog, one of the few primitive bits of country in the neighbourhood of York. Marygate has part of the old wall of St Mary's Abbey, grey, crumbling and crazy. From the grounds of St Mary's Abbey I peered through iron railings at the tomb of Etty, the York painter.

North-east of Bootham stands the County Mental Hospital, and I am reminded how York Retreat, west and south of Walmgate Bar, pioneered modern methods of treatment for the mentally sick. Its methods made an impressive broadcast in 1946. From Bootham Bar to Monk Bar the city wall commands a commonplace view over the Minster grounds. Once the prospect from these walls to the north was more impressive, for the Forest of Galtres came almost up to the city gates. From Monk Bar by way of Goodramgate and

King's Square I came to the Shambles, more decrepit than they were twenty-five years ago, more ramshackle, yet still important to students of English domestic architecture.

There are streets, or rather gates, not included in this three-hour stroll : Coppergate, Friargate, Colliergate, Peter-gate, Little Stonegate, Dean Gate ; Bedern, Aldwark, Ouse-gate and Whit-ma-whop-ma Gate. I have not yet visited Cattle Market and Hay Market, looked at Kings Staith and Queens Staith below Ousebridge, found that tiny court with the lantern window where John Wesley preached, or exam-ined the churches for Roman stonework built into the walls. Nor have I yet inquired what York and Yorkshire clubs and societies have established headquarters here. Moreover, I have written not a word about Cooke lenses and optical instruments, which are made in York, and not a word about Rowntree's though to thousands of people all over the world Rowntree's and York are inseparably coupled. Nor have I given the impression that York is a busy city of shops, offices and banking-houses, or that town and country mix and mingle here in every street, that it is a farmers' emporium and mecca.

There are, however, two York societies with which I must briefly deal.

Everyone knows how the appearance of a city may change in a mere quarter of a century. It needs only a number of small-scale alterations carried through without vision and without conscience to spoil a whole street or a whole quarter. Here, for example, is a shopkeeper who resolves to bring his frontage up-to-date with plate glass, chromium steel and neon lighting, and he contrives to execute his project without for one moment reflecting that he has destroyed the whole appearance of an eighteenth-century façade. Here again is a highways engineer who determines that cobbles must make way for synthetic stone, or that a handsome lot of old build-ings must succumb to his passion for street-widening. New lighting is needed in this or that ancient street, and up goes a set of lamp standards that might do credit to Main Street. In York, this process of small scale change has, here and there, gone far to destroy the individuality and harmony of buildings and streets. In York, too, as elsewhere, there exists

368

the constant menace that amenities may fall short of high standards of achievement. Moreover, who is there to make sure that, when an old and gracious building stands in need of repair and renovation, the owner will not call in the nearest jerry-builder and give him a free hand? Who will ensure that the tenants of such buildings will respect, for example, an Adam fireplace or a Jacobean staircase?

To preserve the beauty and antiquity of the city, to make sure that amenities shall be in keeping with their surroundings, to encourage good design in public and in private works, a strong society of argus-eyed watchmen is essential, and such a society exists to-day in York. It is called the York Civic Trust for Preservation, Amenity and Design. It is a voluntary society with a powerful membership, which, within the city, will carry out work similar to that of the National Trust. It remembers how York was once the artistic capital of the North and hopes to restore its ancient skills. It has its eye upon the Georgian houses in St Saviourgate, upon the early Tudor building in Patrick Pool, upon the shop-fronts in many parts of the city but especially, perhaps, in Stonegate, upon the rather dilapidated Jacobean frontage in Ogleforth, and upon other properties elsewhere. It has no notion of infringing upon the work of other societies, but aims to lend them, and the city council, its influence and co-operation, and with its funds to purchase properties, and, restoring them to their former dignity and beauty, to educate the public conscience so that what now exists shall not be lost.

The second of these two societies is the Georgian Society, a scholarly association concentrating attention upon eighteenth-century York. Its members were quick to realize that the general tendency nowadays is to praise and value the medieval and the Jacobean rather than the Georgian, and they therefore stand up valiantly for the balance and restraint of Georgian York. They have a hard task, for much of eighteenth-century York is in use as residences, shops and offices, and those who use the properties are inclined on occasion to treat them with discourtesy. First, then, the Georgian Society has catalogued properties of the period 1660 to 1760 from the Mansion House and the Assembly Rooms to the individual houses that stand in almost every

Walmgate Bar, York

street. The Debtors' Prison in the Castle precincts is attributed to Vanbrugh. John Carr designed the Assize Courts
and the Castle Museum. The Judges' Lodging dates from
about 1718, the Queen's Hotel in Micklegate from about
1720. The Red House in Duncombe Place and the Fairfax
house in Castlegate find an honourable place in the list. And
there are many more such properties in High Petergate,
Colliergate, St Saviourgate, Spurriergate, Coney Street,
Bootham, Micklegate, Blake Street and High Ousegate.
Having made its survey, the Georgian Society came rightly
to the conclusion that Georgian York has not been treated
well, and, in the names of Wren, Vanbrugh, Kent, Adams
and the other great men and women of the period 1660 to
1760, resolved to do something about it. Its first pamphlet,
therefore, was entirely practical. It gave advice on tiling,
roof-ridges, brickwork, woodwork, windows, cornices, painting, care of ironwork, stonework and leadwork. It advised
on the treatment of interiors, with notes on panelling, doors,
shutters, firegrates, overmantels, cornices, stair balusters,
cupboards, plaster ceilings and marble floors and hearths.
Finally it recommended that suitably worded and lettered
panels should be provided for the best Georgian buildings,
and pointed out that destruction can be profitable to no one
but such as live by it.

This pamphlet has great informative value. So, too, have
the others in my possession, though they are the fruits of
historical research rather than of utilitarian interest. Miss
Pressly's notes on the Judges' Lodging tells how the kitchen
floor was flagged with ancient sculptured tombstones, and
how a well-baked loaf might come out of the oven embossed
with a *hic jacet*. I believe this legend is apocryphal. Miss
Wright's notes from eighteenth-century newsprint tell us that
in August 1786 Mrs Siddons appeared at Tate Wilkinson's
theatre; that on 22 March 1790, a Jane Austen wedding took
place at Scarborough when Isaac Newton Esq. married a
Miss Baker, an amiable and accomplished young lady, with a
fortune of £5,000; and that in August 1786 Lunardi went up
in a balloon from Kettlewell's orchard behind the Minster.
Such papers as these conform to the aims of the Society,
which, formed in 1939, exists to promote the preservation

and care of Georgian buildings in York and the neighbourhood and to strengthen and develop public interest in
Georgian craftsmanship, art and architecture.

York has now petitioned for the founding of a university in
the city. This ought to have been done in the eighteenth
century, when, according to Gibbon, the monks of Oxford
were steeped in port and prejudice. But eighteenth-century
York thought of little but horse-racing, dancing and public
executions, and the time was not ripe. I am glad that nineteenth-century York did not think of itself as a university city.
Now, I am sure, the time has come. The thing is in the air.
Before ever the petition was sent forward people all over the
North Riding were thinking about such a project—not influential people, but poor scholars, mostly—and discussing it
fiercely. And these people, the poor scholars, want a university in York that shall stand inferior to none, that shall be as
non-vocational as Oxford, Cambridge and the Sorbonne, and
that shall be worthy of the city and the county.

And now I come to Rowntree's of York, and what I am
going to write may, I fear, rather resemble the account of a
works visit in a school magazine. That cannot be helped.

By blurring technicalities and using his imagination,
Kipling romanticized commerce, industry and machinery. I
think he was wrong, but these three, thanks to publicity men,
are now looked upon as romantic by almost everyone. Nowadays the study of great industrial concerns has become
technical, the managerial staffs have become technocrats and
technocracy is discussed in esoteric terms. One needs a lifetime to master the whole subject on the theoretical side, and
then another lifetime about half as long to get hold of the
practical experience. I have not even a lifetime. I should like
therefore to concentrate upon personalities, but great industrial concerns are anonymous and nothing can be done about
that. I am also interested in techniques and in history. I wish
I had space enough to trace the full history of a concern
whose premises cover a floor-space of over thirty-six acres
and whose works estate runs to nearly two hundred acres,
back to a little grocer's shop in York started in 1725 by a
thirty-year-old spinster, a Quakeress called Mary Tuke. This
founder of the Tuke business was not supposed to trade with-

out a licence from the Company of Merchant Adventurers of York, but she successfully defied the whole membership of that body, which was, in 1725, rapidly approaching decrepitude. The Tukes, indeed, were a remarkable family. William Tuke, a grave old gentleman, founded the Quaker girls' school for which Lindley Murray wrote his Grammar. William Tuke also suggested the foundation of a "retired habitation for persons who may be in a state of lunacy or so deranged in mind as to require such a provision," and from this suggestion emerged York Retreat. Henry Tuke was both grocer and literary man. Samuel Tuke loomed large in the movement for the abolition of the slave trade, and backed Wilberforce with all his influence. In 1813 he published a *Description of the Retreat*, an important document in the history of the treatment of the insane. He was also a founder of schools, and himself taught the prisoners in York Castle. A portrait-gallery of the Tukes would be sufficiently imposing; add to it a complete history of the family, and that would be a monument.

Queen Elizabeth drank beer for breakfast. During Cromwell's Protectorate coffee-houses became popular. Queen Anne drank tea, and in her reign the couplets of Alexander Pope testified to a growing taste for chocolate or cocoa. This change marks a domestic revolution, but though eighteenth-century Quakers were, as a rule, quick to take note of change in commercial trends, it was not until 1785 that Tuke Son and Company began the manufacture of chocolate behind their premises in Castlegate. In 1862 Henry Isaac Rowntree took over this side of the Tuke concern, and from a small-scale business it became an expanding enterprise. Joseph Rowntree, Henry Isaac Rowntree's brother, became a partner in 1869, and, when Henry Isaac Rowntree died in 1883, guided the policy of the firm for the next forty-two years.

There are two ways of running an industry, the autocratic way and the democratic. The Rowntree way is the second way, and it is fully explained in Seebohm Rowntree's *The Human Factor in Business*, which every business man, and everyone who is not a business man, ought to read.

I began my tour of Rowntree's at a quarter past ten in the morning and finished at five o'clock in the afternoon. The moment I looked at the place I knew that I could not cover everything in the course of a single day, but by careful time-tabling and knowledgable shepherding by the managerial staff I spent a profitable time. I got an outline of my tour first. Then I went to look at cocoa-beans in mass. They came mostly from West Africa, and, like some other West African products, they looked hard and gritty. I tasted one, and was reminded of compressed dust. From aloft I watched the beans chuted down to a machine that extracted dirt and foreign bodies; I handled a trayful of nuts, bolts, rusty nails, bits of scrap-iron and old washers that, through carelessness or sheer inertia, had found their way into the sacks of beans. Next I saw the first process in the education of the cocoa-bean—its roasting in huge revolving containers with hot gases circulating round them. When the roasted beans emerged, still in their brittle shells, they were, though not delicious, at least palatable. Next I watched the beans being smashed up in another machine, and the shell winnowed out by air-blast. The bean itself suffered pulverization, and, that process completed, the fine paste was mixed with sugar and cocoa-butter, and the minute particles were coated with the cocoa-butter that makes the finished chocolate slide smoothly over the tongue and glide gratefully down the gullet. The mixing-room was warm and very noisy.

I went on to see the covering of assorted chocolates. Along came the centres on a conveyer-belt, moving steadily in parallel lines. Down came a flow of smooth chocolate to cover them. A fan blew away the surplus chocolate, and, emerging from the fan, the chocolates spread themselves on embossed plaques which imprinted the firm's name on the bases of the sweets. Before the chocolate could stiffen, girls put on the piping or other decorative effects. Then on went the chocolates into coolers, after which they were weighed and sent to the packing-room. Of all the departments in the works the assorted chocolates department has the biggest floor-space and the biggest labour force, for, ingenious as the machines are, chocolate creams have to be watched, marshalled, pushed about and ordered into perfection by deft-handed girls from the beginning of their journey to the end. Girls also do the packing. The cartons come to them after being stoved to remove the smell of printer's ink, but they do not arrive as cartons. They come as flat pieces of shaped and printed cardboard, but with a dexterous twist or two they take familiar shape. Each single cream goes swiftly and with mechanical precision into its bed, and there's the finish of one specialized part of the job. The girl to whom I talked about her work gave me a swift glance and a smile but never stopped her work. Did she find her task tiring? Not particularly. Monotonous? Not at all. Had she time to think of anything else but packing creams? She supposed she had. Did she enjoy her work? Yes, she did.

I asked my questions because my notions of mass production and specialized labour had been drawn from René Clair's *A Nous la Liberté* and Aldous Huxley's *Brave New World*. From all my observations at Rowntree's I drew conclusions : first, that René Clair's film contains an element of exaggeration; secondly, that an elaborate process of conditioning human beings to modern factory labour is superfluous. All that is needed is to get the right sort of person for the job, and after that you won't have breakdowns and emotional crises in the labour force. You should also find it fairly easy to cultivate a team-spirit. The lads I saw using a gargantuan guillotine for cutting corrugated paper worked as a team. The girls putting on the cellophane wrappings and adding the packer's number and the date-stamp worked as agents in a co-operative concern, not as cogs in a soulless machine.

In the department where block chocolate is made I plunged into a racket where the men pick up lip-reading to save their voices, and I concentrated upon one of those super-machines that pretty well look after themselves. This machine filled trays of moulds from overhead tanks of liquid chocolate. The moulds moved along a conveyer-belt into a chamber where an air-blast cooled them, and in this chamber they performed complicated evolutions; they rounded the corners, moved along upside down, cornered again and again, righted themselves, turned over once more and came back to a vibrator that shook out the blocks of chocolate. They dropped down on to a conveyer and vanished from my sight. The trays of moulds then turned right way up again to be refilled from the tanks and start their journey afresh.

In the next room the blocks of chocolate were packed by machine. Foil was cut to size, wrapping papers were whisked along at the rate of one a second, the blocks of chocolate were pushed upward. What happened in the next second was too rapid to follow. Then a chocolate block, completely wrapped, slid from the machine. Hour by hour the girls recorded their output.

Through sheer accident or mischance it is remotely possible that some foreign body may have got into the chocolate. Each specimen, therefore, goes through its X-ray test. I crowded in to watch the outers of the blocks passing their final examination. They slid along, their images out of focus, in focus, out of focus again, and so they vanished from the screen. They came through that green glow in batches of four or five. A half-crown slipped under one of them came through like a moon in total eclipse, for the machine magnifies, or seems to magnify, the objects subjected to scrutiny.

Some manufactured chocolate is at the moment for export, and the packing process here is slower because the cartons, to be quite damp-proof, must be carefully sealed by individual hands. Even so, to note how the girls work by touch and not by counting, to see the unfailing accuracy with which, in ten seconds, they complete an operation that would take me ten minutes, is to wonder at the adaptability of the human mechanism. These girls are subjected to motion-study, and are taught how to execute their movements with the optimum efficiency and the minimum expenditure of energy, and, wherever a machine can help, a machine helps.

In the afternoon I went first to the department where gums and pastilles are made, saw the sacks of acacia gum from the Sudan, watched the machine that cleans the gum from bits of bark and other impurities, saw the gum powdered, dissolved in water, sieved and sieved and re-sieved through mesh so fine as to give a gum-liquor as transparent as glass. This liquor was then stored in great tanks, and next to these stood similar tanks for glucose and syrup. Then I went down to the room where, the various flavours having been added to the mixture, the gums and pastilles were moulded. The room was warm, and men worked in singlets and white slacks. The trays of starch, carried forward on a conveyer-belt, were smoothed over and then stamped so as to give perfect impressions of the various shapes. Into these impressions the gum was filled through pumps, about thirty at a time every second. After this, the gums in their trays went into hot rooms for a lengthy drying process. Finally, the superfluous starch was blown away and the sweets received their final treatment of glossing. The packing of the threepenny tubes was an example of mechanical ingenuity at its most ingenious. From a series of hoppers illuminated to show the various colourings the gums dropped one by one into the slots of a conveyer-belt and, the full number made up, slid into a machine that wrapped and sealed each cylindrical tube.

Lastly I went round the card box mill, where austerity still governed production. The room where work was in progress exemplified the beauty of function. Its floor-space took up more than an acre, its window-glass was continuous all round the walls, there was any amount of air-space and plenty of room to walk about between the machines. Here were cut out in strawboard and card the shapes of cartons and boxes, by this machine at the rate of a thousand an hour, by that at the rate of four thousand. Other machines cut out the corners of lids, and still others, each with one operator, stitched the boxes together with copper wire. Before 1939 this mill turned out millions of boxes a year, and half the floor-space was given up to the making of fancy boxes. Here, too, are made the dummies used in window-dressing. I had not given dummies a thought. Still less had I thought about the boxes made before the war, and they gave me a shock. Looking at them, I realized how lacking in colour is 1947 as compared with 1937; how grey, how grim, how uniformly patterned these post-war years are, and how so accustomed to the patterning we have grown that we scarcely miss the colour and individuality of pre-war production. In that small room where the boxes were laid out for display the silks and satins and velvets in blues and greens and rose-pinks seemed almost too rich. Here was individual workmanship, too, and the manual dexterity I had grown to expect.

So much for the actual manufacturing processes. But I saw more than these. I went into the classrooms of the firm's day continuation school, where instruction is given in English, current affairs, domestic science and other subjects. I looked into one of the best-equipped gymnasiums in York. I saw the girls' canteen. I had lunch and tea in the works restaurant. I got a glimpse of technocracy at close quarters. I went to the movies in the Joseph Rowntree Theatre, and wandered backstage to look at a first-class lighting-set. I saw the results of psychological research all over the factory, I noted the air-conditioning, the cleanliness of the workrooms, the cloak-rooms where in spells of wet weather garments are dried on their separate coat-hangers, the suggestion-boxes, the trade union notice-boards, the hanging baskets of ferns, the steel flooring in places where heavy traffic moved along. And, too, I noted intangibles as important as the material processes of manufacture.

What were these intangibles? Slowly I grew aware that the whole factory was alive on two planes. On the first, the men, the girls, the overlookers, the managerial staff and the machines worked together for material ends. Their aim and purpose was smooth, efficient production of goods. This plane was the plane of organization. On the second plane, the men, the girls, the overlookers and managers worked together on the human level, and this plane was the plane of organic life. Upon this plane there was room for education, sport and recreation; for the lunch-hour cinema show, the dramatic society, the youth club, the week-end camps; for the medical, dental and psychology services; for the library, the pensions and savings schemes and the works magazine, for all the functions that mark the difference between organization and organism.

I grew aware, too, that these two planes of activity were co-ordinated and interdependent, that workers, staff and directorate were in constant contact on both planes, and that without the one the other would cease to function healthily. Harmonious working had imperatively to maintain equilibrium between the two, and, since industrial conditions often change quickly, awareness and goodwill were vital. It was not enough that the few at the top should be aware; everyone had to be.

I was left with a lurking suspicion that I had found not a pure democracy but something that approached the democratic as closely as industry would permit. My fear was lest it should be subject to the taint of parochialism in a world where parochialism is outdated, lest its life should be limited by the potentialities of a little brown bean tasting rather like compressed dust.

J. B. S. Haldane has said that happiness does not summate; that the happiness of a thousand is not a thousand times the happiness of one. Yet I am persuaded that Rowntree's Cocoa Works is a place where happiness is sought diligently and studiously mated, when caught, with industry.

York, then, is not a place where the shards of the past are recklessly flung away, not a place where antiquity lingers in dusty segregation or is brightened up for the showcase, but a city where active life permeates the background of the past, where historic and modern are blended together in a unified spiritual existence. The old is still in daily use, but the modern takes increasing note of the organic unity of past and present. This persuasion of continuity is something not merely English. It is essentially European, and it is partly what we mean by civilization. Perhaps York is not yet completely aware of itself, but it grows steadily in awareness, and inquiry reveals that the public conscience now lies in the keeping of more than a few choice and master spirits. The visitor to York will be mostly conscious of the past. The resident is conscious of the vigorous pulsation of life in the present. He goes about his affairs. He will never allow his city to become a mere showplace parasitic upon the rest of the community. York is cathedral city, county, and county town. It differs from other cathedral cities and other county towns because somehow it is like London, like Edinburgh. Despite the size, the wealth, the importance of the great industrial cities, York still is and still must remain the Capital of the North.

EPILOGUE

THUS in the North Riding of Yorkshire I have played my part as an inquiring spirit, and have tried to do so without self-assertion. In the actual writing of this book, however, I felt that, if it were not to be repetitive of the records and visions of my predecessors and my contemporaries, it would have to be a faithful setting-down of my own impressions however inadequate and however distorted. This I have tried to do, and perhaps the result upon the reader may not be altogether happy. Yet since each observer has his individual impression, his personal vision, that must remain my justification. I have tried, too, to record the visions and impressions of people clearer of eye and more sensitive of mind than I am. Wherever I have gone I have met men and women with the expert's knowledge of North Riding life and history, yet I, expert in nothing and conscious of faltering inadequacy, found no expert who did not cheerfully share his knowledge with me, willingly answer my questions, and listen with patience and tolerance to my comments. To these experts I owe my thanks, and to those I did not contrive to meet I owe my apologies. Within the limits of this volume I have done my best, and now I should like to write another, just as long, on the same subject.

Morra Head
   Wetherby

INDEX

2c

Lealholm, 128
Leavening, 203
Lebanon, cedars of, 288
Lebberston, 9–11
Leckby Carrs, 301
Leeming, 300
Lees, Dr G. M., 118
Leland, 61, 287
Leven, River, 113, 170, 284
Levisham, 103
Leyburn, 209, 214, 222, 238, 243, 257–258
Lias clay, 13
Liddell, Sir Henry, 257
Lilburne, 176
Lilla Cross, 62, 120
Lilla Howe, 203
Limestone, Carboniferous, 236; Estuarine, 55; Jurassic, 14, 82, 236; Magnesian, 342, 349; Yoredale, 213, 222, 258, 261
Linthorpe Pottery, 275
Linskill, Mary, 70
Linton-upon-Ouse, 174
Little Ark, 119
Little Beck, 131
Little Haw, 234–5
Little Whernside, 234–6
Littlebeck, 72
Liverton, 128
Loftus, 78, 128
London Lead Company, 269
Long Nab, 55
Lord, Miss, 218
Low Mill, 164
Low Moor, 128
Low Row, 257, 260
Lower Dunsforth, 177
Lowestoft, 65, 66, 68
Lumley, Peg, 301
Lun Rigg, 119
Lune Forest, 269
Lune Moor, 269
Lune Water, 263
Lunedale, 269
Luther, Martin, 354
Lyke-Wake Dirge, the, 280
Lythe, 129
Lythe Bank, 75

Macaulay, T. B., 210, 270, 340
Macbeth, 70
Maclean, Alick, 19
Maiden Bower, 301
Maiden Castle, 259
Maize Beck, 263, 266
Mallyon Spout Hotel, 122
Malton, 101, 108, 203
Malvern Hills, 49
Manorial system, the, 175–6, 249

Manx crosses, 143
Marishes, 108
Marmions, the, 311–12
Marrick Priory, 255, 259
Marseilles, 15
Marshall, 46, 94, 101–6, 328
Marske, 79, 257, 280
Marston Moor, 303
Martin, Jonathan, 338
Marton, 90, 205
Masham, 207, 210–14, 233, 315
Mauley Cross, 121
May, Phil, 61
Maybecks, 129
Meerbeck, 240
Melanchthon, 354
Meldon Fell, 266
Melsonby, 285, 287
Merrils, 99
Metcalfes, the, 239–40
Mickle Fell, 263, 267
Mickleton Moor, 269
Middleham, 213–14, 243
Middlesbrough, 5, 67, 78–80, 102, 169–70, 272, 275
Middleton, 136
Middleton, Conyers, 248
Middleton Tyas, 285, 288–9
Midgley, the Rev. R., 35
Mill Gill, 241
Millstone grit, 229
Millstones, 87
Milward, 18–20, 37, 38
Ministry of Works, the, 27, 33, 146, 250
Montrose, 64
Moorjocks, 119, 165
Moorpouts, 117, 219
Moors, North York, 44, 58–9, 105, 112, 129
Moraine, the York, 339
Morley, Henry, 70
Morris Grange, 286
Morris, William, 240
Mortham Peel, 270
Mortimer, 115
Mount Grace Priory, 170–3
Mount Misery, 48–51
Mount Pleasant, 205
Mowbray, Roger de, 176, 180
Mowbray, Vale of, 2, 174, 260, 270, 284–5, 288, 306
Mowthorp, 46
Muker, 261, 262
Mural paintings, 82, 101, 133, 250–1
Murray, Dr, 35
Murton Fell, 263
Muscoates, 144
Musk, 46
Muston, 10–12

389